Designing & Delivering
Scientific, Technical, and Managerial
Presentations

Designing & Delivering
Scientific, Technical, and Managerial
Presentations

Peter J. Hager
James Madison University

H. J. Scheiber
Right First Time Department
Hoffmann-LaRoche, Inc.

With a chapter on international presentations by
Nancy C. Corbin
Loral Corporation

A WILEY-INTERSCIENCE PUBLICATION
JOHN WILEY & SONS, INC.

New York / Chichester / Weinheim / Brisbane / Singapore / Toronto

Copyright © 1997 by John Wiley & Sons, Inc.

Library of Congress Cataloging in Publication Data:

Hager, Peter J.
   Designing and delivering scientific, technical,
   and managerial presentations / Peter J.
   Hager, Howard J. Scheiber : with the assistance of Nancy C. Corbin.
      p.   cm.
      "A Wiley-Interscience publication."
      Includes bibliographical references and index.
      ISBN 0-471-15564-0
      1. Oral communication.   2. Public speaking.   I. Scheiber, Howard
   Jeffrey.   II. Title.
   P95.H34   1997   96-22145
   302.2'242--dc20

Printed in the United States of America

10 9 8 7 6 5 4 3 2 1

To Maria and our son Peter
P. J. H.

To Noam Julian Scheiber,
Dean's Honor Scholar
H. J. S.

Preface

A small but growing number of books on the market today address the topic of communicating complex technical, scientific, or business information through the use of oral presentations. The majority of these books are aimed at readers who need to deliver presentations in technical/industrial environments or within business organizations. While a handful of books address the needs of *both* technical and business audiences, no current text explores

(1) the function and use of presentations in *technical* and *scientific* contexts within organizations
(2) the function and use of presentations in *managerial* contexts.

These dual functions combined constitute the focus of our book, *Designing and Delivering Scientific, Technical, and Managerial Presentations.*

This text is targeted toward a range of professionals in technical, scientific, or managerial environments and university or college students interested in enhancing their skills in preparing and delivering concise, organized, and persuasive presentations to audiences in industry, business, government, or academia. Regardless of whether readers present regularly or only occasionally, our book includes and underscores components of presentation design and delivery that are often overlooked or under-emphasized:

- The process of designing and delivering presentations, such as, defining your purpose(s) in presenting as well as the audience to whom you will be speaking, researching primary and secondary data and information to develop a persuasive presentation, designing and using effective visual aids, projecting a confident delivery technique, managing nervousness, and handling Q & A.
- Complete sample scripts of presentations delivered by technical, scientific, and managerial professionals with AT&T Applied Digital Data Systems, Inc., Grumman Technical Services, and Pfizer Inc.

- A global perspective of how best to script and graphically present data and information to international and multicultural audiences and the use of technical or scientific translators for international audiences.
- Troubleshooting such logistical components of the presentation as scheduling, seating arrangement, room acoustics, and lighting.

PURPOSE OF THE TEXT

The purpose of our book is to train professionals to design, prepare, and deliver concise, effective, and interesting presentations whose content, organization, style, and visuals will vary according to

(1) the informational needs and technical backgrounds of target audiences
(2) the uses to which target audiences might put presented data and information.

Our text, as you will soon see, specifically addresses the presentational needs of *technical, scientific,* and *management* professionals by examining the unique communication requirements of these speakers and their audiences. In addition, we will be sharing with you the theory, principles, and best practices associated with designing and delivering effective, listener-centered professional presentations.

While our text will profit professionals relatively inexperienced in planning and delivering presentations, even those readers who have moderate to extensive experience in delivering presentations should profit from our process-oriented "tutorial" detailing how speakers can

- identify and clearly define their aims, purposes, and motivations in constructing their presentation
- define and analyze their audience(s) to ensure that their message hits the mark
- research the topic (or question) under discussion thoroughly
- draft and revise a concise, precise, and interesting presentational script
- design and integrate effective visuals into the presentation
- cultivate an effective stage presence to maintain listener interest and involvement
- manage the logistics involved in conducting a successful presentation
- elicit audience response so speakers can improve the process of planning and delivering their presentations.

WORK-WORLD MODELS

Beyond exploring the process(es) involved in designing and delivering a successful presentation, our book also provides readers with sample scripts of three professional presentations planned and delivered in work-world environments. The three scripts involve situations in which presentations are designed and delivered by a technical professional, a scientist, and an executive-level manager—each one directed to, and involving, a different target audience. We accompany each of these scripts with an examination of

- the speaker's purposes and aims in delivering the presentation
- the informational needs, technical and educational backgrounds, and "motivation profile" of the target audience and their intended uses of the data and information presented
- the function and use of visuals included in the presentation
- the content, organization, style, form/format, and time frame of the presentation itself.

GLOBAL PERSPECTIVE

Because we believe that our intended readership will likely comprise a truly global "network" of professionals, this book addresses the special demands placed on speakers who must design and deliver presentations before international and intercultural audiences. Consequently, we have included a special "guest chapter" written by Nancy Corbin of the Loral Corporation (Manassas, Virginia), an expert in the field of international presentation. This guest chapter explains in considerable concrete detail how our readers can most profitably design and deliver successful presentations to international audiences composed of technical, scientific, and managerial professionals.

LOGISTICAL EMPHASES

Within this book we have devoted much space to discussing such key logistical elements as scheduling, seating arrangements, and lighting and sound requirements, and we explore how these basic concerns are properly handled by professional presenters. We even offer specific suggestions for overcoming the difficulties—logistical and otherwise—inherent in working with foreign-language translators who often prove central to the process of preparing and executing useful, well-paced presentations to international audiences.

ORGANIZATION OF THE TEXT

In keeping with our process orientation, the book has been divided into six parts and a postscript:

Part I: Preparing Your Presentation
Part II: Designing and Using Effective Audio and Visual Media
Part III: Managing the Logistics of Your Presentation
Part IV: Delivering Your Presentation
Part V: Professional Presentation Models
Part VI: Presenting in International Environments
Postscript

Part I explores the role of presentation in scientific, technical, and managerial contexts. It opens by defining what a professional presentation entails and discussing the various types of presentations frequently delivered in today's organizations.[1] Moreover, this first section, like much of the book, is process-oriented, providing a detailed discussion of central steps to follow in the planning phase:

- Selecting presentation delivery techniques
- Identifying presentational aims and objectives
- Defining and delimiting audiences
- Outlining the presentation (viewing it as a whole)
- Researching the presentational topic or question
- Practicing (or "rehearsing") the presentation.

In addition, Part I examines how to (a) construct an effective organization for your presentation and (b) adopt a clear, concise, and relevant style for the presentational script.

Part II focuses on how readers can learn to determine what visual aid graphics would best help to clarify, simplify, explain, or explore ideas expressed in the presentation. The section also discusses how readers can determine which visual aids would be most effective in integrating those graphics seamlessly into their presentation. Part III examines important logistical concerns: arrangement of room seating; setup of visual aids; adjustment of room acoustics, lighting equipment, lecterns, and microphones; and consideration of room ergonomics to ensure audience comfort.

Part IV discusses central considerations in delivering your presentation: eye contact, body movement, voice control, the use of props. Because many well-designed and well-rehearsed presentations fall short of the mark due to the presenter's nervousness during delivery, we examine effective ways to prevent or diminish stage fright. Part IV also explains how presenters can prompt listeners (in various forms) for feedback on the effectiveness of the presentation in meeting their information needs.

In addition to providing readers with model scripts for a technical, scientific, and management-based presentation, the chapters that comprise Part V analyze the purpose(s) and objectives that determine the thrust of the presentation: the target audience; the organizational structure; and the script's form and style. This section also examines the logistics (and related issues) surrounding these particular professional presentations.

Part VI presents our guest chapter, "Internationally Speaking . . .", which examines the considerations unique to designing and delivering presentations for international audiences.

UNIQUE FEATURES

While we have constructed this book to be read in a linear fashion, from beginning to end, readers with more or less professional experience in designing and delivering presentations might wish to dip into chapters or sections that simply attract their attention or offer them valuable information they need—right now. Many sections of the book (even many of our chapters) provide self-contained information, hints, processes, or models. So, depending on your needs and experience, you can certainly read, initially, and review material without beginning at the beginning.

---

[1]Portions of the survey-based material we present in our Introduction appear in a different (summary) form in our article, "Oral Communication in Business and Industry: Results of a Survey on Scientific, Technical, and Managerial Presentations," *Journal of Technical Writing and Communication,* 24(2), 1994, pp. 161–180.

Because many of you will want to continue efforts in strengthening your oral communication and presentational skills, we have also included useful "suggested reading" at the end of each chapter—references that offer both practical suggestions and a theoretical foundation for our discussion throughout the text.

Other features that we think you'll find particularly valuable and unique to our text include the following:

- A managerial context in which many technical, scientific, and business presentations are set
- A discussion of effective, audience-based style(s) consonant with, and useful for, the presentation of complex material
- A process-oriented, developmental exploration of script formation
- Model presentations—shown in full, with complete text and visuals—from technical, scientific, and managerial work-worlds
- An international–intercultural perspective.

ACKNOWLEDGMENTS

In producing a book as rich as this one in information, ideas, prose models, textual and visual samples, and industry-based materials that highlight our work-world and professional orientation, we find that we are deeply indebted to a wide variety of individuals, groups, and organizations. First, we'd like to express our appreciation to all of the members of the John Wiley & Sons editorial staff—especially Rosalyn Farkas, Associate Managing Editor, Lisa Van Horn, Managing Editor, and Stephen H. Quigley, Executive Editor—who assisted us in designing, editing, and producing a book whose content and emphases will, in our opinion, prove of lasting value and continual interest to our readers—whether highly experienced technical, scientific, and managerial professionals or university students just now about to embark on a career involving oral, or public, communication.

Next, we'd like to acknowledge Professor Lois Rew, of San Jose State University, to whom we are indebted for providing a careful review and discerning preliminary reading of our book in manuscript form.

We want to extend the sincerest appreciation to all of those individuals and organizations who contributed to our effort in constructing and completing this book. We would like, therefore, to acknowledge the following very important people who shared with us their valuable time, insights and encouragement, presentational materials, documents, checklists, graphics and visuals: Bruce Cone, formerly of the NCR Corporation; Lynn Dixon, Brenda Hurst, and Robert Diegelman of the Management and Planning Staff, Justice Management Division, U.S. Department of Justice; Randall Estep, Comsonics, Inc.; Dr. Raymond W. Hackney, Jr., Office of Health and Safety, The University of North Carolina at Chapel Hill; Dr. John L. LaMattina, Vice President of U.S. Operations at Pfizer; Dr. John A. Lowe III, Principal Research Investigator, Central Research Division, Pfizer, Inc.; Ray McCormick, Deputy Director, Integrated Ground Operations (Engineering Support), GTS; Andrea McMakin and Nancy Burleigh, Senior Technical Communication Specialists, Pacific Northwest Laboratory, Battelle Memorial Institute; Robert W. Oliver, General Manager, the X-Station Business Unit, NCR Corporation (now AT&T Applied Digital Data Systems, Inc.); J. L. "Skip" Olson, Program Vice President,

Shuttle Processing Contract, Grumman Technical Services (GTS); Clifford R. Pelchat, Customer Service Manager, Metretek, Inc.; and Deirdre A. Sheetz, Supervisor of Operations and Maintenance Documentation, GTS.

In addition, we'd very much like to publicly offer our gratitude to the following individuals and organizations for their support and their time, the sharing of documents and vital information, the sharing of books and reference tools, and the preparation of graphic materials: Dr. Richard F. Whitman, Provost, and Dr. David K. Jeffrey, Associate Provost, College of Arts and Letters, James Madison University; Gloria A. Reece, now of The University of Memphis; Dalia Sofer-Scheiber, Management Information Services, Watkins Motor Lines, Inc.; Blanchard Training & Development, Inc.; and Mary Flekke, Reference Librarian, Roux Library, Florida Southern College.

Our debt to Nancy Corbin, author of Chapter 13, our guest chapter ("Internationally Speaking . . ."), is huge. We thank, you, Nancy, for a fruitful collaboration, for your patience, your insights, and your nuts-and-bolts approach to presenting technical material to professionals at forums composed of international and intercultural audiences.

One final note of acknowledgment is called for here and is long overdue: Professor Mitchell A. Leaska, friend and New York University mentor, will surely see his influence in various sections of this book (and in our previous book) where matters of style are discussed and stylistic principles are invoked.

PETER J. HAGER
H. J. SCHEIBER

September 1996

Contents

Part V Professional Presentation Models

Part VI Presenting in International Environments

Preparing Your Presentation

Introduction

The Role of Presentations in Technical, Scientific, and Managerial Environments

Professional presentations, as we are all now learning, have become increasingly essential to the ultimate success of just about every major enterprise in business, industry, and government, both in the United States and throughout the world. In fact, many organizations—large and small, national and global—rely on some kind of oral presentation for survival and for growth. An oral presentation can be used to (a) attract external business via bidding for contracts, (b) inform, and sometimes persuade, internal clients (e.g., senior-level management) about a program, a strategy, or a new technology, (c) market products, services, or ideas, and (d) attract investors, venture capital, or a board of directors.

RATIONALE AND FOUNDATION

Because the clear and effective presentation of technical information and data (computer-related, electronic, biotechnological, medical, astrophysical, financial/economic, chemical-engineering, geological, architectural, managerial/decisional) has become so important to just about every corporate entity and government agency, we believe that a book covering all facets of the presentation field would now be fully justified. That is, a book directed at meeting the needs of all those technical professionals who must develop, design, and make presentations routinely, as a large part of their work life, would clearly prove welcome.

But this book is not merely based on our hunches about the presentational needs of technical specialists, scientists, managers, or decision makers working at a broad range of jobs and professional levels within contemporary organizations. Instead, we have based the theory we present here and the practices we recommend throughout our book on research we recently completed.

Our Survey on Oral Communication

Before beginning to write *Designing and Delivering Successful Presentations,* we surveyed 210 professionals employed in technical, scientific, and managerial arenas.[1] Our survey subjects were randomly selected from mid- and large-size organizations involved in a range of activities, including aerospace, artificial intelligence/expert systems, banking, computer manufacturing, computer services, insurance, research and development, and space systems design. (Table A.1, appearing in Appendix A, presents a complete list of participating organizations.[2]) Of the 210 questionnaires we mailed out, respondents returned 106, for a very respectable 50.47 percent return rate.

Our survey—and our research goals in general—addressed the following 10 elements which we consider central to designing and delivering successful presentations by technical professionals and managers working in business, industry, and government:

(1) Frequency of presentations made

(2) Target audience(s) of presentations delivered

(3) Presentation objectives

(4) Types (or forms) of presentations made

(5) Presentation length

(6) Types of data or information presented

(7) Types of visuals used

(8) Equipment most frequently used

(9) Obstacles to delivering effective presentations

(10) Presenters' training in designing and delivering presentations.

The theories presented throughout our book, as well as the practices reviewed, illustrated, and recommended, are based largely on (a) responses to survey questions we posited to participants in our study, (b) descriptive responses and "anecdotal" commentary we obtained from many of the survey participants, and (c) additional business/industrial "probes" and consultation activities in which we have recently been involved.

Survey participants responded to our 10 issues-oriented questions and, also, to an eleventh question which simply asked participants to "add (or attach) anything important or relevant to *you* about making scientific/technical presentations (e.g., outlines, summaries, photocopies, or graphics) that has *not* been examined via this brief survey." As directed, some participants—about 26 percent of the total survey population—did append useful comments to this and other survey questions. Many of the practices, techniques, and habits offered to us by survey participants have been shared (and sometimes even mod-

[1] Secondary research for this project uncovered no published empirical studies on the nature of oral presentations in technical, scientific, or managerial environments. However, we direct interested readers to L. E. Corder's unpublished doctoral dissertation, "A Descriptive Study of Presentation Skills Training in *Fortune* 500 Industrial Companies" (University of Pittsburgh, 1990) for a survey- and interview-based examination of a wide range of current corporate presentational skills training practices.

[2] The survey also queried respondents for such demographic information as job title or profession (Table A.2), academic and professional degrees held (Table A.3), years of related professional/technical experience (Table A.4), and sex (Table A.5). For a copy of the survey used in our research, contact either author in writing or on the Internet (via e-mail) at HAGERPJ@JMU.EDU.

eled) within our book. (Complete survey response data are shown in Appendix A, Tables A.1–A.5.)

Some Fundamental Conclusions

An examination of our survey results—the proverbial "bottom line"—validates the fact that professional presentations are, indeed, regularly (a) made in business, industry, and governmental contexts and (b) delivered to a wide range of technical, scientific, and managerial audiences primarily up the organizational hierarchy. We also found that professional presentations are increasingly aimed at a variety of technical audiences, namely, technical customers, potential customers, and marketing and customer service "reps."

In addition, we found that professional presentations generally tend to be of what we termed "medium" duration, between 15 and 30 minutes. However, a bit more than a quarter of our survey respondents (some 27 percent) noted that their presentations usually last up to an hour. Still another quarter of our respondents (about 24 percent) reported that their presentations last more than one hour. For example, comments made by those who typically delivered presentations lasting an hour or more included the following:

- "Many [presentations] are more than one hour because of questions and answers during presentations."
- "Usually about an hour . . . including interaction with my audience regarding their experiences involving the subject matter or questions and answers."
- "Technical discussions often lengthen the time span . . . [to] two hours or more."
- "Design reviews take two hours minimum, depending on levels of responsibility and complexity of overall design."

Addressing the presentational time frame issue, one noteworthy group of survey respondents focused directly on audience concerns. Some of their comments included the following:

- "Length of time depends [first] on audience . . . and second on degree of technical information conveyed and questions asked."
- "Length of time [is] frequently dependent on degree of audience interaction. If they don't like what's being said, it can be a *very* long time, objectively as well as subjectively."
- "Depends on audience—try not to go over 90 minutes . . . ever."
  (We'll be addressing audience variables and related concerns at length in Chapter 2 of this book.)

Our findings suggest to us that messages contained in respondents' presentations represent more than mere routine or basic briefings. Presenters seem to be involved in detailed explanation—that is, producing and delivering *informative,* and what we call *decisional,* oral reports. More on these (and related) findings below.

Primary Objectives. Most of our survey respondents (some 66 percent) reported that the primary objectives of their presentations are to *inform* and to *instruct* or *train.* Many suggested that their professional presentations routinely involve "*sharing* information."

Surprisingly, fewer than 20 percent noted persuasion as a primary objective in giving their presentations. This finding regarding the *persuasive* aim suggests to us that those who teach oral communication skills to technical employees and technical managers—in both college courses and training seminars—might consider deemphasizing this presentational aim. As our data suggest, students and professionals alike might want to spend more classroom time on presentational skills involving informing, sharing data, and instructing. James G. Gray (1986) seems to agree with this point: "On most occasions, presentations are designed to be informational, a product update, for example" (p. 67). Gray adds, though, that professionals do "need to be prepared for occasions that call for highly persuasive presentations" (pp. 67–68). We certainly agree with this view. As we all have learned, and as we will show in this book, many seemingly informational or instructional presentations are really persuasive events in disguise (in intent).

Presentational Forms, Types, and Content. The most common forms of presentations identified by our respondents were technical messages (initiated by the respondents themselves) and messages geared toward decision-making and training activities. Respondents also indicated that their presentations are often more than mere superficial briefings; that is, they are more in the nature of informative and decisional (recommendations-based) reports which require substantial time for development and explanation.

Individual survey participants focused primarily on the content of their presentations; they indicated that the data and information they most frequently present involve the following:

- Technical information
- Marketing technology
- Financial data
- Project status reports
- Issues and recommendations reports
- Design reviews
- Product(s) reviews
- Assessments of organizational plans
- Analyses of budget submissions
- Technical aspects of system design(s)
- Pre- and post-hurricane disaster recovery planning
- SLOSH models and storm plotting.

Visuals or Graphics. To communicate both data and information clearly and quickly, our survey respondents noted that they most frequently rely on simple graphs, charts, and tables. Most of the employees we surveyed tended to eschew the fancier, more complex visuals and high-tech graphics. Respondents reported, for example, that they rarely use photographs, formulas, maps, or diagrams frequently found in scientific discourse, such as cutaways and exploded diagrams.

A small number of our survey participants (fewer than 10 percent), however, indicated that they do, in fact, regularly use more sophisticated means to support and enhance their presentations. Among the visuals, graphics, and presentational tools this group employs are the following:

- Block diagrams
- Schematics
- CAD
- Narrative statement charts
- Hierarchical level signal flow(s)
- Live computer demos with software or computer display(s)
- Computers and expert systems software connected to LCD/VGA-compatible overhead projectors that permit BITMAPS and animation.

Equipment Used. To present information involving visuals or graphics, about 23 percent of our respondents indicated they most frequently use overhead projectors. Roughly 20 percent of those we surveyed reported that they regularly use handouts of one sort or another, while 15 percent noted that they (still) use blackboards as adjuncts in delivering their professional presentations. Very few respondents in the population we surveyed, however, reported that they use opaque projectors, film, or recordings. While few in our sample noted the use of slides, we suspect that 35-mm slides might be used more regularly in formal presentations, as one respondent noted, as the medium for sharing or representing data and information. And, quite surprising to us, were the relatively small numbers of respondents (only 6.3 percent) who indicated that they use video technology in their professional presentations.

Descriptive comments we received from survey participants tended to ratify the results discussed in the previous paragraph (above). That is, many respondents indicated that they commonly use the overhead projector and handouts:

- "For most presentations I use vu-graphs."
- "[My] formal presentations utilize slides . . . but most presentations use viewgraphs."
- "I *always* have 'hardcopy' for the attendees, either as handouts or [as] published session notes."

One respondent noted the frequent use of "whiteboard"; another emphasized the use of "actual device demonstrations—prototypes, models, screen dumps to portray [the] look and feel of a future product."

Major Presentational Obstacles. For most of the technical, scientific, and managerial professionals we surveyed, the major obstacles to designing and delivering effective presentations can be summarized as follows:

(1) Attempting to cram too much information into a chosen presentation format and within a limited time frame (nearly 20 percent of respondents)
(2) Devoting (or allowing) insufficient time for preparation (about 13 percent)
(3) Selecting an appropriate organization and structure (about 12 percent).

In addition, a sizable portion of our respondents indicated that nervousness (about 11 percent) and the technical level of the information communicated (nearly 12 percent) were central obstacles to the successful delivery of presentations as well.

The question we posed about obstacles inhibiting effective presentations and typical difficulties met in delivering them elicited the greatest number of participant comments. Of those who provided a descriptive response to this question, about a third suggested that their presentations tend to be flawed because they consistently have "too much to say in a brief period." Another group—slightly larger than a third of those commenting on this issue—noted that they often had "difficulty fielding questions on the spot" or "difficulty with Q & A." Indeed, we will be addressing these obstacles (and many others) in various sections of subsequent chapters of this book.

Several respondents mentioned related areas and identified these as "my big" or "my biggest" problem(s):

- "Putting too much information on a single vu-graph."
- "Converting data to presentation form. . . . A mistake here can cause a very good idea and presentation to go right down the drain. It can . . . cause numerous questions and lead to lengthy discussions."
- "Preparing [for] technical presentations. . . . I find that . . . [when] I spend enough time on a presentation . . . usually 3 revisions . . . it goes well."

While only one participant cited nervousness as an obstacle ("The butterflies usually go away in approximately 10–15 seconds . . . which, I'm told, is normal."), several commented on various audience-related difficulties. All of the following difficulties were listed as major obstacles to overcome: adjusting to the level of a nontechnical audience, preparing for a specific audience, not knowing the composition of an audience, and using the "language" of a particular professional audience. Comments concerning various aspects of "audience analysis" included the following:

- "Determining the level of detail to satisfy the audience."
- "Presenting technical data to technical people in other . . . unrelated disciplines."
- ". . . Tailoring presentation to audience—many times background of attendees is not known."
- ". . . Presenting data to mixed audiences . . . [of] technicians who want nitty-gritty details and managers who want top-level summary only. In general, engineers have difficulty tayloring [*sic*] their presentations to the needs of the audience."
- ". . . Not knowing [your audience] and [not] adapting your presentation to . . . [that] audience. . . . Not being flexible enough to adjust your presentation based on what's already been said in the meeting."
- "Language type/level . . . matching the audience; converting professional lingo into language that matches the audience."

College Courses or Training Seminars Attended. The participants we surveyed reported having had some training in basic presentational skills (about 22 percent), oral communication (about 14 percent), and listening skills (14 percent). However, most of the participants reported only minimal training in more specific categories:

(1) General speech making

(2) Advanced oral communication

(3) Small-group communication

(4) The use of presentational visuals.

Indeed, very few respondents reported that they had ever enrolled in college courses or participated in training seminars dealing with "professional" speech making, advanced oral communication (technical or managerial), or small-group communication. And only about 6 percent of our survey respondents indicated that they had had training in the use of visuals for technical, scientific, or managerial communication purposes.

Comments made by survey participants focusing on college courses and training seminars devoted to making professional presentations were mixed and many. A few respondents noted having taken a Dale Carnegie course at some point in their careers; two respondents identified Toastmasters as a source of presentational skills development; another mentioned Justin Joseph's "The Power Presenter" seminar. Still other respondents mentioned in-house seminars in such areas as "state-of-the-art presentation skills," "effective presentations," and "train-the-trainer."

One participant, a director of corporate training at a major international organization, stated that she had had a professional development seminar entitled "Speaking as a Management Tool for Women." Other courses or seminar "experiences" in which survey participants had been involved included the following: the U.S. Navy's Instructor Training School course in oral communication, computer training seminars (for Harvard Graphics, BITSTREAM, computer graphics), speech in college, and the oral component of a college-level technical writing course.

A Final Note on Survey Responses

Many of the professionals who participated in our survey provided us with extensive and often insightful comments on a number of issues and problems—that is, comments on their careers, their communication training experiences, their ability to make presentations, and the elements of sound presentations, as well as advice on giving effective presentations and, of course, comments on our survey as well. We've included a small assortment of these comments here (below) to kindle your interest in reading our entire book.

We believe that we've provided our readers with much useful information, sound presentational techniques and strategies, ideas of all sorts, and possible solutions to the problems raised by our survey participants. We've addressed a wide variety of issues concerning oral communication in professional/technical contexts. Some of the issues we've decided to address in this book were, in fact, directly precipitated by the comments of our survey participants. Here are just a few:

- "I really enjoy all aspects of preparing and delivering presentations . . . as long as I have been given adequate preparation time."
- "I recommend to all my instructors that they need to complete . . . [our] course on giving presentations. This 2-day course *triples* their ability to give presentations!"
- ". . . [A speaker] should consider the *tone* of the presentation relative to the objective[s]."

- "Rarely . . . [make] formal presentations. . . . [I] use discussions of technical issues in informal, 'broad-based' sessions of 6–12 people."
- "The importance of a good outline cannot be stressed enough. If the presenter knows the subject, he or she needs to lay out a logical format and 'tell the story.' Graphs/charts must be kept simple so the audience pays attention to the speaker."

As an addendum to our survey results—and as prologue to a book on the nature of oral communication in professional/technical contexts—we'd like to present a rather incisive comment here from an aerospace-based business development manager:

- ". . . One must consider . . . the primary constraint[s] that may keep the presentation objective from being met . . . time, background, experience of the audience, size of the room, language, educational level[s], sensitivity of the subject. . . ."

In a very brief space, this aerospace development manager seems to have highlighted the essential elements of the field pretty well, indeed. So let's move on now and begin to consider in depth some of those elements that are particularly useful in developing the skills necessary for making successful presentations.

SUGGESTED READING

Corder, L. E. (1990). *A descriptive study of presentation skills training in Fortune 500 industrial companies.* Doctoral dissertation, University of Pittsburgh.

Fearing, B. E. (1985). Oral presentation and presence in business and industry. In M. G. Moran and D. Journet (Eds.), *Research in technical communication: A bibliographic sourcebook,* pp. 381–405. Westport, CT: Greenwood Press.

Gray, J. G., Jr. (1986). *Strategies and skills of technical presentations: A guide for professionals in business and industry.* New York: Quorum Books.

Weber, J. R. (1989). Professional presentations. In C. H. Sides (Ed.), *Technical and business communication: Bibliographic essays for teachers and corporate trainers,* pp. 201–220. Urbana, IL: National Council of Teachers of English (copublished by Society for Technical Communication).

1

Professional Presentations: Types, Tools, Techniques, and the Planning Process

Professional presentations of the sort we are examining throughout this book come in a wide variety of lengths, content packages, aims or purposes, and types or forms. We're all very much aware, naturally, that nontechnical, so-called "public" speeches often last from just a few minutes (say, 5 or 10) to a half hour (or more) and typical "political" speeches last, perhaps, 30 minutes to an hour (sometimes more). Technical, scientific, and management-oriented presentations also vary widely in the time frame a speaker selects to address a group.

PRESENTATIONS IDENTIFIED

The time frame a speaker must adhere to (or simply selects) in delivering a professional presentation, however, represents only one of the major variables we need to discuss in piecing together our working definition. The overall success of a given speaker, of course, depends on how completely she or he considers what we call the key *presentational variables*—content, audience, form/format, time frame, aims (CAFTA)—and plans with them in mind. Success also depends on how well these CAFTA variables, following close examination and careful preparation by the speaker, all cohere in the execution of the presentation.

In preparing for a professional presentation, then, the speaker must pose, address, and examine answers to a number of key questions during the planning stage to aid in the development of her or his notes, script, handouts, and visuals. Among the questions that speakers might consider during the planning stage are the following:

(1) Has the content been chosen in light of the background(s) and expertise of the audience to be addressed?

(2) Is the audience planned for—say, Cicero's "receptive, well-disposed, and attentive" *hearers*—the very same audience that will, in fact, be addressed?[1]

(3) Does the time frame the speaker has chosen mesh well with the degree of complexity of her or his material?

(4) Are the aims or objectives of the speaker clear and, perhaps, motivating for the members of the professional audience to be addressed?

(5) Does the content of the presentation jibe with the chosen form or format (collaborative, team-based oral technical report; half-day training session; strategic planning round-table discussion; marketing seminar; leadership forum)?

CAFTA Variables

While the remainder of our book will examine, in some detail, all of the presentational variables, our basic working definition must rely on and include those key CAFTA variables mentioned above:

- *Content*: The speaker's subject matter—for example, the degree of detail of the material; its complexity.

- *Audience*: Members of the group addressed—for example, technical, professional; interested, motivated listeners, or neutral or hostile listeners; members of the same "field" as the presenter, or not.

- *Form/Format*: The type of presentation designed and made—for example, a seminar presentation; conference presentation; delivery of academic or professional/technical paper; training program or presentation; collaborative or team-based presentation; panel or round-table discussion; business meeting; videoconference; press conference.

- *Time Frame*: Length of time your presentation will involve—for example, 5 to 10 minutes; 15 to 30 minutes; up to 1 hour; more than 1 hour; 2 hours; one-half day; full day or longer.

- *Aim(s)*: The stated or implied goal(s), objective(s), or purpose of your presentation—for example, to inform (share trends, empirical data, statistical information); to teach or train (focus on a process, product, pattern of behavior, marketing strategy); to persuade (make recommendations and argue for their implementation, present a "decisional" report and argue for the acceptance of key strategic decisions); to sell (an idea, concept, approach, strategy, process, or product).

Toward a Working Definition

As we can readily see from the list of presentational variables delineated above—and from the brief examples we've provided for each of these variables—a definition for the term *presentation* is no easy, clear-cut matter. In fact, attempting to define the breadth and scope of the professional presentation seems as difficult as, say, defining the contemporary automobile (two-seater sports car? subcompact? mid-size "family" car? luxury town car? European touring car? full-size convertible? compact station wagon? off-road, four-wheel

---

[1] For a discussion of the manipulation of the audience or "hearer" variable (within the planning process), according to a "classical" view, interested readers should see Cicero, *Ad Herennium,* I (H. Caplan, Ed. and Trans.), Cambridge, MA: Harvard University Press, 1989, iv.7–v.8, pp. 13–17 (original work published 1954).

drive vehicle? light pickup truck? mini-van?). All of these categories are obvious variants of the "umbrella" term automobile or the more abstract term vehicle. And, while all are fully described, exemplified, priced, and categorized by their manufacturer, category borders for each of these vehicles remain fuzzy. So, too, with professional presentations.

To provide some closure to our search for a working definition of presentations as we see them "manufactured" today by professional/technical speakers, we'll simply summarize. Suffice it to say, at this point in our discussion, that presentations

(1) reflect a wide variety of contents
(2) involve a number of different audiences or listener profiles, depending on levels of interest or motivation, training, expertise, professional experience, or vocation
(3) come in a multiplicity of forms, formats, and types
(4) vary considerably in the time frames during which a speaker presents material or interacts with an audience
(5) include a number of aims and objectives, depending on a speaker's (or an organization's) intended purpose(s).

PRESENTATIONAL TYPES

In this section we'll concentrate primarily on presentational types, forms, and formats. As we have shown in the discussion of our oral communication survey results, professional presentations—whether technical, science-based, or managerial—vary considerably in form, format, or type (see "Our Survey on Oral Communication" in the Introduction).

Although we want to focus on presentational types here, the other variables—content, audience, time frame, and aims—cannot be entirely excluded from our discussion because of the interrelationships that exist between and among them. As a professional situation or occasion triggering the need for a presentation evolves and changes, the type of presentation developed and delivered might also evolve and change. In addition, the CAFTA constellation of presentational variables will change as well.

To paraphrase what Mary Beth Debs (1989) has to say about writers working in industry, the choices that speakers who are working in business and industrial settings must make are generally drawn from the rhetorical situation that is "determined and mediated by . . . [their] organizational context" (p. 42). Typically presentational type(s) and subject matter are determined as much by the particular needs of mid- or senior-level management as by the broader organizational context or occasion.

Most Common Presentational Categories

Presentational types, therefore, will be as numerous and varied as the vehicle types we mentioned above—given the wide range of management needs and organizational occasions that routinely arise in the contexts of business, industry, government, or research. Among the wide variety of common presentational types (forms or formats), the following (often overlapping) categories have proved useful to us both in our research and in practice:

- Seminar presentation (in-house or external)
- Training program or presentation
- Conference presentation

sis is, strictly speaking, scientific. For example, a *conference* presentation or *round-table discussion* on radioactive luminous compounds might involve only (or primarily) "the discourse of science," relying minimally (or not at all) on ancillary technical data or external, practical information. Such a presentation might involve few or no immediate implications for product research or industrial development.

For the most part, the kinds of professional presentations we regularly encounter in business, industrial, and government contexts seem to be hybrid "affairs," with speakers blending the language(s) of science, technology, and business (economics, finance, or law) into a discourse drawing from two or all three domains—technical, scientific, and business/management.

In a pharmaceutical firm, a mid-level manager with scientific training might need to develop and deliver a presentation for sales representatives relying on a mixture of demographic or marketing data and information garnered from such interrelated fields as anatomy, physiology, pathology, and pharmacology. Likewise, a researcher working for a biotechnology organization might be asked to present her or his "findings"—involving the results of lengthy trials on a soon-to-be-patented human hormone therapy—to a team of senior managers with overall financial control of the project area. In each of these contexts, and hundreds of others you might only imagine, a presenter must marshal linguistic, data-based, and informational resources from different but interrelated professional spheres to deliver a complex message.

Whether your message draws from a repository of technical data (engineering, computer science, environmental), reflects the results of pure scientific inquiry (biochemical, geological, medical), or, alternatively, provides a package of information and relevant facts for management decision makers, the same commitment to *preparation* in designing and developing your presentation must be followed. Throughout this book, the presentational variables we examine must be carefully considered whether your subject matter, audiences, and professional field(s) are technical, scientific, or managerial, or, possibly, all three.

PRESENTATIONS AS MANAGEMENT TOOLS

At all levels of contemporary organizations, in every department and division—from R & D, product design, and manufacturing to marketing, finance, corporate planning, and sales—employees, supervisors, managers, and directors need to communicate their ideas to senior-level decision makers. Whether informing (sharing, training) or persuading ("selling"), analyzing, or designing, professionals in all fields need to "package" the outcomes of their work for consumption by organizational decision makers. Managers up and down the corporate hierarchy must, ultimately, share with top management what we call "decisional" materials:

- Data
- Information
- Facts
- Analyses
- Interpretations
- Methods
- Processes

- Solutions
- Results
- Recommendations

And, having received and read, listened to, or viewed these decisional materials, top management can then respond, plan, and act.

Organizational decision makers continually review materials that come to them in brief memos and complex, data-based reports (see Hager and Scheiber, 1992). They query department heads, researchers, project directors, engineers, and manufacturing supervisors—one-on-one—about progress, delivery schedules, training needs, product lines, government regulations, and patents. And they sit through staff meetings and planning sessions where essential data and information are presented in brief, "quick-hit" presentational formats (from 15 minutes to an hour) and in longer, more complex formats (from, say, an hour-long videoconference to a morning-long round-table discussion).

In short, whatever organization or field you work in now or plan to work in and whatever your professional role (supervisor, manager, researcher, design specialist, human resources administrator, systems analyst), you need to learn how to make effective presentations. You'll need to know how to communicate important information—that is, how to present decision-oriented raw materials—to senior management in a wide variety of technical, scientific, and industrial environments. Honing effective speaking skills will prove essential to you throughout your career(s) because of the potential power that resides in presentations as management tools—yes, powerful management tools for proposing new programs, generating knowledge pools, building profits, and increasing productivity.

If you still don't believe us, perhaps you'll be convinced by James A. Newman and Roy Alexander, who tell readers of their book *Climbing the Corporate Matterhorn* (1985) that no matter what your college program, you'd better be sure to to take courses in speaking and writing. "You may think you learned *both* years ago," Newman and Alexander assert, "but for the fast track, you didn't." They offer the following advice you need to ponder:

> . . . Speaking to groups—effectively and persuasively—is a basic requirement of executive life. You'll probably need to continue with business speaking courses later as well. But get on the right foot by studying speech in school.
>
> Some of the world's otherwise-sophisticates quake at facing an audience. Giants of industry become pygmies on a podium. Board chairmen self-destruct at stockholder meetings. Today, more than ever *the ability to speak well in public is critical* [italics added].
>
> . . . With the visibility of business leadership in the media increasing, executives often have to appear at public forums, before Congressional hearings, and at conventions.
>
> . . . Good speech can be the cutting edge in out-pointing a competitor who's almost as good but suffers from hoof-in-mouth disease. (pp. 25–26)

ORAL REPORTS AND WRITTEN REPORTS—A BRIEF COMPARISON

Designers of oral presentations for delivery in technical, scientific, and managerial environments share planning procedures and construction processes with writers of written reports. In designing both oral presentations (oral "reports") and written reports, for example, an software engineer, biochemical R & D specialist, or accounting manager might engage in the following procedures and processes whether writing an analytical report or designing a professional/technical presentation:

- Brainstorming
- Speculating and jotting down ideas
- Incubating them over a few days or even longer
- Outlining or simply making lists of essential information bits
- Devising a sound model for data collection
- Summarizing, analyzing, and synthesizing data and relevant information
- Presenting research results or recommendations
- Planning the structure of the document or organization of the presentation.

In addition, we find it important to point out here that the *oral* form of reporting technical, scientific, and management-based information and *written* reports reflecting the same content(s) are both "human systems" which, according to Rosenstein, Rathbone, and Schneerer (1964), involve following "the same basic rules of logic and rhetoric" (p. 63). Both oral and written systems "impose certain [obvious] demands upon the originator." These are the following:

(1) Speakers and writers must have information (or data) to transmit.
(2) Speakers and writers must have a legitimate purpose(s) for transmitting information (or data) and also for making demands on their listeners and readers.
(3) Speakers and listeners must encode their messages to fit the "channel capacity" of their listeners or readers—for example, their educational or technical background, their managerial experiences and skill areas, and their professional vocabularies.
(4) Speakers and writers must control the level of "noise" in the system.
(5) Speakers and writers must separate their functions as originators of language and information—as information sources, encoders of messages, and transmitters of messages.[3]

---

[3] This material has been adapted from A. R. Rosenstein, R. R. Rathbone, and W. F. Schneerer, *Engineering Communications,* Englewood Cliffs, NJ: Prentice-Hall, 1964, Chapter 6, pp. 63–66. Their term *noise* in item 4 of this list refers primarily, but not exclusively, to qualities of written reports and can be subdivided as follows:

(1) *Semantic noise,* "faulty word choice . . . improper sentence structure, failure to put words into a meaningful context . . . and poor organization of thought."

(2) *Mechanical noise,* "errors and inconsistencies in typography, poor physical layout of illustrations, overcrowding of text, poor reproduction qualities [*sic*], and even . . . a binding that prevents the reader from keeping the report open at a given page."

(3) *Psychological noise,* "any emotional reaction by the reader [or listener] that decreases his channel capacity, thus distorting the message. Doubt, disagreement, boredom, and even anger are . . . common negative reactions of technical readers [or listeners]. The source of psychological noise may be the message itself, semantic or mechanical noise in the message, or . . . [an] external stimulus" (Rosenstein et al., 1964, p. 53). Naturally, noise of all three varieties might well affect a writer's ability to communicate effectively with readers; psychological noise, particularly, might affect a speaker's ability to communicate successfully with listeners. Presenters should note, of course, that the emotional responses of members of your audience might distort your message—wholly or in part.

Finally, we need to mention that the format(s) of both oral and written reports—whether technical, scientific, or managerial—are, at least in part, dictated by the location (or hierarchical position) of speakers or writers within an organization and by their relationship to those who will use the report (listeners or readers). Where individuals or audiences are situated—internal, external, senior or executive level, professional level, entry level—with respect to a speaker or writer also has an impact on the format and, perhaps, even length of an oral or written report.

Indeed, the variation in format(s) of both oral and written reports is also directly related to the level of formality inherent in, or to be achieved by, the communication situation (see Hager and Scheiber, 1992, pp. 46–49). In the most general terms, both oral and written reports might involve communication situations that appear somewhere on the following three points of a continuum:

- *from* . . . relatively informal—for example, internal and, perhaps, in close proximity to the speaker or writer
- *to* . . . semi-formal—for example, an audience of mixed mid-level professionals from various locations (units, divisions) throughout an organization
- *ending up with* . . . formal—for example, a report aimed at, or a presentation designed for, top-level decision makers residing at (or near) the pinnacle of an organization.

(Rosenstein et al. [1964, pp. 63–64] maintain that the order presented above "represents the frequency of use and order of importance of the three types as far as communication is concerned.")

SELECTING PRESENTATIONAL DELIVERY TECHNIQUES

Whether your presentational aim or purpose involves informing, instructing, persuading, or entertaining—or, perhaps, more than one of these aims—you need to examine carefully the range of delivery technique(s) that are available to speakers. You might want to use any one or some combination of the following four basic delivery techniques:

(1) *Reading* from a prepared script

(2) *Speaking extemporaneously* from prepared notes

(3) *Memorizing* the complete presentation

(4) *Presenting in impromptu* fashion.

Each of these presentational techniques has advantages and disadvantages for both speakers and audience (see Hager and Scheiber, 1992, pp. 488–490).

The selection of any one (or more) of these techniques will depend on the particular business situation at hand and on the needs or constraints of a given speaking occasion: the specificity of your time frame; the needs of your audience; and, of course, the degree of complexity of the content or subject matter of your presentation. In short, a diligent examination of the various presentational variables—the CAFTA variables—discussed above should aid you in your process of selecting one (or more) delivery technique(s) that seems right for the speaking occasion.

Reading from a Prepared Script

Reading directly from a prepared script seems most appropriate when you are delivering a highly complex technical, scientific, or management-oriented presentation. In such a situation, because of the complexity of the material, a major consideration must be to communicate all of your data and information as precisely and accurately as possible.

If, for example, your presentation involved communicating the specifics of a "warhead replacement tactical telemetry" (WRTTM) system to decision makers within the Department of the Air Force, you might want to read from a prepared script (report, proposal). In this kind of situation, surely, you would not want to make even the smallest error or digress at all from the central thrust of your presentation. And to ensure for the utmost precision and accuracy in your delivery of such complex and detailed material, you would almost certainly follow a strategy of reading your entire presentation. In fact, in industrial, governmental, or military contexts, formal briefings or presentations of proposals are generally read from prepared texts.

Presentations designed for and delivered at scholarly, scientific, or technical conferences are often read from prepared texts (or papers) as well. Were a chief scientist from a national research facility to present her or his recommendations on the control and removal of radioactive contamination in laboratories, that scientist, because of the inherent complexity of the information, would do well to select a strategy of reading from a prepared text. In this case, the scientist would normally present a painstakingly researched, well-organized, and carefully structured "traditional" scientific paper, replete with finely wrought results, discussion, and recommendations.

Reading from a script, paper, or prepared text might also prove to be an advantageous strategy when your time frame must be strictly followed—as at a scientific or technical conference, a news conference, or any formal briefing. A speaker can much more easily gauge the length of her or his presentation when it is fully scripted and when that script is read from directly and thereby meet the dictates of a specific and allotted time frame.

However appropriate and advantageous it might seem to you to read through a scientific or technical paper or a management-based script, three disadvantages of this technique are worth noting. The primary disadvantage of reading anything aloud consists in the reader's inability to maintain eye contact with members of an audience for most of the presentation. And if eye contact is not continually made between speaker and listeners, then the possibility of losing your audience's attention to your message increases dramatically.

Moreover, when your ability to make eye contact with members of an audience has been diminished, then the necessary "barometric reading" you need from that audience—input, say, derived from body language, facial expressions, and the like—will also be diminished. Being attentive to the "pulse" of your listeners by maintaining eye contact with them can provide you with continuous audience input. You need that sort of input from members of your audience to gauge their needs—and their level of attentiveness—from one moment to the next during a presentation to ensure that you are, in fact, communicating your message successfully.

A second major disadvantage in employing a reading strategy involves the speaker's (or reader's) need to remain at a lectern or behind a podium. Because reading from a lecturn or podium generally prevents a speaker from moving around and about a stage area, such a lack of movement tends to alienate audience members rather than garner their attention. A speaker's movements often serve to punctuate topics and underscore key statements in a presentation. A static presentation delivered without movement from behind a podium, however, tends to discourage active listening, diminish involvement, and, thus, reduce the overall level of an audience's attention.

A third and final reason why reading from a script or prepared text might not prove successful concerns the skill level of most readers. Apart from those rare and uniquely gifted individuals, most readers read aloud in a rather dull or monotonous presentational style, quickly alienating potentially "connected" listeners and transforming them into bored and passive members of a captive audience.

Speaking Extemporaneously from Prepared Notes

Speaking extemporaneously from notes that have been prepared in advance is a second technique that you might want to consider using for delivering your presentation. Constructing your notes and organizing them prior to the actual presentation allows you as a speaker to communicate directly with your audience while effectively maintaining your course, your plan, and your overall approach to the talk. Because your presentation has been thoroughly planned in advance, you may, with some degree of ease, stray from your plan; that is, you may want to modify the content or even the overall structure of the presentation on the spot during the course of delivering your material.

You might, for example, find the material that you had prepared just a bit too formal, your anticipated time frame too long, or the structure of your talk too rigid for a particular audience or the physical setting when you enter that venue. Perhaps either your intended audience (now, say, a smaller group of program managers or fellow researchers) or the room you had scheduled (now a medium-sized conference room) has changed and you feel the need to modify your presentation. As you speak, then, you can easily accommodate your new group of listeners, readily adhere to a new time constraint, and even perform better within your newly found (smaller) physical setting. In any event, through extemporizing a business speech or technical presentation, a speaker's eyes can remain focused on members of her or his audience and need not be glued to the printed page.

Although extemporaneous speaking is the delivery technique chosen by most business professionals most often, this strategy can be an invitation for a speaker to digress too far from the original, planned presentational message. Additionally, timing an extemporaneous presentation with great precision might prove a bit more difficult than it would for simply reading a presentation word-for-word from a text.

Memorizing the Complete Presentation

Committing a technical, scientific, or management-based presentation to memory requires considerable skill and, of course, intense work. Memorizing the content of your presentation—your message—does, though, have two distinct advantages:

(1) No podium or lectern will be required because you need not have your prepared notes, written report, or presentational outline handy. You can simply move around and about that portion of the room allocated to your "performance" while continually maintaining eye contact with members of your audience.

(2) Flexibility to alter the content (message), structure, or length of your presentation can be maximized. In the same way that an extemporized presentation—based on prepared notes—enables you to change the content or structure of your talk in midstream, a memorized presentation permits that same degree of flexibility.

Memorizing the complete "text" of your presentation, however, has a major downside as well. Designing a clear, complete, absorbing, and entertaining—in a word, *effective*—technical, scientific, or managerial presentation can itself be a daunting task. If you add the preparation and practice time involved in committing your talk to memory, you increase your work load significantly. Indeed, most of the professionals in business, industry, and government we meet simply do not have the available time necessary to memorize even the most important presentation.

Obviously, for most mere mortals, the act of memorizing sophisticated statistical data, complex "bottom-line" figures, detailed conclusions and recommendations is no easy matter. What's more, even after memorizing the complete presentational text, a speaker never receives a guarantee that she or he will recall the text of the talk verbatim while under the stress inherent in such an event. A word, phrase, or sentence forgotten, or perhaps a "chunk" of your talk misstated or misplaced, can easily disorient and frazzle even the most confident speaker and most diligently memorized presentation.

And, finally, most speakers in business and industry who attempt to deliver memorized presentations frequently sound "staged" or wooden and seem only artificially in command of their subject matter. Thus, the lengthy preparation time you would need to invest in memorizing your presentation might be more productively spent in carefully reviewing the critical points of your message as well as the peripheral issues you intend to include.

Presenting in Impromptu Fashion

The *Oxford American Dictionary* defines *impromptu* as "without preparation or rehearsal." Thus, an impromptu professional presentation, the least formal of the four delivery techniques we've examined, is an unrehearsed, minimally planned presentation. Presenters adopting an impromptu delivery strategy do not memorize their messages verbatim nor do they speak from note cards or prepared outlines. Rather, they draw from their own general knowledge of the subject matter—or their own repository of key issues, ideas, or themes that have been internalized—delivering the essentials of their message spontaneously and as they deem appropriate for their audience during the presentation.

While it might prove useful to commit key phrases or data "bits" to memory, the greater portion of the impromptu presentation is spontaneous—that is, completely off the cuff. Following an impromptu strategy enables a presenter to (a) create an informal atmosphere for the duration of the presentation and (b) establish a more personal tone for the delivery of the message. When an impromptu strategy is employed, audience members will be put at ease and made to feel sufficiently comfortable to interact with a presenter. Employing such a strategy seems to encourage listeners to comment on topics or issues discussed, to share data or information, or query the speaker for answers or greater detail.

Presenters who adopt an impromptu strategy for delivering their presentations employ a delivery technique that can be extremely demanding. The successful impromptu speaker must work from, and depend on, a thorough knowledge of the subject matter and a profound understanding of the material to the extent that it has become almost second nature. The success of this strategy hinges on the speaker's ability to

- retrieve data rapidly from the recesses of memory
- generalize from prior experiences and apply acquired knowledge, behaviors, or solutions
- listen attentively and adroitly

- handle questions with dexterity
- maintain a high level of composure and poise.

On the downside, the use of an impromptu presentational strategy might tend to give speakers an artificial sense of security. Presenters might develop the false notion that scrupulous preparation and sufficient time devoted to designing and researching the presentation is, simply, not necessary. Of course, nothing could be further from the truth: successfully delivered impromptu presentations must appear fluid and well-paced and must communicate the information needed by the audience with precision and completeness.

Effective impromptu presenters, then, must (a) thoroughly research their topics, (b) methodically define their audience's backgrounds, interests, and needs, (c) anticipate an overall structure and general organization for their material, and (d) develop a polished, carefully modulated, and well-paced delivery style.

THE PRESENTATIONAL PLANNING PROCESS—AN OVERVIEW

Regardless of your subject matter, your time frame, your audience, your aim(s) or purpose(s), or even what type or form your presentation might take, putting together a successful technical, scientific, or managerial presentation necessarily involves considerable planning. Indeed, the more scrupulously your presentation has been planned, the more likely your presentation will prove to be a success. Where your ability to deliver successful presentations may be crucial to your success on the job, careful planning will become critical to your success as a presenter.

Planning, of course, cannot simply be a haphazard, last-minute affair; rather, you must develop and follow a strict planning process, one that works for you on a regular basis. The planning process you need to develop—and to which you ought to routinely adhere—should concentrate on the following areas, taken together as a series of recursive (or cyclical) stages: (1) Identify your aim or purpose and your presentational objectives, (2) define your audience, (3) select a format and outline your presentation, (4) collect and organize data and information, (5) draft your presentational script, (6) design and integrate effective visuals, and (7) practice (rehearse) your presentation.

While we submit that adhering to a strict planning process—within a reasonable time frame—is, ultimately, essential to a successful presentation, we also recognize that we aren't always granted a sufficient amount of time during which to plan properly. And this dilemma leads to one of the most fundamental questions that we find presenters consistently posing: "How can I plan my presentation effectively when I'm given only a very short notice to do so?" In his book, *The Persuasive Edge: The Executive's Guide to Speaking and Presenting,* Myles Martel (1989) provides us with "the basic answer" to this perennial question: "Don't leave out any of the steps [i.e., our *stages*] that you would rely on if you had weeks or months to prepare; just devote less time to each of them" (p. 147).

We believe that your preparation or planning process can most effectively be broken down into these *seven* stages—major stages in the design and development of your professional presentation (see Figure 1.1).

We'll briefly discuss a basic context to be established for each of these seven planning stages here (below); we'll examine the content of each of these stages in far greater detail throughout the rest of this book in the chapters that follow (e.g., see Chapter 2, "Presentational Aims/Objectives plus Audience Analysis," Chapter 3, "Researching Your

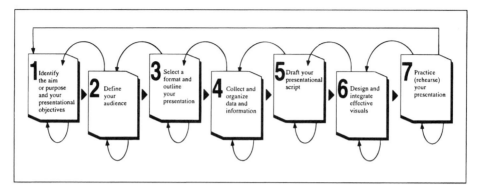

FIGURE 1.1. *The presentational planning process: a seven-stage, recursive process.*

Presentation," Chapter 4, "Organizing Your Presentation," and Chapter 6, "Selecting and Using Audio and Visual Presentation Media").

Stage 1: Identify Your Aim or Purpose and Your Presentational Objectives

Early in the preparation process, you must determine the aim or purpose of your presentation and identify your major objective(s). The basic aims or purposes of oral presentations are to

- Inform
- Instruct (or train)
- Entertain
- Persuade (or "sell").

Presentational objectives must, of course, be tailored to your overall aim or purpose; they must also reflect the entire constellation of CAFTA (content, audience, form/format, time frame) variables discussed earlier in this chapter.

If, for example, your aim is *instructional,* you might want to introduce human resource staff members to methods of implementing and following a variety of new benefits/compensation policies and procedures. If your aim, however, is *persuasive,* you might want to "sell" programmer/analysts on a best practice for retrieving files from your newly installed database system.

At times, of course, your aim might be twofold—for example, to inform and persuade. You might need to do the following:

(1) "Brief" or "update" your intended audience about a new (personnel) process or procedure

(2) Convince audience members of the merits of a new software product (e.g., a database system) to make that new process or procedure much easier to implement and follow.

Additionally, your persuasive or instructional presentation might also entertain. While entertainment is rarely the main aim or purpose of a technical, scientific, or management-oriented presentation, entertainment can increase the overall impact or effectiveness of an informational, instructional, or persuasive speech or presentation. More on presentational aims and objectives in Chapter 2.

Stage 2: Define Your Audience

While identifying your presentational aims and objectives will generally seem the best and most likely place from which to begin your preparation, defining your audience is perhaps the most essential element in the overall planning process. The skill and time you devote to defining, or *delimiting,* the membership of your intended audience will prove crucial to the ultimate success of your presentation.

Your broadest purpose is, of course, to *communicate.* And to communicate most effectively—to "connect" with your listeners—you must diligently examine

(1) the needs of those who will (or might) comprise your audience
(2) the possible uses to which they will put the information you provide.

After all, defining the membership of your intended audience and identifying their needs is, arguably, the most fundamental component in the communication "equation." Indeed, your message will become increasingly meaningful and significant to members of your audience as you begin to analyze and understand the needs of those individuals (or groups) who will listen to your presentation (or speech).

In short, your presentation will become *audience*-centered—that is, it will be shaped and molded according to the informational needs, professional experiences, backgrounds, and educational level(s) of your listeners. Your own, *speaker*-centered, needs must become subordinate to the needs of your listeners. After all, you know the material you are sharing well enough; your listeners, however, have come to your presentation to learn, to grow professionally, to be informed, instructed, or persuaded, and, possibly, to take some kind of action based on what they have heard.

In Chapter 2 we will examine in some detail the concept of audience analysis and its importance, demonstrate the central role of the audience variable in the CAFTA constellation, and describe how to analyze your audience most effectively.

Stage 3: Select a Format and Outline Your Presentation

The form, or format, your presentation will take depends, of course, on the other CAFTA variables we have isolated and examined earlier in this chapter—including your content, audience, time frame, and aim(s).

In many instances, we can form or mold our own presentational content (e.g., in developing and delivering a conference paper). In other speaking situations, however, our content, allotted time frame, and aim(s) dictate or merely suggest particular presentational forms or formats, such as the following:

- **Collaborative or team-based product development reports** (progress or periodic) to senior-level progam management (1- to 1½ hour time frame per month)

- **Training program modules** aimed at software product users (1- to 2-hour modules, depending on length and complexity of documentation to be covered)
- **Panel or round-table discussion(s)** on industrial safety (OSHA) and pollution control standards to be videotaped for all corporate professional and "exempt" employees (2-hour time frame, to be viewed when managers can schedule unit/department sessions)
- **Press conference(s)** announcing a biotechnological firm's latest product, the Aleppo 2100/DNA Synthesizer, and contribution to genetic research (½ hour, invited local and national news media)
- **Business meeting presentation(s)** at two distant corporate sites (Atlanta, GA and Melbourne, FL) to inform managers from marketing, finance, and planning sectors of fourth-quarter figures on product sales compared to those of the previous fiscal year (15- to 20-minute presentations by several key team leaders).

While methods of organizing your professional presentation will be offered in a later chapter, we want to comment briefly here on the need for *outlining* your data and information—prior to refining your working notes, ordering your content, or constructing your script. Whether you generate a formal topical outline, a paragraph (or "chunk") outline, or an informal outline simply "roughing out" central points you intend to make during your presentation, an outline will help you to

- *forecast* the direction of your oral "report"
- *dissect* it into major parts or subsections
- *visualize* the whole as an extended unit.

The use of some kind of outline—however brief, personal, or idiosyncratic—will surely aid you in (a) envisioning the scope, length, and limitations of your undertaking, (b) assembling your data and information, (c) drafting the sections of your script (whether you plan to follow one strictly or not), (d) revising your script (your formal paper, or the written version of your oral "report"), and (e) organizing or reordering your finished product.

Stage 4: Collect and Organize Data and Information

The outline you generate (see Stage 3) will enable you to collect appropriate data and information needed to enrich and strengthen your presentation. Your outline will also help you to conduct an efficient search—logical, ordered, systematic—for data and information relevant to your presentation topic. Putting together an outline, and tinkering with it, will help you to (a) clarify your topic further (for yourself), (b) narrow its scope to a manageable size, and (c) focus your search toward appropriate issues and key subtopics.

Your search for primary data (data, perhaps, that you've collected) and secondary information (library-based books, journal articles, reports) will prove considerably easier and more efficient if you've clarified your presentational topic and effectively narrowed its scope via some variety of outlining process. For a detailed discussion on conducting secondary and primary research for your report or presentational needs, see Hager and Scheiber (1992, Part III, pp. 161–252).

Following the collection of data and information from secondary or primary sources, you will need to *organize* your material into some kind of logical order for the most successful presentation of that material to an audience. You must, for example, decide the following:

- What must be included in your presentation and what might be effectively left out
- How, exactly, your material might best be arranged for oral (and visual) consumption
- Where emphases in your presentational material might most appropriately be placed
- How best to interpret the data and information for listeners so that your conclusions appear clear and well-founded and your recommendations justified.

Stage 5: Draft Your Presentational Script

Your data have now been collected, your information tentatively organized, your rough outline refined, and your working notes ordered. At this point in the planning process, you will want all of the various strands of your research—data, information, outline, notes— to meld into a solid structure as your presentation continues to evolve. Stage 5, therefore, involves drafting a presentational script to provide the necessary structure, or foundation, on which to build your presentation.

While you may not choose to use the script during your talk or presentation, we believe that developing or "drafting" such a script is essential to the planning process. Constructing a complete script will, ultimately, provide a degree of coherence, consistency, and clarity necessary for the transmission of complex technical, scientific, or management-based material orally.

All of this preparation adds up to what we call *audience awareness* and ensures that you, the speaker, center your presentation on the needs of your audience. Without doubt, any complex professional presentation that appears incoherent, inconsistent, muddled, or aimless to the members of your audience will result in communication failure. We believe that a scrupulously constructed script is your proverbial ticket to the successful presentation of complex ideas.

We'll have considerably more to say about developing and drafting presentational scripts in Chapter 5.

Stage 6: Design and Integrate Effective Visuals

Complex technical, scientific, and management-based presentations tend to be more convincing and more memorable when visuals are used and skillfully integrated within and throughout your script, or the text of your material.

Researchers suggest that just a few days after your presentation, listeners will generally recall roughly 10 percent of what they heard you say. However, if your presentation involves the effective use of visuals, members of your audience might well retain 50 percent—some authorities say 65 percent or more—of what they've both seen and heard even three days after the event.

We'll discuss how to design and integrate effective visual aids later on (see Part II, Chapters 6 and 7). We'll focus on choosing the right visual, designing dynamic visuals, and integrating visuals into your presentation. Now, though, we simply want to underscore the persuasive potential of even the most common, least expensive visuals—for example, chalk boards, overhead transparencies, posters, flip charts, or 35-mm slides.

We're not talking here about sophisticated video displays, stand-alone computer technology, or the use of hypermedia; we're not talking about what Suzanne Watzman, in a recent *ITC Desktop* article, has dubbed presentations with "technical razzle-dazzle." Nope, just the use of plain vanilla visuals to enhance your technical, scientific, or management presentation.

A study conducted at the University of Pennsylvania's Wharton School, among graduate-level (MBA) students, found that the mere addition of overhead transparencies to basic business presentations tended to

(1) strengthen the impact of the overall presentation on audience members

(2) increase the perceived organization of the presentation

(3) elevate the *ethos* or credibility of the speaker and the believability of the presentational content

(4) increase audience support for a given position (i.e., say "yes" to, and act on, a recommendation).[4]

Stage 7: Practice (Rehearse) Your Presentation

Finally, we want to emphasize the importance of practicing your presentation, preferably *more than once* and in an environment that simulates the venue you will actually use at the time of your presentation. We believe that successful professional presentations are a result of careful, scrupulous practice sessions and at least one final dress rehearsal.

If you intend to give your presentation in a small conference room with chairs around the conference table, with a package of handouts and a whiteboard, try to match that sort of environment during your practice session(s). If, on the other hand, your presentation is scheduled to take place in a mid-size hotel banquet room or auditorium and you plan to use 35-mm slides and a slide projector, make every effort to practice at a similar site.

Whatever time frame you are scheduled to speak within, whatever your ultimate presentation format and venue, whatever visuals and equipment you intend to use, be sure to practice your presentation in a manner that matches your actual presentation as closely as you are able. In addition, visit the actual site—the training room, conference room, hotel banquet room, board room, local auditorium—in order to get a feel for the layout, the acoustics, the seating arrangements and chairs, and the lighting.

Three final comments on practicing and rehearsing your speech, talk, or professional presentation:

(1) Practice delivering your complete presentation before a trusted colleague, organizational peer, candid friend, or your spouse. And that means practicing from beginning to end, including a summary if you've prepared one.

(2) Be certain, too, to elicit critical feedback from that colleague, peer, or friend. Ask for an in-depth analysis of all aspects of your presentation as delivered during the practice session(s) or final rehearsal. Bert Decker, a communication trainer we respect, suggests that you garner three positive comments about your presentation during the practice session(s) coupled with three negative.

---

[4] For additional comments on this Wharton School study, see D. A. Peoples, *Presentations Plus: David Peoples' Proven Techniques,* New York: John Wiley & Sons, 1988, p. 68.

(3) Make use of either videotaping or audio taping to review your presentation, to gauge your effectiveness yourself, and, also, to stimulate evaluative feedback from reliable colleagues and interested peers whose technical or professional training might be relevant.

Kenneth Koehler (1991), a partner in the firm of Peat Marwick Stevenson & Kellogg who consults in financial and general management studies, neatly sums up what is frequently missed in developing a presentation—appropriate *planning* and *practice:*

> *Planning* should place a great deal of emphasis on *the visual elements* of a presentation. And *practice* should result in the best use of time and an appropriate marriage between the visual and audio elements—resulting in a truly effective presentation [italics added]. (p. 25)

SUGGESTED READING

Debs, M. B. (1989). Collaborative writing in industry. In B. E. Fearing and W. K. Sparrow (Eds.), *Technical writing: Theory and practice,* pp. 33–42. New York: Modern Language Association.

Decker, B. (1991). *You've got to be believed to be heard.* New York: St. Martin's Press.

Forbes, M. (1993). *Writing technical articles, speeches, and manuals.* Malabar, FL: Krieger Publishing Co.

Gray, J. G., Jr. (1986). *Strategies and skills of technical presentations: A guide for professionals in business and industry.* Westport, CT: Quorum Books.

Hager, P. J., and Scheiber, H. J. (1992). *Report writing for management decisions.* New York: Macmillan.

Koehler, K. G. (1991). How to make an effective presentation. *CMA Magazine,* February, 25.

Martel, M. (1989). *The persuasive edge: The executive's guide to speaking and presenting.* New York: Ballantine Books.

Newman, J. A., and Alexander, R. (1985). *Climbing the corporate Matterhorn.* New York: John Wiley & Sons.

Peoples, D. A. (1988). *Presentations plus: David Peoples' proven techniques.* New York: John Wiley & Sons.

Rosenstein, A. B., Rathbone, R. R., and Schneerer, W. F. (1964). *Engineering communications.* Englewood Cliffs, NJ: Prentice-Hall. See especially Chapters 5 and 6.

2

Presentational Aims/Objectives Plus Audience Analysis

As we noted in the previous chapter, Stage 1 of the presentational planning process involves carefully identifying your aim(s) or purpose(s). If you haven't determined your primary aim or purpose—say, to instruct or train a dozen senior programmer/analysts in the basics of a newly purchased relational database system called TechnoQuest 1.0—you simply cannot further refine your presentation into discrete sections with concrete objectives. And a presentation without concrete, clear-cut, or stated, and thus achievable, objectives will surely never succeed.

IDENTIFYING PRESENTATIONAL OBJECTIVES

In identifying presentational objectives, you must initially ask yourself what you want your audience to *learn,* to *know,* or to be able *to do.* What information—or new skills—do you want your listeners to leave your presentation with? You must also determine the number of presentation sessions you will need—or, more likely, you will be "allowed"—to train the group thoroughly or partially or minimally in the use(s) and application(s) of the system. Moreover, you must decide how much information you can legitimately cover during three or four or even five three-hour (morning) training sessions. And, following these initial training sessions, you must determine whether full mastery of the software can be achieved or, more reasonably, whether only an introduction can be provided to the uses and applications of such a complex software package.

Keeping this same example in mind, should these programmer/analysts leave your presentation with a thorough knowledge of the TechnoQuest software? Should they have learned how to use the database for a wide variety of both common business queries and sophisticated, "special" applications? Or, following this initial phase of the training, should they simply have learned to use the software for only the most routine business applications?

So, while you've succeeded, perhaps, in identifying your aim—in this case, *training* or *instructing*—you will certainly have found that isolating three or four (or even five) major presentational objectives must be done only in the context of examining all of the other CAFTA variables. That is, since an examination of each variable affects the evolution of your presentation, you, the presenter-trainer, must make reasonable and appropriate decisions about all aspects of your presentation:

- The degree of difficulty of your *content* or subject—that is, of training senior programmer/analysts to use TechnoQuest 1.0 and (all?) its applications.
- The skill level and composition of your *audience*—their interest and motivation as professionals in the data processing field, as well as their need for the training in order to succeed daily on the job.
- The *form/format* of the training—for example, a single trainer (you) with all trainees working "hands-on" in a corporate data processing training lab; a team of two or three trainers working with the group in a conference room setting via an overhead monitor, computer, and real-time screen; and so forth.
- The *time frame* overall needed for, or allocated to, the training sessions and the length of time per day that each individual session should (or will) involve.

STANDARD PRESENTATIONAL AIMS

In our discussion of the major presentational (or CAFTA) variables in the previous chapter, we outlined a variety of standard presentational aims. We'll repeat some of those aims here so that we can further refine and subdivide these aims into useful presentational objectives.

If you recall, we have defined a presentational *aim* as a stated or implied goal or purpose—that is, the goal or purpose of your presentation, speech, or talk. Whether your aims address or evolve from technical, scientific, or management-based subject matter, they will very likely fall into the following broad categories:

- **To inform**—for example, sharing trends, ideas, empirical (or tabular) data, payroll data, statistical information, descriptive information, inventory figures, manufacturing cost-benefit analyses.
- **To teach** or **train**—for example, focusing on a process (like team building), a product (new chemical compound, microminiature modem technology), a pattern of behavior (techniques for creative problem solving, language skills training for bicultural business and technical communication contexts), a new marketing strategy (Merck's "revenue hedging model" as optimal marketing tool), or software use (a relational database system).
- **To persuade**—for example, presenting manufacturing-oriented recommendations along with concrete "arguments" (i.e., data and information) for their immediate (or long-range) implementation; arguing for the acceptance of key corporate-level strategic market decisions examined and developed in a series of decisional reports written for senior-level executives; arguing for a substantially enlarged departmental budget and presenting your arguments graphically emphasizing more efficient product marketing strategies, increasingly complex needs, and spiraling costs; presenting recommendations for a research staff increase at the professional–scientific level to develop a significantly more effective, more compact "pump" design for single-organ chemotherapeutic use.

- **To sell**—that is, "selling," or targeting, addressing, and convincing members of your audience to "buy" or "buy into" your idea (designing and marketing programming system software based exclusively on natural language processing techniques), concept (operating with self-directed work teams), approach (changing behaviors of manufacturing related employees through team-building activities), strategy (developing an investment portfolio consisting only of no-load growth, balanced, sector, bond, and global funds), proposal ("reengineering" the culture of your organization toward maximum and measurable efficiency of human resources at all levels of the corporate hierarchy), process (incorporating the dual-delivery document design process in the product development cycle), or product (creating newly designed, aesthetically appealing newspaper vending machines).

TYPICAL PRESENTATIONAL OBJECTIVES

Presentational objectives for any of the above aims or aim categories must, minimally, be (a) clear and briefly stated, (b) concrete (where and when possible), (c) action-oriented (if appropriate), and (d) audience-centered (as strictly as might prove useful to your specific, well-defined audience).

Following up on training senior programmer/analysts to use TechnoQuest 1.0, the relational database software system we discussed above, let's now place a group of these same senior programmer/analysts into a somewhat different training context—that of "leadership training" for supervisors and team leaders.

Naturally, in designing and developing a training program in situational leadership for this group of data processing supervisors, we need to delimit a set of clear presentational objectives based on our examination of the other major CAFTA variables (content, audience, form/format, time frame). If, as before, in the TechnoQuest scenario we want to

(1) conduct in-depth skills training (*aim*) in order to

(2) hone the situational leadership skills (*content*) of data processing supervisors, potential supervisors, and team leaders (*audience*), we might design a training program to take place over the course of three three-hour morning sessions (*time frame*) to be held in a conference room, employing two instructors to present material via small seminar groupings (*format*).

The *objectives* for the first morning of the three-day training seminar on situational leadership[1] might consist, for example, in the following:

DAY 1: OBJECTIVES

Part 1

- What are the major "leadership styles"?
  - Directing
  - Coaching

[1] These presentational objectives were derived by us from "Leadership Training For Supervisors—Situational Leadership II" (Module 2), Blanchard Training and Development, Inc., 1990, a training seminar conducted for data processing staff at Watkins Motor Lines, Inc., Lakeland, FL during the spring of 1994. We have developed this brief series of objectives—loosely adapted from the Blanchard material—for the exclusive purpose of illustrating the teaching/training presentational aim.

- Supporting
- Delegating
- How might we observe leadership styles on the job?
  - Observe your boss's leadership style
  - Observe your own leadership style
  - Examine your use of different styles with various employees

Part 2

- How do effective supervisors . . .
  - Use different approaches (or styles) for *different* employees?
  - Use different approaches (or styles) for the *same* employees, depending on the task at hand?

Part 3

- How might we best define an employee's development level regarding the task at hand?
  - How might we measure an employee's *competence?*
  - How might we measure an employee's *commitment?*
  - How might we assess an employee's *motivation* level for a given task?
  - How might we assess an employee's *confidence* level for a given task?
- How might we diagnose an employee's *development* level for a specific task?
  - What skill(s) does the employee bring to the task?
  - Can the employee perform the task without help?

These objectives, developed for a training-based presentation and in conjunction with the training aim, are relatively brief, clearly subdivided into three parts, generally concrete, action-oriented, and, perhaps most important, audience-centered. The data processing professionals addressed here seem to be targeted as an audience of interested listeners eager to gain (a) insights into basic leadership theory and (b) skills in applying that theory to specific tasks, employee types, and supervisory or management contexts.

SHAPING YOUR AIM(S) AND OBJECTIVES INTO A UNIFIED AND COHERENT PRESENTATION

Once presenters have identified their aim or aims (e.g., to inform, train, persuade, etc.), they will want to adhere to Stage 1 of the presentational planning process (see Figure 1.1) and, thus, generate at least a rough list of major (and minor?) objectives. Some presenters, though, might wish to move on to Stage 3 and produce an outline (however rough) of their presentational script—that is, even prior to developing their list of objectives. Still other presenters might move quickly on to Stage 5 and construct an initial "draft" of the presentational script.

Whichever planning strategy you adopt, some amount of *brainstorming* will necessarily be undertaken to solidify the goal you intend to pursue:

- What facts relate to the problem?
- What's causing the problem?
- What information sources are available?
- What bite-sized "chunks" can I (we) assimilate?

Step 2: Define the problem.

- What type of problem has been identified (e.g., analytical, judgmental, creative)?
- Does your problem statement encourage creative responses?
- What other related problems seem to exist?

Step 3: Generate bright ideas.

- What are some possible responses? What raw ideas can we list?
- What are some possible combinations and recombinations of these ideas?
- What seem to be the most imaginative ideas?

Step 4: Allow your ideas to incubate.

- What new ideas have surfaced?
- What are your more unconventional ideas?
- What requirements must be met (individual, organizational)?

Step 5: Evaluate your ideas.

- What categories do your ideas belong to?
- What "tools" might be used for evaluating your ideas?
- Which of your ideas might need to be combined, modified, or somehow improved?
- What restrictions need to be considered?

Step 6: Select the best solution(s).

- Which ideas seem to be most useful?
- What criteria might you follow for selecting the best solution(s)?

Step 7: Test your solutions.

- Does your idea work?
- Does the idea meet your needs or requirements?
- Are there (now) any new alternatives to consider?
- Does your idea need any reworking? If so, at what level?

Step 8: Use your solutions.

- How can your idea best be communicated to others?
- Who will support your idea? Which audience members will support your idea?
- What level of "buy-in" will you need to launch your idea?
- How might your idea best be executed?

Finding answers to these kinds of questions during the presentational planning process will surely help you to develop an effective individual or team presentation. Generating creative solutions, based on answers to these and similar questions, will surely help you to succeed whenever you become involved with—and must present to others—technical, scientific, or management-oriented material of a complex or controversial nature.

DEFINING YOUR AUDIENCE

Arguably the most important of the seven stages in the presentational planning process—and the one most often only partially attended to or neglected altogether—Stage 2 involves defining (and delimiting) the membership of your intended audience. As we mentioned in our brief discussion of the CAFTA constellation in Chapter 1, defining your audience with care and completeness will prove crucial to the ultimate success of your presentation.

While your broadest purpose remains to communicate, to communicate most effectively, as we keep arguing, means to "connect" with the members of your intended audience, your hypothetical listeners. But, to connect with your listeners in the deepest and most practical way(s), you must scrupulously examine their *needs* and the potential *uses* to which they might put the data and information you provide during your presentation.

Delimiting Your Audience

Identifying the purpose(s) of your presentation, as well as determining the objectives for delivering your oral "report," certainly comprise major stages in the planning process. Nevertheless, structuring your presentation (i.e., collecting the data, producing your outline, drafting your script) so that it meets the informational needs, professional expertise, and skill or ability levels of your listeners will prove a futile task unless and until you take the time to analyze, or *delimit,* your audience.

Oral presentations, as we've said in another context, must be *audience*-centered, not *speaker*-centered. The more completely you understand your intended listeners, the richer and more meaningful your technical talk or professional presentation will appear to them. Just as potential readers of organizational documents vary in many ways—for example, in job title or job function—your "organizational" listeners (whether senior scientists or senior managers, or both) will differ, too, with regard to the following categories:

1. *Informational Needs.* Their interest in, and need for, data and information, method(s) or approach, results, recommendations.
2. *Intended Uses.* Uses to which data and information, method(s) or approach, results, and recommendations will be put (and the relative priorities "assigned" for each use).
3. *Knowledge of the Presentational Topic.* General knowledge of the topic; specific knowledge of the subject matter, the background details, and the overall "context" out of which the material has evolved.
4. *Range of Experience in the Presentational Topic Field.* Practical experience on the job, in the general field, in the lab, or in a particular industry or organization.
5. *Preconceptions of You and the Upcoming Presentation Itself.* Motivation to attend and to listen carefully; degree of interest in your topic (neutrality toward it, hostility); allocation of time (and money) to attend.

6. *Demographics.* Formal education, professional/technical training, skill and ability levels; organizational responsibilities, duties, and specialties; ratio of male to female, English-speaking to non-English-speaking audience membership.

7. *Size of Your Intended Audience.* Small seminar size, mid-size training classroom, large-scale conference presentation or hotel ballroom venue.

When you have delimited your intended audience, you will be able to perform your presentational planning activities much more purposefully. Clearly and carefully delimiting your presentational audience will surely help you to do the following:

- Modify your topic, content, organization, format, and delivery mode at any convenient point in advance of your delivery date so that the presentation best fits the needs (backgrounds, skill levels, priorities, time constraints, etc.) of your listeners.
- Anticipate and prepare for potential obstacles or difficulties that could obstruct the communication of your message (e.g., enclaves of unmotivated or unreceptive listeners, blocs of hostile listeners, drifting audience sentiment that just might turn against your message, latent biases that even your listeners might not be able to acknowledge).
- Adjust, adapt, or alter your message (content, point, even objective) more adeptly during the presentation so that adjustments to your original script might appear seamless to the members of your audience.
- Design and include the most appropriate visual aids (or graphics) to clarify, simplify, explain, or review key ideas presented.

Refining Your Audience Analysis Technique

To delimit your presentational audience effectively and to refine your objectives in the process, you might want to pose a broad range of audience-directed questions to answer throughout the planning stages of your project. Formulating answers to these audience-directed questions will likely help you to structure your overall presentation as well.

Informational Needs. Because you probably have isolated far more points (ideas, objectives) in planning your project than you can ultimately include—points that you deem important enough to warrant inclusion in your "finished" presentation—you might want to rethink these points and their number. You might consider evaluating them for inclusion solely on the basis of the specific informational needs of your listeners rather than for your own professional gratification. Distinguish between what they *want* to hear, what they *expect* to hear, and what they *need* to hear. For example, employees of *XYZ* Corporation—at all organizational levels—invariably want to hear that the company they work for is in superior financial health. Nevertheless, what you might need to tell them, in your role of vice president for corporate affairs, is that for a variety of reasons the company must adhere to an "austerity track" during the next 2–3 years in order to survive.

Intended Uses. Additionally, in preparing your presentation, you would do well to explore the possible uses to which your listeners will put the material you intend to provide.

So that the members of your audience can best use (act on, or profit from) the data and information you intend to provide, how general, abstract, specific, concrete, or detailed must your material be? Naturally, if you aim to deliver a training-oriented presentation based on the new text-editing program, *LOGOS,* you would surely want to provide sufficient information and enough concrete detail so that members of your audience will be able to use the software independently, as expected, according to your published objectives.

Impact of Prior Knowledge and Professional Experience. Prior knowledge of your topic and experiences within the field that your listeners will bring with them to the presentation also impact your presentational planning process. Therefore, in order to meet the needs of your listeners, you must mold the content and structure of your developing presentation according to your best estimate of an audience's knowledge-base and experience level. You might consider these kinds of questions in planning:

- What general knowledge base and experience level(s) might members of your expected audience have in common?
- What specific knowledge and experiences do audience members possess in relation to your presentational subject matter?
- What, exactly, do members of your audience already know about your intended message? And, how much more do they *need* to know?
- How much training have they had in your (broad) field? How much experience in your (particular) discipline?
- What is the technical level of their training or the precise nature of their experience? Where did they receive their training or gain such experience? Within your organization? With another, competing organization? In an American work environment (or university)? Abroad?

Because speakers tend to immerse themselves so completely in their presentational topic—or are so thoroughly familiar with every aspect of their theme—they often assume that their audience is equally knowledgeable about their topic. Eager to share their in-depth knowledge and armed with the misconception that their listeners know (or care) as much about their theme as they do, speakers frequently launch into presentations far too advanced or content-specific for their audience. If the occasion for your presentation calls for (and attracts) a self-selected group of listeners with shared experiences, relevant academic or industrial training, or professional interest in your particular field, you'll be just fine. More likely, though, your presentation will prove a (predictable) communication failure—producing boredom or disappointment, confusion, and irritation.

Suppose, for a moment, you are asked to design and deliver a presentation on the new relational database software, TechnoQuest 1.0, the system we mentioned earlier in this chapter. Unlike before, when we were training data processing technical professionals, on this occasion you are persuading a dozen (or so) managers from marketing, sales, human resources, manufacturing, and accounting to implement the system and thus connect all isolated databases currently in use in their divisions.

On such an occasion, your aim is to persuade this group of nontechnical managers that the new ("networked") database software should be implemented for two essential reasons: (1) to improve organizational (interdivisional) efficiency and (2) to reduce operational expenses.

message? Certainly you could easily gauge in advance the possible response and motivation level of your intended audience if you were to speak about either of the following subjects:

- **A new package of employee benefits,** including longer yearly vacation periods, a more substantial and inclusive medical/dental plan, a more elaborate college/university credit reimbursement program (including graduate-level education), and an extensive open-access professional development/training component.
- **A recently purchased database software system,** which will save the organization, and a number of divisional managers, significant amounts of two prized commodities, time and money.

Conversely, if you were to deliver a presentation whose central message happened to reflect a universally perceived *negative* event, say

- an impending series of "downsizing" (or "outsizing") corporate maneuvers, or
- the results of a series of experimental protocols which will *delay* the market release of an important and potentially profitable new drug, you would certainly want to
  (a) anticipate the depth of possible hostility your listeners might bring with them to the presentation (aimed, presumably, at you) and
  (b) plan for the inevitable hostile response by selecting strategies you believe can reduce and diffuse audience resentment.

Demographics and Size. Another important factor to consider in analyzing audiences, and fundamental to effectively planning your presentation, involves audience demographics. A number of essential questions should be posed (and answered) as you attempt to delimit the *demographic* characteristics of your intended audience. Some questions about the nature of your audience might be the following:

(1) What is (are) the level(s) of formal education of your listeners? College educated? Managers/administrators with MS or MBA degrees? Researchers with PhDs in technical or scientific areas?
(2) What is the nature of their technical/professional training? What kinds of technical skills and abilities do they bring to your presentation?
(3) What are the organizational duties and responsibilities of the members of your intended audience?
(4) What is (are) the cultural background(s) of your audience? What are their political, social, trade, or labor affiliations? What portion of your audience is English speaking? Non-English speaking?
(5) What is the male-to-female ratio of your intended audience? What is their average age? The average number of years working in your organization? The average number of years working at their current job or in their profession? What is the average income level of your listeners?

One final factor to consider in analyzing your audience is, of course, the *size* of the group expected to attend. The size of your audience will necessarily affect your planning process and will be determined largely by the overall aim (e.g., training, selling) and specific objectives of your presentation. Naturally, you will want to include in your presentational audience all those individuals with some sort of vested interest in your message.

If you intend to train corporate employees in the use of the database, TechnoQuest 1.0, you might initially include only senior divisional managers and their immediate administrative staffs, a relatively small group of 12 or 15 people. However, if you intend to train programmers and systems analysts in the various, in-depth technical applications of TechnoQuest 1.0, you might need to involve, and plan logistically for, 50 (or more) professionals working in your organization's data processing or MIS division. In the case of the former group of divisional managers, you'd probably decide to hold your presentation in a relatively small conference room simply working around a table. In the case of the latter group, the programmers and systems analysts, you might want to consider a few alternatives. For this group, comprising a large number of technical professionals, you might opt to use

(1) a mid-size auditorium for the training, relying heavily on a mixture of 35-mm slides, overhead transparencies, manuals, and workbooks, or

(2) a classroom or conference room and deliver the training to smaller groups of data processing people scheduled on different days or in different time slots.

Be forewarned, though, that unnecessarily large audiences tend to become counterproductive for a variety of reasons, including the following:

- Large audiences necessitate the use of large auditoriums, conference halls, or hotel ballrooms that often become logistical and acoustical nightmares; indeed, making yourself heard with ease in these sorts of surroundings may prove particularly difficult. In large halls or auditoriums you may be working with unreliable sound systems—systems that are incapable of reaching those sitting in the rear sections and that often produce distracting background noise or even loud hissing sounds against which your own voice will be forced to compete.

- Large audiences make for impersonal, sometimes inhospitable, presentational environments. Any kind of "personal contact" becomes virtually impossible when you must address an excessively large number of listeners. When speaking before groups of more than 15, 20, or 25 people, sharing ideas successfully on a one-to-one basis becomes extremely difficult and distracting for participants.

- Large audiences rarely possess common informational needs, professional expertise, training, or demographic profiles. A larger, more diverse group will invariably require that your overall message be considerably more general than would be the case in a presentation before a more homogeneous group.

AUDIENCE ANALYSIS WORKSHEET

Professional Objectives
1. What do you want listeners to learn from your presentation?
   _____
   _____

2. What will listeners be able to do with the information given to them during your presentation?
   _____
   _____

Audience Demographics
1. What is the size of your audience?
   ___ Fewer than 10   ___ 10–25   ___ 25–50   ___ More than 50
2. From what levels of the organizational hierarchy will your listeners come?
   ___ Senior executive   ___ Mid-level management
   ___ Supervisory   ___ Office technical/professional
   ___ Line/staff workers   ___ Other (please specify: _____)
3. What is the average educational level of your audience?
   ___ High school   ___ MBA/MM/MS/MA degree
   ___ AA degree   ___ JD/LLB degree
   ___ BA/BS degree   ___ PhD/EdD degree
4. What are your listeners' technical level(s) of expertise in the subject matter to be covered by the presentation?
   ___ Nontechnical   ___ Semitechnical   ___ Technical
5. What experience might your listeners have in the subject matter of the presentation?
   ___ None   ___ Limited   ___ Moderate   ___ Substantial

Audience Motivations and Expectations
1. Why is your audience attending this presentation? What is the *occasion* for the presentation? _____
   _____

2. What are their expectations for coverage, tone, and applicability of the information to be provided in your presentation? _____
   _____

3. How receptive will your audience be to your message?
   ___ Very receptive   ___ Moderately receptive   ___ Neutral
   ___ Unreceptive   ___ Hostile   ___ Unknown
4. What audience-related "barriers" do you anticipate in successively communicating your message? _____
   _____
   _____

FIGURE 2.2. Audience analysis worksheet.

Application

1. What content area(s) should you communicate to achieve your presentational objectives and meet audience needs?

_____

_____

2. What organization (or structure) should you employ to best communicate this information?

  ____ Deductive   ____ Inductive   Other (specify: _____)

3. What presentational techniques are most appropriate for communicating this content to your particular audience?

  ____ Lecture   ____ Demonstration   ____ Workshop

  ____ Panel discussion   ____ Computer/video   ____ Round table

  ____ Press conference   ____ Other (specify: _____)

4. What visual aids will you need to convey your data and information most effectively?

_____

_____

FIGURE 2.2. *(Continued)*

Using Audience Analysis Worksheets

Knowing *what* to look for and examine in analyzing your listeners is, really, only a portion of your task. You must also know *where* to look for answers during the presentational planning process. One of the most obvious ways to find out more about your audience is, simply, to ask those individuals who will be involved. Such a direct "query" method might prove fruitful to you in planning presentations involving small groups of readily accessible colleagues within your organization. The method, however, might become impractical, burdensome, or just plain impossible when you are planning to speak before larger, external groups that are, perhaps, somewhat unknown to you—as in keynote speeches or conference presentation sessions.

An effective technique for delimiting your intended audience, for aiding you in clarifying your objectives, and for further developing or structuring your project involves the use of *audience analysis worksheets.*

To help you to form a clear image of your audience(s), you might consider designing an audience analsysis worksheet to fit your own professional or organizational needs—for your own use as your presentation develops. The audience analysis worksheet we have provided for your use consists of four major components:

1. Identifying presentational objectives
2. Analyzing audience demographics
3. Speculating about audience motivations and expectations
4. Applying a knowledge of your audience to forecast what content, organization, delivery technique(s), and visual aids might prove most useful to you in developing your presentation.

These four components might, of course, be modified as your own needs for increased (self-) guidance evolve (see Figure 2.2).

SPEAKER PREPARATION WORKSHEET

Audience/Situation Analysis

The occasion: _____

Audience profile (summary): _____
_____

Type of presentation: _____

Content and Organization

Purpose: □ Inform   □ Solve problems/arrive at decisions   □ Persuade
□ Agree on a course of action   □ Sell (fund projects, etc.)   □ Other: _____
Action you want audience to take: _____
Take-home message: _____
Key points: 1. _____
             2. _____
             3. _____
Timing: ____ minutes + ____ minutes for Q & A = ____ total minutes
Can exclude if necessary: 1. _____
                           2. _____
                           3. _____
Background info audience needs to understand topic: _____

Delivery

□ Seating: _____   □ Lights: _____
□ Sound System: _____   □ Lectern: _____

Visuals

Visuals on these topics are needed: _____

Arrangements for room equipment made: □ Overhead projector   □ Slide projector
□ Video player   □ Flip chart   □ Pointer (standard or light)   □ Table
Visuals you will bring (appropriate for audience and room size): _____
_____

Handouts: _____
Alternate plans for visuals in case equipment not available or malfunctions: _____
_____

Questions and Answers

Likely questions: 1. _____
                   2. _____
                   3. _____
Wrap-up after last question: _____

FIGURE 2.3. *Speaker preparation worksheet. Source: The Technical Presentation (a workbook), N. Burleigh and A. McMakin, Pacific Northwest Laboratory, Richland, Washington (Courtesy of Battelle), 1992.*

For your reference, we have included two additional audience analysis worksheets here as well. Please feel free to adapt these materials to your best advantage; they should prove especially useful within the context of your own presentational planning process. Figure 2.3, "Speaker Preparation Worksheet," and Figure 2.4, "Audience and Situation Worksheet," were both developed by Nancy Burleigh and Andrea McMakin, Senior Technical Communication Specialists at Batelle / Pacific Northwest Laboratory, Richland, WA.

AUDIENCE AND SITUATION WORKSHEET

1. Who are my audience members? _____
2. What do they have in common? _____
3. No. of people: _____   _____ % men, _____ % women   Age range: ___ to ___
4. _____ % domestic   _____ % foreign
5. Their backgrounds/jobs: _____
6. Likely education? ☐ High school   ☐ College   ☐ Postgraduate
   Likely areas of study: _____
7. Why are they there? _____
8. What do I have in common with them? _____
9. What specifically do they know about my topic? _____

10. What attitudes do they bring? _____

11. How much more do they need to know? _____

12. What do I want to accomplish? _____

13. How will they use my information? _____
14. Where in the program am I scheduled? _____
    ☐ Right before meal   ☐ Right after meal   Time of day? _____
15. Room size? _____   Lightning: ☐ Variable control
    ☐ Lights either on or off
16. Equipment needed: ☐ Overhead projector/screen   ☐ Slide projector/screen
    ☐ Video player/monitor   ☐ Lectern   ☐ Table   ☐ Other: _____
17. Sound system: ☐ Stationary mike   ☐ Clip-on mike   ☐ No mike
18. Format: ☐ Panel   ☐ Workshop   ☐ Q&A at end   ☐ Q&A throughout
    ☐ Other: _____
19. Previous speakers and their topics: _____

FIGURE 2.4. *Audience and situation worksheet. Source: The Technical Presentation (a workbook), by N. Burleigh and A. McMakin, Pacific Northwest Laboratory, Richland, Washington (Courtesy of Battelle), 1992.*

3

Researching Your Presentation

Of the CAFTA variables, you've by now determined the audience, format, time frame, and aims of the presentation that you intend to deliver. You also probably have a general idea of the content that you'd like to include in the presentation but have yet to consolidate information or data with which you'll defend the hypotheses or arguments contained in your presentation. At this point in the presentation planning process, then, you're ready to begin researching your presentation topic and to arrange the information and data collected from that research into a coherent and unified organization.

To be persuasive, you must supply listeners with sufficient evidence collected from primary or secondary sources to support your central argument as well as any subarguments. A thorough and orderly research effort is key to building a successful presentation. The steps involved in researching an oral presentation are as follows:

(1) Conducting primary or secondary research
(2) Evaluating your sources.

CONDUCTING PRIMARY OR SECONDARY RESEARCH

Research is the systematic process of collecting, organizing, and evaluating information or data, and it is central to the successful planning of presentations. Regardless of the specific type of research that you might be asked to perform for your organization, you will collect your research from primary or secondary sources.

Primary Research

Primary research involves synthesizing, analyzing, and evaluating information or data culled from your own observations or studies through such methodologies as experimentation, surveys, and interviews. Such investigations are designed to answer questions and to solve problems relating to the specific focus of your presentation. Consequently, primary sources can provide extremely detailed and relevant information and data. Planning and performing the kind of primary research that will provide you with accurate and reliable data can, however, be prohibitively time-consuming and expensive if you are constrained by tight deadlines and restrictive budgets. While secondary research can provide excellent background and contextual information on industrywide, national, or international issues, it is primary research that typically supplies the up-to-date material needed for people to make intelligent managerial decisions in dynamic technical, scientific, and managerial environments. The most common methods for collecting primary information and data are observation research, survey research, and experimental research.

Observation research and *survey research* are passive in nature; that is, the researcher uses these methods to gather information or data—whether through analytical observation, personal or phone interviews, or mail surveys—without altering the research environment and, thus, without biasing the results of the study. In effect, the researcher simply describes events as an interested but objective observer. This type of investigation is often called *descriptive* or *ex post facto* research.

The methods for conducting *experimental research* are intrinsically different from those of descriptive research. Experimental researchers test hypotheses on which a study is based by (1) intentionally controlling and modifying the research environment and (2) measuring how the altered environment has affected the study's results. Although hypotheses are often only vague, speculative theories or hunches, they can also be specific, studied, yet still unproved, explanations. Whether speculative or studied, however, all hypotheses require corroboration through empirical testing before audiences feel confident enough to base decisions on them.

Primary research offers researchers various benefits. First, primary research often brings to light new information and data that cannot be found in secondary sources. For example, how could strategic planners thoroughly investigate and accurately assess current hiring needs within their company if they did not use interviews with company managers and labor leaders as part of their research methods? No secondary source could provide this type of immediate, company-specific information, nor could secondary information cover the production and sales ends of the equation which would invariably influence the company's future hiring needs. When performing primary research for the first time on an organizationwide level, many companies are shocked to discover the large discrepancy between how they *thought* their businesses operated and how their businesses *actually* operate.

Second, if you have properly conceived, controlled, and executed your primary research, the resulting data should reveal ways to make the organization more effective and efficient. Often the investigation produces cost savings that pay the price of the primary research many times over. Third, primary research provides information that is significantly more accurate than data collected haphazardly by audiences using their own business experience to eyeball a problem, or by researchers extrapolating data collected from secondary sources. Finally, some subjects or problems simply cannot be studied in workworld situations because of associated costs, time constraints, or inherent dangers.

Regardless of which primary research method(s) you might employ in conducting your study, you will normally perform your investigation in five basic steps:

(1) Planning the report focus and research method
(2) Collecting the data

(3) Organizing the data

(4) Analyzing the data

(5) Reporting the synthesized and interpreted information.

While an extensive discussion of primary research is outside the scope of this text, you can find a thorough explanation of primary research methodology in relevant texts listed in the Related Reading section at the end of this chapter.

Secondary Research

Secondary sources contain information that other researchers have already collected, analyzed, and reported in either published or unpublished form. Books, journals, magazines, and newspapers comprise the bulk of secondary sources; however, you should not overlook unpublished works—such as business reports, operating and procedural manuals, and doctoral dissertations—which can often provide highly specific and detailed information that could be valuable to your research.

Secondary research offers a number of important benefits. By conducting a thorough search of secondary sources, you can determine whether other researchers have already completed and published similar research on a subject. Uncovering and using such related research in your presentation can save you considerable time, energy, and cost which you may otherwise have spent in performing your own primary study.

In addition, secondary sources can help you better define and focus your presentation topic. Inexperienced presenters too often select topics that are so broad and ill-defined that their talk can be little more than a superficial and general overview on a subject. While researching, you can learn much about how successful researchers in your own field have limited the parameters of their own studies. Although the general subject of your presentation may have already been decided for you by superiors, examining how other presenters handle topics related to your own helps you to (1) decide what specific content should be included in your discussion and (2) determine how that information might best be organized to meet your audience's informational needs, technical backgrounds, professional interests, and intended uses of the information.

When used as substantive evidence in your presentation, secondary sources also lend credibility and authority to your discussion of issues. A thorough investigation of secondary sources illustrates to listeners that you've done your homework and that you understand the significance of your own research as it relates to the work of other researchers in the field. By discovering where other researchers stand on the subject, you can determine where your approach to and research on the same, or a related, issue(s) fits into the general pool of knowledge. In addition to their value as supportive evidence, many secondary sources provide bibliographies which may offer still more useful references pertaining to your topic.

Finally, your investigation of secondary sources can reveal areas within your field of study that deserve further attention. As a result, you may decide to redefine the focus or expand the scope of your presentation to cover those unexplored topics. If you cannot alter the scope of your presentation to address gaps in your research, at least the recognition of the shortcomings might help generate future research on the subject.

Researching secondary sources is often the most time-intensive phase of the presentation process. To use your time efficiently, it is important that you design a logical and ordered system for collecting, organizing, and evaluating data. The following *preresearch* steps should aid you in starting your research off on the right foot:

(1) Clearly define the focus, scope, and purpose of your presentation. Try to state your purpose in a single sentence. (Stating the purpose in the form a question often helps to identify the problem as well as possible solutions.)

(2) Select a method for researching secondary sources that offers you the chances of finding the required information quickly and conveniently.

(3) Decide if you will need special research expertise—such as a librarian knowledgeable in computer database searches—to successfully complete the research phase by a predetermined deadline.

(4) Begin your research at a point that immediately attracts you and where you some basic knowledge or preliminary understanding.

Because most secondary research is found in libraries, it is often referred to as *library research*. University and public libraries are the most common source of secondary information and may prove to be a productive resource for your research. However, many professionals often benefit significantly by beginning their research in company libraries as well as those of private organizations.

Company and Private Libraries. Company and private libraries could prove invaluable to your research because they could well represent the only source of information specific to your company's historical, scientific, technical, financial, managerial, or operational context. Company and private libraries are typically maintained by businesses, professional associations, and trade and technical organizations. Company libraries can be especially useful because they often contain relatively complete archives of in-house (*internal*) information (e.g., annual reports, company memoranda, employee handbooks and manuals, company newsletters and newspapers, policy and procedural directives, sales proposals, and strategic planning reports) as well as recorded interviews with company personnel. Company libraries also contain *external* materials (including books, government documents, journals, newspapers, and trade magazines) that, although generated outside the company, are directly related to the organization's mission.

The advantages of investigating secondary sources within your company are threefold. Such research is

- often the only method of uncovering detailed, company-specific information
- convenient to the researcher and possible interviewees
- relatively inexpensive.

The disadvantages, however, of investigating secondary sources within your company are that company records can be disorganized and incomplete, and company turf battles may constrict a researcher's access to important information.

Apart from a company's central library facilities, many departments within the firm support smaller, decentralized libraries that provide information specific to the regular duties of those organizational units. No research investigation within your company is complete, however, until you make use of the expertise of colleagues. If your research concerns departmental- or company-specific issues, the notes, files, bookshelves, and compiled research of fellow employees can save you significant time and energy. Some of your colleagues may already have performed studies similar to your own and can provide insights into your topic which you could gain nowhere else.

Public and Research Libraries. After you have thoroughly researched relevant materials available in private libraries, you should investigate the resources of public and college or university libraries. Public libraries are sometimes referred to as *general libraries* because they satisfy the varied reading needs of diverse audiences. General libraries typically offer materials on a broad range of topics and at various reading levels to meet the informational needs of their users. However, you may find that the coverage offered by general library resources is inadequate for extensive research in a specialized area, as normally required by business or technical research projects.

Because they must support faculty and students in their research efforts, college and university libraries provide a vast array of resources on general as well as specialized topics. Also referred to as *research libraries,* college and university libraries normally offer modern search methods—including computerized card catalogs, CD-ROM databases, and access to networked on-line databases—for locating sources. In addition to providing standard secondary sources (e.g., books and periodicals), research libraries maintain useful unpublished materials, including brochures, theses, dissertations, manuals, and pamphlets. Some college and university libraries are also depositories for federal government documents covering such areas as Congressional legislation, scientific and technical research, committee findings, and public service records. Take advantage of these valuable resources and determine if your local college or university library is a depository of federal documents. For an extensive listing of private, public, college and university, and government libraries, consult the *Directory of Special Libraries and Information Centers* published by Gale Research Company.

Computerized Database Searches. Because time is a critical factor in an organization's ability to compete, the speed with which you access essential information during a search of secondary sources can make the difference between a presentation succeeding or failing to deliver timely, relevant, and complete information. Just as the use of computers has been integral in enabling organizations to become more efficient and effective, computer technology is also playing an increasingly important role in expediting a researcher's library search.

The *on-line search* of secondary sources is an interactive, computerized method of accessing bibliographic citations and complete abstracts on particular subjects. On-line searches enable researchers to query large computer databases which can electronically store literally millions of pages of data. A database, in a conceptual sense, is like a filing cabinet into which people place files of information pertaining to an assortment of subjects. Files containing secondary sources can be organized in any number of ways, but are typically ordered by author, date of publication, subject, document title, and title of publication. The information provided by the database can be word-oriented, number-oriented, image-oriented, or sound-oriented. The types of information most frequently sought by users are chemical and demographic data, trademark information, biographical sketches, patent information, news stories, and software programs.

A growing number of database producers design and build databases that reference sources on a vast range of subjects. Database producers offer access to their databases directly to users or through *database search service* companies. Database search services work as database clearinghouses as they sell access to a variety of databases to on-line customers—libraries, businesses, government, and private individuals. Most databases are updated monthly and serve as the computerized counterpart of printed abstracts and indexes. The number of database producers, database search service companies, and databases has increased significantly over the past 20 years, as has the use of database searches. In 1975, there were 15 database producers and 105 database vendors providing users with access to 301 on-line databases.[1] By 1993, these numbers had risen to 3007 database producers, 1437 database search service companies, and 7907 databases. The average number of records in a database grew by a factor of 87 from 1975 to 1993. In 1975, the average database contained 647,000 records; by 1993 the average database contained 173 million records. The growth in the average size of databases, however, is skewed by a minority of very large databases. Of the 657,000 databases in 1993, 288 contained more than 1 million records; 10 percent of these 288 databases contained more than 100 million records. In 1975, users conducted 750,000 searches from databases; in 1993, users performed 44.4 million searches. The profile of database producers has changed dramatically as well over the past 20 years. Consistent with the dramatic increase in the number of database services is the sudden rise in the use of databases as a key research tool. In 1975, 50 percent of databases were produced by the U.S. government. By 1993, this percentage dropped to 15 percent, while private corporations and industry produced 75 percent of databases. Because access to databases is through global computer networks, database sites are spread throughout the world. The host countries for most of the world's databases include the United States, Canada, Great Britain, Germany, France, Japan, Hong Kong, Taiwan, India, Russia, Singapore, and Australia. Table 3.1 lists the largest database producers and vendors as well as the most commonly used on-line databases.

The advantages associated with using online searches are as follows:

- *Speed.* The time and energy saved by researchers, who otherwise may have invested days or weeks in manual searching, can make database searches worth the fee charged by search service companies. Within minutes of accessing an on-line database, you can accumulate an extensive bibliography on your topic and print off the list of citations on your terminal's printer. Even if the search results have to be printed at an on-line service's computer facility, you can receive the citations by mail within a few days. Some libraries can also provide electronic facsimiles of documents (FAX services) accessed through the database search.

- *Thoroughness.* Database searches are also comprehensive, because they offer you access to far more sources than a typical library could support in printed form. Some databases provide exclusive information which has no printed form equivalent and, thus, can only be accessed through on-line searches. One hour of on-line searching might provide a range of sources and information that a manual search would require weeks to collect. During one on-line session, you can access citations on nearly all sources available a specific topic, including books, periodicals, newspapers, government documents, doctoral dissertations, conference papers, and patents.

- *Currency of Data.* Because they are updated monthly, biweekly, or even weekly, database searches provide some of the most current information available. Some on-

---

[1] We extract these data from K. Y. Marcaccio's *Computer-Readable Databases: A Directory and Data-Source Book,* published by Gale Research Co., 1993.

TABLE 3.1. Database Producers, Database Vendors, and Popular Databases

Database Producers and Vendors

DIALOG Information Services, Palo Alto, CA
BRS Information Technologies (Bibliographic Retrieval Services, Inc.), McLean, VA
CISTI CAN/SND, Ottawa, Ontario, Canada
Compuserve Information Services, Columbus, OH
Data-Star, Bern, Switzerland
Dow Jones & Company, Inc., Princeton, NJ
DRI/McGraw-Hill, Lexington, MA
Mead Data Central, Dayton, OH
NewsNet, Inc., Bryn Mawr, PA
Orbit Search Services (Online Retrieval of Bibliographic Information and Text), McLean, VA
Reuters Information Services, Toronto, CA
U.S. National Laboratory of Medicine, Bethesda, MD
West Publishing Company, St. Paul, MN

Databases	Profile
ABI/Inform	Provides citations and abstracts of more that 500,000 sources and abstracts of significant (UMI/Courier) articles in such research areas as business, economics, and management. Articles appear in more than 800 major business and management journals published worldwide. Time span: Since August 1971.
Accountants' Index (American Institute of Certified Public Accountants)	Serves as the online counterpart of *Accountant's Index* directory. Although does not provide abstracts for cited articles, its database offers a wealth of sources relating to accounting, data processing, financial reports, industrial securities, management, and taxation. Time span: Since 1974.
AGRICOLA (U..S. National Agricultural Library)	Provides complete bibliographical and cataloguing information for all monographs and serials held by the National Agriculture Library as well as indexing records for articles from agriculture literature. Time span: Since 1970.
Biological Abstracts (BIOSIS)	Provides references and abstracts of biological and biomedical journals articles and other publications dealing with research in the life sciences. Time span: Since 1976.
CHEMSEARCH (DIALOG Information Services, Inc.)	Offers a list of chemical substances registered since 1965. Includes substances that have been cited one or more times in Chemical Abstracts since 1967. Time span: Since 1965.
Compustat Series (Standard & Poor's Compustant Services, Inc.)	Provides full citations, abstracts, and text of literature such areas as science, finance, business, banking, technology, and demographics. Time span: Current.
Compusearch Business Information (Compusearch Market & Social Research, Ltd.)	Provides information on more than 570,000 Canadian corporations and their business characteristics. Time span: Current.
Computer Library (OCLC Online Computer Library Center, Inc.)	Contains full bibliographic and cataloguing information for English and foreign language materials on the topic of computers. Time span: Varies.
Dissertation Abstracts Online (University Microfilms International/UMI)	Provides author, subject, title, and abstract of doctoral dissertations approved by accredited institutions since 1861. Time span: Since 1801.

TABLE 3.1. Database Producers, Database Vendors, and Popular Databases *(Continued)*

Dow Jones Business and Financial Report (Dow Jones & Corporation, Inc.)	Offers edited and complete news stories from the Dow Jones News Service, *The Wall Street Journal,* and *Barron's.* You can search either database by using company stock symbol, industry, or government codes. Free-Text database also lets you search entire texts by descriptor(s). Access both databases through Dow Jones and Company, Inc. Time span: Current.
LEXIS Corporate Law Library (Mead Data Central, Inc.)	Contains the complete text of case law for each of 50 U.S. states relating to corporate industry decisions from the State Supreme Courts, Courts of Criminal Appeals, Courts of Civil Appeals, Courts of Appeals, Superior Courts, Circuit Appellate Courts, and lower courts. Time span: Varies.
Management Contents Database (Management Contents, Inc.)	Besides listing sources in business, economics, and management, also indexes proceedings of major business association meetings and conferences. Contains citations and abstracts of more than 800 business publications. Time span: Current.
MEDIS (Mead Data Central, Inc.)	Provides the complete text of selected journals, textbooks, and access to other related databases covering all areas of medicine. Divided into six libraries: General Medical Library (GENMED), Drug Information Library (PHARM), Cancer Information Library (CANCER), Medline Library (MEDLNE), and MICROMEDIX Library (MDEX). Time span: Varies.
Moody's U.S. Corporate News (Moody's Investors Services, Inc.)	Covers business and financial news on about 21,000 publicly held U.S. corporations, including industrial companies, banks and other financial institutions, insurance companies, public utilities, and transportation companies. Provides annual and quarterly financial statements, mergers and acquisitions news, management changes, capital financing, and operations. Time span: Since 1983.
Moody's International Plus (Moody's Investors Services, Inc.)	Provides comprehensive descriptions of more than 5,000 non-U.S.-based companies operating in more than 100 countries. Offers detailed company histories and in-depth coverage of company financial statements, long-term debt, and capital stocks. Time span: Since 1989.
PTS Promt (Predicasts)	Provides abstracts and complete text of journal articles, newspaper articles, and other sources of the worldwide market. Subjects areas include technology information relating to more than 20,000 companies, new products, plant capacities and expansions, market spread shares, sales, mergers and acquisitions, and government regulations. Time span: Since 1972.
Public Affairs Information Service Bulletin (PAIS) (Public Affairs Information Service)	Monthly updates on international coverage of economic, political, and social affairs around the world. Time span: Since 1972.
Reuters Business Report (Reuters Information Services, Inc.)	Reports significant developments in major U.S. economy and in world markets for stocks, commodities, money, energy, and foreign exchange. Includes regular columns by specialists in oil, energy, agriculture, and consumer trends. Time span: Since 1987.

line services even list sources before publishers can print and distribute the same sources in printed form.

- *Convenience.* On-line searches provide added flexibility and convenience. Thousands of researchers, for example, can concurrently search the same database independent of one another and from different locations.

Despite their many benefits, database searches have important shortcomings. For example, the depth of source listing can be limiting. Although databases were first made commercially available in the late 1960s, the large majority of databases were established in the early 1970s. Consequently, material published prior to that time is often *not* listed in the database. Moreover, although databases normally provide remarkably current information, the process of transferring printed information to electronic media is time-consuming. Lag times for information transfer can vary from a matter of days to weeks or months. For these reasons, you'll have to manually search sources published very recently or earlier than the time coverage of the database (e.g., using the card catalog or indexes).

Because many users of database searches have little expertise in the technical side of computers, search services have simplified the database search to the point that researchers, in most cases, need only respond to a series of menus. Most database services offer citations, abstracts, and full text of cited publications. In addition, printing citations from the screen provides you not only a good working bibliography but also a convenient reference sheet for locating the sources.

Database services offer access to a variety of databases. The assortment of databases provided by one service will depend on the discipline (e.g., computer science, engineering, chemistry, biology, management, medicine, law) that service emphasizes. For example, while ABI/INFORM offers access to hundreds of databases relating primarily to business and financial information and data, BRS Information Technologies offers more than 100 databases that provide an extensive number and range of sources in business, education, medicine, and the sciences. On the other hand, databases accessed through Mead Data Central focus on information and data relating to medicine; the JURIS database service is a principle source of information centering on law; and CAN/SND databases offer an impressive amount of technical and scientific information and data. For research during off-time hours at a lower cost to users, BRS offers BRS After Dark, which offers users access to more than 30 databases from BRS's full assortment. While some databases restrict their records to only abstracts of texts, most database services provide users with the option of receiving research information in both abstract and full-text form. Major database search service companies include DIALOG Information Services, ORBIT Search Service, PFDS Online, the U.S. National Library of Medicine, BRS, Mead Data Central, West Publishing Company, NewsNet, Inc., DataTime Corporation, WEPA Group, Reuters Information Service, DRI/McGraw-Hill, CAN/SND, and STN International.

Effective database searches require skilled searchers. In short, your database search can only give you what you've asked it to find, as defined by your search request. If you don't have experience in on-line search procedures, you should consult a reference librarian skilled in computerized database research. The charge for using the search services databases is typically based on a formula that considers the amount of time you spend on the on-line system, the number of titles found, and the number of citations, abstracts, or copies of full text that you print. On-line search fees can range from $10 to hundreds of dollars.

For a complete listing of available databases, consult Greg Byerly's *Online Searching: A Dictionary and Bibliographic Guide,* Capital Systems Group Inc.'s *Directory of Online*

Information Resources, Amy Lucas and K. Y. Marcaccio's *Encyclopedia of Information Systems and Sciences,* Kathleen Young Marcaccio's *Computer-Readable Databases: A Directory and Data-Source Book* and *Directory of Databases,* or Regina Rega's *CD-ROMs in Print.* For information specific to federal government activities, legislation, and public services, consult Information USA's *Federal Data Base Finder.*

CD-ROM and Internet Searches

Most libraries now offer database material on CD-ROM laser discs. CD-ROM storage allows libraries to store immense amounts of information on a plastic disc about the size of the common stereo compact disc. You can retrieve information from CD-ROM in the same way you search other databases—for example, by title, author, or subject. Apart from its being compact, CD-ROM offers the advantage of providing researchers with a wide range of database subjects. Table 3.2 lists some popular CD-ROM databases that are available at most university research libraries, and Figure 3.1 provides a sample CD-ROM search on the topic of nonpeptide tachykinin antagonists, the subject of the presentation offered in Chapter 11 and recently delivered by Dr. John A. Lowe III, a Principal Research Investigator working primarily in the area of medicinal chemistry at the Central Research Division of Pfizer Inc. of Groton, CT. The CD-ROM search is of the 1995 General Science Index of the WilsonDisc database offered by the H. W. Wilson Company.

It is not surprising that the search found no entries in the CD-ROM database that addressed all three key words in the search subject line of *nonpeptide + tachykinin + antagonist* because of the specificity of the subject. This null response we anticipated. What we had not anticipated was the abundance of the entries offered under the subjects of *nonpeptide* and *tachykinin* that were very close to they kinds of research that we were seeking. Several of the articles cited by WilsonDisc could well have proved helpful to Dr. Lowe in his research prior to presenting.

Although you can search databases stored at sites around the world through database service companies or through database networks accessible through a library, you can also access and retrieve vast amounts of information through your personal computer at home. Using your personal computer as the starting point of your electronic search, you can search any database in the world that is connected to a telephone communications network, such as the Internet, Bitnet, and World-Wide Web networks (and their associated software). Many of these services are free to the public and normally only require that you add communication software and a modem to your personal computer. Table 3.3 lists some of the most popular networks and network software.

The Internet is essentially a vast, global electronic network that allows users to communicate each other from millions of sites via an array of computers—personal computers, workstations, minicomputers, mainframes, and supercomputers. As long as the computers of two users speak a common protocol, they can exchange data in textual, numerical, graphic (still images or video), or audio form. The Internet is most used as a tool for communicating, transferring documents or files, researching, or sharing information by posting it to electronic bulletin boards read by an Internet community. Users communicate on the Internet using four basic software technologies:

- E-mail to exchanges textual messages
- FTP (File Transfer Protocol) to move electronic documents, images, and sounds
- Telnet to access the databases or archives of remote system
- Usenet to read or post messages on a bulletin board.

TABLE 3.2. CD-ROM Databases

GENERAL DATABASES	COVERAGE
Reader's Guide	Articles in popular and general-interest periodicals.
Newspaper Abstract On Disc	Articles in nine major U.S. daily newspapers.
Biography and Genealogy Master	Biographical materials in reference sources.
HUMANITIES AND BUSINESS DATABASES	
ABI/INFORM	Articles on business and management.
Business Periodicals Index	Articles in business periodicals.
COMINDEX	Articles in communications and journalism.
Compact Disclosure	Profiles and financial data on publicly held corporations extracted from Securities and Exchange Commission documents.
ERIC (Educational Resources Information Center)	Articles and documents written in academic contexts.
Humanities Index	Articles in humanities periodicals.
PAIS (Public Affairs Information Center)	Publications on public policy, economics, and social issues.
Predicasts F & S Index Plus Text	Abstracts and full text of articles published in trade and business journals.
PSYCLIT	Articles and books in psychology and behavioral sciences.
Social Sciences Index	Articles in social sciences periodicals.
SCIENCE DATABASES	
Applied Science and Technology Index	Articles in applied science and technology periodicals.
Biological and Agricultural Index	Articles on biology and agriculture.
General Science Index	Articles in science periodicals.
HEALTHPLAN	Articles on health care administration and planning.
Life Science Collection	Publications in the life sciences.
Nursing and Applied Health (CINAHL)	Articles on nursing, biomedicine, and health.
GOVERNMENT INFORMATION DATABASES	
1990 Census of Population and Housing	The most current source for demographic information.
CDP File	Bibliographic database on chronic diseases, including AIDS.
County and City Data Book	Compilation of statistics about U.S. cities, counties, and states.
County Business Patterns	Information on the number of businesses, total payroll, and number of employees for U.S. cities, counties, and states.
GPO (Government Printing Office)	General reference to all U.S. government publications.
NESE (National Economic, Social, and Environmental Data Bank)	Government information on such areas as crime, education, transportation, and the environment.
NTDB (National Trade Data Bank)	Files and programs relating to domestic and international trade and commerce.
Occupational Safety and Health CD	Information and regulations on health and safety in the workplace.
Toxic Release Inventory, 1987-1992	Data on toxic chemical releases and chemicals.

```
┌─────────────────────────────────────────┐
│                                          │
│          WILSONDISC Version 3.1          │
│           Copyright 1995 by              │
│         The H. W. Wilson Company         │
│                                          │
│        PRESS SPACE BAR TO START          │
│            Press ESC to exit             │
│                                          │
└─────────────────────────────────────────┘
```

General Science Index start-up screen of the WilsonDisc CD-ROM database, software offered by H. W. Wilson Company, 1995.

Enter your local search request for GENERAL SCIENCE INDEX

    Subject Words: nonpeptide
      2nd Subject: tachykinin
      3rd Subject: antagonist

Person's Name:
   Title Words:

Journal Name:
 Organization:

         Year:

    Press the END key when you have finished.

```
┌─────────────────────────────────────────────────────┐
│                                                     │
│   The Boolean OR can be used on Subject and Title Word lines.│
│   If the Boolean OR is not used, an AND connects terms on    │
│   that line. The Boolean AND also connects all search lines. │
│                                                     │
└─────────────────────────────────────────────────────┘
```

F1-Help   F2/ESC-Multiple Subject Search (Wilsearch) Menu End-End Input

WilsonDisc prompt for search key words.

GENERAL SCIENCE INDEX   Data Coverage: 5/84 thru 01/25/96

                                                    READY

SEARCH SET	Multiple subject search (Wilsearch) COMMAND	NUMBER of ENTRIES
1	FIND NONPEPTIDE (BI)	22
2	FIND TACHYKININ (BI)	14
3	FIND ANTAGONIST (BI)	189
—	FIND 1 AND 2 AND 3	0
	(ss # 1) . . . . 22 Entries	
	(ss # 2) . . . . 14 Entries	
	(ss # 3) . . . . 189 Entries	

FIGURE 3.1. *Search sequence of the WilsonDisc CD-ROM database for the subject* nonpeptide tachykinin antagonists.

```
YOUR SEARCH FOUND NO ENTRIES
YOU WILL RETURN TO THE WILSEARCH MENU SCREEN
PRESS ENTER          TO CONTINUE
```

Fri Mar 22 09:58:52 1996

F1-HELP F2/ESC-Multiple Subject Search (Wilsearch) Menu

Search results

AUTHOR: Geppetti, Pierangelo; Bertrand, Claude; Bacci, Elena
  TITLE: Characterization of tachykinin receptors in ferret trachea
          by peptide agonists and nonpeptide antagonists
SOURCE: American Journal of Physiology (ISSN: 0002-9513) v 265 p
          L164-L169 August '93 pt1
CONTAINS: bibliography; illustration(s)

SUBJECTS COVERED:
Neuroreceptors
Neuropeptides
Smooth muscle/Contraction
Tracheae/Secretion

AUTHOR: Gether, Ulrik; Yokota, Yoshifumi; Emonds-Alt, Xavier
  TITLE: Two nonpeptide tachykinin antagonists act through epitopes
          on corresponding segments of the NK[sub 1] and NK[sub 2]
          receptors
SOURCE: Proceedings of the National Academy of Sciences of the
          United States of America (ISSN:0027-8424) v 90 p 6194-8
          July 1 '93
CONTAINS: bibliography; illustration(s)

SUBJECTS COVERED:
Protein receptors
Substance P
Antigens and antibodies

AUTHOR: Schambye, Hans T.; Hjorth, Siv A.; Bergsma, Derk J.
  TITLE: Differentiation between binding sites for angiotensin II
          and nonpeptide antagonists on the angiotensin II type 1
          receptors
SOURCE: Proceedings of the National Academy of Sciences of the
          United States of America (ISSN:0027-8424) v 91 p 7046-50
          July 19 '94
CONTAINS: bibliography; illustration(s)

SUBJECTS COVERED:
Angiotensin receptors

FIGURE 3.1. (Continued)

AUTHOR: Gully, Danielle; Canton, Maryse; Boigegrain, Robert
TITLE: Biochemical and pharmacological profile of a potent and selective nonpeptide antagonist of the neurotensin receptor
SOURCE: Proceedings of the National Academy of Sciences of the United States of America (ISSN:0027-8424) v 90 p 65-9 January 1 '93
CONTAINS: bibliography; illustration(s)

SUBJECTS COVERED:
Binding sites (Biochemistry)
Neurotensin
Chemoreceptors
Inhibitors, Metabolic/Proteins

Sample citations that might prove useful to research on nonpeptide tachykinin antagonists.

FIGURE 3.1. *(Continued)*

The World-Wide Web is not a network but, rather, a user interface that serves to simplify users' entry to the Internet as well as many Intenet tools, including FTP, Telnet, Usenet, and gopher. Originally developed by CERN (the European Laboratory for Particle Physics), the "web" was initially intended to simplify the exchange of text, numerical data, graphics, and databases between scientists at different computing sites using hypertext (a term coined by Vannevar Bush in 1945), a system of storing information and data in a non-hierarchical structure. Through a series of software "links" that it creates between computer systems and their constituent databases, hypertext allows users in a single search to move seamlessly between databases stored on computers that may be thousands of miles apart. By typing in a subject to be searched or by clicking a computer mouse on an icon, a user could move from his or her host computer to a database in Madrid, Hong Kong, or Australia within seconds, search for needed information or data, download that material to his or her host computer, and print out the information on a local printer.

Many new "browser" software packages make such searches as easy as two or three clicks of the mouse away. Having logged onto his or her computer and accessed a browser software with a click of the mouse, the user is ready to enter the research topic on the browser's subject search line. Although users can search the Internet using *line browsers* (e.g., a *Lynx browser*, typical of Unix-based computer host systems) requiring users to use line commands to search topics, the most popular browsers are *graphical browsers* that allow users to click on icons or highlighted words (usually color-coded on the computer display) to move quickly through subject menus. When the user clicks on a menu topic, the browser moves the user through Internet to the database referenced by that menu subject. Though graphical browsers do involve some text input from the user, they emphasize heavily the use of the mouse. Some of the most popular graphical browsers on the market today include Netscape's Navigator, Spyglass' Mosaic, and Oracle's PowerBrowser.

Evaluating Your Secondary Sources

Although you may have collected many promising secondary sources of information, not all will be useful to your presentation. Consequently, you must evaluate each source to de-

TABLE 3.3. Computer Network Software

NETWORKS

Internet	A global information and communications network that connects the resources of thousands of corporations and small business, government agencies, libraries, computer user groups, professional societies, and private individuals. Internet also provides access to such commercial database service companies as America Online, Compuserve, DELPHI, Dialog, and Dow Jones as well as other networking software, including GOPHER, E mail services, and UseNet Newsgroups.
Bitnet	A global information and communications network primarily linking academic users.

NETWORK SOFTWARE

World-Wide Web	A leading-edge communications network designed to offers users easy access to all global networks. This networking system acts much like a relational database system that links into a variety of networks, including Internet and Bitnet.
LIBS	LIBS software allows users to log onto remote library catalogs, Campus-Wide Information Systems (CWIS), and other Internet services. The menu-driven LIBS software simplifies the process of connecting to and logging onto remote computers. For example, after finding a library catalog in the LIBS menu system, you can follow connection prompts with the LIBS program to direct LIBS to connect you to the desired catalog. To connect to LIBS, access a networked computer and type *LIBS* at the system prompt.
Telnet	Telnet is a command in the Internet standard protocol for connecting your computer to another computer across town or across the world. You can log onto that remote computer as if you were logged onto it directly, and when you terminate your session Telnet returns you to your local computer system. To access Telnet, log onto your local host system and type *telnet* at the system prompt (for example, telnet pac.carl.org). Then type the address of the target remote system. After you've connected to the remote system, you must log in.
Gopher	Gopher is an information delivery system that searches for, retrieves, and displays requested information from remote servers on the Internet. It allows you to browse for resources on the Internet using a hierarchy of menus. You can select from the resources the Gopher list of resources. Depending on your resource selection, Gopher will establish a Telnet (terminal-type) connection, establish an ftp (file transfer) connection, connect you to a text file (as document), connect you to an image or a sound, or connect you to another Gopher or directory for further searching. All Gopher systems are interconnected to create "gopher space" in which you can explore such Gopher as Campus-Wide Information Systems (CWIS) and subject-based Gophers. Gopher nodes include Duke University (gopher.duke.edu), Florida State University (gopher.fsu.edu), Virginia Tech (gopher.vt.edu), University of Maryland (gopher.umd.edu), and University of Pennsylvania (gopher.upenn.edu).
Archie	Archie tracks the contents of more than 1200 separate anonymous FTP (file transfer protocol) archive sites around the world. These sites, containing more than 2.1 million files, are updated on Archie once a month. Archie's database describes more than 3500 public domain software packages, documents, and data sets that are stored in anonymous FTP Archie sites throughout the Internet system. The best way to connect to an Archie server is through Telnet. Archie servers include Rutgers University (archie.rutgers.edu), University of Nebraska (archie.unl.edu), Canada (archie.mcgill.ca), United Kingdom (archie.doc.ic.ac.uk), Finland (archie.funet.fi), Australia (archice.au), and Taiwan (archie.ncu.edu.tw).

TABLE 3.3. Computer Network Software *(Continued)*

LISTSERV	LISTSERV is a software program that enables electronic discussion groups to communicate through e-mail. This tool offers computer users ongoing dialogue with other users with common interests. LISTSERV allows you to subscribe to and unsubscribe from a discussion group, identify other members of the discussion group, search the archives of past messages sent to the discussion group, and retrieve files distributed to the group its moderator.
FTP	File transfer protocol (FTP) is a method of moving a file (e.g., a short message, an article, a book) from onecomputer to another across the Internet, regardless of the file's storage format or operating system software. With few exceptions, FTP allows you to open a session on a remote host computer any where in the world and transfer files quickly to your local computer. To identify FTP archive sites, check an Internet bibliography, ask a colleague for site pathnames, search an Archie server, or query such major archive sites as the National Science Foundation (nnsc.nsf.net), (ftp.nisc.sri.com), (nic.ddn.mil), (ftp.sura.net), (ftphost.nwnet.net), (hydra.uwo.ca), (infolib.murdoch.edu.au), and (ftp.unt.edu).
E-Mail	E-mail (electronic mail) is a vital communications medium with academia and, increasingly, in industry and government. Perhaps the most popular application of the Internet, e-mail assists users in sending messages to colleagues around the world. To use e-mail, log onto your host computer and type *mail* at the system prompt.
Veronica	Veronica is an enhancement of Gopher that allows users to search many gopher databases during a single computing session.
WAIS	WAIS is s powerful tool for searching selected large databases.

termine which ones should be read in full. Evaluate the usefulness of the source by asking the following questions:

- Is the source truly useful in substantiating the thoroughness and validity of my analyses and conclusions contained in my presentation?
- Are the data current or dated? If less current, does the source's information necessarily lose its validity or usefulness to my project?
- Are the data accurate and reliable? Have they been collected and analyzed using proven methodologies?
- What is the expertise of the author? Has she or he published other work in the same or related area?
- How reputable is the publication in which the work appears?

Although current and timely information on a topic is often the most useful, older material can also be integral to developing background on a subject. The credibility and validity of a source often depends on the degree of expertise which authors bring to their collection and analysis of the information. However, evaluating the qualifications of authors is not always easy. Some articles and books provide author profiles that illustrate the author's expertise in the area of her or his writing, including the writer's professional affiliations, teaching or career experience in the field, noted awards received, and other works by the same author on related subjects. You might also consult the *Who's Who* series of directories for more background on authors' credentials.

To evaluate accurately a journal, book, or publisher, you should spend time researching other articles that have been published in the same publication or by the same publisher. Do they seem well researched, complete, consistent, and objective in their findings? Do they include substantive bibliographies? Are their authors recognized experts in their

IDENTIFY YOUR CENTRAL ARGUMENT

Identifying the central argument or topic of a presentation is an ongoing process of refinement, not a static decision made when you begin planning the presentation and never reconsider. Although you may have initially assumed that you would discuss one subject or argue one side of an issue, you might discover that your choice of subject or your stand on the selected issue changes as you learn more about the topic from your analysis of the collected research. As you analyze your research, work at refining the thrust of your presentation by continually asking yourself these questions:

- Now that my research has taught me more about the scope and complexity of my topic, what issues surrounding my subject had I not considered when planning my presentation?
- What issues do I need to address? What issues should I not address in the presentation?
- How do these new issues and their associated information or data affect the scope of my presentation? Do I narrow, or expand, my topic? How, then, should I refine my subject?
- How should I adjust my research efforts so that I can sufficiently cover this new subject and scope?
- Would a change in subject or scope benefit my audience? If so, how?

As you consider your answers to the last few questions, consider the limitations placed on you by the logistics surrounding the presentation. How much of a shift from your original subject and scope can your schedule and budget support? Can the research resources available to you provide you with sufficient material on the revised topic? Would others involved in the presentation (e.g., colleagues, co-presenters, management) approve of such a change of topic? Would such a shift still be in line with your listeners' informational needs and professional interests?

IDENTIFY YOUR SUBARGUMENTS

After refining the central subject or argument of your presentation, you'll need to factor that argument into subarguments (or subtopics) in order to (1) narrow the scope and depth of your research and (2) understand fully how you should categorize and order the research information or data that you collect. When factoring your central argument into subarguments, be sure that all subtopics relate directly to the main argument. Also, ensure that all subarguments carry comparable weight and importance. You should normally limit the number of subarguments to three, unless you are delivering a presentation that is expansive in both time and coverage. This narrowing of presentation scope often proves difficult for experts who, often because of their enthusiasm for the subject, unconsciously overinform listeners by trying to cover too many subtopics and their constituent evidence.[1] Figure 4.1 illustrates how factored subarguments and associated evidence fit into the *opening, middle,* and *close* presentation structure discussed later in this chapter.

---

[1] From our recent survey discussed in "Oral Communication in Business and Industry: Results of a Survey on Technical, Scientific, and Managerial Presentation," *Journal of Technical Writing and Communication,* **24**(2) pp. 161–180.

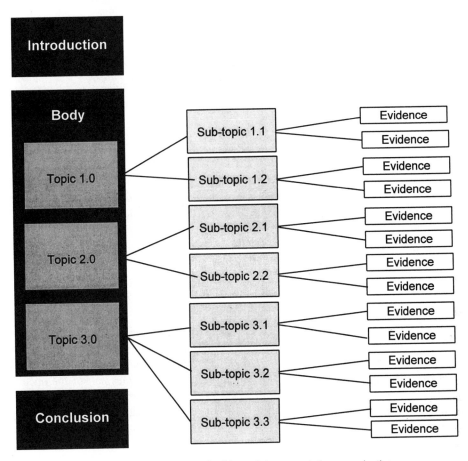

FIGURE 4.1. *Integration of evidence into presentation organization.*

ORGANIZE YOUR PRESENTATION: THE OPENING, MIDDLE, AND CLOSE

Review the steps you've taken thus far in the planning process. In light of all the modifications you've made to the emphasis and direction of your research over the past days, weeks, or months, decide on the purpose and scope of your presentation as well as the information or data (i.e., the evidence for your argument and subarguments) that you wish to include in your presentation. The following discussion explains how you can organize this material into a logically ordered presentation in three parts: the opening, middle, and close.

The Opening

The primary purposes of the presentation opening are to

- grab the attention and arouse the curiosity of your listeners
- state the central focus of the presentation

- create audience interest in the presentation subject
- establish a sense of mutual respect and goodwill between you and your audience
- establish your credibility as a trustworthy and objective expert in the topic area of the presentation
- convince listeners of the importance of the presentation topic by explaining how it relates to their informational needs and interests (i.e., benefits gained by listening to your message)
- provide a brief background on your topic
- forecast the range of major topics (scope) to be covered in your presentation.

When planning your introduction, remember to keep it simple and short (usually no more than 10 percent of the length of entire talk). Introduction components include the

- Attention-getting component
- Identification component
- Forecasting component

The Attention-Getting Component. Grabbing listeners' attention is critical if you are to hold your audience's interest long enough to introduce the topic of your presentation. You can grab and hold the attention of your audience by integrating into the introduction any of the opening devices listed in Figure 4.2. Figure 4.3 provides part of the opening used by J. L. "Skip" Olson, Grumman Program VP for NASA Shuttle Processing, in his presentation "Journey to Excellence" (full script provided in Chapter 12). In his opening, Olson successfully employs humor to engage his audience and then smoothly leads into

---

- Thought-provoking question (avoid loaded questions)
- Direct appeal for information about audience's concerns
- Meaningful and relevant quotation
- Personal experience or self-disclosure relevant to the central point of your message
- Vivid example that illustrates the central point of your message
- Significant statistic(s)
- Insightful story or anecdote
- Historical achievement or tradition that emphatically exemplifies the topic or problem at hand
- Startling statement or report of an unusual event
- Demonstration
- Unusual or impressive visual aid
- The significance of the occasion itself
- The significance of the presentation topic
- Hypothetical situation
- Interesting definition of a word central to your presentation theme
- Suitable humor

FIGURE 4.2. Attention-getting devices for introduction openers.

"Journey to Excellence"

We are encouraged by NASA to speak to others about Grumman's total commitment to quality and the road that led to receiving the George M. Low Trophy.

[Slide 1]

To begin, I'd like to share a little story about a country pig and a chicken.

Well, it seems the two of them were walking along one day when the pig realized that he hadn't had breakfast. Just as he mentioned that to the chicken, the chicken noticed a restaurant across the street. As they were walking across the street, they saw a sign on the restaurant window that said, "Special: Ham and Eggs—99 cents."

Man, the chicken was ready! She practically flew up them steps. The pig, on the other hand, paused. The chicken shouted back, "Come on pig, I'm hungry." The pig replied, "Ham and eggs for you chicken is a *contribution,* for me it's a *total commitment."* [italics added]

. . . *pause* . . . Don't fret, it took me two days to get it.

Well now, Grumman's first attempts at TQM over four years ago were sort of like the chicken's, a contribution. But we quickly learned that to make it

[Slide 2]

work, we had to make a total commitment. It didn't happen all at once and not without a lot of effort first from management, then from our employees. Fortunately, we got a lot of outside help along the way from involvement in various award programs.

FIGURE 4.3. *Sample use of humor in presentation opening from "Journey to Excellence," delivered by GTS staff and Grumman Program VP for Shuttle Processing, J. L. "Skip" Olson (Chapter 12).*

central issue to be addressed in presentation. Whenever you use these or other techniques for winning audience attention, there is always the chance that such "dramatic" strategies may go awry and prove counterproductive to your introduction and presentation in general. While humor can start off a presentation on the right footing, ineffectively delivered humor or inappropriate humor may be the most common errors committed by inexperienced presenters. And such errors invariably affect the success of the entire presentation. To avoid the abuse or mismanagement of attention-getting techniques, follow the guidelines provided in Figure 4.4.

Identification Component. In the identification component, you establish

- the significance of the presentation topic and its relevance to the informational needs and professional interests of your audience
- your credibility as an expert in the presentation area by projecting a positive image and supplying your credentials (i.e., your *bonafides*)
- needed background on the topic to inform listeners on what events brought us to the current problem
- the main argument of the presentation.

Forecasting Component. An effective introduction depends largely on preparing listeners for the subarguments and supporting evidence that are to follow in the body and

When organizing your presentation, ask yourself these questions:

- Specifically what information is needed by my audience for me to realize the presentation objectives?
- In what order does the audience need to know this information and in what detail?
- How much information can I effectively communicate in the time available for the presentation? Subtract 20 percent of the available time for the presentation's introduction and conclusion; then divide that time by the number of key points I must cover in the body of the presentation. Remember also to subtract the time needed to introduce and conclude your presentation. If my presentation runs long, what information do I delete?
- At what points during the presentation body should I insert the needed visual aids? Remember that visual aids are effective in highlighting key points for listeners.
- Is there a need for a question-and-answer period? Is there time?

When ordering the information or data collected through primary or secondary research, keep in mind that the attention span of your audience is limited and that listener interest will fluctuate throughout your presentation. The audience attention curve shown in Figure 4.6 illustrates how audience attention normally drops dramatically following the presentation introduction as the level of listener attention wanes. Audience attention remains low throughout the body of the presentation, but then it rises to approximately the same level during the conclusion as that during the introduction. You can significantly enhance the attention of listeners throughout the presentation by carefully organizing and focusing your message to meet audience needs and interests.

Help Listeners Build Long-Term Schemata. A logically ordered presentation enables listeners to access information more easily and, thus, enhances readers' comprehension of the material. A well-arranged message helps audiences to identify your movement from one topic to another and to store this information in a logical "mental database" of schemata. For example, as you introduce a new subject in your presentation and then provide evidence to develop that topic, listeners create a schematum in their minds. A schematum works much like a computer database file. Audiences listen for your announcement of a key topic and then extract a key word or two from that topic sentence to identify the schematum. Listeners then file all key information pertaining to that topic or argument into the schematum. When you introduce a different topic, listeners close the existing schematum and open a new one, tagging it with a different key word. Each distinct key word allows them later to access the information stored in that particular schematum. If properly identified with a distinct key word, a schematum becomes a part of a listener's both short-term memory (e.g., for a few minutes or the length of the presentation) and long-term memory (i.e., an indefinite amount of time).

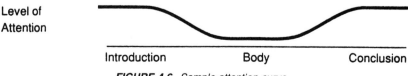

FIGURE 4.6. Sample attention curve.

Understandably, a well-organized presentation with clear transitions and a logical progression of argumentation significantly aids listeners in constructing useful schemata that they can then access easily and quickly at a later time. Conversely, a presentation lacking a clear objective, scope, and transitions—one that rambles with no structured information that listeners can convert into long-term schemata-serves little purpose.

Use the Iterative, Building-Block Approach. The thesis and scope statements at the end of your introduction should forecast for listeners the general order in which you will discuss the major points of the presentation. Dale Carnegie, widely known for his training seminars and texts on public speaking from the 1920s through the 1940s, argued, and correctly so, that speakers should organize their presentations using what we call the *3-T iterative (repetitive) approach*[2]:

- Tell the audience what you are about to tell them (Opening).
- Tell them what you said you were going to tell them (Middle).
- Tell them briefly what you just told them (Close).

Although this arrangement strategy may at first glance seem unnecessarily repetitive, we should remember that redundancy is not duplication but, rather, can be a useful teaching tool that helps listeners to grasp the structure of a presentation. Unless supplied with a written text of a presentation, listeners get only one chance to receive the message you are sending them, interpret that message, and then fully grasp its meaning and significance.

The iterative 3-T strategy prepares listeners for what you are about to tell them by providing them with a clear framework for the presentation, as outlined in your opening's scope statement which defines the topical parameters of the presentation. After supplying the previewed information or data in the presentation middle (consisting, in effect, of arguments and evidence in support of your main idea), you review the key points of the presentation in the summary.

You need not limit your use of the iterative strategy to the macro level of the presentation (i.e., opening, middle, and close). You can significantly enhance your listeners' ability to build long-term schemata by applying the iterative approach in the presentation middle (on the micro level) where you examine each key point in appropriate detail. A presentation middle using an iterative organization is constructed in building-block fashion. After dividing your presentation into major subtopics, you introduce each subtopic with a "mini-introduction" (i.e., topic sentence) which has already been forecasted in the presentation opening. This prepares listeners for the following relevant information or data that you use as evidence to support your claims, as done by Dr. John Lowe in his presentation "Nonpeptide Tachykinin Antagonists: SAR and Receptor Interactions." Dr. Lowe is a Principal Research Investigator working primarily in the area of medicinal chemistry at Pfizer's Central Research Division in Groton, CT. The passage in Figure 4.7 is extracted from the middle section of Dr. Lowe's presentation. The full text of Dr. Lowe's script is presented in Chapter 11. In addition, because your audience may miss the importance or relevance of specific pieces of evidence due to its complexity or technical nature, it's a good idea to summarize the key points at the end of each subtopic section. This "mini-conclusion" usually consists of one or two sentences that stress central ideas just covered.

---

[2] Dale Carnegie does a fine job explaining his philosophy toward public speaking in *How to Develop Self-Confidence and Influence People by Public Speaking*. New York: Pocket Books, Simon & Shuster, 1956.

Opening Scope Section	I'll begin with some background on substance P and show why it represents an attractive target for novel therapeutic agents. Then I'll describe our discovery of the first nonpeptide substance P receptor antagonist, CP-96,345, and discuss its SAR and pharmacology. We'll next look at SAR work in two areas designed to probe the interaction between the receptor and the quinuclidine nucleus. And finally, I'll describe our efforts in molecular biology to define the binding site for CP-96,345 and to understand something about the mechanism of competitive receptor antagonism.
Topic #1 Topic Sentence	2 Substance P is an undecapeptide discovered in 1931 and sequenced in 1970, and is a member of the tachykinin family of peptides which includes neurokinins A and B. . . .
Discussion of Results on Topic #1	4 And these effects enable SP to play a major role in coordinating the pain and inflammation response, as depicted here. We begin with a wound or other trauma,

[Slide #4]

which is communicated to the CNS via these afferent C-fibers which use SP as one their primary neurotransmitters . . . . Any mediator which is centrally involved in coordinating pain and inflammation is likely to be implicated in the pathophysiology of numerous diseases, and some of the diseases in which SP is thought to play a role . . .

[Slide #5]

Transition to Discussion of Testing	5 . . . are shown here. And this is what makes SP such an attractive therapeutic target, and an SP receptor antagonist such a worthwhile goal. 6 To that end, we set up a screening protocol, using bovine caudate membranes as a source of NK1 receptors. 13 SP can be proposed to play a role in inflammation based on its control of endothelial\ permeability, as

[Slide #13]

shown on this slide. Thus SP, released by a proinflammatory stimulus, can increase the permeability of the endothelial lining of blood vessels, allowing neutrophils to pass from the circulation into adjacent tissue, where they migrate to the site of the trauma and initiate the inflammatory response . . . .

Transition to Second Experiment	15 In the next experiment, capsaicin, a releaser of endogenous SP, was administered to guinea pigs and dye-spreading measured in the ureter, with CP-96,345 again providing dose-dependent blockade, with an ED50 value of 0.83 mg/kg p.o., and CP-96,344 showing no activity.
Transition to Final Experiment	16 Finally, mustard oil, another releaser of endogenous SP, was applied to the rat paw, producing this control dye-spreading response, which was inhibited by CP-96,345, with an ED_{50} value of 4 mg/kg p.o., and again, CP-96,344 had no effect. These experiments provide definitive evidence for the NK1 receptor as the site which mediates SP control of endothelial permeability. But the next question is whether or not this phenomenon is really relevant to inflammation. To answer that question, Dr. Nagahisa and his colleagues studied a classic model of pain and inflammation used it to profile NSAIDs, the acetic acid-inducing writhing model in mice . . . .

FIGURE 4.7. *Forecasting elements from opening and middle of sample script "Nonpeptide Tachykinin Antagonists: SAR and Receptor Interactions" presented by Dr. John Lowe, a Principal Research Investigator with Pfizer, Inc. (full script in Chapter 11).*

Figure 4.8 provides a conceptual diagram of the iterative organization strategy. Finally, besides helping listeners to retain key information, the iterative organization strategy enhances the transition in your presentation body by clearly delineating shifts between subtopic sections.

Organization and Development Strategies

Choosing just the right organization strategy, or combination of strategies, for your presentation is critical if you are (1) to develop sufficiently the body of your report and (2) to provide readers with a clear and logical route through the premises, evidence, and interpretations presented in the complete work. However, a discussion of organization strategies should always begin with a word of caution. You should select and subsequently apply no strategy in a contextual vacuum. Base your decision for choosing an organization strategy for your presentation on such rhetorical concerns as the purpose and scope of the presentation, the nature of the report content, the hierarchy of your audience, listeners' informational needs and their intended uses of the information, listeners' receptivity to your message, and the audience's technical expertise in the presentation's subject area.

Table 4.1 defines the most common organization strategies and explains briefly their use in presentations. All the strategies may be applied in reports that are inductively or deductively arranged. The use of one strategy also does not preclude the use of several oth-

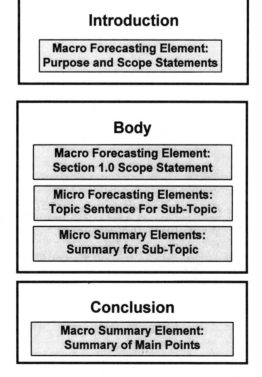

FIGURE 4.8. Schematic diagram of the iterative organizational strategy.

TABLE 4.1. Organizational Strategies

Organizational Strategy	Characteristics
Chronological (or sequential)	Use this arrangement strategy to document a sequence of events, either past, present, or future in time. A presentation organized chronologically may begin with the first occurrence of an event and move to the last and most recent occurrence. The same topic might also be discussed in reverse chronology, with the most recent occurrence developed first and other occurrences covered in reverse order. In reverse chronology, the first occurrence is, in effect, discussed last. Because everything in life is inextricably linked to time and because time can be viewed as a linear phenomenon, all events, processes, and even thoughts can be seen as linear and, thus, chronological. Processes, such as instructions for performing a computer database search or conducting a marketing survey, lend themselves naturally to chronological or sequential organization.
Classification or division	Order by classification and division are the complete opposite of each other. When you divide a topic, you factor that topic into its subparts. When you order by classification, you seek a commonality among separate topics or problems so that you -parts might combine them into a unified problem or topic.
Comparison or contrast	When comparing or contrasting topics or arguments, you normally based your comparison or contrast against a common set of *criteria*. You could compare or contrast all topics against one criterion at a time or compare or contrast against all the criteria only one topic at a time. In longer middles that involve many topics, you'll find the first arrangement more effective, because listeners can compare or contrast how all topics compare or contrast against a single criterion before moving on to a subsequent criterion. This pattern helps audiences in storing the comparisons and contrasts in short- and long-term memory.
Cause-to-effect	Ordering the body of a presentation according to cause and effect provides listeners with information or data on which (1) to understand the causes that led to an action and (2) to forecast the possible outcomes of the same causes if placed in a different context. In presentations organized by cause-to-effect, researchers know the causes but not the results. Thus, organization by cause-to-effect offers audiences a basis from which to answer the quintessential question of speculation: *What if?*
Effect-to-cause	Order by effect-to-cause is the opposite of order by cause-to-effect. Presentations arranged according to effect-to-cause uncover and explain the cause(s) of a particular action or situation. In presentations organized by effect-to-cause, researchers know the results but are left to discover the causes. Arranging a report body by effect-to-cause is much like describing to readers the shards of a shattered vase as a basis for explaining how the vase came [[T T11]to be pushed from the table to the tile floor and its destruction. In using the effect-to-cause organization, you are, in fact, conducting a process of reverse engineering wherein you present the known product or result first, followed by the discovery of how it came to be.
Familiar-to-unfamiliar	A presentation arranged according to the familiar-to-unfamiliar would begin with information that you and listeners would hold in common before progressing on to information less known or unknown by your audience. Because it essentially teaches listeners in patient increments, this organization is effective in building audience trust. It is also useful when you are communicating to which your listeners might be hostile. Because it begins by establishing a common ground of ideas and understanding, this organization can

TABLE 4.1. Organizational Strategies *(Continued)*

Organizational Strategy	Characteristics
	maximize your chances of successfully defusing listener hostility and winning some measure of audience receptivity and acceptance.
Geographical location	If your presentation contains information related to location, you may decide to arrange the presentation middle using geographical boundaries (i.e., maps).
Importance	When choosing to order your findings and interpretations according to their importance, you might begin with the most significant item and end with the least significant, or begin with the least significant and close with the most important item. Researchers normally open the body of their presentation with their biggest guns—the most significant topic of the study. Most listeners want to be first told the information that is most significant and central to the research. However, in some cases, researchers hold the most important item until the end of the presentation body if contextual information, thought less important, were needed to lay a foundation for the more significant item that is to follow. Such a strategy also leaves audiences with the most important item fresh in their minds. You might also experiment with the "sandwich" variation of these two arrangements: Place the most important information first and the next to most important information last, leaving the less important information (or that you wish to deemphasize) in "the middle of your presentation middle." This is a sound compromise. Listeners hear the most crucial information first and remember key information presented last; less pressing information (or information you might prefer to bury) is deemphasized.
Problem–cause–solution	Because this arrangement strategy adheres to the linear procedure followed by troubleshooters, it is commonly referred to as the *troubleshooting strategy.* Presentations organized according to this strategy first explain the problem before analyzing its causes and offering solutions which are often delivered as preventive measure to avoid a reoccurrence of the problem.

ers with your presentation. You will often find that your presentation requires a combination of strategies to communicate information most effectively.

You should explain the findings and analyses contained in the presentation middle in whatever detail is required to attain the objectives of your oral report. Your evidence may take many forms, such as explanations, descriptions, definitions, examples, and statistics. You should sequence your ideas and evidence using an organization pattern that allows your presentation to progress in a logical and coherent fashion toward your conclusion.

Effective Persuasive Strategies

As we argue in the Introduction, the primary objective of most professional presentations is to inform; thus, it must deliver the kinds of information or data needed by listeners to make informed decisions. This type of presentation is not meant to convert listeners to a specific way of thinking or to motivate them toward to perform a desired action. Presentations designed to persuade, on the other hand, are meant to do exactly that—to change listeners' attitudes on a topic or idea, to alter their behavior or way of thinking, to urge them to accept a particular view, or to motivate them to act in a certain way. You are essentially presenting an argument—an arrangement of evidence and appeals to convince an audience to accept your message.

Informative presentations are by nature persuasive to some degree as well. All speakers must convince audiences that what they say is valid and meaningful. Thus, they must be sufficiently persuasive in their delivery of the material to appear a credible source of information for the audience. And persuasive presentations contain an informative component as well. How could you persuade listeners to accept your message if you did not include informative evidence to support your arguments?

But, while persuasive presentations are informative, they go beyond the presentation whose central purpose is to inform. The objectives of informative presentations are to reveal and clarify options to a particular problem, offering listeners alternative ways of seeing things. Conversely, persuasive presentations ask listeners to adopt a particular alternative. Persuasive presentations normally offer recommendations as to which option listeners should select. As an informative presenter, you're a teacher defining problems and explaining options. As a persuasive presenter, you're a leader directing listeners to accept your ideas and to implement your recommendations. And, while informative presentations ask for minimal commitment from listeners, persuasive presentations ask that listeners commit themselves to doing something based on its recommendations. Finally, persuasive messages also require slightly different organizational and developmental strategies that enable you to draw listeners into the presentation so as to gain their cooperation and their commitment to your ideas. Figure 4.7 offers guidelines to increase the persuasiveness of your presentation.

The Organization of Persuasive Presentations. Persuasive messages often adhere to what is commonly called the *AIDA* (*a*ttention, *i*nterest, *d*esire, *a*ction) arrangement. In the *attention* component of the AIDA model, you expose listeners to the persuasive message itself and gain their attention. In effect, you orient listeners to the problem by stating the argument (and whatever needed background) on which your presentation is based in a clear and forceful manner that grabs your audience's attention.

After you have involved listeners in your argument, you need to win their *interest*—that is, to engage them to the extent that they are sufficiently committed to hearing how you argue your message. You gain their interest by demonstrating your credibility as a presenter and researcher, by emphasizing how listeners' acceptance of your argument would benefit them, and by employing convincing evidence. These appeals often center on multiple levels of listener needs, as defined by Abraham Maslow in 1954—whether self-actualization (creativity, wisdom, self-realization, self-fulfillment); esteem and status (respect, community recognition, uniqueness); social (friendship, affection, group acceptance); safety and security (personal competence, protection from enemies); or physiological (air, food, water, sleep, shelter). Frederick Herzberg (1966) ordered human needs in a slightly more organizational context, starting with what he calls *hygiene factors* (salary, working conditions, job security, company policy and administration, interpersonal relations with supervisors, peers, and subordinates) and ending with *motivation factors* (status, recognition, advancement, responsibility, achievement).[3]

In the *desire* component, you build listeners' desire to adopt and implement your solutions to the central problem addressed in the presentation by providing enough evidence to support your subarguments. You should arrange your proofs to persuade listeners to

---

[3] Maslow's *Motivation and Personality* and Herzberg's *Work and the Nature of Man* are especially helpful books on these topics.

agree with your subarguments, to retain the information in long-term memory, and to integrate your ideas into their own base of knowledge and understanding of the presentational problem.

In the *action* component, you push for listeners to implement your proposed solution to the problem. You also try to make it easy for them to demonstrate their commitment to your ideas. This might be as fundamental as asking listeners to consider and accept your ideas. But more often than not, you would urge listeners to act on your recommendations—for example, by modifying existing or implementing new procedures or policies, initiating new or closing current projects, performing additional research on a particular subject, redefining problems, or revising existing perceptions or practices.

You might apply the AIDA model in the following way:

(1) Establish your argument, your credentials, and good will early in the presentation.

(2) Lay the groundwork for areas of agreement (common ground) before introducing areas of disagreement.

(3) Work toward acceptance of general values before proposing specific changes.

(4) Employ evidence from experts whom and sources that listeners will respect and accept.

(5) Set modest goals for change.

(6) Offer a multisided presentation in which you discuss the advantages of your position in comparison with others.

(7) Urge listeners toward integration and action. (Osborn and Osborn, 1991, p. 336)

Figure 4.9 offers guidelines when faced with a "tough sell" in a presentational situation.

Criteria for Building a Persuasive Ethos. How can you project to your audience an image of competence, credibility, and honesty—the foundation of a persuasive *ethos?* The first step is to ensure that (1) you understand your audience's informational needs and professional interests and (2) you will provide them the information they need in the order they need it. You then must be sure that the information or data that you provide are credible—that is, that they are accurate, reliable, and thoroughly researched.

Third, you must project a positive image of yourself as an honest person and expert on your presentation subject. Show enthusiasm in your presentation and sincerity and commitment in conveying information objectively. Also, show that you understand your listeners' needs and that you are genuinely working to meet those needs. You might strengthen your relationship with listeners by illustrating how you and they share beliefs, attitudes, or backgrounds. Consequently, you're keeping their interests in mind. In addition, as a presenter of solutions to technical, scientific, or managerial problems, you must remain open-minded and flexible in working with audiences. Be willing to negotiate throughout the presentation, especially during question-and-answer periods when you and listeners are attempting to consolidate messages from both sides into a synthesized message with which the audience can feel sufficiently comfortable to implement later. Finally, as we discuss in Chapter 9, learn to deliver a smooth, well-organized presentation and dress the part of a respectable and reliable communicator of valuable ideas.

Argumentation Designs. Regardless of how thorough or incontrovertible your evidence might be in support of your argument, you must present the crux of your argument in such a way that your audience clearly understands the general logic behind your argu-

---

- Establish good will with audience from beginning.
- Identify yourself and your needs with those of audience.
- Don't try to convince your audience of too much the first time around (avoid *boomerang* effect.).
- Start with common ground, those areas or topics you and audience agree on, before addressing areas of contention; reinforce that common ground and your common interests and values.
- Stress significance of problem.
- Stress direct and indirect benefits to audience if your ideas are accepted and implemented.
- Stress your credibility.
- Acknowledge positive points of views contrary to your own and represent those views objectively and fairly.
- Be honest and candid about the shortcomings of your arguments.
- Prepare for counterarguments and your answer to them.
- Win audience's acceptance of your general message before addressing specific issues or ideas.
- Employ strong evidence, reputable sources that the audience recognizes—expert testimony, thorough library or primary research, etc.
- Make your proposed plan of action easy for listeners to accept and implement.
- Stress urgency of implementation.

FIGURE 4.9. Guidelines for winning the "tough sell."

ment; otherwise audiences might have difficulty recognizing how your evidence fits together. Argumentative designs lay the groundwork for your entire presentation. They are the foundations of logic upon which you build your argument and present your evidence. The three most central argumentative designs are

- Deductive reasoning
- Inductive reasoning
- Reasoning by analogy

Deductive reasoning is based on a premise that is linked to a given truth and which is then followed by a conclusion derived from that relationship:

Major Premise: Desktop publishing software not only can significantly enhance the quality of corporate manuals but also can reduce the time and cost associated with producing that documentation.

Minor Premise: DeskPro is one of the more versatile and powerful desktop publishing packages on the market today.

Proposition: DeskPro should be considered a prime candidate for use in our company.

Because they assume that audiences will accept the major and minor premises, arguments using deductive reasoning work best with *pathos* and *mythos* appeals. Deductive reasoning also includes counterarguments. These arguments against your proposition normally attack the truth and credibility of the major or minor premises using such appeals as *logos, pathos,* and *ethos* (which we discuss later in this chapter). To prevent your deductive argument from being rejected by astute doubters in the audience, ensure that your evidence is reliable, accurate, and precise and that both your premises are true.

Inductive reasoning works in reverse fashion from that of its deductive counterpart. Whereas deductive reasoning begins with a general truth or argument which is later supported by specific pieces of evidence, an argument based on inductive reasoning begins with specific pieces of evidence that lead to a general conclusion:

> *Evidence:* DeskPro publishing software is one of the more versatile and powerful desktop publishing packages on the market today.
>
> *Evidence:* DeskPro has markedly increased employee productivity levels of our competitors.
>
> *Evidence:* DeskPro is compatible with all our existing software.
>
> *Evidence:* DeskPro costs roughly the same as comparable desktop publishing software packages.
>
> *Conclusion and Argument:* DeskPro not only can significantly enhance the quality of corporate manuals but also can reduce the time and cost associated with producing that documentation. We should purchase the software into our existing software structure.

Because arguments based on inductive reasoning encourage significant amounts of evidence, they can be quite compelling to audiences. Confronted with an array of coherently arranged pieces of convincing evidence, listeners can't help but consider your conclusions seriously, if not accept them outright.

Because you are not relying on a generally accepted truth as a premise for your argument, you must make sure that your evidence is sufficiently thorough, accurate, and reliable to persuade audiences that your concluding premise is believable. Counterarguments to inductively reasoned arguments usually attempt to undermine the validity and reliability of the evidence presented.

Inductive and deductive arguments need not be exclusive to each other. You might use inductive reasoning to formulate a hypothesis or an argument for your presentation and deductive reasoning to support that argument with evidence.

A presenter using *reasoning by analogy* draws a parallel between his or her topic and a second topic with which it has important similarities or dissimilarities, depending on the speaker's needs. Analogies are a distinct type of comparison in which the two items, while not normally compared, have certain important features in common. Based on the strength of these similarities, you might make additional comparisons between features of the items even though only one of the items possesses that feature. For example, you might assume that, as Item A and Item B have Features 1, 2, 3, and 4 in common, both share Feature 5 even though only Item A exhibits that feature. In structuring your reasoning by analogy, you will normally make the comparison using metaphors or similes (a type of metaphor using "like" or "as"):

> *Common Features:* Both the DeskPro and PubPro desktop publishing software packages offer users advanced word processing, the ability to produce graphics, the abil-

ity to import graphics from other graphics packages, and leading-edge networking capabilities.

Added Feature: DeskPro provides users with full conversion capabilities that allow users to convert files from the most popular word processing software packages.

Assumed Commonality of Added Feature: Both DeskPro and PubPro provide users with full conversion capabilities that allow users to convert files from the most popular word processing software packages.

To construct a persuasive analogy, you must ensure that the two items being compared have more similarities than dissimilarities and that the similarities are more significant in the context of your argument than are the dissimilarities. Because they involve two unrelated items, well-constructed analogies can inject a sense of calculated drama and surprise into your presentation.

Those who might attempt to challenge your reasoning by analogy will argue (1) that the dissimilarities between the two compared items far outweigh whatever similarities they might share and (2) that the connections you make between those similarities are weak or inaccurate. Anticipate these counterarguments and select analogies that are not only unusual and interesting but also functional in establishing the significant similarities or dissimilarities that you wish to emphasize in your argument.

Argumentation Appeals. The four appeals used in argumentative discourse are

- *Logos*
- *Pathos*
- *Ethos*
- *Mythos*

Like any syllogism, an argument appealing to *logos* is based on facts, figures, and reasoned interpretation of that information. Arguments appealing to *logos* contain three elements:

(1) A statement that must be proved
(2) The evidence to support that statement
(3) A conclusion that unifies the statement and evidence.

The following hypothetical syllogism establishes causational links between three items, then concludes with a unifying statement that connects the first and third items:

Premise 1: Widget A is more efficient than Widget B.
Premise 2: Widget B is more efficient than Widget C.
Conclusion: Widget A is more efficient than Widget C.

An argument based on *pathos* is appealing to the emotions of an audience. Such arguments often appeal to topics to which we normally attach strong emotions, including social acceptance, security, love, happiness, self-esteem, health, adventure, creativity, fear, guilt, looking good, feeling good, friendship, compassion, competition. Emotional appeals can be very effective in dislodging audiences from their inertia. The following argument is based on the emotional appeal to fear:

mally attack the truth and credibility of the major or minor premises using such appeals as *logos, pathos,* and *ethos* (which we discuss later in this chapter). To prevent your deductive argument from being rejected by astute doubters in the audience, ensure that your evidence is reliable, accurate, and precise and that both your premises are true.

Inductive reasoning works in reverse fashion from that of its deductive counterpart. Whereas deductive reasoning begins with a general truth or argument which is later supported by specific pieces of evidence, an argument based on inductive reasoning begins with specific pieces of evidence that lead to a general conclusion:

> *Evidence:* DeskPro publishing software is one of the more versatile and powerful desktop publishing packages on the market today.
>
> *Evidence:* DeskPro has markedly increased employee productivity levels of our competitors.
>
> *Evidence:* DeskPro is compatible with all our existing software.
>
> *Evidence:* DeskPro costs roughly the same as comparable desktop publishing software packages.
>
> *Conclusion and Argument:* DeskPro not only can significantly enhance the quality of corporate manuals but also can reduce the time and cost associated with producing that documentation. We should purchase the software into our existing software structure.

Because arguments based on inductive reasoning encourage significant amounts of evidence, they can be quite compelling to audiences. Confronted with an array of coherently arranged pieces of convincing evidence, listeners can't help but consider your conclusions seriously, if not accept them outright.

Because you are not relying on a generally accepted truth as a premise for your argument, you must make sure that your evidence is sufficiently thorough, accurate, and reliable to persuade audiences that your concluding premise is believable. Counterarguments to inductively reasoned arguments usually attempt to undermine the validity and reliability of the evidence presented.

Inductive and deductive arguments need not be exclusive to each other. You might use inductive reasoning to formulate a hypothesis or an argument for your presentation and deductive reasoning to support that argument with evidence.

A presenter using *reasoning by analogy* draws a parallel between his or her topic and a second topic with which it has important similarities or dissimilarities, depending on the speaker's needs. Analogies are a distinct type of comparison in which the two items, while not normally compared, have certain important features in common. Based on the strength of these similarities, you might make additional comparisons between features of the items even though only one of the items possesses that feature. For example, you might assume that, as Item A and Item B have Features 1, 2, 3, and 4 in common, both share Feature 5 even though only Item A exhibits that feature. In structuring your reasoning by analogy, you will normally make the comparison using metaphors or similes (a type of metaphor using "like" or "as"):

> *Common Features:* Both the DeskPro and PubPro desktop publishing software packages offer users advanced word processing, the ability to produce graphics, the abil-

ity to import graphics from other graphics packages, and leading-edge networking capabilities.

Added Feature: DeskPro provides users with full conversion capabilities that allow users to convert files from the most popular word processing software packages.

Assumed Commonality of Added Feature: Both DeskPro and PubPro provide users with full conversion capabilities that allow users to convert files from the most popular word processing software packages.

To construct a persuasive analogy, you must ensure that the two items being compared have more similarities than dissimilarities and that the similarities are more significant in the context of your argument than are the dissimilarities. Because they involve two unrelated items, well-constructed analogies can inject a sense of calculated drama and surprise into your presentation.

Those who might attempt to challenge your reasoning by analogy will argue (1) that the dissimilarities between the two compared items far outweigh whatever similarities they might share and (2) that the connections you make between those similarities are weak or inaccurate. Anticipate these counterarguments and select analogies that are not only unusual and interesting but also functional in establishing the significant similarities or dissimilarities that you wish to emphasize in your argument.

Argumentation Appeals. The four appeals used in argumentative discourse are

- *Logos*
- *Pathos*
- *Ethos*
- *Mythos*

Like any syllogism, an argument appealing to *logos* is based on facts, figures, and reasoned interpretation of that information. Arguments appealing to *logos* contain three elements:

(1) A statement that must be proved
(2) The evidence to support that statement
(3) A conclusion that unifies the statement and evidence.

The following hypothetical syllogism establishes causational links between three items, then concludes with a unifying statement that connects the first and third items:

Premise 1: Widget A is more efficient than Widget B.
Premise 2: Widget B is more efficient than Widget C.
Conclusion: Widget A is more efficient than Widget C.

An argument based on *pathos* is appealing to the emotions of an audience. Such arguments often appeal to topics to which we normally attach strong emotions, including social acceptance, security, love, happiness, self-esteem, health, adventure, creativity, fear, guilt, looking good, feeling good, friendship, compassion, competition. Emotional appeals can be very effective in dislodging audiences from their inertia. The following argument is based on the emotional appeal to fear:

Premise 1: Seismologists predict that the San Francisco Bay Area will suffer the worst earthquake in 100 years by the year 2000.

Premise 2: More than 90 percent of homeowners in the Bay Area either do not carry home insurance that protects their investments from earthquake damage or carry insufficient coverage for such destructive acts of nature. Consequently, an such a devastating earthquake as the one predicted would place most San Francisco homeowners in financial ruin.

Conclusion: All San Francisco homeowners should reevaluate their home insurance policies.

The central drawbacks to an argument appealing to *pathos* are as follows:

- Any persuasion realized through this appeal is often short-term.
- Emotional appeals can also backfire (audiences can feel manipulated or react in an unexpected or undesirable manner).
- Emotional appeals are often misused as substitutes for strong logical arguments and evidence.

Arguments appealing to *ethos* (or image) rely on the credibility and reputation of the speaker or the sources of information used in the presentation to persuade audiences. When relying on your credibility as a presenter, you must ensure that your audience perceives you as a person with integrity who is competent in the field about which you are speaking. Briefly stating in your opening the depth of experience or research that you bring to the presentation topic can build a strong sense of *ethos* which you hope to project to your listeners.

When you appeal to *mythos,* you are tapping into the common identity shared by members of your audience. *Mythos* refers to the myths, or stories, that illustrate our self-identity as a member of a town, a state, a country, or of the human race. These stories define who we are as members of our society. They define the common values, history, beliefs, and aspirations of our culture. Arguments based on an appeal to *mythos* often refer to stories of our cultural heritage for which the audience has strong emotions, including those relating to national pride and patriotism, famous heroes and enemies, religious doctrines, liberties and freedom, and personal aspirations. For example, the argument that U.S. citizens should buy "American" is based, for the most part, on the emotional appeal (and pull) of patriotism. When employing emotional appeal in your argumentation, however, remember that this appeal strategy requires that members of your audience share the *mythos* on which you are building your argument.

You will probably use a combination of appeals in your presentation. Keep in mind to select the appeal(s) that is most appropriate to your speaking situation, and use your evidence development strategies effectively. For example, you might begin your presentation by emphasizing your extensive experience in the subject area and your intention to help listeners solve a current problem *(ethos).* You might then build a strong foundation for your argument by supplying plenty of facts and figures *(logos)* and urge your audience to accept your recommendations by appealing to their social values and traditions that would support such recommendations *(mythos).* A combination of appeals strengthens the enduring power of a presentation by providing listeners with a variety of ways in which they might respond to your presentation.

Fallacies in Reasoning. Occasionally you might find yourself unintentionally employing or intentionally tempted to use arguments based on flawed reasoning drawn from erroneous inferences. If not always alert, you might also base your arguments on flawed evidence, or *grounding,* or no evidence at all. Finally, you might attempt to conceal the weaknesses in an argument(s) by misdirecting your audience's attention toward irrelevant issues that seem to support your view. Ultimately, if listeners are to accept your arguments as reasoned and logical, you must ensure that

- your evidence is reliable, valid, recent, and consistent
- the knowledge base from which you are speaking is extensive
- your analysis of collected information or data is objective
- your presentation of the evidence is fair.

Tables 4.2–4.4 list the fallacies in reasoning, grounding, and misdirection that are most commonly used in technical, scientific, and managerial presentations. The presence of any one of these fallacies in your presentation, whether intentionally or unintentionally included, can significantly reduce not only your credibility as a speaker but also the acceptance of your message.

THE CLOSE

Your presentation close should summarize the key points of your presentation that you want listeners to remember most. This is also your last chance to encourage listeners to integrate your message into their own thoughts on the presentation topic and to implement any recommendations that you might have made. Your close, then, should do the following:

- Restate the thesis of the presentation and reinforce its central ideas by summarizing main points.
- Identify for the audience the meaning and significance of key points presented in the body of the presentation.
- Leave the audience with a sense of goodwill toward you and an interest in remaining current on the presentation topic.
- Recommend plans of action based on the conclusions.
- Motivate listeners to action (either to physically *do* something or to actively reexamine their attitude toward your topic).
- Provide a sense of closure to the presentation.

A presentation that has captured listeners' attention and provided an interesting discussion of topics of direct concern to the audience will usually simplify the task of concluding the oral report. When preparing your close, follow the guidelines offered in Figure 4.10. Figure 4.11 offers ideas for constructing "clinchers" to end your close.

TRANSITIONS

Transitions are logical bridges between ideas, and they are critical rhetorical components of your presentation because they serve as road signs that signal the way for listeners

TABLE 4.2. Fallacies of Faulty Reasoning

Fallacy in Reasoning	Definition
Circular reasoning (*circulus in probando*)	Circular reasoning, a form of begging the question, uses a restatement of the argument as proof—for example, "in other words, *A* because *B*, *B* because *C*, *C* because *A*."
Either-or reasoning	Sometimes referred to as the "black-or-white" fallacy, either-or reasoning falsely argues that there are only two responses to a given situation and that only one of the responses is advantageous to the audience—for example, "We either include Barbados as a port on the new cruise or forget about increasing our share in the Caribbean market."
False analogy	A false analogy results when your comparison of two objects or ideas does not satisfy the rules of comparison and opposition—that is, whether the two objects or ideas being compared are sufficiently alike and whether there are any significant differences between them. A false analogy, then, compares two things or ideas that are not alike in significant ways of that have important differences. The comparison in the argument "Our marketing approach to owners of Luxury Car A in the United States should work equally well to owners of Luxury Car A in Japan" is a false analogy.
False cause (*post hoc*)	A *post hoc* fallacy mistakenly assumes that because two ideas or events happen one after the other the second event is caused by the first. *Post hoc* comes from the Latin *post hoc ergo propter hoc,* which means "after this therefore because of this." The *post hoc* fallacy, then, mistakes temporal sequence for causality.
Hasty generalization	A hasty generalization draws a conclusion about an object, idea, or event based on too few or atypical examples. To be reliable, generalizations must ensure that enough members of a class have been observed and that those members are typical of all members in the class. The following hasty generalization does not satisfy these criteria: "The real estate market in our region of the country has been soft recently; therefore, the national real estate industry must be weak as well."
Imprecise wording of premise	If you do not clearly define the premises supporting your deductive argument and the relationship(s) between those premises, you ill-advisedly leave your audience with the difficult task of interpreting your syllogism for themselves. You should never leave unclear the meaning of your message, much less that of your syllogism (the building block of your argument), because it invites listeners' misinterpretation and, more times than not, dooms your presentation to ending as a senseless jumble of misdirected evidence.
Slippery rope	The slippery rope argument consists of a faulty connection between momentum and cause and effect. A speaker using this strategy would argue that the simple fact that an event occurred establishes momentum—a series of following events that will ultimately and unavoidably cause a highly undesirable end. The central flaw in the slippery rope argument is that one event does not necessarily establish causation or predict later related events, positive or negative.

TABLE 4.3. Fallacies of Grounding in Argumentation

Begging the question (*petitio principii*)	You "beg" the issue (or question) you are presenting. This argument uses itself—for example, "We need to broaden our marketing efforts because our current efforts are too narrow." There is no evidence for either case.
Comparing noncomparable data	When we attempt to compare apples and oranges we are comparing noncomparable data. For example, comparing data on the health care systems of the United States and that of Spain would be meaningless unless we established some common foundation for comparison within the highly dissimilar context of the two systems.
Espousing opinion as fact	While a *fact* is information that is verifiably true, an *opinion* is a persona interpretation of information, whether a fact or not. Presenting opinions as facts or facts as opinions can cost your presentation credibility in the minds of your listeners.
Myth of the mean	Figures don't always mean what they appear to be saying. The mean is the mathematical average of two or more numbers. Averages, however, can be misleading. For example, the median income of $55,000 for bank workers does not describe the range and frequency (frequency distribution) of salaries. A minority of very high salaries for bank managers could easily offset the low salaries of the majority of bank employees.
Non sequitur	This Latin phrase means "it does not follow." The *non sequitur* fallacy argues a claim that is irrelevant to or unsupported by the evidence given—for example, "Reduction of the armaments industry in the United States will create economic and social unrest in regions heavily dependent on an armaments-based economy. Unemployment in the Northeast has more than doubled in the last year and the number of welfare recipients in that same region has tripled in the sample time span. In addition, violent crime has increased 225 percent in the Northeast, and the illiteracy rate has climbed 20 percent."
Quoting out of context	Extracting selected words or phrases from their context in whatever source—such as a comment, speech, or document—can significantly distort the meaning of the original message. When quoting in your presentation, be sensitive to presenting accurately both the explicit and implicit meanings of the original source. Also be sure to identify fully the source so that listeners might evaluate its credibility. You might include such important information as the name and title of the quoted author or speaker, a very brief background of his or her qualifications, and the date of the source's publication or speech.
Red herring	If you feel that your presentation lacks sufficient evidence to support your argument, you might be tempted to buttress the argument with an emotionally charged subargument that, although irrelevant to the reasoned evidence to defend your message, is successful in distracting listeners from your initial argument. Because audiences rarely gain their rational bearings in order to return to the original argument, they don't notice the absence of convincing evidence to support that argument.
Self-evident truths	This fallacy proposes arguments founded on premises whose truth is unsubstantiated by fact but that are generally unquestioned in a particular culture—for example, "Because the United States is the greatest nation in the world, we have the responsibility to spread democracy to all corners of the globe."

TABLE 4.4. Fallacies of Misdirection in Argumentation

Argumentum ad hominem	When we attack the person putting forth an argument with which we don't agree, instead of the premise or evidence on which that argument is based, we are committing the *ad hominem* fallacy in grounding. The *ad hominem* strategy diverts attention from the merits of an argument and criticizes it through its association with its arguer—for example, "It's clear why Frank argues for a massive reduction in social security payments. He's wealthy an can well affor such a cut."
Appeal to emotion	When you appeal to your audience's emotions (e.g., fear, hopes, guilt, pity), you are basing you argument not on reason and fact but on often illogical feelings—for example. "If we don't act immediately, we'll lose the largest share of the market."
Appeal to ignorance (*ad ignorantiam*)	This fallacy argues that, because a claim has not been proven wrong, it is right—for example, "We can accelerate the speed of our current microcomputer chip because there's no indication that we couldn't enhance its performance *ad infinitum*."
Appeal to In appropriate authority (*ad verecundiam*)	When we cite an authority who is not in the area of discussion in order to buttress an argument, we are appealing to an inappropriate authority.
Appeal to popular values (*ad populum*)	An argument based on this fallacy appeals to the attitudes, beliefs, and associated emotions of an audience with no regard to the logical or reasoned foundations of the argument.
Bandwagon appeal	The bandwagon appeal is a commonly used form of the *ad populum* fallacy in which you appeal to your audience's need for social acceptance to win support for your argument—for example, "Most Americans are switching from Potato Chip A to Potato Chip B. Why don't you?"
Straw man	When you present an opposing argument in a cursory and inaccurate manner merely as a means to springboard yourself into a more complete discussion of your own message, you are committing what is known as a straw-man argument. Such a distortion of an opposing view calls into question your ethics as a speaker and reduces the credibility of your argument. Always represent opposing views objectively and fairly. Straw-man arguments are undignified and imply a weakness of argumentative design, appeal, or evidence in the speaker's argument.
Tu quoque	An argument based on the *tu quoque* fallacy involves a response to a counterargument made against an initial argument. In defending the primary argument, you might turn the counterargument back on itself, thus shifting the accusation from you to the counterargument—for example, Initial argument: "We need to shorten the research-and-development process." Counter argument: "Do that would undermine the quality of our product." *Tu quoque* response: "Your opposition to an accelerated R & D effort would undermine the product by not allowing us to get it more promptly to market." anything else." As you'll note, *tu quoque* is a close cousin to the circular reasoning fallacy.

- Don't just stop. Abrupt endings—such as "Well, I guess that's all I have for you today. Thank you for coming"—leave audiences hanging. Signal the end of your presentation with clear transition sign posts (such as "In conclusion . . ." or "In summary . . .").
- Provide a sense of closure for the presentation.
- Restate the central argument of your presentation and reinforce it by summarizing its constituent subarguments.
- Identify for listeners the overriding meaning and significance of your central argument and subarguments.
- Keep the conclusion brief. The summary is meant to recap only *key* points and analyses, not to rehash the entire body of the presentation.
- Don't get bogged down in providing explanation or details associated with the main points you summarize in the conclusion. You should have placed this material earlier in the presentation body.
- Include no new information in the conclusion that has not already been discussed, mentioned, or implied earlier in the presentation.
- Be specific when recommending a plan of action; a persuasive analysis is of little use if your listeners don't know exactly how (or where) they should *apply* the information. To aid listeners in understanding the scope and sequence of your recommendations, you might list suggested actions highlighted in a visual aid for greater emphasis.
- Leave the audience with a sense of goodwill and an interest in remaining current on the presentation topic.
- As is true throughout your presentation, don't apologize in your conclusion. Apologies—such as "Well, I'm sorry I couldn't offer you more information on this topic" or "This is all I have for you today; I apologize for not being able to provide you with some useful recommendations"—reduce your credibility and leave listeners with a negative aftertaste toward the entire presentation.
- End with a *clincher* to intensify the closure of your presentation. Figure 4.11 provides a list of popular clinchers.

FIGURE 4.10. *Guidelines for constructing your close.*

- Use direct quotations from respected sources relating to your final conclusions or recommendations.
- Challenge listeners to action.
- Ask a closing question that harkens back to the thesis statement in the presentation's introduction.
- Tell a story that figuratively amplifies your central message.
- Tell a joke that sums up the central point of your presentation.
- Use a visual aid or prop that emphasizes your message.
- Demonstrate the device or procedure on which your talk is focused as a capstone for the presentation.
- End with a striking example that illustrates your central argument.
- Challenge and motivate listeners to implement your recommendations by emphasizing the resulting benefits to the audience.
- Appeal for your audience's help in solving the presentation problem. Seek their suggestions to establish a mood of cooperation.

FIGURE 4.11. *Clinchers for the close.*

throughout your talk. Remember that one significant difference between presenting information or data orally and presenting the same material in written form is that listeners don't have the advantage of replaying what you just said whereas readers can re-read an important or complex passage in a text. Consequently, you must clearly forecast for listeners what you plan to discuss as you open a new line of argumentation and then highlight key points during the discussion. In effect, prevent your listeners from wandering off the central highway of your discussion and getting lost on side roads; provide them with easily recognizable roads signs in the form of explicit transitions between major ideas or arguments.

Transitions come in various forms. Sentence definitions explicitly state the upcoming shift in topic: "Having addressed the causes of the explosion, let's now turn to how we can keep this mishap from happening again." Pronouns are useful in moving listeners from one idea to another by referring to a previous person or thing: "Jane Goodall proved that chimpanzees can learn how to use tools. *She* also proves that they have a rudimentary understanding of how to make tools." Transition words and phrases are perhaps the most commonly used form of transition. Table 4.5 provides a list of the frequently used transition words and phrases along with the relationships that these transitions create between the ideas that they logically link.

Forecasting elements contained in your presentation also serve as highly effective forms of transition. The scope statement, such as the one shown earlier in Figure 4.5, orients listeners to the subarguments that you will make in your presentation and the order in which you will discuss them; it also announces the macro organization of your talk. This forecasting component prepares listeners for what is to come. As you begin discussion of a subargument by repeating some of the key words mentioned in the scope statement, listeners are able to get their bearings and place this new subargument in the context with other scope subarguments. Topic sentences are another form of forecasting component because they summarize for listeners the gist of each subargument you are about to present, as illustrated in the sample topic sentences in Figure 4.12 which are extracted from the middle of the presentation "Nonpeptide Tachykinin Antagonists: SAR and Receptor Interactions" delivered by Dr. John A. Lowe III, a Principal Research Investigator working primarily in the area of medicinal chemistry at the Central Research Division of Pfizer Inc. (Groton, CT). Dr. Lowe's presentation explores the history of his research team's discovery of the first nonpeptide substance P receptor antagonist, CP-96,345.

TABLE 4.5. Transition Words and Phrases

Relationship	Transitions
Addition	Also, and, finally, first (second, etc.), furthermore, in addition, likewise, moreover, similarly, again
Comparison	In the same way, likewise, similarly, in comparison
Contrast	But, however, nevertheless, on the other hand, yet, in contrast, otherwise, to the contrary, conversely, notwithstanding
Illustration	For example, for instance, in other words, namely, specifically
Conclusion	As a result, because, consequently, hence, so, therefore, thus, to conclude, to summarize, in brief, in conclusion, all in all, on the whole, to sum up, in closing, accordingly, thereupon
Time	First, second, next, then, meanwhile, later, now, meanwhile, subsequently, while, since, before, after

---

Likewise, we function as a team with NASA. At KSC, we accomplish what we do because of the attitude that everyone works for the same team and safely launching the Space Shuttle is our goal. To quote one of our NASA teammates, "Our guys work so well together that the only way to tell who works for who is the name on the bottom of their badges."

Unquestionably, this has been the best year for SPC. In the past twelve months, SPC launched eight shuttles, landed three at KSC, integrated into the fleet and launched the newest shuttle, Endeavor, and brought on-line a third Orbiter Processing Facility. Records for processing time continue to be broken each "flow" while, at the same time, our safety record continues to improve. For these and many other reasons, we're proud to be part of the SPC team.

Our mission statement spells out what we do best: we provide safe, reliable, and on-schedule operations & maintenance support for launch processing, instrumentation systems, and calibration support for shuttle processing. For the past eight years we have been committed to continuous improvement. Unquestionably, we achieved our success through communication and teamwork with our customers.

[Slide 6]

In everyday terms, we do a host of functions for the SPC team. Our work force of about 700 people operate, monitor, and maintain over 400 computer subsystems in what is called the Launch Processing System . . . .

FIGURE 4.12. *Topic sentences forecasting the central themes of paragraphs in "Journey to Excellence," developed by GTS staff and Grumman Program VP for Shuttle Processing, J. L. "Skip" Olson (full script of text in Chapter 12).*

To maximize the ease with which listeners can move through your presentation, offer a clear thesis and scope statements in your introduction, highlight your topic sentences, and employ transition words or phrases that establish the appropriate relationship between ideas. Lastly, you can enhance transitions even further by using visual aids (e.g., overhead transparencies or flipcharts that list the scope areas in the order they will be discussed) to forecast topics to be addressed and to emphasize the transitions between these topics when they occur. We examine the use of visual aids in Chapters 6 and 7.

OUTLINING YOUR PRESENTATION

An *outline* is an orderly plan for arranging most effectively the ideas you wish to include in your presentation. The outline should illustrate the relationships between the ideas as well as their significance in relation to each other. A properly designed outline clearly shows which ideas are most important in the presentation and which are subordinate. Outlines are invaluable in helping you determine not only the organization but also the content of your presentation. In effect, outlines function as the architectural blueprint for your message. They keep the entire presentation and its constituent sections thematically unified. A well-structured outline also helps you to maintain coherence in your writing so that ideas flow in a smooth and logical progression of related topics and evidence. They can also prevent you from digressing from the focus of discussion or from including irrelevant information.

In addition, outlines provide you with "the big picture" of your presentation. Acting as the skeletal framework, the outline illustrates how the parts of the presentation fit together. The use of an outline can reveal arguments that may be inadequately developed. Outlines can also suggest to you ways in which you might restructure the presentation by moving entire sections or subparts of sections. Constructing a successful outline involves a process of writing multiple outlines, with each subsequent outline building upon the previous in any number of ways—for example, the specificity and precision of the presentation's stated purpose and central argument, the completeness of the presentation, the depth to which an argument is developed, and the reference and inclusion of visual aids. As shown in Figure 4.13, take the time to truly prepare yourself for delivering a professional presentation by completing the three-step outlining process which involves writing the

(1) Brainstorming outline
(2) Presentation outline
(3) Note outline (used instead of presentation script)

Brainstorming and Presentation Outlines

To construct an effective outline for your presentation, begin by writing a brainstorming outline, which places ideas into logical organization. The brainstorming and presentation outlines shown in Figures 4.14 and 4.15 illustrate how a computer scientist organizes her study on the feasibility of using a meta-design scheme (a structured development tool) to

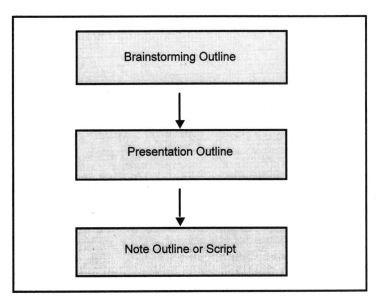

FIGURE 4.13. *The three-step outlining process.*

Presentation Topic: Analytical Study on the Feasibility of Using a Meta-Design Scheme to Implement an Enhanced Software Design Process

Date and Time of Presentation: November, 1995; 1:30 p.m.

Location of Presentation: ThinkWare, Inc., 1015 K Street, N.W., Washington, D.C. 20015

Occasion of Presentation: Internal briefing (30 minutes) to Maria Ortega (Manager of ThinkWare-Washington D.C. facility), Kent Norton (Director of Research and Development), and Jane Peters (Director of Marketing and Sales) on the viability of meta-design to generate better software more quickly.

Purpose of Presentation: To brief decision makers on the benefits of understanding the meta-design process and by applying that process to our own software development procedure.

Central Argument: As a fundamental activity of almost every creative discipline, the design process is understandably critical in the development of software that successfully meets users' computing needs. By better understanding the meta-design process and how it can be best implemented in the software industry, we at ThinkWare can accelerate our software development process and, at the same time, improve the usability of the software.

Introduction

Significance of Presentation to Audience: ThinkWare is currently reexamining current software development practices. Management wants to know how we can improve the productivity of software designers while also enhancing the marketability of our products.

Benefits to Audience: Most disciplines incorporate a design process at SOE point in their product development. ThinkWare can employ the meta-design process to improve effectiveness, usability, and sales of its software.

Your Credentials: I hold an M.S. in software design and analysis and have been working in the profession of software design for five years with ThinkWare at its Palo Alto and Washington, D.C. offices. Maria Ortega personally asked that I conduct the study into the possible uses of the meta-design process at ThinkWare—Washington D.C.

Purpose Statement: Meta-design processes exist in many leading-edge companies today. ThinkWare should implement a structured design process modeled on other established meta-design processes that have already proven themselves to be highly successful in companies comparable to ours.

Scope Statement: I will explain the global design structure of the meta-design process, similarities and common concepts between the meta-design processes of companies comparable to ours, and the means by which we can effectively and efficiently implement our own meta-design process for software development.

Body

Main Point #1: The global (meta-design) process

Subpoints or Supporting Evidence: Explanation of each phase in the meta-design flowchart, design specifications, constraints, and common design principles (simplicity, modularity, information hiding, user focus, feasibility, manufacturability, maintainability, ability to document)

Main Point #2: The need to use the meta-design principles correctly to achieve effective design

Subpoints or Supporting Evidence: Explanation of common examples to illustrate this argument, beginning with basic examples (scissors and "hingeless" door) and ending with a sample ThinkWare computer program.

Main Point #3: The need to implement a meta-design process at ThinkWare

Subpoints or Supporting Evidence: Explanation of how companies comparable to ours have successfully implemented meta-design processes in such areas as mechanical and electrical engineering; the costly penalty for implementing a faulty design; and the cost-savings to R&D, manufacturing, and software maintenance of implementing a workable design.

FIGURE 4.14. Brainstorming outline for meta-design scheme.

Conclusion

Summary of Main Points:

- Existence of a common meta-design process across many industries
- ThinkWare currently lacks a central meta-design process
- Importance of following specifications, constraints, principles for effective designs
- Importance of implementing a structured design process that is appropriate for ThinkWare and its line of software

Recommendations:

- We need to reexamine our current design process.
- We should consider implementing a meta-design process that meets the seven criteria of an effective design (simplicity, modularity, information hiding, user focus, feasibility, manufacturability and maintainability, and good documentation).
- We should ensure that ThinkWare software designers fully understand the meta-design process and know how to implement in their own work on a regular, consistent basis.
- We should fully document our motivations for changing the design process.
- We should require uniform deliverable to customers, user, and design review team at each phase of the design process.

Statement of Closure:

- The meta-design process is an important concept central to the competitiveness of all leading-edge companies in the software development industry.
- ThinkWare can quickly build its own meta-design process by using models from other industries, such as mechanical and electrical engineering.
- By implementing an effective meta-design process, ThinkWare will not only market software that better meets user needs but also realize cost-savings to R&D, manufacturing, and software maintenance of implementing a workable design.

FIGURE 4.14. (Continued)

implement an enhanced software design process. Having completed brainstorming and presentation outlines, she condenses the information contained in the presentation outline into note outline form (Figure 4.16). In effect, she uses the brainstorming and presentation outline exercises as a way to develop, organize, and then condense her thoughts. These forms help her to understand more fully her purpose in presenting this material, her essential message, the needs and interests of her audience, the central argument and associated subarguments, and key evidence to support those arguments. She then, very adeptly, delivered her 30-minute presentation from that skeletal outline.

When writing your brainstorming and presentation outlines, be sure to do the following:

- Use parallel wording.
- Keep balanced in depth and range.
- Write full sentences.
- Coordinate ideas that belong together.
- Subordinate ideas that belong under a larger, encompassing idea.
- Check for explicit and smooth transitions between subarguments as well as between key ideas within subarguments.

Presentation Topic: Analytical Study on the Feasibility of Using a Meta-Design Scheme to Implement an Enhanced Software Design Process

Date and Time of Presentation: November, 1995; 1:30 p.m.

Location of Presentation: ThinkWare, Inc., 1015 K Street, N.W., Washington, D.C. 20015

Occasion of Presentation: Internal briefing (30 minutes) to Maria Ortega (Manager of ThinkWare-Washington D.C. facility), Kent Norton (Director of Research and Development), and Jane Peters (Director of Marketing and Sales) on the viability of meta-design to generate better software more quickly.

Purpose of Presentation: To brief decision makers on the benefits of understanding the meta-design process and by applying that process to our own software development procedure.

Central Argument: As a fundamental activity of almost every creative discipline, the design process is understandably critical in the development of software that successfully meets users' computing needs. By better understanding the meta-design process and how it can be best implemented in the software industry, we at ThinkWare can accelerate our software development process and, at the same time, improve the usability of the software.

I. Introduction

    A. *Attention-Getting Device (Opener):* How many of you have tried to push a door open when you needed to pull, or have tried to push the door open from the wrong side? Most people have been in this situation; you usually feel foolish, right? The truth is, however, that you aren't the one who should feel foolish; the designer of the door is the one who made the mistake, not you. Design is the most important part of almost every creative discipline. The design process, if established correctly, should catch errors such as the lack of visual clues on how a door might work.

    B. *Identification Component:*

      Significance & Benefits:

      • Most disciplines will incorporate a design process somewhere in their work. A high-level design process exists in most disciplines.

      • By understanding how meta-design works and the principles behind meta-design, we at ThinkWare will be able to implement a uniform meta-design process into how we design and manufacture our software. As many of you know, the later the development process an error is found or a revision is made, the more expensive it is to correct. The time and money expended for software revisions grow exponentially through the development phases. By implementing a meta-design process, we would be able not only to market software that better meets user needs but also to realize cost-savings to R&D, manufacturing, and software maintenance of implementing a workable design.

      Credentials: I've had the chance to work with most of you over the past three years here at the ThinkWare-Washington D.C. office in my capacity as the director of Systems Design and Analysis. Some of us even go back to the early '90s when I was a systems designer at the Palo Alto office.

      Background: On any account, I'm glad that Maria Ortega offered me the opportunity to talk with you today about the importance of meta-design to ThinkWare. It's an industry practice that has significantly improved the productivity of many of our competitors, and for that reason and for others it makes sense that we consider where meta-design might fit in at ThinkWare.

FIGURE 4.15. *Presentation outline for meta-design scheme.*

Purpose and Thesis Statements:
- Meta-design has become because it allows designers to design and manufacturers to build a product that better meets users' needs and that saves companies money in manufacturing, maintenance, and documentation.
- In this brief talk today, I want to show how we can use existing meta-design processes currently employed by organizations similar to our own as models from which to create a meta-design process that makes sense for ThinkWare.
- I also want to show how implementing a structured meta-design process as soon as possible will not only enable us to design better software but also make our jobs much easier and considerably more enjoyable.

C. *Forecasting Component:* The procedure for implementing a meta-design process into our software development phases at ThinkWare is to
1. Study the meta-design process and its global concepts and principles to identify the fallacies in our design and those of other companies
2. Compare the successful designs of companies similar to ours
3. Determine how we can implement parts of those meta-design processes into our software development process

D. *Transition into Presentation Body:* Let's examine, then,
1. How the meta-design process works
2. The need to follow meta-design requirements and principles
3. The importance of building a structured design process here at ThinkWare

II. Body

A. *Main Point #1:* The existence of global design (meta-design) process.
1. Meta-design flowchart [overhead].
2. Explain each meta-design phase.
3. Baking a cake [example].
4. Explain specifications of meta-design process.
5. Explain constraints of meta-design process.
6. Outline and explain common design concepts and principles.
    a. Simplicity—Don't make original requirements limiting; all parts requested are necessary.
    b. Modularity—Create design and factor into smaller components
    c. Information hiding—Only show necessary component of design.
    d. User Focus—Know audience/user and appropriate clues/feedback.
    e. Feasibility–Know when to say when.
    f. Manufacturability and Maintainability—Have realistic specifications and constraints.
    g. Effective documentation—Provide deliverables through the process.
7. Transition into Point #2: Now that we have a better idea regarding what meta-design is all about, let's consider the meta-design concepts and principles to see why some designs work while others don't.

B. *Main Point #2:* The need to use design requirements and principle correctly to create effective designs.
1. Example of computer keyboard (good clues of action, definition of parts, good feedback).
2. Example of "hingeless" door (no clues, aesthetics versus usability)

FIGURE 4.15. (Continued)

3. Transition into Point #3: From the previous examples, we can see why it is so important to implement structured design process. Now let's look at some examples that illustrate why we at ThinkWare should adopt a structured design process.

C. *Main Point #3:* The importance of having a meta-design process here at ThinkWare.

1. Explain some disciplines that are more structured than others (mechanical engineering, electrical engineering, software engineering).
2. Show tree-swing design [overhead].
3. Explain how faulty designs can result from the lack of communication within an organization.
4. Explain how the design stage affects the entire life development of a software product.
5. Show how we can identify and correct errors early in the development process.
6. Show how much more time and money would be lost if we were to revise the software later in the process.
7. Show the influence of design on manufacturing costs [overhead].
8. Show how the end product better meets users' needs.
9. Transition into Conclusion: Well, what does all this mean to how we develop software at ThinkWare?

III. Conclusion

A. *Summary of Main Points:* To improve our method of designing and building leading-edge software that will out-perform that of our competitors, we need to

1. Recognize that meta-design is here to stay as a central tool for designing better software
2. Recognize the absolute importance of following specifications, constraints, and principles for effective designs
3. Recognize that we have a lot to learn from other companies that already have successfully implemented meta design into their operations
4. Recognize that we need to implement a meta-design process into ThinkWare software development as soon as we can

B. *Recommendations:* How do we go about implementing the meta-design process at ThinkWare?

1. We form a special design group to study how other companies have successfully implemented a meta-design process into their operations.
2. We ask that group to recommend a specific meta-design process that will work at ThinkWare, one that will keep the user and customer involved in the design process and one that will document motivations, change of actions and design throughout the entire design process, and one that will require deliverables to users, customers, and design review team at each phase of the design process.
3. We implement the best design.
4. And we start this procedure now.

C. *Call for Action:* We have little time to waste. Some of our competitors are out in front of us on the implementation of meta-design process into their software development. But with the exceptional talent we have at ThinkWare we'll not only eliminate that advantage now held by our competitors but overtake them if we begin the implementation process now.

D. *Clincher:* In ten years, I think we'll look back and point to this time in our company's evolution through the use of meta design as the key to much of the growth and success we'll enjoy in the future. Thank you.

FIGURE 4.15. *(Continued)*

IV. Key Works Cited

Ayer, Steve, and Patrinostro, Frank. *Documenting the Software Development Process.* New York: McGraw-Hill, 1992.

Dieter, George E. *Engineering Design: A Materials and Processing Approach.* New York: McGraw-Hill, 1983.

Markus, Aaron. *Graphic Design for Electric Documents and User Interfaces.* New York: ACM Press/Addison-Wesley, 1992.

Norman, Donald A. *The Psychology of Everyday Things.* New York: Basic Books, 1988.Petroski, Henry. *To Engineer Is Human.* New York: Vintage Books, 1992.

Pugh, Stuart. *Total Design: Integrated Methods for Successful Product Engineering.* New York: Addison-Wesley, 1991.

Ullman, David G. *The Mechanical Engineering Process.* New York: McGraw-Hill, 1992.

V. Visual Aids

The Global Design Process (Meta-Design Process).

Tree Swing Design. Deiter, 33.

Design Influence on Manufacturing Cost. Ullman, 8.

FIGURE 4.15. *(Continued)*

Presentation Notes and Scripts

When presenting using a note outline (or any outline for that matter), use note cards. Using full sheets of paper might tempt you to include too much information on the page which could result in disorganization, digressions, and confusion. Remember to write in large letters (but not in all uppercase letters, because they are difficult to read). This strategy allows you (1) to restrict the amount of information you can place on each card to one idea and (2) to read the information in a glance. Cramming the note card with small print makes reading the card difficult and a quick referential glance nearly impossible. Note cards are not designed to hold much information, and for good reason. Note cards can be reshuffled and reorganized easily and rapidly. You can also simply delete cards when you need to cut presentation length or when you find yourself running short of time during the presentation.

When reading from a script containing the full text of your presentation, remember that sheets of paper tend to distract listeners. Leave them on the lectern where they are out of sight. When reading from a note card or script, you might also color-code key components of the presentation—such as your central argument, subarguments, transitions between main points, and introduction of visual aids—so that you can easily identify them during your delivery. For example, you might use a green highlighter to identify your central argument or hypothesis, a yellow highlighter for subarguments, and a blue highlighter for points in the presentation when you wish to refer to a visual aid. Also leave plenty of white space at the margins of the note card or page and around headings. In addition, bulleted or numbered lists emphasize information and make quick reference easy. Don't forget to number your pages. Dropping a stack of unnumbered note cards or pages on the floor has ended many a well-conceived and exhaustively planned presentation.

I. Introduction
A. *Attention-Getting Device*
- Push door on wrong side.
- Feel foolish.
- Not your fault—designer's fault, insufficient clues.

B. *Identification Component*
Significance & Benefits
- Design process is in all our futures.
- Understand how meta-design works before implementing uniform process in designing and manufacturing
  - to save time and money
  - to market better software that meets user needs
  - to realize cost savings to R&D, manufacturing, and software maintenance.

Credentials
- Worked with most ThinkWare-Washington, D.C. designers as director of Systems Design and Analysis.
- We go back to the early '90s while at Palo Alto.

Background: Maria Ortega offered opportunity to talk about importance and implementation of meta-design.

Purpose and Thesis Statements
- Meta-design allows designers to design and manufacturers to build a product that
  - better meets users' needs
  - saves companies money in manufacturing, maintenance, and documentation.
- In this brief talk today, I want to show how we can use existing meta-design processes currently employed by organizations similar to our own as models from which to create a meta-design process that makes sense for ThinkWare.
- I also want to show how implementing a structured meta-design process as soon as possible will not only enable us to design better software but also make our jobs much easier and considerably more enjoyable.

C. *Forecasting Component*
1. Study meta-design process to identify the fallacies in our design.
2. Compare successful designs of other companies.
3. Implement useful parts of those meta-design processes at ThinkWare.

D. *Transition into Presentation Body*
1. Meta-design process.
2. Meta-design requirements and principles.
3. Building structured design process at ThinkWare.

II. Body
A. *Main Point #1:* Existence of global design (meta-design) process.
1. Meta-design flowchart [overhead].
2. Each meta-design phase.
3. Cake example.
4. Specifications of meta-design process.
5. Constraints of meta-design process.
6. Common design concepts and principles.
   a. Simplicity
   b. Modularity
   c. Information hiding
   d. User focus

FIGURE 4.16. *Note outline for meta-design scheme.*

  e. Feasibility

  f. Manufacturability and maintainability

  g. Effective documentation

  7. Transition into Point #2: Meta-design concepts and principles.

B. *Main Point #2:* Need to use design requirements and principle correctly.

  1. Computer keyboard example.

  2. "Hingeless" door example.

  3. Transition into Point #3: Need to implement structured design process . . . . Should adopt structured design process.

C. *Main Point #3:* Importance of meta-design at ThinkWare.

  1. More structured disciplines.

  2. Tree-swing design [overhead].

  3. Faulty designs.

  4. Design stage.

  5. Identification and correction of errors early.

  6. Alternative: loss of time and money.

  7. Influence of design on manufacturing costs [overhead].

  8. Better end product.

  9. Transition into Conclusion: Significance of all this to ThinkWare?

III. Conclusion

A. *Summary of Main Points*

  1. Assured future of meta-design.

  2. Importance of specifications, constraints, and principles for effective designs.

  3. Learning from other companies.

  4. Implementation of meta-design into ThinkWare software development ASAP.

B. *Recommendations*

  1. Form a special design group to study other companies' use of meta-design.

  2. Have group recommend a specific meta-design process that will work at ThinkWare.

  3. Implement best design.

  4. Start now.

C. *Call for Action*

  • No time to waste.

  • Competitors are out in front on the implementation.

  • Exceptional ThinkWare talent will win out.

D. *Clincher*

  • Turning point in our ThinkWare's evolution.

  • Thank you.

FIGURE 4.16. *(Continued)*

SUGGESTED READING

Biddle, P. R. (1966). *An experimental study of ethos and appeal for overt behavior in persuasion.* Dissertation, University of Illinois.

Brembeck, W. L., and Howells, W. S. (1976). *Persuasion: A means of social influence,* 2nd ed. Englewood Cliffs, NJ: Prentice-Hall.

Bunch, J. (1991) The storyboard strategy. *Training and Development,* July, pp. 69–71.

Carnegie, D. *Develop self-confidence and influence people by public speaking.* New York: Pocket Books, Simon & Shuster, 1956.

Chapman, A. J., and Foot, H. C. (Eds.) (1977). *It's a funny thing, humour.* Elmsford, NY: Pergamon Press.

Conway, D. A., and Munson, D. (1990). *The elements of reasoning.* Belmont, CA: Wadsworth.

Curtis, F. (1990). Use of humor by engineers in oral presentations. *Journal of Professional Issues in Engineering,* **116**(3), pp. 293–301.

Dawson, R. (1992). *Secrets of power persuasion: Everything you'll ever need to get anything you'll ever want.* Englewood Cliffs, NJ: Prentice-Hall.

Frank, M. O. (1986). *How to get your point across in 30 seconds—or less.* New York: Simon and Schuster.

Gruner, C. R. (1970). The effects of humor on dull and interesting informative speeches. *C S Speech Journal,* **21,** pp. 160–166.

Hager, P. J., and Scheiber, H. J. (1992). *Report writing for management decisions.* New York Macmillan.

Hart, T. B. (1976). The effects of evidence in persuasive communication. *C S Speech Journal,* **27,** pp. 42–46.

Herzberg, F. (1966). *Work and the nature of man.* Cleveland: World Publishing.

Humes, J. (1975). *Podium humor: A raconteur's treasury of witty and humorous stories.* New York: Harper & Row.

Karlins, M., and Abelson, H. I. (1970). *Persuasion: How opinions and attitudes are changed,* 2nd ed. New York: Springer.

Kupsh, J., and Graves, P. R. (1993). *How to create high impact business presentations.* Lincolnwood, IL: NTC Business Books.

Kusher, M. (1990). *The light touch: How to use humor for business success.* New York: Simon and Schuster.

Leeds, D. (1991). *Powerspeak: The complete guide to successful persuasion!* New York: Berkley Books.

Littlejohn, S. W. (1989). *Theories of human communication,* 3rd ed. Belmont, CA: Wadsworth.

Markiewicz, D. (1974). Effects of humor on persuasion. *Sociometry,* **37,** pp. 407–422.

Maslow, A. H. (1954). *Motivation and personality.* New York: Harper & Row.

Meuse, L. F. (1980). *Mastering the business and technical presentation.* Boston: CBI Publishing.

Mills, J. (1966). Opinion change as a function of the communicator's desire to influence and liking for the audience. *Journal of Experimental Social Psychology,* **2,** pp. 152–159.

Morreall, J. (1987). *The philosophy of laughter and humor.* Albany, NY: SUNY Press.

Osborn, M., and Osborn, S. (1991). *Public speaking,* 2nd ed. New York: Houghton Mifflin.

Rodman, G. R. (1978). *Speaking out: Message preparation for professionals.* New York: Holt, Rinehart and Winston.

Rosenburg, R. C. (1983). The engineering presentation—Some ideas on how to approach and present it. In D. F. Beer (Ed.)., *Writing and speaking the technology professions,* pp. 216–218. New York: IEEE Press.

Ruggiero, V. R. (1990). *Beyond feelings: A guide to critical thinking,* 3rd ed. Mountain View, CA: Mayfield.

Sawyer, T. M. (1979). Preparing and delivering an oral presentation. *Technical Communication,* **26**(1), pp. 4–7.

Scheiber, H. J., and Hager, P. J. Oral communication in business and industry: Results of a survey on technical, scientific, and managerial presentations. *Journal of Technical Writing and Communication,* **24**(2), pp. 161–180.

Sharp, H., Jr., and McClung, T. (1966). Effects of organization on the speaker's ethos. *Speech Monographs,* **33,** pp. 182–183.

Simmons, S. (1991). *How to be the life of the podium: Openers, closers & everything in between to keep them listening.* New York: AMACOM.

Simons, H. W. (1986). *Persuasion: Understanding, practice, and analysis.* New York: Random House.

Snyder, E. (1990). *Persuasive business speaking.* New York: AMACOM.

Thompson, E. (1960). An experimental investigation of the relative effectiveness of organizational structure in oral communication. *Speech Journal,* **26,** pp. 59–69.

Warnick, B., and Inch, E. S. (1994). *Critical thinking and communication: The use of reason in argument,* 2nd ed. New York: Macmillan.

Whittaker, J. (1965). Sex differences and susceptibility to interpersonal persuasion. *Journal of Social Pyschology,* **66,** pp. 91–94.

5

Drafting Your Presentational Script: Style and Language

In this chapter we'd simply like to confine our discussion to important matters of style and language that you might need to review to successfully draft your own presentational script(s)—with clarity and precision, appropriate tone, and optimum audience impact.

The three chapters that compose Part V of this book focus on what we have identified as "presentational models." Each of these chapters offers a sample real-world, full-length script and examines the CAFTA variables that were instrumental in developing, or "crafting," that particular presentational model. Using actual professional scripts and related visual materials (e.g., photos, screen captures, charts, tables), we'll examine the components, the "nuts and bolts," of three models—models we've taken from technical, scientific, and managerial environments. By way of these "models," we intend to mirror your job of constructing an entire script and, thus, guide you through the making of effective presentations.

WHAT ACCOUNTS FOR AN EFFECTIVE PRESENTATIONAL STYLE

Before we examine what comprises an effective presentational style, and which style might work well for you in a specific presentational context, we'd like to undergird our discussion with the following foundation: The most successful professional presentations will typically project a "sense of style" that

- captures the *audience's* interest and maintains their attention
- projects something of the *speaker's* personality, individuality, or imagination
- jibes with the speaker's intended aim(s), goal(s), objective(s), or purpose
- enhances the speaker's *subject matter* and intended *meaning* in the specific presentational context.

Naturally, the style you opt to project in your presentational script should mirror the style you intend to project in your oral presentation, a style you feel comfortable projecting. That is, the style of your oral delivery must mesh well with that of your written script. If, for example, your oral style is colorful, flamboyant, and forceful, so too must your script reflect these stylistic traits.

Of course, your oral delivery style and your presentational script will both be dependent on the CAFTA variables we have outlined and examined earlier: the technical, scientific, or managerial nature of your presentational *content;* the *audience* you will address, whether neutral, supportive, or potentially hostile; the *form* or *format* you have chosen or been assigned, whether academic conference presentation or informal, round-table business meeting; the *time frame* you must adhere to (i.e., a ten-minute speech might warrant a very different script stylistically than a three-hour technical training session); the *aim(s)* or *objective(s)* of your presentation, whether to inform, teach or train, persuade, or entertain—all of these important presentational variables will clearly influence the style you ultimately choose to employ, orally and scriptwise.

Designing/Developing Scripts for Use by Others

While you will often be called upon to design and develop your own script for your own presentation, we should note here that presentational scripts (including transparencies, 35-mm slides, video, and other visuals) are frequently developed by technical writers/editors, speech writers, subject matter specialists, training personnel, graphic artists, photographers, or videographers. That is, scripts are often designed and developed by a team of professionals for use by a presenter (e.g., another manager, VP, technical communicator, trainer, sales or marketing staff member, medical researcher).

At times, a work team might design and develop the presentation (script, visuals, video, computer "real-time" display) under the editorial "guidance" of the presenter; at other times, a work team or individual writer might prepare a script and visuals without concurrent input from the presenter. In either case, of course, team members or individual writers will be generating a script for use by another professional—with her or his own *oral* style (pace, timing, diction, expertise, sense of humor, and so forth). With direct and concurrent input from the presenter, the task of preparing a presentation—script and visuals—should not prove to be particularly difficult. Preparing a presentation without regular access to the presenter, without her or his concurrent input, will prove a bit more challenging.[1]

Nevertheless, whether you are preparing a script for your own presentation—or for that of a colleague, manager, systems analyst, or corporate VP—you need to carefully weigh the stylistic choices we review in this chapter. Ultimately, you should strive to develop a script which projects an oral style that will seem both natural and comfortable to you or to that other professional presenter with whom you are working.

---

[1] For useful information on team building and teamwork, we refer you to "Suggested Reading" at the end of this chapter. See the following sources: Parker, *Team Players and Teamwork* (1990); Quick, *Successful Team Building* (1992); and Varney, *Building Productive Teams* (1989).

A Note on the Nature of Prose Style

We could devote considerable space in this section to the concept of *style* (some have said the *problem of style*).[2] But we'll keep our discussion here focused on the nature of prose style primarily in relation to the presentational script and how that script might best be delivered orally. Attacking the problem from this angle, we feel sure, should prove most useful to you, the professional presenter.

Most contemporary theorists studying language and style tend to agree that style is a matter of the linguistic *choices* that speakers (and writers) make as we draft, revise, and develop a text for oral or written presentation. Our stylistic choices ultimately define us and reflect our individuality as they emerge and evolve over time on a consistent basis. These choices also surface and solidify when we examine *why* and *for whom* we are speaking, or writing, or developing, say, a presentational script.

A speaker's own experiences (whether personal or professional), attitudes, likes and dislikes, hopes and aspirations, and accumulated (personal) knowledge shape the script or document (any text) that is being developed for presentation to an audience of listeners or readers. Thus, if style is the aggregate of an individual's linguistic choices, experiences, and attitudes, then style might best be characterized as the linguistic equivalent of *personality*—the personal imprint or "stamp" we place on the language we use.

Assuming that we accept this view, style becomes not a hoary linguistic concept but rather a dynamic force that professional speakers can marshal in various ways as we confront various business situations and diverse audiences demanding our prose. Contingent upon what a given business situation or organizational audience might demand, we can consciously *choose* or, even, unconsciously *apply* (adopt or manipulate) an appropriate style for a particular professional purpose.

When described in these dynamic terms, then, the concept of prose style really becomes a matter of personal power and control over the language we use. Or, even more emphatically stated, and following a widely accepted current axiom about communication: Effective speakers (and writers) manipulate language in powerful ways to control their listeners' (or readers') responses. If you want to design successful professional presentations, then you too must learn to manipulate language to your own advantage in the development of your written scripts, as well as in their oral delivery.

Style, Script, Situation

In drafting and developing scripts for technical, scientific, and management-based presentations, we might most profitably consider the question of style in a purely functional context:

- Style is a way of writing and a matter of personal choice.
- Style is *situational* and context-based.
- Style reflects, and is closely associated with, a speaker's *intended* meaning and a listener's *perceived* meaning.
- Style is not an external element that can be isolated from a speaker's content; it is neither a frill nor an afterthought.

---

[2] For a complete discussion of the concept of *style* in the context of business, management, and professional prose (replete with numerous examples), see our text *Report Writing for Management Decisions,* New York: Macmillan, 1992, pp. 135–151.

- Style is a matter of having a *point of view,* a unique way of looking at, and talking about, the world.
- Style is a matter of *applying* that point of view wisely in different professional/technical situations to make meaning and shape listeners' responses.[3]

The stylistic choices we make in drafting our technical, scientific, and managerial scripts—the words and phrases we select to inform, to teach/train, to persuade or "sell"—become integral to the *content* we develop and the *meaning(s)* we wish to articulate. In other words, the style of our script (and our delivery) becomes the substance of our presentation. Style is substance.

What stylistic options, then, might we consider in developing our presentational scripts—whether technical, science-based, or managerial? How might a specific business situation, and consequent speaking task, affect our choice of style? To what degree does a particular stylistic decision mirror, or even mold, a speaker's professional relationships?

STYLISTIC OPTIONS AND THEIR BASES

As professional communicators, we have a variety of stylistic options at our disposal. We might, for example, consider selecting a powerful or forceful style; a breezy, professional or "consultative" style; a plain, unadorned, and straightforward "training" style; or even a chummy or intimate style.[4] While options for developing our presentational scripts and their delivery styles are numerous and varied, our ultimate choices necessarily depend on two basic *situational* assumptions:

(1) What is the *organizational context*—or individual-business context—in which we will be speaking?

(2) What is the *rhetorical occasion*—the interpersonal situation or specific purpose—out of which our presentation has evolved?

Organizational Context, Professional Relationships, Style(s)

Technical, scientific, and management-oriented speakers do not design and develop presentations (i.e., subject matter, scripts, and visuals) in a professional "vacuum"; rather, we develop speeches and presentations within very definite organizational contexts. We develop presentations for audiences up and down the hierarchy of our own organizations—for example, for professional finance or accounting staffs, data processing supervisors, senior-level scientific researchers, and members of organizational management (such as divisional or corporate VPs). We also develop presentations regularly for audiences outside of our own organizations—for example, for members of the scientific community at large, the press or media representatives, our clients or customers, marketing/advertising firms, and the general public.

---

[3] For an elaboration of some of this material on style, see out text *Report Writing for Management Decisions,* New York: Macmillan, 1992, pp. 136–138.

[4] For an informative and entertaining discussion of language (usage, register), style (frozen, formal, consultative, casual, intimate), and "the situations in which we communicate," see Martin Joos' *The Five Clocks: A Linguistic Excursion into the Five Styles of English Usage,* New York: Harcourt, Brace, & World, 1967.

We believe that successful professional presenters—speakers who deliver complex data and information on technical, scientific, or business subjects—must choose a presentational style appropriate for

- the specific professional *situation*
- the narrow (or more "global") organizational *context*
- the intended group of listeners—members of our *audience,* however homogeneous or diverse, broad or narrow.

Throughout the process of developing our presentational scripts, we must consider our relationships with colleagues, supervisors, and other professionals—with possible individual listeners and with broader organizational audiences. We must carefully define and delimit the nature of our relationship(s) to our (intended) listeners. Whatever the genesis or character of the business relationship—whether formal and distant, consultative, casual, chummy, or even intimate—the professional presenter must adopt a style consistent with, and reflective of, that relationship for both script and oral delivery.

Choosing an Appropriate Presentational Style

Of course, presenters at all organizational levels—and in all organizational contexts—have a wide variety of professional relationships and thus would do well to adopt a presentational style directed toward each individual or unique group of listeners and for each particular business or professional situation. In short, we professional presenters should be able to effect any one of a number of useful styles wherever and whenever we need to. Presentational styles readily available to us might include the following:

- Formal
- Official (impersonal, objective, legal, bureaucratic)
- Unadorned or plain
- Professional or consultative
- Forceful or tough
- Vigorous or active (perhaps direct)
- Personal or friendly
- Casual
- Chummy or intimate.

Professional speakers today, however, tend to gravitate toward the middle range(s) of this list of stylistic options. In developing presentational scripts and (parallel) oral delivery styles for the transmission of complex technical, scientific, and management material, speakers generally avoid the stylistic extremes—a more formal style at one end of the continuum and a casual or intimate style at the other. Professional speakers presenting complex material in business, industrial, governmental, and academic contexts generally opt for and exhibit some kind of stylistic middle range, often an amalgam of consultative, friendly, active, and vigorous styles.

Whichever presentational style you opt for, you must nevertheless ensure that the style chosen

- communicates appropriately, effectively, and comfortably with individual listeners and your specific organizational audience(s).
- mirrors preexisting (or newly established) relationships between you (the speaker) and your listeners.
- jibes with the interpersonal and organizational demands of the rhetorical occasion (the situation out of which your presentation has evolved).
- parallels or even elevates your presentational content.
- projects your organization's corporate culture when (and if) desired.

PRESENTATIONAL MODELS . . . STYLISTIC SAMPLES

In Part V of this book we examine three fully developed, complete presentational models and we provide commentary on the stylistic decisions that these professional speakers have made in constructing their presentational scripts. Furthermore, we review the CAFTA variables, organizational contexts, rhetorical occasions, and other considerations involved, for each, in selecting the most appropriate (the "right") style for the finished written portion—the script—of their presentation.

While we've discussed the bases for choosing an appropriate presentational style(s) in the preceding sections of this chapter, a few specific samples reflecting widely used (or more "typical") professional presentational styles might be helpful at this stage of our discussion.

In the samples that follow, notice foremost how the speakers have carefully constructed each script segment to convey their material with maximum attention to listeners' need for the following:

- Clarity
- Precision
- Conciseness
- Fluency . . . of *expression.*

Whenever we intend to present complex material on any subject matter or from any domain of inquiry—whether technical, scientific, or business—the speaker must strive for a certain quality of written (your *script*) and oral (your *delivery*) expression. See if you agree that these samples from "quality" scripts might easily evolve into effective, high-quality oral presentations:

Sample 1: Consultative-Professional Style
[From Leadership Training Module]

During peak work periods, you hold daily morning meetings with your people in order to get the work of the team organized. They have many of the skills necessary to perform as a team. They have been struggling with the problems the unit faces and have expressed a lot of frustration with their progress and with each other. Lately, people have been participating and acting in a positive manner. Meetings have been more productive. You are making a decision about how to conduct tomorrow's meeting. You would . . .

(1) Identify the problems to be dealt with at the meeting, develop solutions, and allocate work assignments.

(2) Allow them to conduct the meeting. Intervene only if you are asked.

(3) Direct the meeting, but get and include their ideas and suggestions in your decisions.

(4) Encourage their participation, and facilitate their problem solving.

(*Source:* Blanchard Training and Development, Inc., from "Situational Leadership," Module 2, 1990.)

Comment. This sort of consultative-professional style might be used with ease and appropriate impact in technical training or management development presentations. In these (or similar) training seminars your listeners might

(1) function at (or near) your own organizational, educational, or professional level.

(2) hold similar degrees of organizational power or authority.

(3) reside either within or outside your own organization.

The script appears friendly but business-like, reflecting a sense of professional commitment, involvement, and skill, as well as a genuine concern for the ongoing, mutually engaged-in enterprise.

Sample 2: Consultative-Friendly (Active) Style
[From Professional Development Resource Materials]

Analyze Audience. One of the most important things you'll need to do to be a successful presenter is to connect with your audience. To be able to do that you need to know something about them. How many people will be in the audience? 10? 50? 100? How much do they know about the topic you'll be discussing? What is their level of education and experience in your field? Do they have any biases against your subject?

Select Subject. Narrow your subject down as much as you can, and then make only three to five points on the narrow subject.

Define Purpose. Your presentation must not only have a topic, it must have a purpose. Are you trying to sell something—for example, a program, a project, or a point of view? Do you want to encourage your audience, share a new idea, or discuss the results of your work? Only you know what your purpose is, but try to be as clear about it as possible. . . .

(*Source:* Pacific Northwest Laboratory, Richland, Washington, from *The Technical Presentation,* by N. Burleigh and A. McMakin, Workshop Leaders, 1992.)

Comment. Much like the script exhibited in Sample 1, this consultative-friendly (active) style appeals directly to the professionals being addressed. Many active verbs are used throughout the script (e.g., "Narrow your subject down as much as you can . . ."), as well as lots of pronouns, especially *you, your,* and *you'll* (e.g., "One of the most important things *you'll* need to do to be a successful speaker is to connect with *your* audience."). The pronouns incorporated in this script, while directly addressing audience members (i.e., *you*) tend to soften the consultative-professional style somewhat, ultimately making the script and presentation a bit more friendly and personal. Certainly the style illustrated in Sample 2 might be used effectively in a wide variety of presentational situations—in staff training, professional development seminars, informal business or technically based meetings, even in video conferencing—where speakers aim to address members of their audience both as friendly colleagues and as receptive listeners.

Sample 3: Stylistic "Mix" [From Academic/Technical Conference Presentation]

Introduction. Imagine this: You're an operations engineer at Southern California Edison Utility Company. Your firm has recently purchased an XA/21 System from Harris Controls Division, which has been installed for two weeks now. Today is Thanksgiving Day. You're on duty for the holiday.

It's 12:30 P.M. when you observe that one console shows an alarm alert. You notice that one town is out of power. The XA/21 System failed. The town is in a blackout. In homes across the town, turkeys aren't cooking—a crisis situation for many families.

Thousands of pages of documentation surround you on 10-foot high shelves that stretch the length of one corridor. You'll need weight training and a three-foot ladder to lift the trouble-shooting binder from the top shelf. Then, it may take you several days to understand the structure of the new documentation set that is essential to understanding the system. You've hit the documentation barrier—what an intimidating situation! There's little time to waste on the printed word—those turkeys may spoil! Instead of "getting started," you're "getting frustrated." But, you ask yourself, shouldn't there be an on-line troubleshooting manual? . . .

Dual Delivery Document—Concepts About On-Line.

What Is an On-Line Document? An on-line document is an electronic file that uses hypertext links to call up topics within a document or across documents, sequentially or nonsequentially, using a predefined hierarchy.

How Does Hypertext Work? Hypertext documents use nodes that contain software links to other nodes. Readers can go to other nodes sequentially or nonsequentially. All hypertext documents contain nodes and links which readers view as a web (see Figure 5.1).

What Is a Dual Delivery Document? A dual delivery document is a document that is designed for both on-line and paper and requires minimal reworking by information designers to create the on-line document.

The Process Model of Dual Delivery—Test: Phase 3

- Evaluate the document plan for accuracy.
- Field-test and evaluate the prototype of the on-line schedule.
- Evaluate the prototype of the directory structure.
- Implement template software on a prototype and map the software development process.
- Evaluate the writer's software.
- Examine the methodology for hypertext authoring.

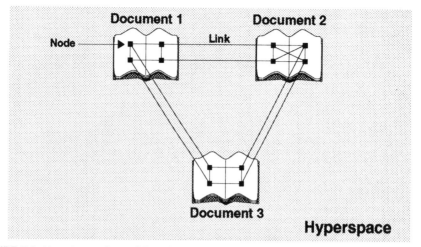

FIGURE 5.1. *Hypertext nodes and links. Hypertext documents use nodes that contain links to other nodes. Readers might move from node to node sequentially or nonsequentially. Legend:* ■, *node;* ——, *link.*

(*Source:* "Designing for Dual Delivery: On-Line & Paper," from *A Presentation on On-Line Document Management and Methodology: A Hypertext Solution,* by G. A. Reece and H. J. Scheiber, IEEE/IPCC International Professional Communication Conference, Philadelphia, PA, 1993.)

Comment. At times, speakers might want to mix script and delivery styles, incorporating two or more styles into their presentations for some special effect or simply to arouse interest in what follows. Sample 3 does just that. The Introduction recounts an anecdote in a light, breezy, and casual, *you*-oriented style; other sections provide conceptual material and definitions in unadorned, impersonal, objective, academic/scientific prose; and still other sections of the presentation introduce material in a vigorous, active, and direct (bulleted) style.

Sample 4: Objective-Impersonal, Technical Style
[From Technical, Industry-Based Conference Paper]

Proper grounding of electronic or electrical installations is necessary for two reasons:

(1) To make the installation electrically safe for technicians and gas company personnel who will come into contact with the installation

(2) To protect the installation from damage caused by electrical surges.

Reason number 1 above is well understood and easily accomplished by following standard electrical wiring practices as outlined in the National Electrical Code (NEC), article 250 on grounding. This standard also applies when trying to protect equipment from electrical surges caused by outside forces. The purpose of this paper [presentational script] is to discuss (a) lightning as an external cause of electrical surges and (b) some specific steps to be taken to protect sensitive electronic equipment. . . .

By definition, lightning is the visible discharge of static charges of electricity within a cloud, between clouds, and between clouds and the ground or earth. These charges are always in pairs, one positive and one negative. Generally, negative charges accumulate near the base of thunder clouds, and positive charges accumulate on the surface of the earth and its projecting objects: trees, antennas, telephone poles, gas pipes, metering stations, fences, and electronic installations, to name a few (see Figure 5.2). The air gap separating the cloud and the earth acts as an insulator. When the charges reach a sufficient potential, they puncture this insulator and the negative charges rush toward the positive charges, causing an ionization of the atmosphere or "large spark" that we see as lightning. Since this is a phenomenon of nature with tremendous power, nothing can be done to divert the enormous energy levels involved. . . .

(*Source:* Technical paper entitled "Electrical Grounding of Electronic Instruments," by C. R. Pelchat, Metretek, Inc., Melbourne, FL, 1994.)

Comment. The style adopted here by the speaker for his presentational script is, appropriately, objective, plain, and impersonal; it is a style that, roughly, typifies the prose routinely found in technical-scientific journal articles. This style generally incorporates few active verbs, instead opting primarily for *passive* constructions (e.g., "Proper grounding . . . is necessary for two reasons . . ." or ". . . electrical surges caused by outside forces"), often coupled with nominalized expressions like "an *ionization* of the atmosphere."

Reading through this script, we soon realize that we are functioning within the traditional language domain of science and technology: The discourse unfolds in a slow, sound, particularly logical fashion; it is unadorned, without flare, yet precise (in the sense of *exact* or *correct*) but not necessarily concise. While patently neither friendly nor chummy, this style appears clear, straightforward, and authoritative.

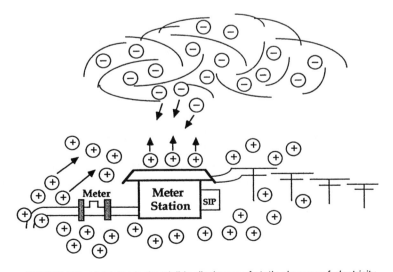

FIGURE 5.2. *Lightning is the visible discharge of static charges of electricity.*

Sample 5: Objective-Impersonal, "Scientific" Style
[From Medical–Dental, Research-Based Conference Presentation]

. . . The initial concept that prompted this research was a need for a surveillance/monitoring methodology to detect operatory contamination for use by dental researchers or public health organizations to evaluate asepsis. The oral cavity offers a normal flora from which indicators of "oral contamination" might be selected. The presence of such indicator organisms on instruments, equipment, and other surfaces in the dental operatory should reveal information about the effectiveness of infection control practices or about how well dental personnel adhere to them. Biological indicators are used in other areas of public health such as the use of coliform bacteria to indicate fecal contamination in drinking water and swimming pools.

Oral bacteria were evaluated as biological indicators of dental asepsis according to (a) the number present in human saliva, (b) ease of cultivation and identification, (c) survival in the environment, (d) occurrence in the nondental general environment, (e) detectability on operatory surfaces, and (f) field evaluations in private dental practices.

The viridans streptococci are numerous in the mouth, and many strains are alpha-hemolytic which produce a green zone of partial hemolysis around a colony grown on blood agar. This characteristic makes them easy to distinguish from other flora growing on blood agar. This project was undertaken to study the validity of using alpha-hemolytic oral streptococci as indicators of oral contamination.

A survey of 47 dental patients showed that there are about 60 million alpha-hemolytic streptococci (AHS) per milliliter in saliva. . . .

(*Source:* Medical-dental conference paper entitled "Oral Bacteria as Biological Indicators to Evaluate Operatory Asepsis," by Raymond W. Hackney, Jr., presented at the Society for Infection Control in Dentistry, Cincinnati, OH, March 6, 1990.)

Comment. The style used for this medical-dental (scientific) presentation manifests many of the same rhetorical attributes of the previous technical sample (Sample 4). Here, of course, we remain wholly within the realm of scientific discourse—an objective, impersonal presentational script, linguistically reminiscent of, and structurally parallel to, the scientific paper or journal article upon which the script is based.

In this script, we are confronted most notably with the following stylistic trends: a reliance on passive voice constructions (e.g., "The initial concept that prompted this research was a need for . . ." and "Oral bacteria were evaluated as . . ."); the use of few active verbs, but lots of verbals and the use of some form of the copula, *to be* (as in "will be present," "AHS were detected," or "Biological indicators are used in other areas . . ."); the use of acronyms and requisite scientific abbreviations (AHS, ml; or, later on, RH, "the *D* value"); the use of abstract nouns and noun phrases (like "ease of cultivation and identification," "nondental general environment," "detectability on operatory surfaces"); and, finally, professional, research-related terminology, expressions, or jargon (such as "coliform bacteria," "operatory contamination," "viridans streptococci," and "alpha-hemolytic").

Of course, all of this scientific language and the linguistic–stylistic trends we have noted above are certainly appropriate to, and consistent with, the scientific discipline—that is, medical–dental research—under examination. But, most importantly, it all adds up to a clearly developed, precise, and richly detailed scientific presentation readily comprehended by those who are familiar with the subject matter ("infection control") and who share overriding concerns relative to this variety of medical-dental research. (We should point out, too, that many useful, well-crafted colored slides were incorporated into this presentation which graphically explore the abstract content and research strategies discussed and summarized.)

OTHER CONCERNS ABOUT LANGUAGE AND STYLE IN YOUR PRESENTATIONAL SCRIPTS

Now that you've seen a variety of styles from five sample presentational scripts, we'd like to review a few other considerations about language and the style(s) you might employ. In your presentational scripts, we want to reemphasize your listeners' central need for clarity, precision, and conciseness. In other words, whatever you present, no matter how technical and how seemingly "complex," as a public speaker you owe it to the members of your audience to be consistently *clear* and as *brief* as possible. (Of course, such variables as aim and purpose, the interest and educational level of the targeted audience, and the occasion for and organizational context of your presentation will all impact on and define what you and your listeners mean by clarity and brevity.)

Fluency of Expression

We'd also like to remind you about what we like to call *fluency of expression.*[5] Whether you read from your scripted material or simply present it using some combination of visuals (transparencies, slides, computer graphic aids, flip charts) and talk, the language you adopt must be both fluid and fluent. Naturally, your choice of words, selection of phrases, and reliance on, say, vague or abstract words will affect the style of your presentational script and, thus, listener comprehension. To achieve a higher degree of fluency, revise your script by excising from it any diction-related problems you might be creating that will confuse your readers.

Try to reduce your reliance on vague terms or abstract words and phrases or, where possible, eliminate them completely. Try to incorporate concrete, specific, vivid words and expressions into your script. If, for example you need to refer to an institution's "lack of facilities," be concrete and specific about a "lack of state-of-the-art personal computer facilities" or a "lack of up-to-date graphics production facilities."

While the conventions of your discipline and subject matter, your specific purpose(s), or presentational situation, will, at times, dictate a reliance on the passive voice, we urge you to speak in the *active voice* where and when possible. For example,

Use

"*Cryoptics* management *recommends* eliminating its electromagnetic and robotics divisions."

Rather than

"A recommendation has been proposed by *Cryoptics* management calling for the elimination of its electromagnetic and robotics divisions."

---

[5] For numerous examples dealing with specific aspects of fluency in language—for example, diction, nominalizations, passive voice versus active voice constructions, and revising negative words and phrases into positive (helpful) statements—we refer you to our text *Report Writing for Management Decisions,* New York: Macmillian, 1992, pp. 142–149.

Adherence to the active voice—and editing your scripts for active sentence constructions, filled with strong, active verbs—will foster fluency of expression in the drafts of your scripts and, if consistently done, will make your presentations much more intelligible to your listeners.

To achieve overall clarity, precision, and fluency—as well as to enhance the acceptance and accessibility of your ideas—you will be far better off avoiding negative words and phrases in your presentational scripts. Creating a positive tone tends to enhance the attention level of your listeners. Therefore,

Use

If you want to ensure the highest performance level of your equipment, install your unit properly.

Rather than

Failure to properly install your equipment will result in *degradation* of your unit's performance level.

Use

Dr. Savino's leadership strategies for managers working in this organization have merit.

Rather than

Dr. Savino's leadership strategies for managers working in this organization are *not* without merit.

Professional Jargon

In editing successive drafts of your presentational scripts for clarity, precision, and fluency, we submit that the overuse of, and over-reliance on, professional jargon must be tempered. Depending on the make-up of your audience and the content of your presentation—and, most importantly, the relation between these two CAFTA variables—you might want to excise all of the profession-related jargon in your presentation.

On the other hand, you might feel fully justified and quite comfortable retaining the following hypertext-related material in your technical presentation:

KMS [Knowledge Management System] is a commercial hypermedia system marketed by Knowledge Systems, Inc. that runs on Sun and Apollo workstations. KMS is based upon the ZOG system developed at Carnegie Mellon University from 1976 to 1984. KMS/ZOG systems have been applied to a wide range of applications including project management, technical manuals, policy guidelines, and electronic publishing.

The basic element of a KMS database is called a "frame," which can contain text, graphics, or digitized images. Each frame has a name, title, body, tree items, annotation items, and command line. . . . The tree items serve as **links** . . . to other frames as shown in Figure. . . . The annotation items can be used to provide comments, formatting instructions, or cross-reference links.

The **user interface** . . . of KMS has some interesting design features. User control is almost completely via **direct manipulation** . . . using a three-button mouse. The functions of the mouse buttons are dynamic . . . and this allows the mouse to have broad functionality. KMS makes no distinction between navigating and editing . . . .

In what kind of environment, exactly, might you feel comfortable (and justified) presenting this kind of complex, jargon-freighted material? Perhaps at an academic or technical conference—replete with hypertext users—or within a technical training environment. An audience analysis, for example, performed during your presentational planning process might have revealed that you will, in fact, be speaking before a group of previously "initiated," computer literate, data processing professionals and database managers. If so, go with that kind of content for that kind of technical talk.[6]

In any case, you must fully weigh the consequences of using professional jargon in your presentational script and in the (parallel) oral presentation itself. **Remember:** The ultimate success of any presentation depends largely, oftentimes entirely, on *access* to your material—that is, on the ease with which your material can be digested, comprehended, and internalized by members of a particular audience.

And so, if ease of access is a speaker's major concern—and, indeed, it is—you'd do well to follow James Garland's "advice" to novice physicists, useful, really, to any technical or science-based speaker:

> Equations make a talk harder to understand, they slow the pace, and they are prone to create confusion. If overdone, they also cause resentment; one literally will hear groans from an audience when a speaker flashes an equation-filled transparency on the screen. Audiences are especially scornful of speakers who load their presentations with equations because of a misguided belief that the mathematics alone will imbue their work with a more scientific or rigorous flavor.[7]

Mathematical equations are, of course, just another form of complex professional/technical jargon. Professor Garland advises the following:

- Gauge the members of your audience to determine "at what level to pitch a presentation when the audience consists of both novices and experts."
- Use mathematics and (and rely on) equations only sparingly.
- "Make absolutely certain that the equations are necessary, and if they're not, toss them out." (pp. 42–43)

Sexism and Linguistic Bias

Remnants of sexist language and linguistic bias (ethnic, national) continue to appear in business documents and in industry-based forums of all kinds. Engineeering and scientific presentations, management-level briefings, shareholders meetings, and technical training seminars—any of these forums might contain some content filled with sexist language (like "chairman," "spokesman") or linguistic stereotyping ("aggressive Oriental sales associate," "black senior VP"). Yes, we still hear a good amount of high-level professional "talk" reflecting the "good-ole-boy" argot of decades past, embarrassing to some but, really, demeaning to all listeners.

---

[6] The complete context for this material can be found in Ben Shneiderman and Greg Kearsley, *Hypertext Hands-On! An Introduction to a New Way of Organizing and Accessing Information,* Reading, MA: Addison–Wesley, 1989, pp. 83–85.

[7] From James C. Garland, "Advice to Beginning Speakers," *Physics Today* (July 1991), pp. 42–45. In this article, Professor Garland offers much useful advice on how to give talks "that won't wreck your career or humiliate your thesis adviser."

Although engineers, managers, researchers, and government officials are becoming increasingly sensitive to bias and stereotyping in language—whether sexual, racial, ethnic, or national—the use of such language persists and perpetuates outdated attitudes and offensive habits. Individuals who tend (still) to use such language in their business reports and professional presentations are contributing to the institutionalization of sexist or, perhaps, racist policy in their organizations. Whether used out of habit, simply mechanically, or unwittingly, such language can be abusive and condescending and must be consciously eliminated from the work place.

Professional presenters, especially, should learn to use gender-*neutral* language (like "head," "chair," "speaker," or "moderator") instead of gender-*biased* language (like "chairman" or "spokeswoman"). Discriminatory and potentially offensive words or phrases and terms that might engender racial, ethnic, or other varieties of stereotyping should also be avoided (e.g., "newly hired handicapped programmer/analyst," "stealthy Pakistani laboratory supervisor," "tight-lipped Taiwanese team leader").

In addition, gender-neutral pronouns should be incorporated into your presentation whenever possible. For example, instead of using *he* or *she* as a referent for the generic titles "manager" or "presenter," simply speak of "managers" and "presenters" and then use the plural referent *they*. If you are speaking in general terms, you might consider revising your script as shown here, removing gender-specific pronouns:

Original Script Version

"Every member of the **Solaris** team should have in *his* possession a copy of the firm's Code of Conduct . . . ."

Revised Script Version

"Every member of the **Solaris** team should possess a copy of the firm's Code of Conduct . . . ."

Original Script Version

"*Her* word processing skills . . . ."

Revised Script Version

"One's word processing skills . . ." or "Your word processing skills . . ."

(Naturally, if the individual team member, manager, or presenter to whom you refer is, indeed, female, do retain the singular referent, *she*.)

The Use of Humor

To paraphrase James Gleason, an IBM "information developer," humor is, indeed, a funny thing.[8] He takes pains to warn us that humor is also quite a delicate matter

---

[8] From James P. Gleason, "Humor Can Improve Your Technical Presentations," *IEEE Transactions on Professional Communication* (1982), **PC-25**(2), pp. 86–90.

. . . best applied to areas of lesser importance to keep from obscuring necessary data [or information]. In addition, humor must be used judiciously to maintain the professionalism of the work. Humor must never be used as a substitute for accuracy or clarity but, rather, must serve to reinforce those qualities. *Humor is a tool that can help a presentation; just don't use a hammer when a feather is sufficient* [italics added]. (p. 86)

We agree, completely. Humor used in the context of presenting complex technical, scientific, or management-based content is an extremely "delicate matter" and should only be integrated into your presentation with the utmost care and skill, and, well . . . delicacy.

If you do decide to "lighten up" your presentational scripts by injecting a bit of humorous material into them—and we think such an idea is generally a good one—be certain that you follow a few simple but essential guidelines:

Avoid

- Jokes and the so-called *funny* (often cloying or embarrassing) story.
- Caustic and potentially offensive humor.
- "Attack" humor, making members of your audience the butt of a joke.

Consider

- Using a cartoon or humorous graphic as an attention-getting device.
- Using a relevant, positive personal anecdote to enliven a point.
- Targeting *yourself* with a humorous anecdote or funny aside (genuine self-effacing, self-depreciating humor tends to work well in professional contexts).[9]

We invite you to spice up your technical, scientific, or managment-based presentations with a dollop of humor, here and there—an initial, attention-getting anecdote; a humorous story to highlight an important idea; a comical note or cartoon graphic to break down the speaker–audience barrier and to put your listeners at their ease. But remember, humor *is* a funny thing; employ it with considerable sensitivity and tact.

A FOOTNOTE ON PRESENTATIONAL STYLE

In summing up this chapter on style, we'd simply like to echo the words of PR and sales/marketing consultant Roy Alexander: "Whatever you say, say it with *style* [italics added]." Say it . . . with enthusiasm, distinction, panache; with appropriate pauses, gestures, boldness and courage; with knowledge, confidence, and, of course, with a smile.[10]

---

[9] Perhaps as far back as 1912, Dale Carnegie recognized that "Audiences open up their hearts, as well as their minds, to speakers who deliberately deflate themselves by calling attention to some deficiency or failing on their part—in a humorous sense, of course. On the other hand, creating the image of the "stuffed shirt" or the visiting expert with all the answers leaves an audience cold and unreceptive." See Dale Carnegie, *The Quick and Easy Way to Effective Speaking* (rev. ed., Dorothy Carnegie), New York: Association Press, 1972, p. 242.

[10] See Roy Alexander, *Power Speech: The Quickest Route to Business and Personal Success,* New York: AMA-COM/American Management Association, 1986; especially Chapter 9, pp. 121–135.

SUGGESTED READING

Alexander, R. (1986). *Power speech: The quickest route to business and personal success.* New York: AMACOM/American Management Association.

Axtell, R. E. (1992). *Do's and taboos of public speaking: How to get those butterflies flying in formation.* New York: John Wiley & Sons.

Document Design Center. (1982). Eliminating gender bias in language. *Simply Stated,* **28,** 2.

Epstein, E. L. (1978). *Language and style.* London: Methuen.

Fielden, J. S. (1982). What do you mean you don't like my style. *Harvard Business Review,* **60,** 128–138.

Gleason, J. P. (1982). Humor can improve your technical presentations. *IEEE Transactions on Professional Communication,* **PC-25**(2), 86–90.

Iapoce, M. (1988). *A funny thing happened on the way to the boardroom: Using humor in business speaking.* New York: John Wiley & Sons.

Joos, M. (1967). *The five clocks: A linguistic excursion into the five styles of English usage.* New York: Harcourt, Brace & World.

McMahon, E. (1986). *The art of public speaking.* New York: Ballantine Books (See Chapter 4, "How to Get Laughs from the Head Table." pp. 32–43.)

Miller, C., and Swift, K. (1988). *The handbook of nonsexist writing: For writers, editors, and speakers,* 2nd. ed. New York: Harper.

Parker, G. M. (1990). *Team players and teamwork: The new competitive business strategy.* San Francisco: Jossey-Bass Publishers.

Perret, G. (1984). *How to hold your audience with humor.* Cincinnati, OH: Writer's Digest Books.

Quick, T. L. (1992). *Successful team building.* New York: AMACOM/American Management Association.

Tichy, H. J. (1988). *Effective writing for engineers, managers, scientists,* 2nd ed. New York: John Wiley & Sons.

Varney, G. H. (1989). *Building productive teams: An action guide and resource book.* San Francisco: Jossey-Bass Publishers.

Williams, J. M. (1990). *Style: Toward clarity & grace.* Chicago: University of Chicago Press.

Part II

Designing and Using Effective Audio and Visual Media

6

Selecting and Using Audio and Visual Presentation Media

Unless carefully packaged in an appropriate form, the complex information and data contained in today's technical, scientific, or managerial presentations can easily overwhelm listeners. Clearly, as we have discussed in previous chapters, presentations whose scripts are poorly written—such as those lacking effective organization, sufficient development, or clear style—are doomed from the start. No presenter, regardless of his or her stage presence or delivery skill, can transform a botched script into a clear and convincing message that can be easily and fully deciphered by listeners and then applied as a decisive decision-making tool.

This is not to suggest, however, that well-written scripts ensure success. Unfortunately, many effective scripts fall short of their presentation's objectives for lack of a vibrant, visual effect. For example, let's assume that you've written a script whose organization, style, tone, and development are perfectly matched with your purpose in giving the presentation and with the informational needs and professional interests of your audience. You insert at the beginning of your script, as an attention-getting opener, a series of disturbing facts relevant to the focus of your message. You then introduce the presentation's central theme and forecast the scope your presentation will take. The remainder of the script flows smoothly, moving from one topic sentence, followed by supporting evidence, to another topic sentence, and so on. Transitions are clear between sentences and paragraphs. You feel confident. All seems to be flowing without a hitch. Then, 10 minutes into your presentation, you look up from your script to discover that you've lost your audience: some listeners are yawning; others are staring up at the ceiling; still others are fidgeting with their ties, hair, or pens or are nervously crossing and recrossing their legs. A few have even gone to sleep. This certainly wasn't the impact you'd expected to attain with your "perfect script."

After reassessing your presentation, you might well find that it wasn't the script's fault at all. Any number of variables can shoot down a great script. The nature of the presentation material itself can be the most difficult obstacle for a presenter to overcome. Highly technical or complex information or data, for example, even when properly focused toward the target audience, can easily confuse listeners. You also must contend with the short attention spans of most audiences. Even among the most interested of audiences, you can only expect 15 to 20 minutes of continuous attention before listeners' attention begins to wane. An unfavorable room setup can also reduce your effectiveness of your communication. It's difficult for audiences to concentrate on your message when seating is cramped or uncomfortable, room acoustics are poor, or ventilation or heating is inadequate. Regardless of the value of your message, you must fight throughout the presentation to hold the audience's attention.

You can greatly increase your chances of overcoming these barriers to effective communication by employing audio or visual media as central components of your presentation. Audio and visual presentation media can significantly enhance your effectiveness in getting your audience to do the following:

- Recognize the meaning of the message being communicated
- Understand its significance
- Comprehend how that message can be applied to meeting their informational needs and professional or personal interests
- Retain in long-term memory important information contained in the presentation.

While preparing your presentation, you've discovered topics that, due to their importance or complexity, require the degree of emphasis, explanation, simplification, or clarification that visual media can offer. By properly designing and integrating visual media into your presentation, you can more efficiently and effectively communicate your message.

When we discuss visual media in this chapter, we distinguish between the two elements of any visual medium: (1) the graphic form of the aid and (2) the medium through which that graphic aid is presented. As we later discuss in Chapter 7, commonly used graphic forms include tables, charts, graphs, drawings, diagrams, and maps. In the present chapter we focus on the selection and use of popular visual medium media, including flip charts, overhead transparencies, slides, and computer graphics displays. Central topics of this chapter, then, include the following:

- Benefits of using visual media
- Types of visual media
- Guidelines for selecting visual media
- Guidelines for presenting visual media.

BENEFITS OF USING AUDIO AND VISUAL PRESENTATION MEDIA

While they should not be used as substitutes for your script, visual media can serve as an excellent complement to your text to maximize audience comprehension and retention of the information or data communicated, thus assisting listeners in whatever decision-making that might be based on that information or data. The following discussion provides some of the strongest arguments for including visual media in your technical, scientific, or managerial presentation.

Presentation Media Increase the Impact of Your Message by Clarifying, Simplifying, Emphasizing, or Explaining Your Ideas. They can explain and simplify for listeners complex information and data. They can also emphasize key material, such as important figures, trends, and concepts, as well as summarize and condense vast amounts of material into a manageable and orderly form. Many topics discussed in today's professional presentations are simply too technical not to be illustrated using such graphical aids as tables, charts, graphs, diagrams, or drawings. The amount of information or data would be too overwhelming if it were not placed in an easily digestible form for listeners.

Presentation Media Increase Listener Retention.   Studies within the field of oral communication reveal that, whereas listeners recall only about 30 percent of what they hear and only 20 percent of what they see, their retention of information rises to about 50 percent when a presentation's text is reinforced by visual media.[1]

Presentation Media Save Time.   Information and data on many technical, scientific, or managerial topics can be more clearly and precisely conveyed in visual rather than textual form. For example, dedicating page after page of script to describe the circuitry of a computer chip maywell be a waste of your and listeners' time if you could show the same circuitry enlarged in a diagram and projected on a large overhead transparency.

Presentation Media Attract Listeners' Attention to the Presentation in General as Well as to Specific Points of Particular Importance.   This reduces the level of viewer resistance to your message, thereby increasing listener interest in and comprehension of the presentation material.

Presentation Media Add Variety to a Presentation.   By adding a conservative mix of visual medium media—such as a flip chart, an overhead projector, a slide projector, a computer projection screen, or a video projector—you can provide a change of pace for the audience and divert their attention from you (the presenter) and your script to key points of discussion. In the next section of this chapter we discuss the various types of visual medium media and their possible uses in technical, scientific, or managerial presentations.

Presentation Media Add Credibility to Your Presentation by Projecting a Sense of Order, Preparedness, and Professionalism.   Well-presented visual media build a positive image—or *ethos*—by conveying to audiences the impression that you are a deliberate and thorough planner and that you have left no stone unturned in preparing a methodical presentation. Effective visual media can mark you as a professional who will be objective and fair in delivering the presentation and in interpreting the presentational material.

Presentation Media Can Help You *Modernize* Your Presentation Through the Use of Technology.   Whether we like it or not, the impact of the visual image is often more forceful, convincing, and instructive than the spoken word. We live in a modern society in which, more times than not, the visual image reigns supreme—from the televised concert, to the politician's 15-second soundbite, to the optical laser disc image on the monitor of your personal computer. Today's visually oriented worlds of business, industry, and government and the associated technology of electronic communication oblige presenters to consider how best to design and present visual media that not only instruct but also attract listeners accustomed to such dynamic visual forms of communication.

Even though technology may not be a thematic component of your presentation, you might still want to make it a part of your visual medium media for presenting your information or data. For example, although the discussion of technology may be absent in your discussion of the migratory habits of Canadian geese, your listeners might more easily

[1] From Anita Taylor, *Speaking in Public* (Englewood Cliffs, NJ: Prentice-Hall, p. 174) and Robert L. Montgomery, *A Master Guide to Public Speaking* (New York: Harper & Row, 1979, p. 36); also referenced in Kenneth R. Mayer, *Well Spoken: Oral Communication Skills for Business* (New York: Harcourt Brace Jovanovich, 1989 p. 112.)

comprehend, appreciate, and remember the material if you were to integrate into your presentation a short video or slide show illustrating the animal's actual habitat, the computerized tracking of their migratory routes on a computer projection screen, or computer-generated tables and graphs of key migratory information and data projected on overhead transparencies.

As They Can Strengthen the Cohesion and Unity of Your Presentation's Organization, Presentation Media Increase the Effectiveness and Efficiency of the Presentation. Well-integrated visual media keep you on topic, working, in effect, as road signs that announce for your listeners (and for you) key topical destinations. For example, you might choose to begin your presentation with a visual medium—say, an overhead transparency—that emphasizes the purpose and forecasts the central issues of your talk (i.e., the presentation's scope). Subsequent visuals might clarify or emphasize important points contained in the body of the presentation and, in so doing, serve as convenient transitions between topics, assisting listeners in following your line of argument while also preventing you from straying off topic. The aids essentially serve as visual cues for announcing key topics contained in your script. A final transparency that notes the crucial conclusions of your presentation would not only help listeners remember previously covered key topics but also assist you in summarizing the main point of your talk.

Well-Timed Presentation Media Serve as Important Visual Pauses Between Long or Complex Passages of Text. Such passages of difficult text can bore audiences and make it difficult for them to extract and retain key points. After having introduced a topic in your presentation, you might insert a visual medium to focus listeners' attention on one key aspect of that topic. This offers your audience time to relax and to shift their concentration from you to a visual representation of what you are talking about. This presentation technique enhances listener comprehension and retention.

Presentation Media Give You, as Presenter, Time to Conduct an On-the-Fly Evaluation of Your Performance. They provide you with a short break from audience scrutiny so that you might take a deep breath, relax, assess the progress of the presentation, make any needed modifications to the presentation coverage or focus, and, in the process, increase your self-confidence and the presentation's effectiveness.

Presentation Media Can Help You to Improve Your Body Language. They can act as the stimulus for leaving the podium, which is essentially a barrier between you and the audience. Your use of models, demonstrations, transparencies, slides, or some other visual medium media provide you with the opportunity to move about the room, gesture toward, for instance, a model or overhead screen, encourage audience interaction, and build an interpersonal relationship with your listeners through eye contact and body proximity that would be impossible if you were anchored behind a lectern. Remember that the most effective communication is not one initiated and totally controlled by the presenter but, rather, one that is *shared* between interested parties, each being free to offer constructive input (whether verbal or nonverbal) into a two-way communication.

Presentation Media Can Provide Insights into a Problem Addressed in Presentation and Offer Possible Solutions That May Otherwise Have Been Overlooked If Relevant Data and Information Were Buried in the Script's Text. For example, a line or bar graph might well illustrate the dynamic nature of one or more items (say, the dramatic increase in sales of German cars in the United States over the past 10 years) that listeners might not be able to retrieve—much less appreciate—if read as a long series of statistics from a script.

By Offering Key Information in an Easily and Quickly Accessible Form, Presentation Media Enable Listeners to Make Informed Decisions.   When supplied with information or data based on visual media that accurately and thoroughly represent key issues, listeners can enhance the quality of any related decision they might make in their organization.

Presentation Media Can Significantly Increase Comprehension by International Audiences.   In this new age of a global economy and interdependent international politics, a growing percentage of your audience will not be native speakers of English. This is a given when you present overseas. But we should also remember that, in our own multicultural and multinational society, the United States, in essence, *is* overseas because we have as U.S. residents representatives of every culture and nation in the world. In fact, non-native speakers of English already constitute a growing percentage of many technical and scientific audiences *within* the United States As Nancy Corbin discusses in Chapter 13 on international presentations, you can appreciably help non-native speakers of English in your audience to extract much of the meaning of your presentation even when they lack advanced language skills in English by inserting into your presentation additional visual media and by "internationalizing" those aids so that they (1) contain a minimum of text and (2) employ images whose meaning can be uniformly understood within a wide range of cultures and languages.

In the final analysis, well-designed visual media that are properly integrated into your presentation can significantly increase listeners' comprehension and their retention of information and data. They also increase the effectiveness of your presentation by raising listener interest in your material, improving its cohesion and unity, and building your credibility as a presenter. As a result, presentations that incorporate effective visual media can leave listeners better informed on a topic of discussion than would presentations without visual media, and better-informed listeners are more able to make wise decisions later down the line.

VISUAL PRESENTATION MEDIA

You can communicate information and data in pictorial and audio form using a variety of visual (and audio) aid media, including the following:

- Audiotapes and record players
- Chalkboards (or whiteboards)
- Flip charts
- Handouts
- Projected media
- Samples and models
- Videotapes and teleconferencing

When selecting visual media for your presentation, consider using a mix of media that can best complement the type of information you are presenting. For example, you might provide in handout form highly detailed information that listeners will most probably want to refer to later. You might consider presenting highly detailed information or data, such as equations, formulas, and statistical information on overhead transparencies (in table, chart, graph, or map form) for discussion purposes as well as in handout form for later reference. Interactive material, such as the operation of a computer software package, might best be demonstrated on a computer projection screen, while presentations designed to acquire audience input would profit from the use of a flip chart or chalkboard. You might use slides in presentations dealing with actual places, people, or animals. If action plays a significant role in the presentation, you might consider using videotapes or audiotapes. Table 6.1 summarizes strengths and weaknesses of each visual medium and suggests the size of audience and nature of the presentation material for which the visual medium might best be used.

You can strengthen your presentation by using a mix of presentation media. For example, you might encourage audience input by first writing their views down on a flip chart. You could then compare those views with your own material already prepared on overhead transparencies. However, to avoid overloading your presentation with visual media and creating a "dog and pony" atmosphere, you should use no more than about three different media per presentation.

Audiotape Recorder and Record Players

Using recorded voices or sounds may occasionally add valuable prestige to or create an appropriate mood for your presentation. An audiotape of an influential person's commentary on a relevant topic, for example, could well increase the credibility of the ideas expressed in your presentation. Likewise, recorded sounds of machinery or animals could help your audience to understand and accept your message. For example, a tape of whales communicating to one another could effectively illustrate to an audience the intelligence of those mammals and, indirectly, exemplify the importance of protecting those animals from mass fishing and possible extinction. If an audiotape is not available, see if the recording is available on record and use the trusted and dependable standby—the record player.

Among their advantages, audiotape recorders and record players are

- relatively inexpensive for even high-quality systems
- convenient to transport and use during a presentation
- dependable
- easy to use
- flexible in synchronized use with such visual media as slides and videos.

One disadvantage in using audiotapes is sound projection. If you do not intend to use a tape that is professionally produced, be sure to record the voice or sound effects in a controlled and acoustically superior studio to eliminate background noise and enhance the sound quality of the tape. A major disadvantage to using record players is content selection. Often you will not be able to locate a professionally produced and commercially distributed record whose sounds are exactly what you need for your presentation.

Chalkboards or Whiteboards

Because it is a throwback to our schoolroom days, the chalkboard (or its modern version, the whiteboard) is probably the visual medium most familiar to us. Professionals integrate blackboards into their presentations nearly 65 percent of the time.[2] Whether a portable or wall-mounted chalkboard or whiteboard, it offers the presenter a number of advantages:

- It is widely available (a basic component in most conference rooms) and inexpensive to use.
- Chalkboard and whiteboards provide you with the flexibility of writing key points on space that you can easily erase to add new information.
- By noting key points on a chalkboard or whiteboard as the presentation progresses, you can inject into the talk a sense of immediacy; listeners often view the information as more current than information prepared beforehand and presented on such visual media as handouts, audiotapes, records, and videos.
- You can modify information presented whenever you sense the disposition of the audience and outside conditions change; if an audience, for example, has difficulty understanding a specific point, you might want to include more explanatory information into your talk by using chalkboards and whiteboards.
- You can use chalkboards and whiteboards to encourage audience participation in the presentation by recording listener responses to questions on the board.
- Chalkboards and whiteboards allow you to control the flow of the discussion, because you can write an idea only at the point in the presentation when it is needed, and not before.
- Chalkboards and whiteboards aid you in identifying and emphasizing relationships between key points by allowing the presenter to draw connecting lines between important ideas relevant to the discussion.

The central disadvantages of using chalkboards or whiteboards are that (1) they demand *neat* handwriting, a criterion that, for many of us, might make chalkboards an impractical, if not a counterproductive, visual medium, (2) the process of writing information on a board breaks your eye contact and, to a certain extent, your rapport with your listeners, (3) chalkboards or whiteboards might seem too low-tech and perhaps amateurish to some audiences, and (4) chalkboards and whiteboards are best used with small audiences and in small rooms where viewers can be close to the board. The guidelines listed in Figure 6.1 will help you to minimize these disadvantages and to make full and effective use of the chalkboard as visual medium.

An electronic version of the chalkboard or whiteboard is the electronic copyboard, a plastic-covered writing surface of standard-size chalkboard dimensions which is either free-standing or wall-mounted. Instead of using a stick of chalk, the presenter writes with a markup pen. After filling the copyboard, the speaker can obtain new writing space (depending on the copyboard model) by simply pressing a button to roll up clean board from a roller at the back of the unit. The copyboard also prints hard copies of any material written during a presentation session. Although the copyboard offers the advantage of convenience and injects a degree of high-tech pizzazz into your presentation, it is too bulky to be used as a portable visual media aid and is relatively expensive.

---

[2] From our recent survey discussed in "Oral Communication in Business and Industry: Results of a Survey on Technical, Scientific, and Managerial Presentations, *Journal of Technical Writing and Communication,* **24** (2), pp. 161–180.

TABLE 6.1. Guidelines for Matching the Right Visual Medium with Your Presentation Environment

Visual Medium	Advantages	Disadvantages
Audiotape	Inexpensive. Adds dimension of a second oral source to presentation. Tape can be reused. You can easily introduce tape only when relevant to discussion.	Might be perceived by audience as too low-tech. Can make listeners become passive.
Chalkboard	Easy to use. Inexpensive. Widely available at presentation sites. Allows you to write information and to show it only when needed. Needs no dark room, thus encouraging audience interaction and eye contact. Information can be changed during presentation, adding spontaneity. Encourages audience participation. Effective in casual situations. Mistakes can be erased.	Requires neat handwriting. Perhaps perceived as too low-tech in a high-tech world. Useful only with small audiences. Does not allow for later reference to material already erased. Chalk dust and ink markers (for white boards) can be messy. Graphic aids are hand-drawn and often lack professional look. Forces you to look away from audience when writing. Not transportable (except for small portable models).
Electronic projectors	Add significant high-tech pizazz to presentation. Permits you to use attractive, computer-generated graphics. Easy to transport. Often does not require dark room, thus encouraging interactive discussion and eye contact. Can be projected onto a large screen for viewing by hundreds of people. Allows for highly advanced video techniques, including multimedia presentations and cinemagraphic fades, wipes, dissolves.	Expensive. Requires technical expertise for creation of graphics and troubleshooting during presentation. Requires that presentation site have compatible projection and computer facilities.
Flip chart	Easy to use Inexpensive. Paper pad is easy to transport. Widely available at presentation sites. Allows you to write information and show it only when needed. Needs no dark room, thus encouraging audience interaction and eye contact. Information can be changed during presentation, adding spontaneity. Encourages audience participation. Allows for easy reference to earlier pages during Q&A. Mistakes can be erased.	Requires neat handwriting. Perhaps perceived as too low-tech in a high-tech world. Best used only with small audiences. Flipping pages can become a clumsy ordeal. Flipping pages can become a clumsy ordeal. Graphic aids are hand-drawn and often lack professional look. Forces you to look away from audience when writing.

Medium	Advantages	Disadvantages
Handout	Provides precision in communicating information and data. Leaves audience with material for later reference. Extensive handouts can become heavy and unwieldy to transport.	Might distract audience away from your speaking. You need a second person to distribute them.
Overhead projectors	Is easy to use. Looks professional. Uses inexpensive transparencies. Requires no technical facilities or expertise to create. Projects range of graphics (e.g., charts, graphs, drawings, diagrams, maps), many of which can be computer-generated. Can project color transparencies and overlays. Does not need a darkened room. Allows you to face audience. Allows you to edit projected material in a real-time exercise. Transparencies allow you to write notes on their cardboard frames. Transparencies are easy to store and transport. Transparencies are easy to re-organize. Transparencies are easy to relocate for later reference during Q&A. Widely available at presentation sites.	Does not work well for large audiences (more than100 people). Light bulb can burn out during presentation. Can be noisy. Bulb produces notable heat during long talks. Takes some attention away from you. Constant flipping of transparencies can be distracting. Projector often obstructs audience's view of screen. Keystoning can occur. Projector itself can be bulky to transport, if needed. Opaque projectors prevent you from facing audience.
Slides	Can be remote-controlled. Projects bright, professional-looking images. Is easy to reorganize slides. Is easily used, stored, and transported. Looks professional. Uses projectors that are available at most presentation sites.	Might require technical expertise or expensive equipment to make slides. Can be expensive to produce slides. Requires dark room, thus inhibiting note-taking and eliminating eye contact. Poses problem of slides being placed upside down or crossways. Bulb might burn out. Dark room discourages interactive discussion. Difficult to relocate for use furing Q&A. Best viewed by only small- to medium-sized audience.
Videotapes and teleconferencing	Adds dimension of motion of your presentation. Impressive when tape or film is specifically made for target audience only. Can be projected onto large screen for viewing by large audience.	Expensive. Requires technical expertise to produce. Normally reuires significant time to produce. Audience retains little detail. Requires projection equipment on site. Can become quickly dated. Audience can become passive. Requires darkened room, eliminating audience interaction and eye contact.

- Write legibly and large enough so that all viewers can read the information easily.
- If you have large amounts of information to place on the board, write the information before the presentation and cover the chalkboard so as not to confuse listeners with the purpose of the material before it is needed in the discussion.
- While writing on the board, try to maintain the pace and direction of your presentation. Don't leave the audience in dead silence while you take time out to fill the board with text; occasionally speak while you write.
- Try to stand to the side of the board when writing so as not to block your audience's view of the information.
- To highlight the key ideas contained in your presentation, set important terms and phrases apart from the rest of the text and employ a logical structure in organizing the information on the board. Writing dense passages of text or cramming the board with spaghetti-like trails of figures or equations will only confuse your audience.
- Use color chalk (or markers for whiteboards) to emphasize only *key* ideas.
- Make sure not to erase information before listeners have had time to read it carefully or to copy it into their notes. On the other hand, promptly erase information once it is no longer relevant to the discussion.

Figure 6.1. Guidelines for preparing and using chalkboards and whiteboards.

Flip Charts

Like the chalkboard, flip charts provide a sense of immediacy to a presentation, because you are able to visually highlight key ideas as they arise during the presentation. Nearly 35 percent of professionals use flip charts in presentations. The flip chart is a large pad of paper (normally 2 feet by 3 feet) mounted on an easel, and it enables the presenter to write key terms or phrases or make simple drawings on the flip chart page using felt-tip marking pens. Some distinct advantages that flip charts have over chalkboards are listed below:

- You need not erase key information that you have written as you normally would on a chalkboard to make room for new information. Having made your point and completing a flip chart page, you merely flip to the next fresh page. (You might want to write on alternate pages if the ink of your marker bleeds onto the next page.)
- You can easily review old material, which you might well have erased on aa chalkboard, by simply flipping back to previous pages, or you can detach those same pages from the pad and tape them to the wall for ongoing reference.
- Flip charts are inexpensive to purchase and maintain.
- Flip charts are easily portable and accessible during the presentation.
- Flip charts can be prepared beforehand at a site different from that of the presentation and then later carried to the presentation. (If you don't want the information to look too "precooked," however, consider tracing key terms or difficult drawings beforehand in pencil so that they can be seen by you and not your audience.)
- Flip charts allow you to conceal information contained on subsequent sheets, thus preventing the audience from jumping ahead of the discussion.

The disadvantages of using flip charts are the same as those of the chalkboards. Flip charts require that your handwriting be neat and attractive. Writing on flip charts also forces you to turn from your audience, thus breaking eye contact with your listeners. In addition, because of their size, flip chart pages are limited in the amount of information they can hold and are most appropriate for small audiences and in small rooms that allow viewers to be close to the flip chart. You may also find that you spend more time flipping pages than writing or drawing. Such constant interruptions in your presentation may reduce the continuity in your message. Figure 6. 2 offers some guidelines for preparing and using flip charts.

Handouts

About 90 percent of professionals delivering technical, scientific, or managerial presentations integrate handouts into their presentations. Handouts are especially effective visual media when used to communicate scientific or technical information to audiences. The advantages of distributing handouts to listeners are twofold: (1) Listeners can more closely examine complex, detailed information when it is in hard copy in front of them, and (2) they can refer back to the information at a convenient time when needed.

When you should distribute handouts during the presentation will depend on the purpose and nature of the handout information and your intended use of it in the presentation. You should normally distribute handouts before or after the presentation. Distributing hard-copy handouts during the presentation typically wastes time, distracts listeners from the topic at hand, and interrupts the flow of the talk. If you expect to work actively with the material during the presentation, you should distribute the relevant handouts *before* the presentation. Handouts distributed at the beginning of the presentation might include sample documents to be analyzed and evaluated during the discussion, printed guidelines of workshop objectives and procedures, or key figures or passages of text that serve as the groundwork on which the rest of the presentation builds. This advice, however, comes with

---

- Write neatly.
- Write lines no more than three or four words long and be sure to write in large letters.
- Write in large, block letters (not script).
- Prepare your pages beforehand.
- Include a title page at the first page of the chart.
- Use plenty of headings to announce main ideas.
- Choose a chart size that is suitable to the size of your audience.
- Use color markers to color-code key topics and their subordinate subtopics.
- Leave a sheet of paper blank to prevent ink from bleeding onto the next page of text.
- Leave blank pages in the middle and at the end of the pad where you anticipate writing additional information, such as input from listeners during interactive sessions.
- Position the pad where everyone in the room can see the information.
- Attach the pad securely to the easel and stand to the side when writing on or referring to information on the pad.

Figure 6.2. Guidelines for preparing and using flip charts.

an important qualifier: Be aware that handouts distributed before the presentation may tempt listeners to read the information rather than pay attention to the presentation.

If the purpose of the information is to provide listeners with important details *supplemental* to the presentation, then the handouts might be distributed *after* the presentation. Materials that might be best handed out after the presentation include tables of financial data, copies of information conveyed in overhead transparencies used during the presentation, audience response forms, works cited page of the experts referred to in the talk, or bibliography of suggested readings. Whether you decide to distribute the handouts before or after the presentation, be sure to refer to them during the talk and to explain their purpose in realizing the objectives of your presentation. If you are convinced that your handouts must be distributed during the presentation, arrange for someone to pass out the copies so as not to interrupt the flow of the discussion.

The central disadvantage of handouts is abuse. It is often tempting to depend too much on handouts, to the point that the entire presentation is provided in handout form. In addition, the excessive use of handouts not only increases significantly the cost of the presentation but, to a large extent, makes the oral presentation superfluous. Be selective in deciding what information, if any, should be conveyed in handout form. Finally, unlike information projected on an overhead projector or computer projection screen, the prepared information or data cannot be revised if needed just prior to or during the presentation.

Projected Media

Projected media are those requiring some type of light projector and screen. The most commonly used projected aids include overhead projectors, slide projectors, electronic projection pads, and computer projection screens.

Overhead Projector. Overhead projectors use mirrors and lights to project portions of a document onto an overhead screen. However, instead of projecting images from a book or other paper-based document, overhead projectors reflect images written on a transparency, a transparent sheet of plastic. Overhead projectors come in all sizes—from compact models that fit into briefcases, to console models designed to project large images for audiences in bigger conference or meeting rooms.

Most office supply stores can make overhead transparencies from your master copy which contains the text, numbers, figures, borders, graphics, or art as you want them to appear on the transparency. You can use various methods to make your transparencies. You can produce transparencies of computer-generated overheads by printing the material on transparency film on a laser printer. In addition, some of today's more sophisticated photocopiers can also produce high-quality transparencies. Moreover, you could use a dedicated transparency-making machine which employs a thermal carbon-lifting process to burn images onto an acetate sheet.

Overhead projectors and the use of transparencies have a number of advantages over other visuals aids:

- Overhead projectors are easy to use and relatively simple to transport.
- Not only are overhead transparencies inexpensive and easy to produce but with per-

sonal computers, graphics software, and high-resolution color printers, you can make highly professional transparencies in the convenience of your own home or office.

- Overhead projectors enable you to face the audience when reading the transparency and, thus, to retain eye contact with listeners.
- Overhead projectors can be used in various degrees of lighting—from a fully lit room, to a darkened one—which enables you and listeners to refer easily to notes or handouts.
- Overhead transparencies are easy to revise during and after a presentation.

Because of these advantages, more than 95 percent of professionals integrate overhead projectors into their presentations.[3] However, using overhead projectors does come with some disadvantages:

- Images can become distorted if conditions require that the projector be placed too near the screen or at awkward angles to the screen, producing *keystoning* in which the top of the image is wider than the bottom.
- Transparencies can be misused when long passages of text are included which the presenter laboriously reads to the audience, instead of including only key words or short phrases.
- Projector bulbs occasionally burn out during a presentation (thus, carrying an extra bulb or two is always a good idea).

Overhead projectors are best suited for use with small audiences of no more than 20 or 30 viewers and in small rooms. When preparing transparencies, ensure that all graphics and text are large enough for the audience to read. Typewriter-size letters are not large enough to be read by audiences in a medium-to-large conference room. Consequently, you may need to use special computer graphics programs or press-on letters from a lettering machine to produce sufficiently large print (normally 18-point type size or larger). When using uppercase type to emphasize text, remember to keep the lines of text short. Research shows that long lines of uppercase lettering are hard to read. Readers recognize words by their typographical profile—that is, the dynamic distance between ascenders and descenders in a line of text:

$$\frac{ascenders}{descenders} \text{ typographical profile } \underline{\qquad\qquad} \times height$$

The following lines of text are two possible titles for the same overhead transparency. The first title, however, is easier to read because only the first letter of the initial and subsequent key words are capitalized:

---

[3] From our recent survey discussed in "Oral Communication in Business and Industry: Results of a Survey on Technical, Scientific, and Managerial Presentations, *Journal of Technical Writing and Communication,* **24**(2), pp. 161–180.

Designing and Delivering
Scientific, Technical, and Managerial
Presentations

DESIGNING AND DELIVERING SCIENTIFIC, TECHNICAL, AND MANAGERIAL PRESENTATIONS

The flat typographical profile of uppercase lines delays viewers' recognition and comprehension of your message. Finally, if you are using a limited number of transparencies, you might consider taping a plastic or paper frame around each transparency to lend a neat and professional refinement to your presentation. Figure 6.3 offers some guidelines for preparing overhead transparencies and for using overhead projectors.

- Focus on only one major idea in each transparency.
- Choose lettering and images for your transparencies that are large enough to be seen by everyone in the room.
- Use phrases of text, never complete sentences.
- Use descriptive titles. (See our discussion of graphics titles in Chapter 8.)
- Avoid flat typographical profiles when capitalizing long lines of text. Instead, use the up-and-down style by capitalizing only the first letters of initial words and key words in your transparency.
- Place your overhead transparencies in sequence next the projector before the presentation.
- Have the title page for your presentation already on the projector when you turn it on.
- When it is time to refer to a transparency, simply turn on the projector and continue your discussion.
- Try to minimize the loss of eye contact with your listeners by not staring at the projector.
- When referring to items on the screen, stand to the side of the screen and use a pointer to highlight specific information for the audience.
- Talk to your audience, not the screen.
- Don't bore your audience by reading the projected text verbatim. Highlight key ideas or trends.
- To prevent listeners from reading upcoming transparencies and jumping ahead of the presentation, lay a sheet of paper over the transparency to cover its contents until you are ready to discuss them.
- Use overlays to control your pace in discussing transparency material. Overlays are sheets, or strips, of transparencies that can be layered over previous transparencies. They normally introduce a new topic related to that of the previous transparency. When working with overlays or transparencies, be sure not to lose eye contact with your audience by looking down at the projector for long periods of time.
- Use colors for emphasis and employ only colors that complement each other. (See our section on the use of color in Chapter 8.)
- For easy handling and space for notes on the transparency's content, tape cardboard or plastic frames to each transparency and number the transparency on the frame.
- To eliminate fan noise and viewer distraction, turn off the projector when you are not using it.
- Carry with you an extra projector bulb, three-prong plug, and extension cord.

Figure 6.3. *Guidelines for preparing overhead transparencies and for using the overhead projector.*

Slide Projector. The versatility, resolution, and attractiveness of slides have made them a popular form of visual medium for scientific (especially within biomedical and engineering disciplines), technical, and managerial presentations. With the wide availability of slide-producing technology—such as cameras, computer graphic programs, and slide-developing equipment—slides have become a primary visual medium to illustrate a variety of graphic aids from simple pie charts, to diagrams, to photographs of people, processes, or products. The use of slides offers a number of advantages to your presentation, but perhaps the most central advantage is that they can incorporate a range of dynamic images, such as photographs of corporate chiefs from a recent annual report, lines and bar graphs of economic indicators from a financial periodical, or graphic drawings of your firm's new product line. Slides also offer you the flexibility to change easily the order of your slides at the last moment so that you can tailor the presentation to fit the particular needs of your audience.

When incorporating slides into your presentation, you should use a slide projector that accepts standard 35-mm (2-inch by 2-inch) slides. A projector with a remote-controlled zoom lens (from 102 mm to 152 mm, $f/3.5$) will enable you to control the flow of slides and focus from your position away from the projector. You may also consider using a projector that works in tandem with a synchronized audiotape recorder that not only plays a prerecorded message but also signals the projector when to change slides. You might also consider videotaping your slides with audio to produce video slide shows that can be shown on television or projection screen.

Despite their ability to attract attention and to present a range of images, slides also have their drawbacks. First, the layout of slide masters and the production of slides from those masters are often complex operations and require the help of computer-graphics systems and graphics professionals. Second, although user-friendly computer software exists today to help you design slides (e.g., Adobe Systems' *Adobe PhotoShop,* Silicon Beach's *Digital Darkroom,* Letraset Graphic Design Software's *ColorStudio*, Computer Presentations' Windows *ColorLab,* Micrographx's *Picture Publisher*), you might still find that you need the aid of graphics professionals. This assistance can significantly increase the cost of using slides while also extending the preparation time needed for the presentation. However, without professional help, your slides, instead of being simple and well focused, might prove ineffective, for example, because they are crammed with too much information or because that information is poorly arranged. As with overhead projectors, slide projectors are best suited for use in small rooms of 20 to 30 people. Figure 6.4 provides some guidelines for preparing and using slides.

Electronic Video Projectors. The electronic video projector is a combination of overhead screen, projector, and personal computer. It allows you to project whatever information is on your personal computer monitor onto an overhead screen where it can be viewed by your audience. Clearly, video projectors can be invaluable when the presentation pertains to computer-related topics, such as on-line tutorials and the operations of a personal computer or supporting software, because viewers can see the actual operation during the presenter's real-time demonstration.

Computer-based video projectors work well when the presentation deals with any process-oriented topic. A workstation personal computer equipped with special graphics capabilities can project stunning motion graphics that will grab any audience's interest. If you have the budget and technological support, you might consider using electronic video projector technology to produce a high-tech, multimedia event that not only sig-

- Design slides with the idea of creating a continuous, coherent message, much like a movie of photographs.
- Use computer-generated graphics whenever possible.
- Use word charts to forecast the scope area of a presentation section and to summarize key ideas before closing that section.
- Start your preparation early. Slide preparation also requires more time than you think.
- Don't cram the slide with information. Limit each slide to one major idea.
- Use headings to emphasize the central point in each slide.
- Use colors for emphasis, but use them consistently (e.g., blue for main ideas, green for subordinate ideas, and yellow for examples).
- Stand near the screen so that viewers can see your face. Avoid becoming the "voice from the dark."
- Know well how the slide projector works. Don't confuse the reverse button for the forward button on the remote control.
- If you use a projectionist, arrange for a hand signal rather than saying "Next" to move to the subsequent slide.
- Double-check the order of your slides just before presenting.
- Carry an extra bulb, three-pronged plug, and extension cord with you.

Figure 6.4. *Guidelines for preparing and using slides.*

nificantly increases audience interest but also greatly enhances the effectiveness of the presentation.

Projection pad technologies are available in two forms: the LCD panel and the LCD video projector. The *LCD panel* is connected by cable to an projection screen via a personal computer. The panel is normally placed on top of the projector platform. The panel then projects the digitized transparency image onto a computer display screen or a standard projection screen. The chief advantage of digitizing the material in this manner is that you can store the information in computer memory and modify it as needed during and after the presentation. Consequently, LCD panels allow you to prepare images for multimedia presentations on highly portable computer disks. Panels are lightweight, making them a convenient visual medium when you're on the road and presenting off-site. LCD panels also add a dynamic dimension to your presentation. You can address the question "What if?" by changing the projected text or images in real time with input from listeners during the course of your presentation. You might, for example, modify figures in the projected image of an accounting spreadsheet or rearrange the parts of an engineering model to examine how these changes might affect your hypothesis.

One type of LCD panel, the briefcase-size *IntelliView* by IntelliMedia, allows you to store on a 3.5-inch disc still text, images, full-motion video, slides, and animation produced on a range of graphics software packages. You can then project this material onto the system's LCD screen or place the unit on top of a standard overhead projector to show the information on a projection screen. Apollo Audio Visual, Telex Communications, Kodak, 3M, Computer Accessories/Proxima, Nview, and Sharp Electronics make comparable models. The primary drawback to using an LCD panel is its price tag—ranging from $1000 to $7500.

A second type of projection pad is the *LCD video projector.* These self-contained units have their own light source and, thus, do not need an overhead projector. While the LCD video projector can produce both static and dynamic images just as the LCD panel, the video projector tends to project better color images and to have faster reaction times in moving stored images from disc to screen than do LCD panels. However, as with the LCD panel, the LCD video projector is relatively expensive—priced from about $3000 to $5000.

Two other types of video projection are the CRT projector and light-valve projector. Often used to show sporting events in public places, the *CRT projector* throws a digitized image onto a large, curved screen. Manufactured by such companies as Electrohome, NEC, and Barco, CRT projectors cost between $3000 and $10,000. *Light-valve projectors* can project extremely sharp images onto very large screens. Made by companies such as General Electric and costing between $35,000 and $350,000, the light-valve projector is usually reserved for special, on-site presentations.[4]

A major advantage of the video projector technology is that its dynamism and high-tech appeal pull listeners into the discussion. Presentations delivered in a room equipped with computer terminals can even make an audience actual participants by allowing them to respond to the discussion through their own keyboards; the video projector then displays their responses on the overhead screen. However, because it is normally projected onto an overhead screen of standard dimensions, video projectors are best used with a small audiences of 20 to 30 people. In addition, the technology involved with running a computerized visual medium often requires that you have computer experience or training. Finally, depending on the budget available to your presentation, the cost of the computer hardware and software necessary to support a computer video projector may be prohibitive.

Samples and Models

Occasionally, you might find that descriptions or pictorial representations of an object or process are insufficient in communicating the full meaning and significance of your message. Consequently, you might supply listeners with a *sample* of the actual object or process being discussed. If, for example, you were proposing marketing strategies for a new product, you might strengthen your presentation by demonstrating or distributing samples of the actual product. Similarly, if you were explaining to a group of radiologists and radiological technicians the benefits and use of a new scanning/imaging system, you would probably want to locate your presentation in a model imaging lab in order to use the necessary medical technology.

Sometimes, however, integrating samples into your presentation, even though they are important in communicating your message, is impractical or impossible. Samples, for example, may prove too costly to obtain; too bulky or fragile to transport to the presentation site; or too dangerous. In such instances, you might consider using working *models* instead of the real thing. For example, let's change slightly our previous example and suggest that you direct your instructional presentation to a group of medical professionals who need to integrate this new scanning/imaging system into their hospital's large radiology center. If holding the presentation in a model lab is impossible, you might use a made-to-scale model of the system in order to illustrate the size, configuration, and components of the scanning/imaging system.

The primary advantage of using samples and models is that both visual media provide

---

[4] From John A. Murphy's discussion of current computer-based projection technologies in "Polishing Your PC Presentations," *Today's Office,* **24**(2), p. 18.

listeners with a three-dimensional view of the object or process under discussion. Samples and models, however, can distract listeners from your presentation. Consequently, you should distribute the samples or models, or refer to them, only when they are to be examined or used. In addition, try to have on hand enough samples or models so that listeners don't have to pass the visual media around. This invariably draws listeners' attention away from the presentation at different times as each examines the aid. Manage samples and models so that the attention of *all* listeners is either on the visual medium or on you and your message. Finally, samples and models are best suited for use in small to medium rooms of 20 to 50 viewers.

Videotapes and Teleconferencing

Videotapes and teleconferencing can enhance the effectiveness of your presentation as follows

- By illustrating dynamic processes whose meaning and significance must be shown in continuous action and sound
- By grabbing the attention of today's audience who are accustomed to television, movies, and VCRs and the dynamic video images those video systems project
- By projecting video images to remote sites with the help of satellites
- By recording and archiving a process or discussion for later examination
- By enabling you to integrate a wide range of graphic images besides processes into your video presentation, including still-action shots of charts, diagrams, tables, and photographs.

Videotapes are commercially marketed and distributed in three sizes: $\frac{1}{2}$ inch, $\frac{3}{4}$ inch, or 8 mm. Most of today's videocassette recorders (VCRs) use either the $\frac{1}{2}$-inch or 8-mm videotapes. A portable video system for oral presentations normally consists of a video player or recorder, monitor, connecting cables, and equipment stand. Major motion pictures can be rented and shown on VCR recorders as well.

In addition to videotapes that prerecord information, real-time video can record and, at the same time, broadcast images to local or remote sites using telecommunications. Teleconferencing has become an important real-time video system for communicating actual images of processes or discussions as they happen. Real-time video, such as teleconferencing, normally involves the use of closed-circuit cameras, satellites, monitors, accompanying cables, and complex computer software that connects and manages the telecommunications network.

When using a video system in your presentation, consider carefully the size of your audience and the size of the image that your video monitor can project. Most video aids are designed for use with smaller audiences, because they project their images with 20-inch to 30-inch monitors or television screens, an image that can easily be seen by 15 to 20 people in a small conference room. Audiences any larger than that will have difficulty reading the image. Some video and teleconferencing systems do support large wall screens; however, their resolution typically is murky for viewers close to the screen.

If you have decided that the commercially available videotapes and movies do not meet your visual needs, you may choose to make your own video. If so, keep in mind that the images projected by effective video aids should be *compressed images* captured. In other words, there is no room for superfluous movement or discussion. If, for example, you are using a video cassette system to illustrate the procedure for loading a computer program onto personal computers, you might show a person performing the key steps but *without* the coffee breaks and chatter of the typical workplace. Moreover, although it is broadcast in real time and is, thus, unavailable for editing, teleconferencing video must still be better planned and more tightly organized than we would normally structure a 15 minute office conference where there are no high telecommunication costs.

In designing your video, be sure to inject *movement* into the film. The simplest type of movement is motion—that is, physical movement of people or objects. The most common flaw in in-house videos (those made by the presenter or an organization without the help of a professional cinematographer) is the static scene of people sitting, or standing, and talking without any movement at all. This is widely referred to as a "talking heads" video. In some cases, the content of your video will be intrinsically static, and the introduction of dynamic, physical movement into the video might be impractical or appear artificial. In such instances, you might give the appearance of movement by regularly changing camera angles of a static scene or by splicing together different but related scenes that, though static, give the sense of movement due to the varying settings, characters, or message.

Some of the disadvantages of using video aids in a business presentation are as follows:

- Designing and producing a technically and dramatically appealing and successful video presentation require the use of complex technology as well as the assistance of video experts.
- The use of such technology and video consultants can significantly increase the cost of your presentation.
- Videotapes or movies whose topics are directly related to your presentation message may not always be available.

GUIDELINES FOR SELECTING VISUAL MEDIA

When selecting visual media for your presentation, first remember to use only those visual media that emphasize, clarify, simplify, or explain the most important ideas in your message. Don't waste your listeners' time or your organization's money by cluttering your presentation with superfluous visual media. To determine whether a visual would prove itself to be functional in your presentation, ask yourself the questions listed in Figure 6.5. If you answer yes to all these questions, you have found a functional visual medium to include in your presentation.

GUIDELINES FOR USING VISUAL MEDIA

Well-conceived and professionally designed visual media are of little use if they are not effectively presented to audiences. Consider the guidelines for using visual media listed in Figure 6.6 when preparing for your presentation.

- Is the visual medium necessary for me to achieve fully my purpose(s) in presenting the information or data. Will it make a lasting impact on listeners in their understanding and retention of the information or data communicated? In effect, is this a visual medium I really need?
- Does the visual medium contain the content and can it present that content in such a way that the key informational needs and professional interests of listeners will be met?
- Have I limited the visual medium to only *one* idea?
- Have I kept the meaning contained in the visual medium direct, clear, and simple?
- Do the capabilities of the visual medium match the nature of the material presented? If, for example, you were presenting measurements of major stress fractures found in tanks containing liquid nitrogen, would you not choose to convey that data in table form, perhaps via handout or overhead transparency media? On the other hand, would not a transparency illustrating a drawing of the cracks, or a videotape of the cracks themselves, be effective in driving home to viewers the seriousness of the fractures?
- Consider the room setup. Would the visual medium be visible or audible to the entire audience? Use such media as chalkboards, flip charts, opaque projectors, and overhead projectors for small audiences (up to 30 people). Use handouts or large-screen visual aids (e.g., light-valve projectors or large-scale movie screens) for large audiences.
- Would the visual medium be easy to access and operate during the presentation?
- Is the presentation medium readily available for my use?
- Can I use all the selected presentation media in the allotted time for the presentation? If a technical glitch occurs in the medium, is there time to fix it and complete the visual part the presentation? Are there backup aids I keep in reserve for such a misfortune?
- Do I have enough lead-in time to prepare the information or data for the presentation media?
- Does this visual medium complement the key information in my script, rather substitute for it? Visual media should not serve as substitutes for clear and developed explanations and arguments.
- Is my audience accustomed to reading and understanding this the type of visual medium? If not, will they be open to my use of it, or should I use another visual medium?
- Can I afford the visual medium? Is its use cost-effective for the length and significance of the presentations? Often, it's a common process of elimination. Start with the perfect visual medium to meet your presentation objectives; then consider your budget and the presentation environment. For example, if you're handcuffed by a small presentation budget and plan to present at a no-frills site with no visual medium facilities other than a projection screen, why not consider using the tried-and-true overhead projector supplemented with handouts.

Figure 6.5. *Guidelines for selecting presentation media.*

You can integrate many graphic aids into your presentation as various presentation media, such as chalkboards, flip charts, handouts, models, overheads, slides, transparencies, computer display screens, audiotapes, videos, and teleconferencing. A slide show at the beginning of your presentation, for example, might prove very effective in gaining your audience's attention while also providing a general overview of the presentation topic. Flip charts or bar charts could be a useful way to illustrate dynamic changes in several items being discussed in the body of your presentation. More complex data and information, however, might be better presented in handouts distributed before the presentation.

- Place the visual medium where everyone can see it.
- Stand out of the way; don't put yourself between your audience and the visual medium.
- Explain the visual medium. Remember that *you* are the presumed expert on the topic of your presentation topic. Leaving viewers to interpret for themselves the meaning of a graphic aid (1) deprives your audience of your valuable insights into the significance of the information and (2) invites inaccurate interpretations of the aid's function, meaning, or significance by listeners who, for the most part, are less knowledgeable in the area of study than you. Therefore, help viewers in their analysis of the data and information that you are providing in the graphic. Highlight for them in the text of your report the key pieces of information contained in the graphic. Then explain how and why that material is important when considering solutions to the problem at hand.
- Speak up. The drone of projector motors and cavernous lecture halls can reduce a normal voice to a whisper.
- Maintain eye contact with your audience as much as possible; don't talk to the visual medium.
- Don't distract the audience by introducing a visual medium before it is needed in the presentation.
- Use visual media as a tool for increasing your body language. Move about the room, using the visual medium as an object to analyze from various angles at different locations in the room.
- Use a pointer if needed to draw viewers' attention to precisely the right detail contained in your visual medium.
- Case out the presentation site beforehand. Check for the location of power outlets, availability of extension cords and extra projector bulbs, ease of darkening room, orientation of lectern or microphone to audience.
- Practice using your visual media. Learn how to integrate them smoothly into the flow of your presentation.

Figure 6.6. Guidelines for using presentation media.

SUGGESTED READINGS

Audiovisual communication. (1978). Special Issue. *IEEE Transactions on Professional Communication,* **PC-21**(3).

Beer, D. F. (Ed.). (1992). *Writing and speaking in the technology professions: A practical guide.* New York: IEEE Press.

Bishop, A. C. L. (1970). The multimedia presentation of technical information. *IEEE Transactions on Professional Communication,* **EWS-13**(1), pp. 24–27.

Blais, W. (1991). When visuals aid in the presentation. *Management Accounting,* **73**(3), pp. 47–49.

Boyd, S. D. (1991). When visuals aid in the presentation. *Canadian Manager,* Summer, pp. 22–23.

Bunch, J. (1991). The storyboard strategy. *Training & Development,* July, pp.69–71.

Byham, W. C. (1992). Six factors to consider when using audiovisual materials. *Across the Board,* **29**(3), pp. 52–53.

Crider, B. (1984). Professional presentations. *PC World,* August, pp. 248–254.

Filson, B. (1991). *Executive speeches: 51 CEOs tell you how to do yours.* Williamstown, MA: Williamstown Publishing Co.

Fletcher, L. (1990). *How to design and deliver a speech,* 4th ed. New York: HarperCollins.

Gray, J. G., Jr. (1986). *Strategies and skills of technical presentations: A guide for professionals in business and industry.* Westport, CT: Quarom Books.

Gregory, H. (1987). *Public speaking for college and career.* New York: Random House.

Johnson, G. (1991). Visual literacy. *Successful Meetings,* January, pp. 2–4.

Kaeter, M. (1991). Slide show savvy. *Presentation Technologies,* November, pp. 11–14.

Kemp, J. E. (1980). *Planning and producing audiovisual materials,* 4th ed. New York: Harper & Row.

Kerfoot, G. (1980). Let the audience see your presentation. *IEEE Transactions in Professional Communication,* **23**(1), pp. 50–52.

Kuzmin, K. (1992). Computer presentations products create better communications. *Office Technology Management,* February, pp. 40–43.

Mambert, W. A. (1985). *Effective presentations,* 2nd ed. New York: John Wiley & Sons.

Mayer, K. R. (1989). *Well spoken: Oral communication skills for business.* New York: Harcourt Brace Jovanovich.

Meyer, J. I. (1977). The effective use of audiovisual media in presenting technical information orally. *Journal of Technical Writing and Communication,* **7,** pp. 45–49.

Minor, E. O. (1979). *Handbook for preparing visual instructional materials.* New York: McGraw-Hill.

Morrisey, G. L., & Sechrest, T. L. (1987). *Effective business and technical presentations,* 3rd ed. Reading, MA: Addison-Wesley.

Moskovitz, R. (1991). Electronic meetings raise effectiveness. *Office Systems,* August, pp. 30–36.

Murphy, J. (1991). Polishing your PC presentations. *Today's Office,* August, 16–19.

Nies, J. I. (1991). How to add visual impact to your presentations. *The Cornell H.R.A. Quarterly,* May, pp. 46–51.

Osborn, M., and Osborn, S. (1991). *Public speaking,* 2nd ed. Palo Alto: Houghton Mifflin.

Pevey, J. L. (1990). Technical support for audio visual communications—Suggestions for improving oral presentations. In *Proceedings of the IEEE International Professional Communication Conference—Communication Across the Sea: North American & European Practices,* September 12–14, 1990, pp .220–223.

Pike, B. (1992). *Creative training techniques.*

Rowh, M. (1992). Six factors to consider when using audiovisual materials. *Office Systems,* February, pp. 23–25.

Scheiber, H. J.,and Hager, P .J. Oral communication in business and industry: Results of a survey on technical, scientific, and managerial presentations. *Journal of Technical Writing and Communication,* **24**(2), pp. 161–180.

Timm, P. (1981). *Functional business presentations: Getting across.* Englewood Cliffs, NJ: Prentice Hall. (1971) *Visual materials: Guidelines for selection and use in training situations.* U.S. Civil Service Commission. Washington, DC: U.S. Government Printing Office.

Wormald, K. (1991). Use transparencies to enhance presentations. *The Office,* July, pp.58–59.

7

Designing Presentation Graphics

Graphics are the textual, numerical, or pictorial presentation of information or data. They are the actual forms in which information or data are arranged and then communicated through visual aid media, such as handouts, flip charts, overhead transparencies, slides, and computer display screens. Apart from enabling us to clarify, simplify, and emphasize complex ideas—making long, complicated explanations unnecessary—graphics, such as tables, pie charts, line graphs, bar graphs, drawings, diagrams, and maps, help listeners to remember key information from a presentation and to apply the knowledge gained from the discussion in their own workplace. Moreover, well-conceived and professionally produced graphics interest viewers. They add a touch of professionalism to your presentation and increase your credibility as an expert presenter. Finally, in today's visual-intensive world of portable microtelevisions, VCRs, and video laser discs, few presentations fail to take advantage of the visual draw of graphics.

The focus of this chapter is to

- examine the types of graphics most commonly used in scientific, technical, and managerial presentations
- provide guidelines for designing and using graphics in presentations
- discuss how computer graphics software can help you to create graphics of professional quality.

TYPES OF VISUAL AID GRAPHICS

Graphics come in the form of either *tables* or *figures.* Tables can be numerical or textual in content. Figures most commonly used in technical, scientific, or managerial presentations include the pie chart, line graph, bar graph, drawing, diagram, and map.

"And that, as my four dimensional graph clearly shows, is why our customers can't understand what on earth it is that we do."

Source: *Courtesy of the American Management Association, New York, November 1994.*

Tables

Tables are effective in providing audiences with accurate, specific, and complex information (especially numerical values) in an easily accessible and compact form. Tables organize information graphically in orderly columns and in rows, as shown in Figure 7.1.

			Spanner Head	
Stub Head	Column Head	Column Head	Column Subhead	Column Subhead
Row Head*	XXXX	XXXX	XXXX	XXXX
Row Head**	XXXX	XXXX	XXXX	XXXX
Row Head	XXXX	XXXX	XXXX	XXXX
"	"	"	"	"
"	"	"	"	"
"	"	"	"	"
"	"	"	"	"
"	"	"	"	"
TOTAL	XXXX	XXXX	XXXX	XXXX

Table XX. Table Title

* Footnote 1
** Footnote 2
Source:

FIGURE 7.1. *Components of a formal table.*

Those that contain nontextual information (e.g., numbers, symbols, equations) are called *numerical tables,* as illustrated in Figure 7.2. *Textual tables* consist of non-numerical information—such as lists of key terms, equations, formulas, phrases, and short sentences—and are excellent summary devices that aid listeners in synthesizing and retaining information central to your presentation (Figure 7.3). When designing your table, consider some fundamental layout guidelines listed in Figure 7.4 for this specific graphic aid.

Table 9
Obstacles to Delivering Effective Presentations

Dichotomy Label	Count	% Responses	% Cases
Too Much Information	53	18.4	55.8
Preparation Time	38	13.2	40.0
Structure	35	12.2	36.8
Technical Information	33	11.5	34.7
Nervousness	31	10.8	32.6
Q & A	28	9.7	29.5
Converting Information	21	7.3	22.1
Voice Loudness	16	5.6	16.8
Reading	14	4.9	14.7
Visuals	13	4.5	13.7
Other	6	2.1	6.3
Total	**288**	**100.0**	**303.2**

Table 3.16. Economic Performance and Literacy Rates, 1995

	GNP per Capita		Adult Literacy
	In 1995 Dollars	Average Annual Growth	
Bangladesh	180	−0.4	38
Bhutan	200	−0.3	—
Somalia	260	−0.5	60
India	360	1.4	36
Rwanda	360	1.4	23
Haiti	520	0.2	23
Kenya	660	2.2	40
Egypt	780	3.3	44
Honduras	940	1.1	57
Spain	6,940	4.2	99
Russia	7,400	4.3	99
United Kingdom	10,060	2.1	99
Japan	14,560	7.6	99
Canada	18,360	3.5	99
United States	19,180	2.4	98
Denmark	19,840	3.2	99
Sweden	20,450	2.5	99
Switzerland	25,010	2.2	99

FIGURE 7.2. *Numerical tables.*

Some Things Just Won't Work: Our Options	
Item Considered	**Comment**
Newly designed FTT	While possibly smaller and cheaper, the schedule, risk and safety certification of a new design make this option prohibitive. We chose to stick with the proven Micro-Systems design.
Use of current MEGS antenna	The MEGS antenna would use up too much of the restricted surface area available for WRTTM antennas. This would have forced us to use FTT and TM antennas with exotic designs and materials. Recurring cost considerations demand a single, three-in-one antenna.
Use of existing TM components	These items are all larger than the multichip module based on subminiature telemetry. This would squeeze the volume so much that we could not use existing items.
Lower power FTT HPA	We could use a smaller (e.g., 600–700 W) high-power amplifier, but it would not produce the required 150-W EIRP at all regions of the roll plane. Because this would significantly reduce FTT safety margin, we selected the 1200-W unit.
Run TM cable through SRTTM	This would allow the antenna to wrap completely around the missile, improving antenna gain. But the aerodynamic impact on the missile as well as the packaging inside WRTTM caused us to abandon this option.
Modify non-GRDCUS-qualified FTT	Our modification of existing non-GRDCUS-compatible requirements might sound like a good idea, but such an option is difficult to achieve. The need for significant new software development, in addition to having to meet the GRDCUS interoperability qualification, imposes unacceptable technical performance and schedule risk.

FIGURE 7.3. *Textual table.*

Tables are excellent graphic aids for communicating detailed and precise information and data. However, use tables only when you believe the data are essential in assisting listeners in understanding the meaning and significance of your message. For audiences with less knowledge or technical expertise in your presentation subject, large tables of complex data may well prove confusing and frustrating. Moreover, tables are not an effective means of illustrating dynamic trends or tendencies in numerical values (e.g., significant growths, dramatic declines, frenetic roller coaster increases and decreases). To emphasize and clarify more effectively important dynamic movements in numerical data, you might, instead, integrate figures—such as the pie chart, line graph, or bar graph—into your presentation.

Line Graphs

Perhaps the most popular and frequently used figures are the *graph* and *chart*. Although the two terms are often used interchangeably, they are, in fact, distinct in both meaning and

- Organize the information logically in the graphic (e.g., by order of importance, alphabetically, chronologically, geographically).
- Identify each column and row of information with clear and accurate headings; include subtitles where appropriate.
- Limit your table to no more than three or four columns.
- Include horizontal **stub lines** to separate the title, **columns heads,** rows and columns, and any subtable material (e.g., footnotes and source lines).
- Insert **spanner heads** to unify any multiple subheads under one general column heading.
- Normally place column and row totals at the end of each row or column, or as needed, though totals may appear at the beginning of rows and columns as well for greater emphasis.
- Convert all fractions into their decimal equivalents.
- Align numerical data in columns by decimal point; round off numbers as the level of precision warrants.
- Where no data are available, use the dash (two hyphens), the abbreviation "N.A.," or three dots (. . .); do not use a zero because it can confuse viewers in their interpretation of the data
- Place unit definitions (e.g., percentage, dollars, kilogram, degree) of numerical data in column heads; use standard symbols and abbreviations for such units as %, $, kg, °C, °F.
- Place the dollar sign (and that of other commonly known currencies) with the first column entry and the total entry only.

FIGURE 7.4. *Guidelines for constructing formal tables.*

function. Graphs are figures that plot values on a coordinate system (i.e., on a grid of columns and rows). Charts, on the other hand, depict relationships between items and their respective values without using a grid. Line, bar, and surface graphs are the most commonly used form of graph in technical, scientific, or managerial presentations.

Line graphs use a printed line to represent and plot the changing numerical values of an item. The line rises and falls as the changing values it represents are plotted across a grid, a field of intersecting vertical and horizontal lines. (Because it can be distracting to the viewer, the grid is usually omitted from the final version of the graphic aid.) Line graphs are most effective when used to illustrate the quantitative changes in one or more items over a period of time. Dynamic quantities—such as prices, sales, income, and production—and the cause-and-effect relationships between them can be clearly and quickly communicated through line graphs than in text.

As shown in Figure 7.5, the *x* (horizontal) and *y* (vertical) axes of the graph provide the boundaries and measurement scale for the grid. The intersection of these two axes creates four quadrants. A line connecting different coordinates plotted between the *x* and *y* axes displays how the numerical value of an item(s) changes over time. Time—in the form of months, quarters, or years—is commonly placed on the *x* axis. The *y* axis frequently serves to quantify the amount of change an item undergoes over specific periods of time. For this reason, the *y* axis is scaled according to relevant measurements of the item being plotted, such as monetary amounts, distances, and weights. To aid viewers in determining the value of key coordinates, you might plot the points of coordinates at important locations on the graph. Figure 7.6 presents an example of a single-line graph, and Figure 7.7 shows a multiple-line graph.

Line graphs can significantly expand listeners' understanding of data as well as reduce the time they need to decode and interpret your message. However, when not properly con-

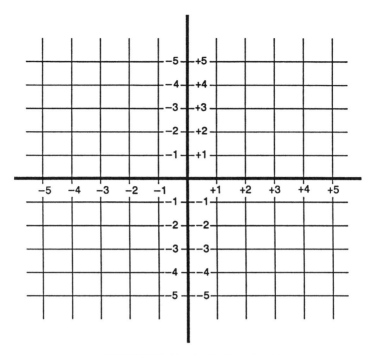

FIGURE 7.5. Quadrants of graph grid.

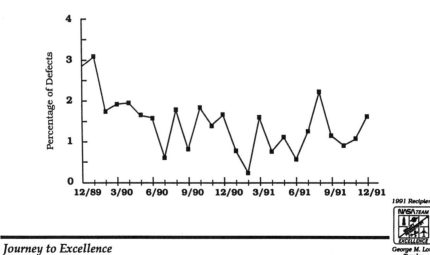

FIGURE 7.6. Single-line graph. Source: *Grumman Technical Services, Kennedy Space Flight Center, Titusville, Florida.*

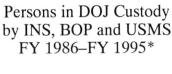

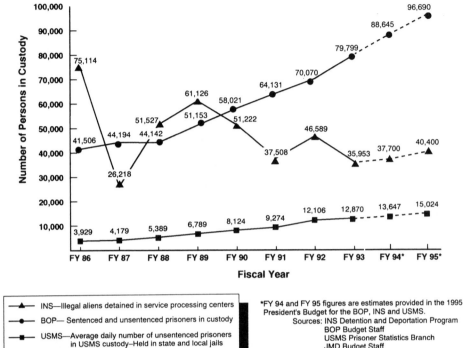

FIGURE 7.7. *Multiple-line graph.* Source: Review of Air Fleet Operations within the U.S. Department of Justice, *Management and Planning Staff, Justice Management Division, U.S. Department of Justice, Washington, D.C., 1994.*

structed, lines graphs, as with any graphic aid, can easily decrease the accuracy, accessibility, and effectiveness of a presentation. When designing and constructing line graphs, consider the guidelines listed in Figure 7.8. Moreover, beware of how distorted calibrations of either the *x* or *y* axes can distort the appearance of data's significance and meaning, as illustrated in Figure 7.9.

On occasion, you may want to measure and plot multiple components of a single item. A *surface graph,* also called a *belt graph* or *band graph,* is a variation of the line graph that allows you to illustrate the numerical changes in subcomponents of an item (Figure 7.10). The total value of all plotted components of a surface chart equals 100 percent. Surface graphs enable audiences to estimate (1) the the value of each subcomponent at any point along its plotted line and (2) the percentage of the whole represented by that component.

Although it resembles a multiple-line graph, the surface graph is read very differently. As you recall, the value of a line in a multiple-line graph is measured from the baseline of the graph to the position of any coordinate on that line. In a surface graph, however, each line represents a percentage of the total value of a single item, which is represented

- As a general rule, integrate no more than five lines into your line chart. A chart crammed with lines, regardless of the care you may take in identifying each line, invariably confuses an audience.
- Color-code lines in a multiple-line graph to differentiate lines. You might also use different line formats to differentiate lines in a multiple-line graph, including solid lines (——). broken lines (– – –), dash-dot lines (– · –), dots (· ·), or any combination of these.
- Identify the item that each line represents by including a legend in a corner of the chart. If space limitations preclude the use of a legend, you might label the items by using a tag line to connect the item to the caption.
- Begin your calibration of the y axis at zero. If the range from zero to the highest value on the axis is too great to be represented within the space of the chart, break the vertical axis by using a **slash** (/) or **zigzag** (/\/\) **graph break** near the zero point.
- Calibrate both the x and y axes using vertical (on the x axis) or horizontal (on the y axis) **hash marks,** or **tick marks,** to denote each calibration. Calibrate values of an axis at equal increments. Unequal increments distort the meaning of data.
- Keep the length of each axis should be roughly equal.
- Label both axes, placing the caption below the x axis and to the left of the y axis. Plot each point where data on the x axis intersect with data on the y axis. Connect these points to form a continuous line.
- Omit grid lines most of the time, because they are not normally needed by viewers to estimate the values of plotted items or variables.

FIGURE 7.8. Guidelines for constructing line graphs.

by the top line. Thus, the value of any coordinate on a line is determined by the distance (or difference in values) between that coordinate and the line just below it.

When constructing your surface graph, place the largest component at the base of the graph; then overlay subsequent components in descending order of size, with the smallest component plotted on the top line, as shown in Figure 7.10. Use different colors, cross-hatching, or shading to distinguish between the various layers of components.

Bar Graphs

By using *bar graphs,* you can compare quantities of different items by representing them as distinct bars of varying lengths: The longer the bar, the greater the quantitative value of the item plotted (Figure 7.11). Bar graphs are most effective in illustrating the growth and decline in quantities over time. The bars may be either vertical or horizontal but must be of the same width. Bar graphs can also represent negative values, as illustrated in the *bilateral bar graph* in Figure 7.12.

Multiple-bar graphs, such as the one shown in Figure 7.13, enable you to compare the values of more than one item in a single graph. Because multiple-bar graphs can easily become cluttered with excessive bars, you should limit your graph to no more than three separate variables (and their corresponding bars) for a each item. For example, if you wanted to compare in your multiple-bar graph the growth in your company's computer ship sales over the past five years, you would want to limit the number of items to the three chip models manufactured by your firm (e.g., Model 30286, Model 30386, and Model 30486) for each year. Moreover, because multiple-bar graphs express more than one item or quan-

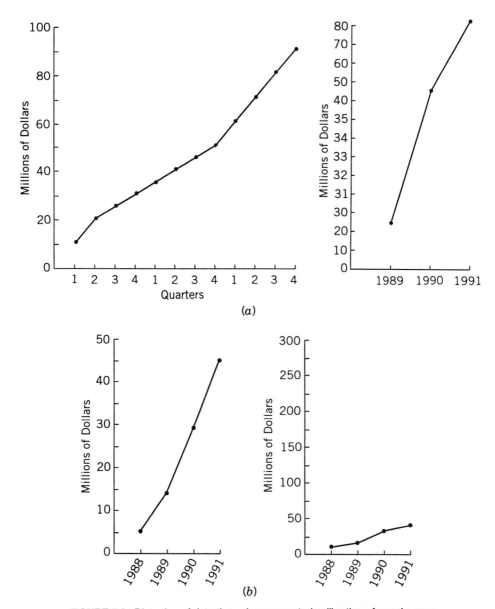

FIGURE 7.9. *Distortion of data through exaggerated calibration of* x *and* y *axes.*

tity, you should distinguish bars from one another by coding them with distinct colors, crosshatching, or shading. Identify each color and item in a legend.

To represent more than one item within each bar depicted in the graph, you might consider integrating into your presentation a *segmented bar graph* (also called a *component bar graph*). Instead of measuring only one variable within each item and bar, as done by simple bar graphs, segmented bar graphs allow you to divide each bar into subordinate components. To distinguish between items within each segmented bar, use different colors, crosshatching, or shading. Start with darker colors and shades near the base axis and

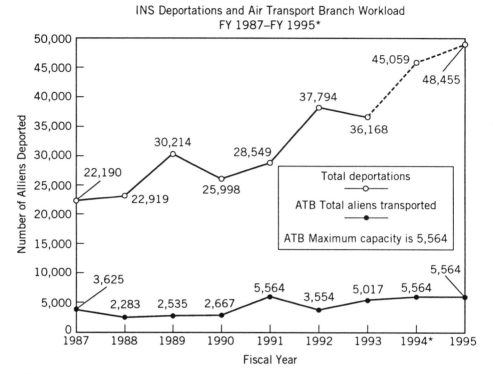

INS Deportations and Air Transport Branch Workload
FY 1987–FY 1995*

* FY94 and FY95 figures are estimates.
(*Source*: 1992 Statistical Yearbook of the Immigration and Naturalization Service,
       INS D & D Air Transport Branch Annual Reports).

FIGURE 7.10. *Surface graph.* Source: Review of Air Fleet Operations within the U.S. Department of Justice, *Management and Planning Staff, Justice Management Division, U.S. Department of Justice, Washington, D.C., 1994.*

alternate contrasting colors and shades to make each segment as distinct as possible. To avoid cluttering the graph, you should generally divide an individual bar into no more than three segments.

We commonly think of bar graphs as vertical in orientation—with the x axis serving as the graph's base and the values of the items plotted represented in vertical bars. A *horizontal bar graph*, however, uses the y axis as its base. Because its bars run horizontally across the page, horizontal bar graphs are visually effective in illustrating items whose values increase or decrease significantly in terms of percentage change, time, or distance. The bar graph in Figure 7.14 is a segmented, bilateral bar graph. When constructing your bar graph, consider the guidelines provided in Figure 7.15.

A *pictogram* is a horizontal bar graph that uses pictures, icons, or symbols instead of bars to represent numerical data and the relationships between data items. Because they are unique in design from other figures, pictograms can effectively attract viewers' attention and communicate simple information quickly, as does the sample pictogram in Figure 7.16. When constructing your pictogram, be sure to illustrate information that can be expressed simply and easily with pictures. For example, you could represent the growth in

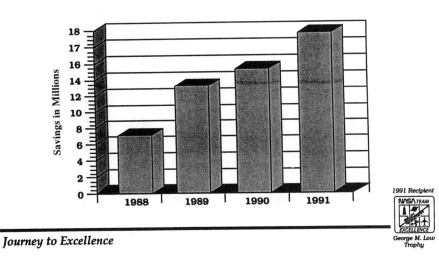

Cost Savings
(Cumulative)

Journey to Excellence

1991 Recipient
George M. Low Trophy

FIGURE 7.11. *Single-bar graph.* Source: *Grumman Technical Services, Kennedy Space Flight Center, Titusville, Florida.*

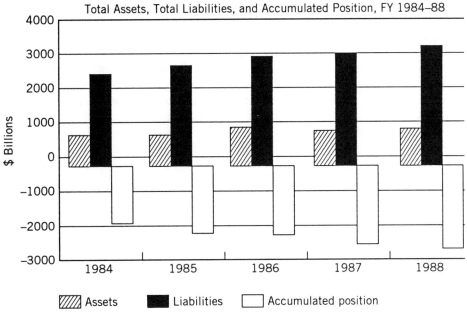

FIGURE 7.12. *Bilateral bar graph.*

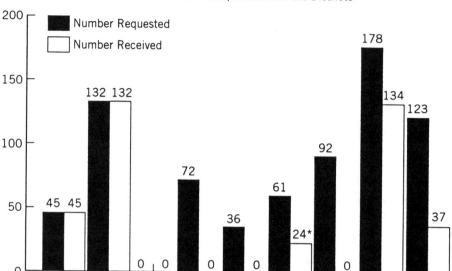

USMS Asset Seizure and Forfeiture Program
Number of Additional Positions Requested and
Received for Headquarters and the Districts

* Reprogramming of USMS budget identified an additional 39 positions
based on workload/time reporting.

USMS currently has 372 ASF positions and 140 contract (EBON) personnel. (*Source*: USMS).

FIGURE 7.13. *Multiple-bar graph.* Source: Review of Air Fleet Operations within the U.S. Department of Justice, *Management and Planning Staff, Justice Management Division, U.S. Department of Justice, Washington, D.C., 1994.*

population of City A over a five-year period with bars comprised of stick figures in a horizontal pictogram.

Because the pictogram, however, is constructed of pictures, icons, or symbols, you cannot segment it. Thus, when representing the five-year population growth of City A, for example, you would not be able to segment the rows of figures to distinguish between male and female populations. Multiple-bar pictograms also prove to be confusing to audiences. Placing three rows of figures, say, for three different cities (as you might do with bars in a multiple-bar chart) would clutter the graphic aid and invariably confuse listeners.

When designing your pictogram, consider the guidelines provided in Figure 17.17.

Word Charts

Word charts are similar to textual tables in that both graphics consist of words, not numerical data or figures. But a word chart is different from a textual table because it includes no column or row heads. It usually consists of a graphic title and a bulleted list of words, phrases, or sentences.

A word chart is most often used as a *forecasting* tool to preview key points that are about to be addressed or as a *summary* tool placed at the end of a presentation section or at the close of the presentation itself to summarize and compress into one list the most im-

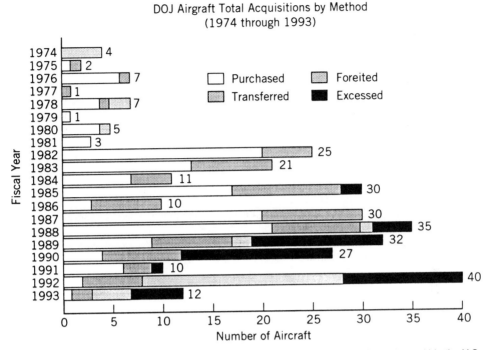

FIGURE 7.14. *Segmented horizontal bar graph.* Source: Review of Air Fleet Operations within the U.S. Department of Justice, *Management and Planning Staff, Justice Management Division, U.S. Department of Justice, Washington, D.C., 1994.*

portant information or data from that discussion. Consequently, many speakers employ word charts to emphasize the purpose and scope of their talk in the introduction of their presentations and to summarize key ideas as they move through each subtopic noted in their scope word chart. When constructing a word chart, consider these guidelines:

- Keep your phrases short, precise, and descriptive.
- Organize the key ideas in the order you addressed them.
- Use the type of bullet (e.g., hollow round, solid round, hollow square, solid square) that is most appropriate for the word, phrase, or sentence entry and use this *bulleting structure* consistently throughout your presentation. For example, you might use solid round bullets for short phrases and use solid square bullets for sentence entries.
- Use no more than two types of bullets in a presentation. Too many bullet types are distracting and can confuse viewers.

The word charts in Figure 7.18 were used as the title page and scope in a safety and health presentation by a professor at the University of North Carolina.

Pie Charts

The most commonly used charts in today's presentations are the pie, organizational, and flow chart. Perhaps the most appealing and easily interpreted graphic aid is the *pie chart*

- Identify each bar at the graph's base with an accurate, concise item caption below the *x* axis (for a vertical bar graph) or to the left of the *y* axis (for a horizontal bar graph).
- Identify the axis (*x* or *y*) representing the quantities of the dependent variable(s) with a scale caption, such as "Millions of Dollars," "Tons of Wheat Shipped," "Kilometers Flown."
- Initialize the units of measurement along the *y* axis (for vertical graphs) or *x* axis (for horizontal graphs) at zero.
- Use grid lines or figures to aid audiences in determining the exact quantities of items. Grid lines should extend out from the base axis; place figures above or within bars (as in segmented bar graphs).
- Organize the bars in a logical sequence (e.g., according to importance, chronology, numerical size, alphabetical order).
- Maintain equal distance between tick marks along the item *(x)* axis and the scale *(y)* axis to avoid distortion of measurements.
- Maintain equal space intervals (usually less than the width of a bar) between bars and keep the width of bars equal.
- Supply a legend to identify any special design effect, such as different colors, crosshatching, or shading used to differentiate bars or segments within bars.

FIGURE 7.15. *Guidelines for constructing bar graphs.*

About 5 Nurses Are Employed for Every Health Practitioner

Distribution of employment among health occupations, 1995

Health practitioners 12%

Nursing occupations 58%

Health technologists,
technicians, and assistants 11%

Therapy and rehabilitation
occupations 4%

Other health occupations 15%

FIGURE 7.16. *Pictogram.* Source: *U.S. Bureau of Labor Statistics, Washington, D.C.*

- Choose only pictures or symbols that are suitable for the information. Common symbols include coins, buildings, stick figures of people, and barrels.
- Measure the value or quantity of the item being charted in terms of units rather than by size of the symbol.
- To add precision to the pictogram, include the exact numerical value for each bar above or to the side of the bar.
- Make all units equal in size and identical in appearance to avoid distorting your presentation of the data.

FIGURE 7.17. *Guidelines for constructing pictograms.*

(Figure 7.19). As its name implies, the pie chart resembles a pie, with each slice of the pie representing a subdivision or part of the whole item. The percentage or numerical values of all the pie wedges add up to 100% of the whole's percentage or numerical value. Pie charts enable viewers to compare the constituent parts to each other but also to the whole. Consequently, they are most effective in representing simple percentage divisions of only one whole. They become confusing and thus counterproductive when cluttered with too many wedges and numbers. In constructing your pie chart, consider the guidelines provided in Figure 7.20.

Pie charts are least effective in communicating detailed data and information. For example, to convey the same information contained in the segmented bar graph in Figure 7.14, you would need 20 pie charts, one for each year plotted on the bar graph. Moreover, like tables, pie charts cannot illustrate the dynamic trends of values over a period of time.

Use of Oral Bacteria as Biological Indicators
to Evaluate Oratory Asepsis

R. W. Hackney, Jr., J. J. Crawford, and J. J. Tulis
UNC School of Public Health and School of Dentistry
Chapel Hill, North Carolina

Criteria for Evaluating Oral Bacteria as
Biological Indicators

- Number of organisms present in human saliva
- Ease of cultivation and identification
- Survival in the environment
- Occurrence in the nondental general environment
- Detectability on operatory surfaces
- Field evaluations in private dental practices

FIGURE 7.18. *Word charts.* Source: *Courtesy of Dr. Ray W. Hackney, Jr., Health and Safety Office, University of North Carolina, 1994.*

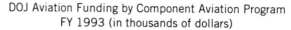

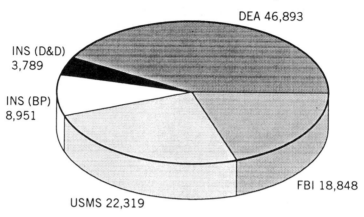

Total Funding = $100,800*

FIGURE 7.19. *Pie chart.* Source: Review of Air Fleet Operations within the U.S. Department of Justice, *Management and Planning Staff, Justice Management Division, U.S. Department of Justice, Washington, D.C., 1994.*

Rather, pie charts serve as excellent introductory graphic aids that provide viewers with a brief and attractive overview, or forecast, of more detailed, specific, or dynamic information presented elsewhere in the presentation and, typically, in the form of other graphics more effective in conveying such types of material (e.g., tables, bar charts, line charts).

Organizational Charts

An *organizational chart* is a graphic representation of an organization's hierarchy. Organizational charts use blocks and connecting lines to indicate the varying levels of authority and the relationships between the positions at different levels of an organization.

- To avoid clutter, limit the chart to no more than 5 but at least 3 wedges.
- After drawing your circle for the pie chart, begin dividing the pie at the 12 o'clock position. Start with the slice representing the largest percentage of the pie; then subdivide the remaining pie in clockwise fashion and in descending order of larger to smaller slices.
- Combine smaller or less significant divisions of the pie into a single wedge labeled "Miscellaneous" or "Other."
- Identify each of its parts by placing a label inside or to the side of each wedge. If space limitations prohibit your putting the external label next to the wedge, use a **tag line** to connect the slice with its corresponding label.
- Keep all labels horizontal for easy reading.
- Because estimating the numerical value represented by each wedge of a pie is frequently difficult for viewers, you might include that value in parentheses below the percentage.
- To distinguish between subdivisions of the pie, use different colors, crosshatching, or shading for each wedge.

FIGURE 7.20. *Guidelines for constructing pie charts.*

USMS SEIZED ASSETS DIVISION

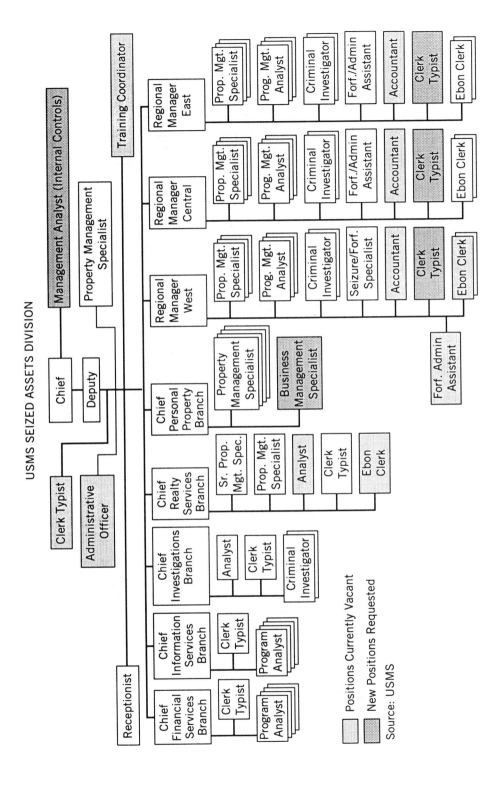

FIGURE 7.21. *Vertical organization chart. Source: A Management Review of the U.S. Marshals Service Asset Seizure and Forfeiture Program, Office of Management and Planning, Justice Management Division, U.S. Department of Justice, 1992.*

Organizational charts enable listeners to visualize the subordinate, lateral, or superior positions within an organization.

Like bar charts, organizational charts can be vertical or horizontal in structure. *Vertical organizational charts,* like the one shown in Figure 7.21, begin with top-level management positions (e.g., president, chief executive officer, chairman of the board) at the top of the chart, which then branches downward to subordinate positions. Horizontal organizational charts begin at the left and branch toward the right. As is the central rule in designing all presentation graphics, keep organizational charts simple. Presenters all too often include positions and hierarchical levels in the chart that are not relevant to the point of discussion. Include in your organizational chart only as much detail as is needed to communicate your main point.

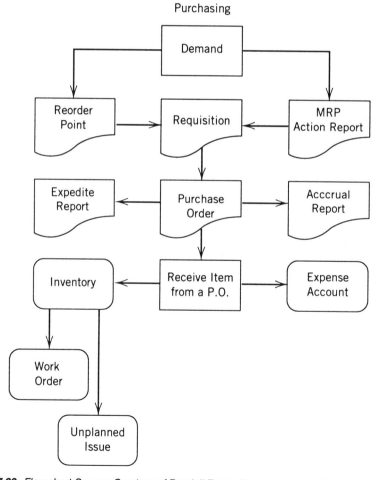

FIGURE 7.22. *Flow chart.* Source: *Courtesy of Randall Estep, Comsonics, Inc., Harrisonburg, Virginia.*

Flow Charts

Flow charts resemble organizational charts in that both present relationships between parts of a whole. However, whereas an organizational chart depicts the relatively static chain of command in an organization, a flow chart represents the "flow" of a dynamic process. Each relevant and significant step in the process is represented by a block (rectangle, square, or diamond); the flow of the process is indicated by lines and arrows connecting the blocks, as shown in Figure 7.22. Each distinct box in the sample flow chart represents a different type of action or decision. For example, rectangles normally represent constants in causation or result, such as "Demand," which begins the flow of action and decisions in Figure 7.22; printout boxes (those with a wavey line at the bottom of the box) mean that results are communicated in document (hard copy or on-line) form; oval boxes represent end results. Although not included in the flow chart provided here, the diamond box represents a decision. Depending on the decision reached by the reader or viewer ("Yes," "No," Maybe," and other), he or she will follow distinct branches that typically lead to different outcomes.

Flow charts are effective in representing an unlimited variety of processes—from depicting the logical flow of calculations in a computer accounts-receivable program, to tracing the flow of written messages in a communication audit of a major corporation. When constructing your flow chart, double-check the logical flow of the chart's sequence of steps. In addition, ensure that the chart contains no *endless loop*—a process (or routine) that has no logical end, but simply "loops" back upon itself indefinitely.

Drawings and Diagrams

A *drawing* is a representational depiction of an item, a person, or a place. It is best used to illustrate relationships that are physical rather than numerical or abstract (Figure 7.23). A *diagram* is a type of drawing that represents (1) an unconventional view of an object or process or (2) an abstraction or concept in pictorial form. It can depict not only an item but also the relationship(s) between that item, its components, and associated items. Diagrams are particularly useful in illustrating abstract relationships between ideas and in illustrating objects (or parts of objects) that could not be shown for practical reasons in realistic form.

One common type of diagram is the *exploded diagram,* which illustrates the distinct parts of a mechanism and how that object is assembled (Figure 7.24). Exploded diagrams are frequently used in technical operation, reference, and maintenance manuals. A second type of diagram is the *cutaway diagram,* which shows the components inside an object (Figure 7.25). Although they can be exhibited as a stand-alone graphic in your presentation, cutaway diagrams are often integrated into exploded diagrams.

The *procedural diagram* is closely related to the flow chart. However, whereas the flow chart illustrates a process using blocks of text, connecting lines, and flow arrows, the procedural diagram presents sequential drawings of major steps in the process, as shown in Figure 7.26. *Conceptual diagrams* illustrate the dynamic relationships between concepts that may or may not be evident or applicable to the physical world (Figure 7.27). Whereas some conceptual diagrams might represent abstract ideas or forces, the *schematic diagram* (a close cousin of the conceptuial diagram) illustrates actual physical objects or processes that, due to limiting factors (such as their complexity, size, location, and scale of operation), are best studied in pictorial form (Figure 7.28).

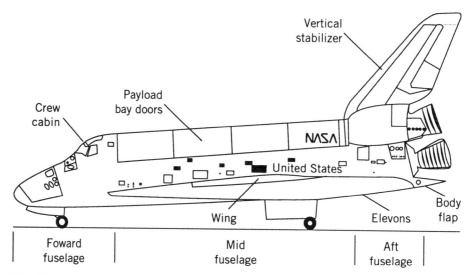

FIGURE *7.23. Drawing.* Source: *National Aeronautics and Space Administration, Washing-ton, D.C.*

Maps

When the data you wish to place in a graphic aid is geographically based, consider placing this information in a *map, or cartogram.* The maps you use should pertain to the specific geographical area (e.g., counties, cities, states, countries, continents, oceans) that is relevant to the data. Types of data commonly placed on maps, such as those shown in Figure 7.29, include population levels, types of agricultural products and production amounts, sales figures, and meteorological information.

You may integrate data into your map by actually placing the numerical values in their respective geographic area. A second choice is to use special graphic techniques—such as color, shading, or crosshatching—to distinguish between regions with different numerical values. A third approach is to integrate pictures (much as a pictogram does) into the map to represent the quantitative data relevant to the geographic region. Another alternative is to place dots on your map, with each dot representing a specific numerical value. When using special graphic techniques—such as color, shading, or crosshatching; pictures; and dots—be sure to include a legend somewhere in the graphic aid to identify the value of each of these special graphic symbols.

Color

In addition to the above guidelines, you should consider using color to make your visual aids more appealing to audiences. Color attracts viewers while also aiding audiences to better read and interpret the information contained in the visual aid itself. For example, use color-coded lines or bars in line or bar graphs to simplify viewers' task of reading the data and comparing the items contained in the graphic. The use of color graphics can significantly enhance viewer comprehension and retention of presentation material as well as en-

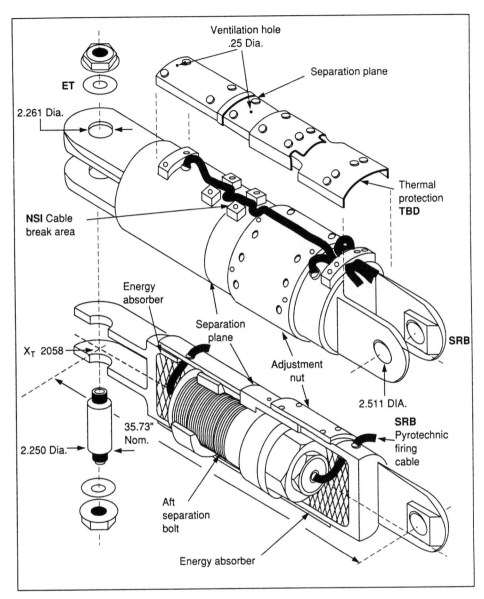

FIGURE 7.24. *Exploded diagram.* Source: *National Aeronautics and Space Administration, Washington, D.C.*

gage audiences so that they are more motivated to learn from and to participate in the presentation. When selecting colors for a visual aid, consider the guidelines provided in Figure 7.30.

Before deciding on a color scheme for your graphic, test the colors for reproducibility. Some shades may reproduce poorly when making photocopies or overhead transparencies. Also consult your local computer software shop. Computer graphics software can help you to design and produce multicolor graphic aids of exceptional quality. In addition, choose colors that are suitable to your audience's physiology. Gerald M. Murch argues that color

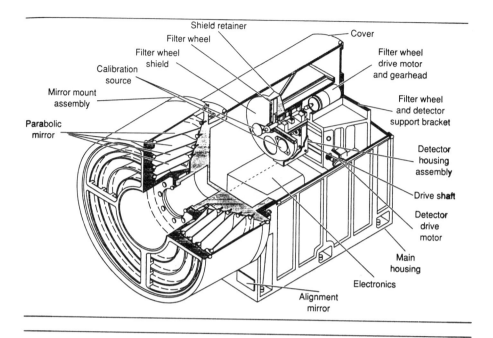

1 – pilot's cabin
2 – ventilation valves
3 – ceiling
4 – rack
5 – cloak-room
6 – toilet

7 – turbine starter
8 – center engine AI-25
9 – entrance
10 – lateral engine AI-25
11 – fuel tanks
12 – entrance door

13 – luggage compartment
14 – removable partition
15 – passenger compartment
16 – folding seats
17 – air conditioner vent
18 – weather radar

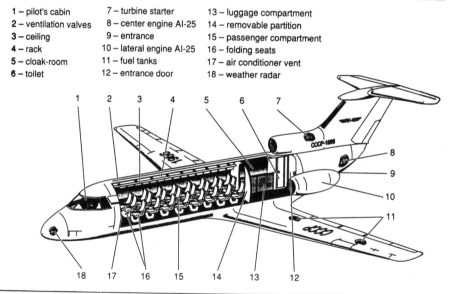

FIGURE 7.25. *Cutaway diagram.* Source: *National Aeronautics and Space Administration, Washington, D.C.*

is not a physical entity but, rather, "a sensation, like taste or smell, that is tied to the properties of our nervous system" (March, 1985). The construction of the lens, retina, rods, and cones of the human eye can make colors appear more, or less, pleasing to viewers because of the eye's receptivity to the light wavelengths reflected by the colors. Murch recommends the following guidelines when integrating color into graphics:

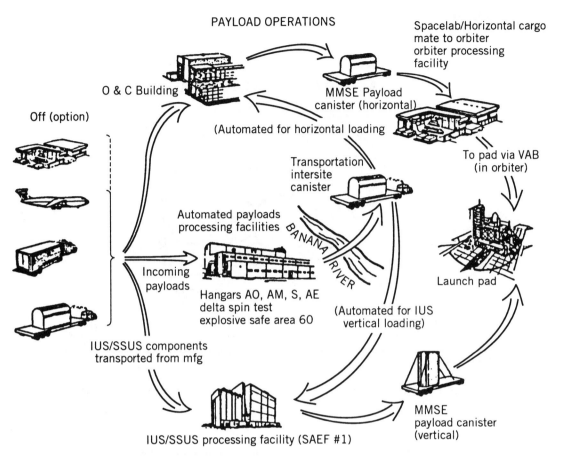

FIGURE 7.26. *Procedure diagram.* Source: *Kennedy Space Flight Center, National Aeronautics and Space Administration, Florida.*

- Don't overuse color. Use it as an attention-getter. Excessive color defeats its purpose. Use a color's brightness and saturation to attract attention.
- Utilize group-related items by using a common background color. Similar colors connote similar meanings. Use the same color or close hues of that color to imply the relationship between ideas. Colors ranging from blue to green typically seen as connoting similarity more than colors ranging from red to green.
- Link the degree of color to the importance of the idea. Likewise, coordinate the degree of change from one color to the next with the degree of difference between ideas associated with those colors. Thus, one bar green and the other red in a bar graph implies significant thematic distance (or perhaps meaning) in the items themselves.
- Avoid "the simultaneous display of highly saturated, spectrally extreme colors" (March, 1985, p. 19), such as blues and cyans, which cannot be viewed at the same time without causing viewer fatigue. Reds, oranges, yellows, and greens are not prone to creating this type of fatigue.
- Avoid colors that change in appearance with changes in ambient light. Changes in fluorescent, incandescent, and daylight intensities can alter the contrast between colors as well as the eye's sensitivity to those colors.

Communication

Management/
Employee
Dialogue

Goals and
Objectives

Morning
Meetings/
Telecons

Team
Building

Hot Line/
Open Door
Policy

Employees

Suggestion
Program

Annual
Employee
Opinion
Survey

Job
Shadowing

Newsletter

Weekly Staff
Meetings

Skip Level
Meetings

Journey to Excellence

1991 Recipient

NASA TEAM

EXCELLENCE

*George M. Low
Trophy*

FIGURE 7.27. *Conceptual diagram.* Source: *Grumman Technical Services, Kennedy Space Flight Center, Titusville, Florida.*

- Use colors whose wavelengths are widely disparate to create sharp lines where the colors meet. Avoid using blue as an edge trim color. It blurs because the eye cannot perceive the short-wavelength stimuli.
- Avoid using red or green in the outside borders of large graphics because the retina's peripheral insensitivity to these colors. Yellow and blue are good periphery colors.

What colors, then, according to Murch, go together in a multicolor graphic? Use opponent colors located at opposite sides of the color wheel—for example, red and green; blue-green and red; yellow and blue; yellow and purple-blue; purple and and green; or purple and yellow-green. Avoid mixing yellow and cyan; blue, red, and magenta; green, red, and black; green, yellow, and white; or white and cyan.

If color proves too impractical as a graphic-enhancing tool, you might try shading or crosshatching parts of such graphics as pie charts, bar graphs, maps, and diagrams with diagonal lines. For example, by varying the angle of the crosshatching, you can effectively distinguish for viewers the wedges in a pie chart or the different states on a map graphic. When using line graphs where crosshatching is not applicable, you might consider diversifying the format of the lines themselves. You could, for instance, use an unbroken line when showing the values of one item, a broken line for a second item, a dash–dot–dash line for a third, and a dot line for a fourth. A central disadvantage of both crosshatching and line diversification is their limited repertoire of variations. Graphics containing more than five or six different items make the use of crosshatching and line diversification confusing and unmanageable.

The Recommended Resistance To Ground
Is 25Ω Or Less

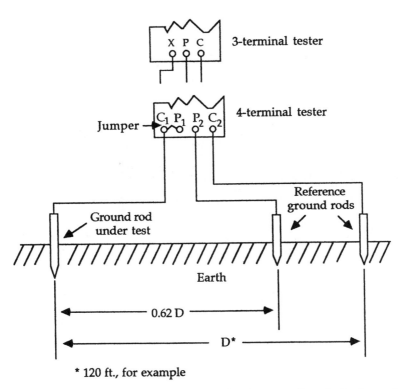

The resistance to ground of a driven grounding electrode can be measured by a ground tester in this manner.

FIGURE 7.28. *Schematic diagram.* Source: *Courtesy of Clifford Pelchart, Metretek, Inc., Melbourne, Florida.*

GUIDELINES FOR DESIGNING VISUAL AID GRAPHICS

As discussed throughout this chapter, the key to realizing some or all of the above purposes is that the graphic aid must be *functional*. Effective graphics are not decoration, but, rather, communication tools whose central function is to enhance the overall effectiveness of your presentation. Well-designed graphics, after having sparked listeners' interest, encourage an audience to delve more deeply into the data and ideas contained in your presentation.

To be functional, graphic aids must serve a specific purpose(s) in order to justify the time, expense, and expertise you invest in designing and producing them. Fully functional graphic aids are not, for instance, last-minute afterthoughts inserted as extra filler to make a presentation look more "professional"; nor are they superfluous "whistles and bells" used to dress up a presentation that is short on substance.

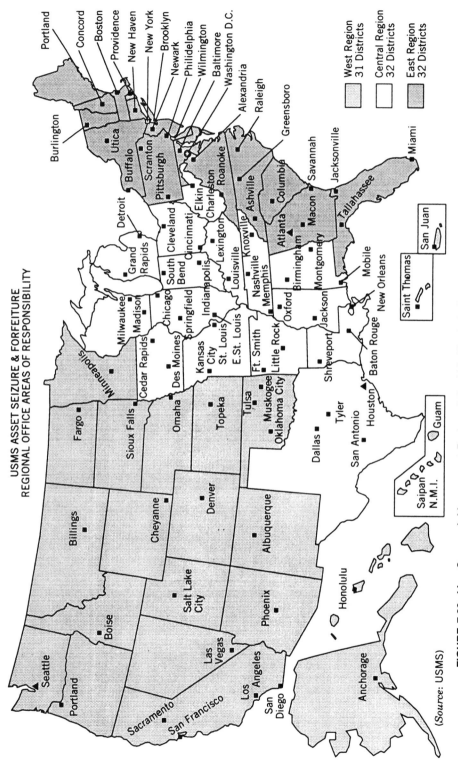

USMS ASSET SEIZURE & FORFEITURE
REGIONAL OFFICE AREAS OF RESPONSIBILITY

West Region
31 Districts

Central Region
32 Districts

East Region
32 Districts

Portland
Concord
Boston
Providence
New Haven
New York
Brooklyn
Newark
Philidelphia
Wilmington
Baltimore
Washington D.C.
Alexandria
Raleigh
Greensboro
Burlington
Utica
Buffalo
Scranton
Pittsburgh
Elkin
Charleston
Roanoke
Ashville
Columbia
Macon
Savannah
Jacksonville
Tallahassee
Atlanta
Miami
Detroit
Grand Rapids
South Bend
Cleveland
Cincinnati
Lexington
Knoxville
Birmingham
Montgomery
Mobile
Milwaukee
Madison
Chicago
Springfield
Indianapolis
Louisville
Nashville
Memphis
Oxford
New Orleans
Minneapolis
Cedar Rapids
Des Moines
Kansas City
St. Louis
E.St. Louis
Ft. Smith
Little Rock
Jackson
Baton Rouge
Fargo
Sioux Falls
Omaha
Topeka
Tulsa
Muskogee
Oklahoma City
Shreveport
Billings
Cheyanne
Denver
Albuquerque
Dallas
Tyler
San Antonio
Houston
Boise
Salt Lake City
Phoenix
Honolulu
Anchorage
Seattle
Portland
Sacramento
San Francisco
Las Vegas
Los Angeles
San Diego

Saint Thomas
San Juan

Saipan
N.M.I.
Guam

(Source: USMS)

FIGURE 7.29. *Map. Source: A Management Review of the U.S. Marshals Service Seizure and Forfeiture Program, Office of Management and Planning, Justice Management Division, U.S. Department of Justice, 1992.*

- Use only colors that stand out from each other. Choose from basic colors, such as reds, greens, yellows, and blues.
- Determine what colors and shades are most appropriate for the nature of information you are attempting to convey. Be conscious of the emotive and cultural associations that most colors carry. For example, white suggests purity, innocence, peace; gray connotes dignity, sobriety, age; black formalizes with its overtones of soberness, conservatism, death. Red communicates warmth, passion, importance, urgency, perhaps even danger, depending on the context in which it is used. Green is wholesome, natural, soothing, refreshing. Blue projects a sense of coolness, pensiveness, power, authority. Yellow is bright, positive, and sunny; orange bold, encouraging, cautionary.
- Select a foreground color only after having selected a background color, and choose foreground and background colors that are compatible.
- Use **analogous colors,** those adjacent to one another on the color wheel (e.g., red, orange, and yellow), to suggest the connection between or relatedness of items.
- Use **complementary colors,** those opposite each other on the color wheel (e.g., red and green), to suggest tension, opposition, or contradiction between items.
- Combine colors to project subtle meaning: white and blue or white and green produce a sense of cleanliness; gold, silver, black, white, navy, and red lend elegance; red, magenta, cyan, and orange evoke excitement; browns, greens, and other earth tones project the calmness and tranquility of of nature.
- Use distinctive shades of a basic color if it must be repeated. Five similar shades of blue in the same bar chart will probably confuse listeners and either delay or prevent your audience from fully grasping the visual's information and its meaning.
- Vary colors without overloading the visual aid (usually a visual can support no more than five different colors).
- Keep your use of colors consistent. For example, if you first use red as a color suggesting danger, don't use it later to invoke a warm, invigorating mood.
- Choose background colors that allow foreground colors to stand out. For example, white serves as a consistently good background color for almost any foreground color. Mixing analogous colors as foreground and background colors, however, normally produces poor results—for instance, blue on green, or red on orange.
- Avoid colors that are overused by presenters in your discipline.
- Avoid colors that make reading more difficult for specific audiences. Llight greens and reds. Viewers who are red-green colorblind cannot will not see this material. Blue and gray aid dyslexic viewers in reading graphic-based information.

FIGURE 7.30. Guidelines for using color.

From the moment you begin organizing and writing your presentation, you should identify what topics require the assistance of graphics. You might make a running list of needed graphics, their planned placement in the presentation, and the type of information each graphic should contain. After you have determined the number and types of visual aids you want to include in your presentation, take the extra time needed to design and produce visual aids that meet or, better, exceed expectations. Poorly designed or produced visuals are worse than no visual at all. When designing and using your graphics, consider the guidelines provided in Figure 7.31. A checklist for presentation visual aids and graphics is included in Appendix B. As we discuss in the following section, your graphic may also require

- Keep them simple.
- Keep them neat and uncluttered. Limit one key idea per graphic.
- Keep them accurate and clear.
- Keep them professional in appearance; obtain the help of a graphics professional if necessary.
- Maintain wide margins.
- Write in large letters and incorporate large figures that can be seen by the entire audience (e.g., 36-point type for titles and at least 18-point type for text).
- Capitalize only the first letter of the initial word in the graphic title or in constituent text to give it a typographical profile, enabling viewers to recognize individual words quickly. If you capitalize throughout, keep phrases short.
- Use short phrases. Don't simply convert a document's paragraphs of text to visual form.
- Don't right-justify the right margin of text in handouts or on transparencies; leave them ragged (unjustified). Studies show that text with ragged right margins is considerably easier to read.
- Use descriptive titles and headings that convey the central message of the graphic.
- To produce an attractive portrait effect in visual aids contain text, leave the bottom 1/4 of the page or transparency free of text.
- Keep the design symmetrical to project a balanced look.
- Use rules and frames to enhance the appearance of your graphic aids and to make it easier for viewers to access and understand the information contained in the graphics. Vertical and horizontal *rules* are lines typically used within tables to separate columns and rows of tabulated data. *Frames,* sometimes called *borders,* are horizontal or vertical lines.
- Use color wisely to attract viewers and to communicate your message forcefully.
- Keep graphics in a complementary role to your presentation text. Don't allow them to become a substitute for your discussion.
- Choose the right graphic for the kind of information or data with which you are dealing. Use figures to illustrate dynamic relationships in items. Use tables to compress data into an ordered form.
- Avoid using too many graphics. Make sure that each graphic has a clear and justifiable function in your presentation.
- Practice repeatedly with your graphics and visual aids. Rehearse such points as standing out of the way to the side of the projection screen (if using a projected graphic), locating on the graphic the exact piece of information or datum you wish to emphasize and explain, and integrating into your talk smooth transitions between graphics.
- Highlight only the most important item from a graphic and discuss its significance to your presentation problem or hypothesis. Don't force listeners to interpret the information by themselves. You're the expert. They're attending the presentation to hear your explanation of the information or data.
- Plan for emergencies. Include a back-up method for presenting your graphics if the primary method fails. For example, distribute hard copies of the most important transparencies in your presentation. Should the overhead projector malfunction (and there not be an available second projector), you can at least speak from the hard copy.

FIGURE 7.31. Guidelines for constructing and using visual aid graphics.

- a label (e.g., *Table, Figure, Exhibit*), number, and title;
- footnotes; or
- source lines.

Label, Number, and Title Visual Aids

Label and number all visual aid graphics, such as *Table 1, Table 2, Table 3* (or *Table I, Table II, Table III*); *Figure 1, Figure 2, Figure 3;* and so on. To simplify and standardize the labeling of all graphics, you might refer to all tables and figures as exhibits (e.g., *Exhibit 1, Exhibit 2,* etc.). Center the label, number, and title of a visual above the aid.

Carefully word the title of each visual so that it presents an accurate and complete picture of the visual's message. To do so, you might answer, as the following title does, the journalist's five *W*s: *who, what, where, when,* and *why:*

**The Impact of the CIA's 1985–1995 Media
Campaign Using Broadcast National Media
and Narrowcast Local Media**

While the *why* is not explicitly expressed in the title, listeners would have no difficulty inferring the purpose of the graphic: to illustrate the effectiveness of the CIA's media campaign between 1985 and 1995. If the title occupies more than one line, single space and center the remainder of the title on the following line. Titles are normally printed in lowercase letters, with the first letter of the first word and all following key words (i.e., usually all words except prepositions and conjunctions) capitalized. Unless the title is a complete sentence, include no end punctuation (e.g., period, question mark).

Footnotes and Source Lines

Use *footnotes* to append commentary to an item in the graphic aid, to explain the absence of data from your table, or to comment on a caveat or idiosyncrasy in the information or data conveyed. Refer to information to be footnoted by placing special footnote symbols immediately after the item—such as one or more asterisk (*), degree symbol (°), dagger (†), or lowercase letters $(^{a,\ b,\ c})$. As shown here, place the special footnote symbols in the superscript position for greater emphasis. Place the footnote itself two lines below the lowest part of the graphic (e.g., below the frame line of a table or the label, number, and title of a figure). Begin the footnote with a special footnote symbol on the left margin, skip two spaces, and close the notation with your brief comment. You may also footnote graphics by using the term *Note* instead of the special footnote symbols. *Note* works well when commenting on the entire graphic, rather than several specific items. Begin the footnote with *Note,* followed by a colon. Skip two spaces and insert the notation.

Use *source lines* to note the actual source of the material contained in the visual aid. Whenever including in your graphics data or information gathered from secondary sources, you must cite those sources at the bottom of the graphic aid. The following source line identifies the secondary source(s) from which the presenter collected all (or part) of the information contained in her visual aid:

Source: Office of Management and Planning Staff, U.S. Department of Justice, 1995, pp. 198–201.

Source lines typically include the name of the work's author (or sponsoring organization), year of publication, and number of the page(s) from which the information was taken.

Information that you have collected from primary research and included in your graphic does not have to be footnoted. However, you may choose to clarify the source of such material by using the following source line:

Source: Primary.

When including both footnote(s) and source line together in the same graphic, place the source *after* the footnote(s). Single space within footnotes and source lines; double space between each component and the graphic itself.

GUIDELINES FOR USING COMPUTER GRAPHICS

Application software for personal computers have significantly simplified the process of designing and producing sophisticated, professional graphic aids. The phenomenal advances in the miniaturization and speed of computer hardware (e.g., microcomputers, portable computers, laptops, briefcase computers) as well as the efficiency and assortment of software programs (e.g., word processors, text editors, graphics application programs, desktop publishing programs) since the mid-1980s have dramatically opened the world of computer graphics to serious and occasional PC users.

The greatest advantage computer graphics programs have over manually created graphics is speed. Graphics programs allow you to choose from a range of existing graphic constructs (e.g., tables, pie charts, line charts, bar charts). Some graphics software packages also allow you to create your own specialized configurations of objects or processes that are specific to your own organization, such as engineering diagrams, architectural drawings, or manufacturing and operations flow charts. Most major software development companies, such as those listed below, offer PC- and Macintosh-based graphics programs that might prove useful in creating anything from accounting tables to technical exploded diagrams:

Software	Manufacturer
Chart-Master	Ashton-Tate Corporation
Diagram-Master	
Map-Master	
Sign-Master	
Diagraph	Computer Support Corporation
Picture Perfect	
ColorLab	Computer Presentations
ColorStudio	Letraset Graphic Design Software
Digital Darkroom	Silicon Beach
Freelance	Lotus Development Corporation
Freelance Plus	
Graph Plus	Micrografx
Harvard Graphics	Software Publishing Corporation
Illustrator 88	Adobe

MacPaint	Apple
MacDraw	
MacDraft	
Microsoft Chart	Microsoft Corporation
PowerPoint	
Mirage	Zenographic
Pixie	
Overhead Express	Business and Professional Software
3mm Express	
Pagemaker	Aldus
PC Storyboard	IBM Corporation
PFS: Graph	Software Publishing Corporation
QuarkXpress	Quark, Inc.
Show Partner	Brightbill-Roberts & Co.
The Graphics Gallery	Hewlett-Packard
WordChart	Digital Research, Inc.
Ventura	Ventura Corporation

The following are central benefits of using graphics programs:

- You can learn how to use most graphics programs easily and quicky (normally in a matter of hours). Graphics software packages typically include user manuals that contain detailed information for first-time users as well as on-line tutorials that teach you step by step how to create graphics.
- You can subsequently update and modify graphics on screen and with the same level of accuracy and precision afforded you by the graphics program when you created the graphic.
- You can save yourself and your organization considerable time and cost with the fast updating and revision capabilities of graphics programs.
- Because graphics programs, used in conjunction with sophisticated laser printers, can produce hard copy or overhead transparencies that are as good or better in appearance than manually produced graphics (and in a fraction of the time), you can significantly speed production time for graphics while also lowering production costs.
- You can choose from an attractive assortment of colors and hues for use in your graphics. Many graphics programs will offer far more colors than are supported by most printers. For this reason, the purchase of a more advanced printer (e.g., laser or ink jet printers) is a wise investment for the manager committed to producing sophisticated, multicolor graphics on paper or transparencies.
- You can select from the program's assortment of special layout features, including different type sizes, fonts, and various thickness of rules, frames, bars, and clip art.
- You can produce three-dimensional effects in your graphic aids by using shading, overlays, changes in scale, and other perspective-enhancing techniques.
- You can design complex models of objects, processes, or systems (e.g., the planning of production, costs, marketing and sales) and—using the speed, power, and memory of the computer—forecast and monitor the condition of those models when different variables are inserted into the formula.

Despite the advantages of speed, accuracy, and advanced graphics capabilities offered by graphics application software, however, computer-generated graphics are not without their drawbacks. Although the prices of computer hardware and accompanying graphic software continue to fall with the continual arrival of new and less expensive computer technologies, investment in a quality graphics system (both hardware and software) can still be expensive. Second, once surrounded by an appealing array of computer-supported graphics capabilities, you may be tempted to overload your presentation with graphics. Finally, with the advanced capabilities of graphics software, you may attempt to integrate too many special features into your graphics, thus cluttering them and reducing their effectiveness. Keep in mind that your use of a graphic aid, and each component within it, must be justified by how effectively that graphic performs its specified function in the presentation.

SUGGESTED READING

Carlsen, R. D., and West, D. L. (1977). *Encyclopedia of business charts.* Englewood Cliffs, NJ: Prentice-Hall.

Dickinson, G. C. (1973). *Statistical mapping and the presentation of statistics.* New York: Crane and Russak.

Cleveland, W. S., and McGill, M. E. (Eds.). (1988). *Dynamic graphics for statistics.* Pacific, CA: Wadsworth & Brooks/Cole Advanced Books & Software.

Curtice, B., and Stringer, S. (1991). Visualizing information planning. *Computerworld,* pp. 63, 66.

Fradkin, B. M. (1975). Effectiveness of multi-image presentations. *Journal of Educational Technology,* **5,** pp. 53–68.

Fritzen, J. (1991). Projecting the best image: Effective graphics help grab an audience's attention. *AGRI Marketing,* pp. 91–92.

Glau, G. R. (1986). *Business graphics with the IBM PC/XT/AT.* Homewood, IL: Dow Jones-Irwin.

Graphic Design. (1979). Rochester, NY: Eastman Kodak.

Green, R. E. (1984, Oct.). The persuasive properties of color. *Marketing Communications,* October, pp. 50–54.

Hoadley, E .D. (1990). Investigating the effects of color. *Communications for the Association for Computing Machinery,* **33,** pp. 120–125, 129.

Johnson, V. (1989). Picture-perfect presentations. *Training & Development Journal,* **43**(5), pp. 45–47.

Johnson, V. (1990). Desktop presentation software. *Successful Meetings,* December, pp. 118–122.

Johnson, V. (1991). Visual literacy. *Successful Meetings,* January, pp. 97–99.

Mason, S. (1989). Seeing red? Feeling blue? *Data Training,* December, pp. 28–29.

Making the most of charts: An ABC of graphic presentation. (1960). New York: American Management Association, Finance Division.

McComb, G. (1988). *Executive guide to PC presentation graphics.* New York: Bantam Books.

Meilach, D. Z. (1990). *Dynamics of presentation graphics.* Dow Jones-Irwin.

Miller, S. (1990). One simple device helps dyslexics to read better. *Los Angeles Times,* December 14, E24.

Murch, G. M. (1985). Using color effectively: Designing to human specifications. *Technical Communication,* fourth quarter, pp. 14–20.

Nies, J. I., and Tas, R. F. (1991). How to add visual impact to your presentations. *The Cornell H.R.A. Quarterly,* **32**(1), pp. 46–51.

Osgood, W. C. (1985). *Using business graphics: Lotus 1-2-3 on the DEC Rainbow.* Burlington, MA: Digital Press.

Planning and producing slide programs. (1975). Rochester, NY: Eastman Kodak.

Pratt, D., and Ropes, L. (1978). *35-mm slides: A manual for technical presentations.* Tulsa: American Association for Petroleum Geologists.

Schaefer, J. H., and Bradshear, M. A. (1989). *Speech communication in business and the professions.* Belmont, CA: Wadsworth.

Schmid, C. F., and Schmid, S. E. (1979). *Handbook of graphics presentation,* 2nd ed. New York: John Wiley & Sons.

Seiler, W. J. (1971). The effects of visual material on attitudes, credibility, and retention. *Speech Monographs,* 38, pp. 331–334.

Spear, M. E. (1969). *Practical charting techniques.* New York: McGraw-Hill.

Truran, H. C. (1975). *A practical guide to statistical maps and diagrams.* London: Heinemann Educational Books.

Tufti, E. R. (1983). *The display of quantitative information.* Cheshire, CT: Graphics Press.

Vardaman, G. T. *Making successful presentations.* New York: AMACOM.

Wilder, C. (1990). *The presentations kit: 10 steps for selling your ideas!* New York: John Wiley & Sons.

Zelazny, G. (1985). *Say it with charts: The executive's guide to successful presentations.* Homewood, IL: Dow Jones-Irwin.

Part III

Managing the Logistics of Your Presentation

8

Managing Presentation Logistics

Regardless of whether you are lucky enough to have a coordinator within your organization who is responsible for handling the logistics surrounding your presentation, it is essential that you review personally the arrangements for your talk. Remember that, regardless of who forgot to do what, *you* are the one who will receive the criticism if the logistics are not properly completed. And it is *your* presentation that will suffer as a result.

When planning or reviewing the logistics of your presentation, be sure to consider the following:

- Room seating
- Visual aids
- Projectors and screens
- Microphones and lecterns
- Room lighting, acoustics, and safety
- Audience comfort, your own (presenter) health, and the inevitable last-minute details (which should not be *last-minute*).

ROOM SEATING

Providing listeners with a comfortable environment in which to listen and respond to your presentation can significantly enhance the effectiveness of your talk. Whether or not you have control over the seating arrangement for your audience, you should be aware of the advantages and disadvantages associated with each of the most common seating patterns so that you can modify your presentation delivery or content to fit the seating configuration:

- Auditorium
- Classroom
- Auditorium classroom
- Herringbone arrangement
- Horseshoe
- Round-table
- Round-table workshop

Auditorium. The auditorium is useful when you want to address a large number of people in a formal setting (Figure 8.1). Auditoriums are normally equipped with large projection screens on which you can project very large images that can easily be seen by all viewers. The central disadvantage to presenting in auditoriums is its size. For small audiences, the auditorium is too large, and its fixed, rank-and-file, stage-directed seating does not make for a personal workshop environment in which viewers can easily interact. The auditorium arrangement realistically allows group interaction only during the question-and-answer period.

Classroom. The classroom provides listeners with tables or desks on which they can write—a key advantage when you want to encourage audience participation in the form of written responses (Figure 8.2). However, because tables are directed toward the front of the room, classrooms are too structured for informal workshopping with listeners. Like the auditorium arrangement, the arrangement pattern realistically allows group interaction only during the question-and-answer period. Also, classrooms can pose a problem for presentations that incorporate a projected visual aid. The projector should only be placed at the rear of the room and operated by a remote control. If placed at the front of the room, the projector will obstruct the view of some listeners.

Auditorium Classroom. The auditorium classroom includes tables or desks arranged in an angular semicircle pattern which requires that listeners only turn their heads slightly to examine both presenter and visual aid (Figure 8.3). This arrangement shares a key advantage with the classroom pattern, in that the audience can use the table or desk to take

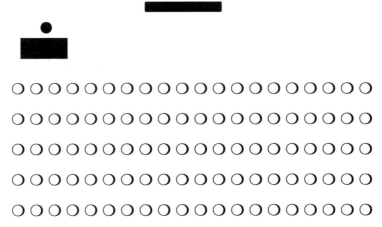

FIGURE 8.1. *Auditorium arrangement.*

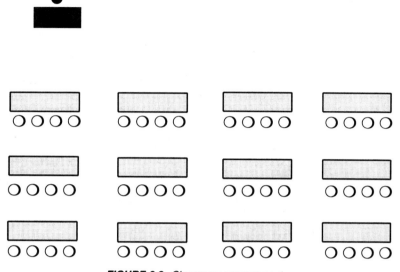

FIGURE 8.2. Classroom arrangement.

notes or to complete, say, a presentation exercise or survey. Like the classroom and auditorium, however, this arrangement does not encourage audience interaction.

Herringbone. The herringbone pattern improves listeners' comfort when viewing the presenter and visual aids even more than does the auditorium classroom (Figure 8.4). It has the added advantage over the auditorium classroom in that its tables or desks are not

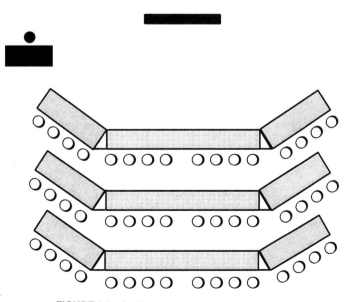

FIGURE 8.3. Auditorium classroom arrangement.

FIGURE 8.4. Herringbone arrangement

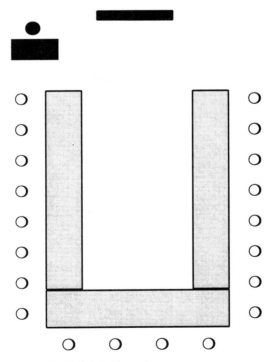

FIGURE 8.5. Horseshoe arrangement.

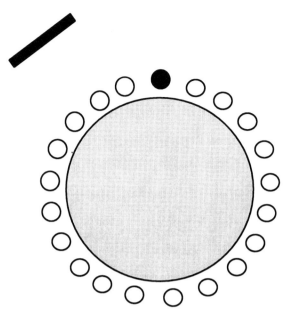

FIGURE 8.6. *Round-table arrangment.*

configured into long lines of continuous table tops. Consequently, the pattern encourages workshopping in small groups of listeners.

Horseshoe. The horseshoe arrangement is best used when you want listeners to face each other or to have an unobstructed view of each other's faces (Figure 8.5). This pattern works well in encouraging small-group discussions. The obvious limitation is that it is inappropriate for large audiences.

Round-Table. The round-table arrangement places listeners in a circle around a large (or small) table (Figure 8.6). Each person has a writing space and an unobstructed view of each member in the group. Like the horseshoe pattern, the round-table arrangement is best suited for small-group discussions and interactive sessions. Moreover, the arrangement is particularly effective in promoting workshop environments. The round-table, however, can make viewing visual aids difficult because the audience must turn in their seats or crane their necks to look around other heads to see the aid.

Round-Table Workshop. The round-table workshop configuration, a modification of the round-table arrangement, is most useful in facilitating small-group workshops in which participants can exchange ideas (Figure 8.7). However, like the round-table pattern, this arrangement can make it difficult for listeners to view a statically placed visual aid.

VISUAL AIDS

Visual aids are central to the success of a presentation. When presenting with visual aids, be certain to address these logistical guidelines:

- Make certain that all visual aids are at the presentation site and that you have access to them.

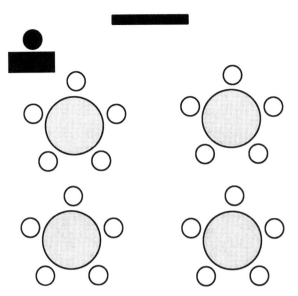

FIGURE 8.7. *Round-table workshop arrangement.*

- Set up the visual aids early and make any necessary alterations.
- Arrange the visual aids well beforehand.
- Stand out of viewers' line of sight to the visual aid.
- Be prepared with the right type of marking instrument (e.g., chalk, felt-tip pen, grease pen, pencil, pointer). You might also bring an extra note pad for yourself.
- Prepare presentation media such as graphics on chalkboards or flip charts before the presentation.
- Check that there is enough paper on the flip-chart easel. Keep an extra pad of paper to the side in case you run out during mid-presentation (or keep a backup easel handy).
- Come with extra copies of your handouts than you think you'll need for the size of audience expected. Also arrange for someone to distribute them at the appropriate time. Keep a master copy of the handouts in case you need to make additional copies.
- Keep master copies of your presentation script and supplements (e.g., transparencies, slides, handouts) in case you lose the presentation-ready copies. You might need to a last-minute rush to the nearby copy center.
- Organize and number your overhead transparencies and place them next to the projector.
- Place slides in the correct order.
- Don't show a visual aid until you're ready to use it. You can cover the flip-chart visuals with a blank page or title page. Don't place a transparency on the projector until you're ready to discuss it. Keep samples or models out of sight until their introduction into the presentation.
- Wait until the presentation is over and most of your audience has left before removing and storing visual aids.

PROJECTORS AND SCREENS

Although projectors (e.g., overhead, opaque, computer display screens) are standard visual aids for professional presentations, you might pay special attention to the following guidelines to ensure that your preparation for the presentation focuses sufficient attention on these aids:

- Know how to use the projector and its parts (e.g., remote control, focus, forward and reverse controls). Know how to replace the projector's bulb.
- Bring with you the pedestrian but essential tools of the visual aids trade: extra projector bulb, extra extension cord, converter plug, extra blank transparencies, and masking tape.
- Locate the outlet closest to your projector. Ensure that the extension cord to that outlet offers no safety hazard to your audience.
- Identify an area within the room in which you can move freely without obstructing your audience's view of the projected image.
- Place the projector so that it does not obstruct the view of your audience.
- Add distance between loud projectors and your audience to prevent fan noise from interfering with listeners' hearing you.
- Ensure that the screen is large enough to produce an image that can be seen by all viewers.
- Keep the bottom of the screen high enough off the floor so that text or graphics projected low on the screen are visible anywhere in the room.
- Close drapes or blinds to eliminate glare on the screen.
- Check that the screen's surface is appropriate for the type of visual aid that you plan to use. Screens with a matte finish are fine for all projected images, but screens with glass-beaded surfaces are best used with slide, computer, or videotape projection.

MICROPHONES AND LECTERNS

Presenters all too often, and unnecessarily, suffer embarrassment not because of their inexperience in using high-tech gadgets but, rather, because of low-tech widgets that we take for granted—until we realize too late that we haven't learned the tricks of operating them. As a result, presenters, for example, who have difficulty moving about the stage or who fumble about with a microphone that projects only enough sound to reach the first few rows of the audience can markedly reduce the credibility and effectiveness that a sound presentation script and impressive visual aids would otherwise merit. When working with microphones or lecterns, consider these guidelines:

- Check the microphone to see that it's working. Ask someone to stand at the back of the room before the presentation to test the carry of your voice. Remember that sound travels better in an empty room; consequently, you might have to increase volume to a room filled with people.
- Don't put your face too close to the microphone. By speaking about six inches away from the microphone, you can avoid your *p*s sounding like popping corn.

- Don't move out of the microphone's range.

- Avoid the whine of *feedback* by keeping the microphone volume at an appropriate level. You might arrange for someone to monitor the sound to prevent your voice from "feeding back" into the microphone.

- Use a wireless remote microphone if available. This eliminates the chance of your tripping over the microphone cable. If a remote microphone is not available, you might choose instead either a hand-held microphone or a miniature microphone that clips conveniently to your lapel or collar.

- If you have to clear your throat, do so *before* the presentation. If during your talk you find your throat getting itchy, drink from a glass of water (you should have placed one near the lectern before the presentation) or cover your mouth and turn your head away from the microphone as you clear your throat.

- Keep the lectern relatively close to the first row of listeners. A distance of more than 10 feet is too much, producing a physical as well as a psychological barrier between you and your audience.

- Adjust the lectern to your height or arrange for a step platform concealed behind the lectern so that you can see your audience and so that they can see your face, shoulders, and chest.

- Determine your route to and from the lectern beforehand. This prevents your getting confused or, worse, tripping over unseen obstacles getting to the stage.

- Move about the stage. Don't stay behind the lectern during the entire presentation; don't use it as a wall to separate you from your audience.

- When stepping out from behind the lectern, make certain that you *step out*. More than one presenter has caught the toe of his or her shoe on the inside corner of the lectern.

ROOM LIGHTING, ACOUSTICS, AND SAFETY

Room lighting, acoustics, and safety are important factors in achieving a completely successful and professional presentation. First, you should make sure that you have enough lighting in the room and that you know how to adjust the lighting. Individual dimmer switches for different sections of the room are most useful for tailoring the lighting intensity for specific phases of the presentation. For example, you might keep the front of the room where the projection screen is darker than the rear of the room. This gradual lighting provides enough light away from the screen to encourage note-taking while also ensuring that the projected image is visible everywhere in the room.

You should also test room acoustics to ensure that there are no acoustically "dead" spots in the room. Any room, especially large auditoriums, can have corners where a presenter's voice has difficulty reaching. Identify these dead spaces and try to arrange seating away from them. You can also reduce (or eliminate) distracting room noise by selecting low-noise projectors and by closing windows and doors leading to outside streets, corridors, or other meeting rooms.

Finally, ensure that the presentation site is safe for your audience as well as for yourself:

- Tape loose electrical wires and cables to the floor.

- Ensure that the room is not filled over its safe capacity, as determined by the local fire marshal.

- Check for room emergency exits so that, if needed, you can direct the audience to safety. Ensure that these exits are not blocked by such obstacles as extra seats, tables, or boxes.
- Should an emergency arise, know how to contact police, fire, and medical professionals for immediate assistance.

AUDIENCE COMFORT, PRESENTER HEALTH, AND LAST-MINUTE DETAILS

To enhance the ergonomic comfort of your listeners, consider these guidelines:

- Keep the room temperature comfortable, usually between 68 and 72 degrees Fahrenheit.
- Ensure that the room is well ventilated. Know how to control heating or air conditioning.
- Ensure that the seats themselves are comfortable and that you have extra seating in case more listeners show up than expected,
- Arrange for the room to be a nonsmoking area. You might reserve a room outside the meeting room for smoking.

You'll invest weeks and even months of hard work into preparing your presentation script and visual aids. But you also need to consider your own physical condition, which invariably influences your mental preparation. The following guidelines are a starting point for addressing this part of your presentation planning:

- Stay fit. Exercise months in advance of the presentation to raise your stamina and self-concept.
- Eat well.
- Get enough sleep.
- Establish self-confidence in your ability to present successfully by practicing your presentation repeatedly. Know your presentation script inside-out until you can visualize your delivering each of its parts and integrating into your talk all accompanying visual aids.

Then there are the last-minute details that should not be left to the last minute, such as

- travel arrangements (for you or for members of your audience) for off-site presentations (e.g., airline tickets, ground transportation, hotel reservations)
- confirmation of the hour and location of presentation as well as the number (perhaps also names) of attendees
- distribution of invitations (e.g., via memo, letter, e-mail, phone call, word of mouth) to your audience in plenty of time before the presentation
- presentation publicity
- registration for yourself or attendees (for conference presentations) or confirmation of attendees (for on-site presentations within your organization)
- preparation of presentation packages and name tags (or tend cards) for speakers or audience members

- "food for thought" (e.g., catered beverages and snacks between sessions, pre-presentation breakfasts, lunches, dinners).

The fact that these aspects of presentation logistics are commonly referred to as "last-minute" details may well indicate the insufficient attention we pay to them. Don't leave these points to the last minute. Plan and review all your logistics earlier than you think necessary to prevent last-minute problems from reducing the effectiveness of your presentation.

SUGGESTED READING

Andrews, J. R. (1979). *Essentials of public communication.* New York: John Wiley & Sons.

McVey, G. F. (1988). The planning and ergonomic design of technical presentation rooms. *Technical Communication,* first quarter, pp. 23–30.

Woelfle, R. M. (Ed.). (1975). *A guide for better technical presentations.* New York: IEEE Press.

PART IV

Delivering Your Presentation

9

Establishing a Professional Delivery Style

The delivery of your presentation is the moment of truth. You can waste significant time spent in researching and preparing your presentation if you cannot draw upon your oral communication skills, poise, and presence to present the information effectively. The major components in the delivery phase of your presentation are as follows:

- Practicing your presentation
- Establishing an effective stage presence
- Maintaining your poise
- Managing your audience effectively
- Gathering and analyzing audience feedback.

The manner in which you present your message is essential to delivering information and its meaning successfully. To deliver presentations effectively, you must commit to and be genuinely enthusiastic about sharing your message with your audience. Our discussion of these major components of the delivery phase will help you to do just this.

PRACTICING YOUR PRESENTATION

A common weakness in many presentations is that speakers, while knowing what they want to say, are not sufficiently prepared before the presentation in *how* they are going to say it. Rehearsing your presentation allows you to do the following:

- Improve your delivery skills
- Practice how you can smoothly integrate each visual aid so that it is introduced at the most efficacious point in the presentation
- Expand your knowledge and understanding of the presentation content
- Time the length of the presentation as well as its pace and assess where it might be shortened or expanded

- Identify possible problem areas in the presentation and make any last-minute adjustments to such presentation components as content, organization, or visual aids
- Increase confidence in yourself.

Begin practicing early. If possible, practice over a number of days to give intervals of time betwen practice seessions. Read the text (whether in presentation outline, note outline, or script form) as many times as you need until the central points become second nature. Practice presenting without the outline. Learn your speech point by point, not verbatim, unless you are using the memorization speech format. Spend extra time practicing beginnings and endings. It's essential that your get off to a good start and that you end well, leaving listeners with a positive impression of you and your message.

Practice with the presentation outline and make complete presentations, not parts of the speech, to check the continuity, coherence, and unity of the whole; otherwise you'll get bogged down and the presentation will seem fragmented to you. Practice your presentation as many times as needed until you are comfortable with how you plan to deliver the information to your audience. If possible, practice in the same room where the presentation will be held. Rehearsing the presentation in front of someone whose background and interests closely match those of the target audience can also provide you with valuable ideas on how the delivery could be improved. Practicing in front of a mirror and taping yourself can also help you to identify and modify delivery flaws. Enunciate and pronounce correctly difficult words, and work through *entire* presentation to get a realistic feel for its flow and length. Videotaping yourself enables you to see your delivery as your viewers will. This preparation technique offers significant learning possibilities that allow you to modify ineffective delivery approaches and mannerisms.

Remember also to practice incorporating visual aids into the stream of text. Simulate as much as you can the actual presentation conditions, including the same type of lectern, placement of visual aids, size of room, placement of light switch, and arrangement of of seating. Moreover, consider how you might improve voice, body movement, gestures, expressions, posture, and pauses as strategies to emphasize ideas or to create a transition between ideas. Finally, practice, but don't overpractice. Be sure to maintain a fresh attitude and a sense of spontaniety to the information. If you're bored with the presentation, you're bound to bore your audience.

ESTABLISHING AN EFFECTIVE STAGE PRESENCE

The human element is significantly more critical in communicating effectively through oral presentations than through written documents. Your poise and appearance, body movement, and voice are central components of the presentation delivery and can greatly affect the audience's perception of both you and the information you present.

Voice

Your voice is perhaps the most important delivery tool for clearly and persuasively communicating your message. It is an important means of building and projecting a credible image—*ethos*—that confirms the expertise and confidence behind your accurate and reliable message. A calm and friendly voice implicitly tells listeners that you are comfortable with what you are saying, that you believe in your message, and that they should believe in it too. Your voice is also crucial in keeping listeners engaged in your message. While a slow monotone can quickly put listeners to sleep, a moderately paced and modulated voice can just as quickly draw and hold an audience's attention through even the most complex discussions. Although most of us do not have the resonant voice or oratorical skills of, say, a Franklin Roosevelt, John F. Kennedy, Martin Luther King, or Margaret Thatcher, we can significantly enhance the clarity, attractiveness, and persuasive power of our voice by better managing the following:

- Volume
- Rate
- Pitch
- Pronunciation
- Enunciation

Volume. Voice volume poses a problem for a significant percentage of presenters. About 32 percent of respondents in our survey identified volume as a major barrier to presenting effectively.[1] The volume, or intensity, of your voice should be sufficient so that all your listeners can hear your message, but not so loud that it overpowers your audience. Moreover, you should use the volume of your voice as a part of your presentation style to emphasize key points and to illustrate your conviction in your message, as the guidelines in Figure 9.1 describe.

Rate. The rate, or tempo, at which you speak can directly affect how much of your message your audience hears and comprehends. As in managing your voice volume, you should vary the rate of your presentation to keep listeners' interest and increase their understanding of your message. In addition, by modulating your voice rate throughout the presentation, you can emphasize key points or distinguish central points from subordinate ones, as explained in the guidelines in Figure 9.2.

Short presentations invite voice rate problems. Regardless of how much information you feel is vital to the presentation, don't cram so much material into your report that you are forced to spit the message out in machine-gun fashion. Slow down. Avoid a rate so slow that listeners' attention wanes, but let your audience hear the full message. A well-placed pause when discussing key ideas can also give an audience just enough time to digest the significance of your message.

Pitch. The pitch, or tone, refers to the voice's lows and highs. Consider the natural intonation pattern of your individual voice—that is, the ups and downs of your voice, the highs and lows, much like a musical scale. You can alter pitch to enhance the character of your voice, as explained in the guidelines in Figure 9.3.

Pronunciation and Enunciation. Often overlooked by inexperienced or unprepared speakers, mispronunciation can be a major obstacle in effectively communicating your message. First, mispronunciation prevents listeners from immediately recognizing the mispronounced word(s), if they can recognize it at all. This makes the listener's task of comprehending your message more difficult.

---

[1] From our recent survey discussed in "Oral Communication in Business and Industry: Results of a Survey on Technical, Scientific, and Managerial Presentations," *Journal of Technical Writing and Communication*, **24**(2), pp. 161–180.

- Speak loudly enough so that all can hear. This means that you must consider such influences as room size, room resonance, residual murmur of the audience's whispering, car noise from from nearby streets, and the noise of air conditioning or heating. Speak to the farthest corner of the room.
- Don't overwhelm an audience with too much voice.
- Breath regularly. Don't run out of breath due to nervousness. Consciously breathe every 10 or 12 words, but try to breathe naturally—not from your throat but from your chest. Avoid too many deep breaths. Practice breathing breaks at ends of sentences, key phrases, and emphasized points.
- Modulate the loudness of your voice to emphasize points. Use varying degrees of voice volume as a dramatic device. Obviously, speaking in louder tones draws listeners' attention to key points. But you can also emphasize parts of your message by modifying your voice volume. A sudden drop in voice intensity, for example, can spark an audience's curiosity—as if you were asking, "Why am I talking so softly now?" This variety in loudness adds character—color and texture—to your presentation.
- Use a microphone if needed. But be sure you know how to use it. Test it first. Make sure it works. When using it, place the microphone about six inches from your mouth, not right against it, which will make your *p*s sound like the popping of corn. Finally, if moving about the lectern, watch the microphone cord; more than one presenter has tripped over it.
- When practicing for your presentation, audiotape yourself to assess and, if necessary, modify your voice quality. Also, before the presentation, practice your voice in the presentation room to evaluate how your voice projects in that particular room. Make voice adjustments as needed.

FIGURE 9.1. *Guidelines for managing voice volume.*

Second, listeners who miss a word or phrase due to the speaker's poor pronunciation are often distracted enough to miss the entire idea expressed in that sentence. In addition to reducing listener comprehension, poor pronunciation erodes speaker credibility. From an audience viewpoint, speakers who do not take the time to check the pronunciation of words in their presentations may also fail to double-check the accuracy of the information being presented. Ensure that your listeners hear your message. If you aren't sure how to pronounce a word, look it up in a dictionary. If you don't know how to pronounce someone's name, ask a colleague of yours or of that person. The following list includes some of the more commonly mispronounced words:

- Avoid one-speed presentations. They can bore listeners, and bored listeners whose minds wander tend to miss key points in a presentation.
- Speak more slowly when conveying more important or technical information. A slower voice rate emphasizes ideas by giving the audience time to hear and comprehend the complete message. A fast voice rate used to communicate technically complex information can significantly reduce audience comprehension of your message.
- Use pauses as a type of oral punctuation to emphasize key ideas.
- Although perhaps effective when summarizing well-established points, a fast voice rate is normally inappropriate when communicating information that is new to listeners.

FIGURE 9.2. *Guidelines for managing voice rate.*

- Maintain a pitch that is natural to you. Use pitch to build a speaking character and a personality, and use for emphasis. A conversational tone is typically the most effective.
- Avoid a monotone pitch. As with voice volume and rate, modulate your pitch to keep listeners interested not only in your voice but, more important, in your message.
- Let your enthusiasm show in your tone. If you are energetic about the information expressed in your presentation, the enthusiasm noted in the pitch of your voice will draw listeners into the discussion at hand.
- Monitor your pitch to avoid tonal extremes. Strong emotions, such as nervousness, can significantly raise the pitch of your voice and reduce your effectiveness as a speaker. Consequently, always be vigilant of your voice's pitch. When you sense yourself becoming emotional because of presentation stress, an emotionally charged subject that you're presenting, or some other reason, modulate your pitch until you compose yourself; otherwise your presentation and your credibility might suffer from the emotion that you project.
- When practicing for your presentation, audiotape yourself to assess—and, if necessary, modify—your voice pitch.

FIGURE 9.3. *Guidelines for managing voice pitch.*

Correct Pronunciation	Incorrect Pronunciation
ask	ast, ax
ath-lete	ath-a-lete
hun-dred	hun-derd
i-dea	I-dear
go-vern-ment	goo-ver-ment
li-brar-y	li-berry
nu-cle-ar	nu-cu-ler
pic-ture	pitch-er

Enunciation is the articulation of words—the way in which you clearly, or unclearly, speak a word or phrase. While a speaker may pronounce a word correctly, he or she may not enunciate it properly. Poor enunciation, as with faulty pronunciation, can prevent listeners from hearing and understanding your message. Achieving clear, crisp enunciation takes practice. Listed in Figure 9.4 are some fundamental, but too often ignored, guidelines toward better enunciation.

Dialects, a speech pattern of a particular region or ethnic culture of a country, are often the cause of mispronunciation and poor enunciation. Dialects are not intrinsically disadvantageous to a presenter in communicating clearly to audiences. In fact, any dialect can add character and personality to a presentation. Try audiotaping yourself during your practice sessions. If you possess a heavy dialect that lends itself to poor pronunciation or enunciation, you may need voice training to modify your accent while maintaining the color and texture of the dialect. Be aware that some audiences may have preferences for certain dialects, such as the Midwestern, Southern, Northeastern, or British. If you're not lucky enough to have an accent preferred by a particular audience, concentrate on delivering a clear and convincing presentation. The strength of your delivery and message should demand all your listeners' attention, leaving little time for them to ponder your accent.

- Don't mumble. Open your mouth. This has two benefits. You speak more clearly, and your jaws muscles will relax, making you feel more comfortable as a result.
- Don't bite off the ends of words. Complete the entire word. Watch out for those words that end in consonants; they're commonly chewed at the end (e.g., "gimme" for "give me," "dontcha" for "don't you," "Haryall?" for "How are you all?").
- Don't round off your *t*s into *d*s (e.g., "liddle" for "little").
- Don't crunch your *th*s into *d*s (e.g., "dem" instead of "them").
- Don't muddle through diphthongs (e.g., "yur" for "your").
- When practicing your presentation, audiotape yourself to assess—and, if necessary, modify—your enunciation.

FIGURE 9.4. *Guidelines for better enunciation.*

Body Movement

How you move during the presentation can communicate to the audience a great deal about you as well as the message you're trying to convey. By the eye contact you maintain with your audience, facial expressions, gestures, and posture, you can strengthen the content of your presentation. On the other hand, ineffective body language, such as poor movement, lack of eye contact, and scared expressions, can ruin a presentation. Body language can help you to do the following:

- Project your enthusiasm toward the topic (and thus encourage the same enthusiasm and attention from your listeners)
- Expend some nervous energy and relax you
- Illustrate your confidence in the importance of your message as well as your ability to express that message effectively
- Capture, or recapture, an audience's attention
- Emphasize central points in your message
- Build a sense of goodwill and mutual respect between the audience and yourself
- Establish a high level of credibility.

Eye Contact

Maintaining eye contact with your audience is an important technique in managing how your message is received by listeners. Regular eye contact, for example, allows you to do the following:

- Establish a personal contact with each person in the audience
- Build listeners' confidence in you and your message
- Hold listeners' attention and draw their interest
- Receive nonverbal audience feedback from which you can decide to adjust the content, organization, or delivery of your message to meet the changing needs of your audience
- Establish goodwill with your listeners by projecting interest in them.

Maintaining eye contact with your audience is not always easy. For instance, looking into the eyes of your listeners, especially hostile ones, can produce nervousness or, worse, stage fright, which could distract you from your line of thought. In addition, some visual aids (e.g., opaque projectors, videotapes, films) may make eye contact difficult. Any exaggerated attempt in this case to maintain eye contact can appear mechanical and ingenuine. Furthermore, presentational media requiring a dark room (e.g., slides) make eye contact impossible. However, failure to maintain eye contact as much as possible might be interpreted by western audiences as an attempt by to you to hide something, a sign that you're lying, boredom on your part, or your disinterest in or dislike of them. The guidelines in Figure 9.5 will help you to integrate eye contact into your presentation as a valuable communication tool.

Establishing a positive rapport with your listeners through the use of eye contact will make you more relaxed and your listeners more receptive to your message. However, remember that the amount of polite and acceptable eye contact is culture-based. In western cultures, eye contact suggests honesty and openness on a direct and equal level. Conversely, in many Asian cultures, prolonged eye contact is considered impolite. When presenting to multicultural audiences, first do your homework into the courtesies of communication to avoid insulting or threatening your listeners through cultural ignorance.

Expressions

As with eye contact, your facial expressions communicate powerful messages to your audience that can either aid or impede your presentation. Unlike eye contact, however, facial expressions are difficult to manage consciously. While you could fake the basic expressions—such as a smile, scowl, a look of surprise, a smirk—such histrionics are difficult to maintain and keep consistently convincing, except for the best of actors. More importantly, why would you want to waste energy trying to fool your listeners instead of concentrating on your message and delivery? You should, however, consciously avoid expressions that are sure to create a negative impression on your audience, such as giving deadpan looks, puckering your mouth into a sour expression, and squinting your eyes.

The most effective expressions are those that are genuine and that come from a positive attitude. To project warm, genuine facial expressions, first try to relax, enjoy the chance to discuss important ideas, and share this enthusiasm with your audience. Smile! Change expressions. Don't be an automaton. The positive and authentic facial expressions will follow naturally.

- Never ignore your listeners. Use eye contact regularly throughout the presentation.
- Move your eyes over the audience. Include everyone.
- When you look at listeners, really *look* at them. Don't gaze about.
- Look to the back of room, where perhaps your toughest and most distant audience is.
- Give listeners a warm, confident smile, not frightened glances.
- If you are prone to nervousness or stage fright, pick out a few friendly faces in different areas of the crowd and talk to them until you are more relaxed. Then make eye contact with the entire audience.
- Rehearse your use of visual aids so that there is time to look up and make regular eye contact with your audience.

FIGURE 9.5. *Guidelines for managing eye contact.*

Gestures

Well-timed gestures that are appropriate to the situation can effectively do the following:

- Emphasize key points in the presentation
- Serve as transitions between topics
- Increase audience interest, and
- Encourage listeners' participation in the talk.

An extended hand held above the head, for example, can draw the audience's attention to an important message, while a short chopping motion with the hand can suggest a change of topic. By holding your open palms up, you can invite the audience's response and active participation. Nodding the head can suggest affirmation of an idea, or thoughtfulness, depending on the situation. When using gestures in your presentation, consider the guidelines in Figure 9.6.

Posture

Your posture can convey much to an audience about your emotional attitude toward them as well as your message. A speaker with poor posture often projects a lack of interest, energy, discipline, or orderliness. For example, leaning against the lectern or wall or slouching suggests a sense of indifference toward the presentation or even disrespect toward your listeners. Moreover, the halting movements of a speaker's walk may imply his or her uncertainty in the meaning or accuracy of the message. The projection of such negative images reduces both the value and effectiveness of your message in the eyes of your listeners.

- Use only those gestures that seem natural to you and the message at hand. Gestures that don't match your personality or the topic usually appear rehearsed and artificial.
- Use gestures that draw listeners' attention to the message, not to the gesture itself.
- Match the gesture to the nature of the point being stressed (raised fist to ram a point aggressively home, open palms to suggest inclusiveness and size, palms down to suggest a slowing effect or control).
- Make sure your gestures are visible from behind the lectern or podium.
- Don't overuse a gesture.
- Avoid gestures that may be considered by your audience to be offensive.
- Don't grab the lectern with your hands. You might appear to be nervous, holding on for dear life.
- Avoid personal habits that might annoy your audience: stuffing your hands in your pockets, playing with your glasses, hair, pen, or paper clips; jiggling the change in your pocket; hitching up your trousers by the belt; licking your lips; pulling at an ear; buttoning and then unbuttoning a coat; continually clearing your throat; crossing and recrossing your arms.
- When practicing for your presentation, videotape yourself to identify and modify ineffective gestures.

FIGURE 9.6. *Guidelines for managing gestures.*

Good posture, on the other hand, suggests that you are alert, interested, energetic, and confident. Strong, brisk movements project confidence and decisiveness. Consider your posture throughout the presentation. Sit erect. Stand and walk straight—shoulders back, head up, chest out, stomach in. You should, however, avoid rigid movements that may imply that you are nervous or uncomfortable with your message, the audience, or both. But always present to your audience a posture that projects a relaxed confidence.

Stage Movement

You'll find that simple physical movement around the environs of the presentation (e.g., lecture hall, board room, office) can improve your delivery and audience acceptance of your message. Movement gives you a chance to work out nervousness that might otherwise cause your hands to shake or your voice to falter. In addition, if you avoid getting pinned to a lectern, you're able to emphasize key points in your presentation. For example, you might walk to one side of the stage to stress one side of an issue and then cross to the other side when addressing an opposing side of the same issue. In addition, you might pause or stop in your movement to place a kinetic exclamation point on a particular idea.

To strengthen your relationship with your audience, you might also use *proxemics*—the study of our use of space in relation to people. By moving close to your listeners, you bring the communication down to a personal level while engaging your audience further into the presentation. Also consider your relation to your audience in terms of elevation. Avoid putting yourself physically above an audience, or below them for that matter. By using proxemics intelligently, you can make listeners more receptive to both you and to your ideas.

However, if used unwisely, proxemics can significantly reduce your effectiveness. First, when attempting to break down physical and attitudinal distance between you and your audience, be certain not to violate listeners' space. Any advance within a listener's personal zone, about two feet, might be perceived as a threat. Second, avoid moving too much. Presenters who pace appear nervous, and listeners must turn their heads to and fro as though watching a tennis match. Finally, as when using any body movement to complement your verbal message, don't allow your movement to seem artificial or "staged." This only increases listener distrust in you and your message.

Dress

Dress the part of a credible, professional presenter. When choosing your dress for the presentation, consider the following guidelines:

- Wear clothes slightly more formal that those of your audience.
- Wear clothes that make you feel relaxed.
- Wear clothes that attract and reinforce your *ethos*.
- Dress neatly and avoid excessive accessories or jewelry.
- Choose styles and colors appropriate for the occasion, usually conservative and staid.
- Wear new clothes at least once before presenting in them. This is to save you from

the possible embarrassment of stepping before a large audience in an ill-fitting suit or dress.

- Wear more conservative clothes to appear older and, presumably, more experienced and credible.
- Remove noisy articles (e.g., change or keys in the pocket, a long jingling necklace or bracelet).

MAINTAINING YOUR POISE

A moderate amount of nervousness is normal and can actually be rechanneled as positive energy to make you more alert and enthusiastic during the presentation. Excessive nervousness, however, can distract you from your message and thereby significantly reduce

---

- Be prepared. Make sure that youíve done your research and that you've mastered your note outline or script. Completing the Brainstorming and Presentation Outlines discussed in Chapter 4 will help you to do this.
- Be prepared to present your message, to defend it, to compromise, and to respond to listeners' reactions (some of which may be negative).
- Rehearse the presentation repeatedly.
- Remember that all except the most hostile audiences want you to *succeed* in the presentation. They want to hear what you have to say. They *don't* want to waste their time or to suffer embarrassment for you as you nervously bumble through the presentation. Don't forget that you have well-wishers out there in the audience.
- Concentrate on *ideas*. Think about your message and how you can most effectively communicate that message.
- Make a good first impression. Stride confidently into the room. Pause before speaking to look your audience over and to give them a chance to look you over.
- Lock into your audience and smile. This will help you and your listeners to relax.
- Speak up. Even if you don't feel very confident at the time, raising your volume slightly at the beginning of your presentation will appear confident, which invariably makes you think you're confident. If you think so, you are.
- Speak directly to a few individuals in the audience to loosen yourself up; then open you presentation to all in the room.
- Set a relaxed and professional tone for the presentation by address the audience with the same respect and courtesy as you would colleagues.
- Use wit, if appropriate. Show that you enjoy sharing your time and ideas with your audience.
- Act, move, and speak in a dignified manner. Avoid appearing stiff or distant, but always maintain good posture and comport yourself in a professional manner.
- Arrive a few minutes early to check out and to become comfortable with the room and audience.
- Mix with audience members before the presentation. Get a general impression of them and promote a sense of goodwill between colleagues.
- Start on time. Don't let the audience become fidgety. The edginess may make you nervous.

FIGURE 9.7. *Guidelines for managing nervousness and poise.*

the effectiveness of your delivery. By projecting an air of relaxed self-confidence, a poised speaker places the audience at ease and implicitly asserts his or her credibility. A speaker who appears nervous can lose credibility as a knowledgeable authority on the presentation topic, which tends to significantly reduce, or even eliminate, the presentation's impact. You can reduce your nervousness while also enhancing the degree of poise that you project to audiences by applying the guidelines listed in Figure 9.7.

MANAGING YOUR AUDIENCE EFFECTIVELY

It is important that you involve your audience in your discussion from the very beginning of the presentation. A participatory audience will typically be more attentive and receptive to your message. Involved listeners tend to comprehend more because they are constantly examining and relating the information to their own base of knowledge and perceptions. Participatory audiences can also provide you with valuable reactions to your message that can help you in improving the content or organization of the message and even aid you in preparing and delivering better presentations later.

Ways in which you can increase audience participation in your presentation include

- Asking listeners questions
- Maintaining eye contact with your audience (as if to say, "I recognize you as a fellow participant in this discussion. And I am open to your views.")
- Encouraging reactions during the presentation's question-answer period.

Occasionally, not all audience participation is welcome. At one time or another you will face an unreceptive or even hostile listener or group of listeners. For example, you might face the argumentative listener who wants to corner you into a one-on-one debate. This person might be a *rational antagonist,* one who has a legitimate argument, or an *intimidating antagonist,* one who has no legitimate argument but who wishes merely to disrupt your presentation and to replace it with his or hers. Such an individual is usually looking for attention or recognition from you and members of the audience. Your first reaction to the argumentative questioner, as with any hostile member of your audience, should be to remain calm. Don't turn the presentation into a war of conflicting points of view or, worse, personal insults. First, recognize the idea put forth by the argumentative listener: "Thank you for raising that idea, Frank" or "You've identified some valuable and interesting points, Ted." Then direct your response so that you can continue with your presentation: "I'd like to discuss that topic in greater detail. Could we talk after the presentation?"

The *loaded question* often has no clear answer and is basically meant to put you on the spot. The best solution to a loaded question is turn the question back on the questioner. Suppose that you are delivering a presentation on the current U.S. trade deficit. In the presentation, you make no recommendations on how to reduce the deficit. How would you react to a loaded question like the following: "Your solution to the trade deficit, then, is to ignore it?" You might do well to remind the questioner that the purpose of your presentation was to examine the causes of the deficit and to consider possible options to solving it, *not* to make recommendations. You might also suggest that a follow-up presentation focusing on recommended solutions to the deficit might be in order.

How many times have you seen a presentation screech to a grinding halt because someone in the audience insists on posing a *long-winded question?* The questioner may simply not know how to phrase the question. In such cases, you might step in and help as a collaborator: "I think what I'm hearing you say is . . . ."; then go on to answer the question. On the other hand, the long-winded question may be posed as a way to control the presentation by a *dominator* or *pontificator.* In this case, you should cut short the question by asking the questioner to actually state his or her question so that the presentation can continue: "Do you have a question?" or "Can we have your question, Bill?"

Regardless of how experienced and knowledgeable you might be in the subject area of your presentation, inevitably a question will arise from your audience that you cannot answer. When this happens, don't panic or make up an answer whose inaccuracy will be discovered during or after the presentation, leaving you embarrassed and your credibility reduced. Instead, pause to give yourself the time to formulate a prudent answer. Some of the most popular and successful pause tactics include

- Asking the questioner to repeat his or her question
- Prompting the questioner for his or her own view on the issue (much as you would do with the loaded question)
- Sounding the audience for their answers to the question
- Writing the question down on a visual aid, such as an overhead transparency or flip chart, until you have had time to construct your answer.

Finally, you can answer a question that, for the moment, confounds you by simply saying, "That's an interesting and thought-provoking question. I wish I could tell you that I have a quick answer to it, but I don't. Could we get together after the presentation and discuss it when we have more time?"

GATHERING AND ANALYZING AUDIENCE FEEDBACK

You can evaluate the effectiveness of your presentation by recording and interpreting the reaction of your listeners throughout your presentation. Based on the *nonverbal* or *verbal* feedback of your audience, you can modify your report so that (1) the content, organization, or delivery of your message remains in line with changing audience needs and (2) you can modify the presentation to achieve your objectives.

Nonverbal audience feedback is most often reflected in the body language of your listeners, such as their facial expressions and body movement. Are their eyes glazed over with sleep, or do they look alert and interested? Are they weighed down by boredom and slouched deep in their chairs, or are they attentively perched on the edge of their seats? Are they restlessly fidgeting, or are they calmly attentive to each word you speak? Read the nonverbal messages of your audience. They are trying to tell you something. You can influence the nonverbal feedback of your audience so that it is consistently more positive by altering and improving the content, organization, or delivery of your presentation.

You can elicit verbal feedback from your audience by milling about the room before

- Plan for Q&A as carefully as you prepared for the presentation. Anticipate questions and formulate answers.
- Set a relaxed and professional tone for the presentation by address the audience with the same respect and courtesy as you would colleagues.
- Use Q&A as a chance to refine your message to direct it more precisely to the informational needs of specific audience members.
- Use Q&A as a chance to clarify possible confusion audience might have construed in their minds.
- Use Q&A as a chance to solidify relationship and goodwill that you created during presentation or to patch up differences that might have occurred during presentation.
- Give listeners time to formulate their questions, Don't wrap up the presentation and rush to get out the door.
- Welcome questions. Don't scowl and look down at the floor. Look at audience, smile, urge them to ask.
- Repeat a question if others did not hear it.
- Close the Q&A component when your time is up.

FIGURE 9.8. *Guidelines for the question-and-answer session.*

or after the presentation to get a sense of their informational needs and interests. You can also encourage feedback during the presentation by asking your listeners questions relating to the topic at hand. The most useful verbal feedback, however, comes during the question–answer period when listeners have heard all or part of your message and can intelligently respond to it.

Placement of the question-answer period will depend on your personal preference. Question–answer periods placed at the end of the presentation, however, may be most effective in obtaining an accurate sense of listeners' views because the audience has had the chance to hear the entire message prior to responding. While questions or responses accepted before or during the presentation can contribute valuable responses to topics as they are addressed, such verbal feedback is invariably registered by listeners ignorant of the rest of the message that is to follow. Consequently, this type of audience response is often distorted in its context. In addition, verbal feedback encouraged or accepted during the presentation can disrupt your delivery of the message by (1) anticipating topics that the speaker will address at a more appropriate point later in the presentation and (2) forcing the speaker to digress in order to touch on a valuable but peripheral issue. When planning the Q & A component of your presentation, consider the guidelines listed in Figure 9.8.

Another popular method of obtaining audience feedback is the postpresentation questionnaire. The survey, distributed either before or after the presentation, prompts listeners for their evaluation of presentation components—such as the value of its content, the appropriateness of its organization, and the effectiveness of the speaker's presentation style—as well as a self-analysis of their own expectations of, and participation in, the presentation. A sample postpresentation survey is provided in Figure 9.9. In addition, Figure B.1 in Appendix B contains a sample survey you might use for evaluating group presentations.

Presentation Evaluation Survey

Topic: _____

Presentor: _____

Occasion of Presentation: _____

Content and Organization

Introduction

1. How effectively did the introduction create interest in the presentation?
   Very Well _____   Good _____   Fair _____   Poor _____
2. Was the purpose of the presentation clearly stated?
   Yes _____   Somewhat _____   No _____   Not Sure _____
3. Did the introduction sufficiently forecast for you the key topics that would be addressed in the body of the presentation?
   Yes _____   Somewhat _____   No _____   Not Sure _____

   Comments: _____
   _____
   _____

Body

1. Were all the key topics promised in the introduction later presented in the body?
   Yes _____   Somewhat _____   No _____   Not Sure _____
2. Were the speaker's ideas clearly and convincingly presented?
   Yes _____   Somewhat _____   No _____   Not Sure _____
3. Were the supporting data and information

Interesting?	Yes _____	Somewhat _____	No _____
Varied?	Yes _____	Somewhat _____	No _____
Directly related?	Yes _____	Somewhat _____	No _____

4. Were the content and organization of the presentation successful in meeting your

Informational needs?	Yes _____	Somewhat _____	No _____
Interests?	Yes _____	Somewhat _____	No _____
Area of training/expertise?	Yes _____	Somewhat _____	No _____
Technical level?	Yes _____	Somewhat _____	No _____

   Comments: _____
   _____
   _____

Conclusion

1. Did the conclusion summarize the purpose(s) of the presentation as well as the central interpretations of the data and information presented?
   Yes _____   Somewhat _____   No _____   Not Sure _____
2. If the conclusion included recommendations, did they effectively urge a plan of action and did the action seem appropriate and feasible?
   Yes _____   Somewhat _____   No _____   Not Sure _____
   Comments: _____
   _____
   _____

FIGURE 9.9. *Presentation evaluation survey.*

Delivery

Visual Aids
1. Were the supporting visual aids
   Interesting?   Yes ____   Somewhat ____   No ____
   Varied?   Yes ____   Somewhat ____   No ____
   Directly related? Yes ____   Somewhat ____   No ____
2. Were they easy to read and understand?
   Yes ____   Reasonably so ____   No ____
3. Were they introduced into the presentation at the appropriate time?
   Yes ____   No ____   Not sure ____
4. Were the aids sufficiently discussed in order to make their relevance and significance to the message clear?
   Yes ____   Reasonably so ____   No ____
   Comments: _____
   _____
   _____

Delivery Techniques
1. Did the speaker seem poised and relaxed, in control of the situation?
   Yes ____   Reasonably so ____   No ____
2. Were the speaker's posture and body movements appropriate?
   Yes ____   Reasonably so ____   No ____
3. Were gestures appropriate in communicating the speaker's message?
   Yes ____   Reasonably so ____   No ____
4. Did the speaker maintain sufficient eye contact with the audience?
   Yes ____   Reasonably so ____   No ____
   Comments: _____
   _____
   _____

Voice
1. How were pitch and voice quality?
   Good ____   Too high ____   Too low ____
   Flat and monotonous ____   Nasal ____   Harsh ____   Other ____
2. How was the rate of the presenter's speech?
   Good ____   Too fast ____   Too slow ____
3. How was the intensity of the presenter's speech?
   Good ____   Too loud ____   Too soft ____
4. How was the speaker's pronunciation and enunciation?
   Good ____   Fair ____   Poor ____
   Comments: _____
   _____
   _____

General
1. How would you evaluate the overall effectiveness of the presentation's content and organization?
   Outstanding ____   Good ____   Fair ____   Poor ____
2. How would you evaluate the overall delivery of the presentation?
   Outstanding ____   Good ____   Fair ____   Poor ____

FIGURE 9.9. (*Continued*)

Please offer any additional comments that might help improve the presentation:

FIGURE 9.9. (Continued)

SUGGESTED READING

Addington, D. W. (1971). The effect of vocal variation on ratings of source credibility. *Speech Monographs,* **38,** pp. 242–247.

Addington, D. W. (1968). The relationship of selected vocal characteristics to personality perception. *Speech Mongraphs,* **35,** 492–503.

Ailes, R. (1988). *You are the message: Getting what you want by being who you are.* New York: Doubleday.

Anderson, J. B. (1989). *Speaking to groups eyeball to eyeball.* Vienna, VA: Wyndmoor Press.

Axtell, R. E. (1992). *Do's and taboos of public speaking: How to get those butterflies flying in formation.* New York: IEEE Press.

Baird, J. E., Jr. (1981). How to overcome errors in public speaking. In D. F. Beer (Ed.), *Writing and speaking in the technology professions,* pp. 232–236. New York: IEEE Press.

Brigance, W. N. (1926). How fast do we talk? *Quarterly Journal of Speech,* **12,** pp. 337–342.

Brooks, W. T. (1988). *High impact public speaking.* Englewood Cliffs, NJ: Prentice-Hall.

Brownell, J. (1991). Designing and delivering effective presentations. *The Cornell H.R.A. Quarterly,* May, pp. 41–45.

Bruskin, R. H. (1973). Fears. *Spectra,* **9,** p. 4.

Carle, G. (1989). Handling a hostile audience—with your eyes. In D. F. Beer (Ed.), *Writing and speaking in the technology professions,* pp. 229–231. New York: IEEE Press.

Carnegie, D. (1956). *How to develop self-confidence and influence people by public speaking.* New York: Pocket Books.

Cheever, E. (1992). Personalized presentations increase message impact. *Public Relations Journal,* February, pp. 28–29.

Cobin, M. (1962). Response to eye contact. *Quarterly Journal of Speech,* **48,** pp. 415–418.

Ellsworth, P. C., and Carlsmith, J. M. (1968). Effects of eye contact and verbal content in affective response to a dyadic interaction. *Journal of Personal Social Psychology,* **10,** pp. 15–20.

Eisenson, J. (1974). *Voice and diction: A program for improvement.* New York: Macmillan.

Fearing, B. E. (1990) Oral presentation and presence in business and industry. In Michael Moran and Debra Journet (Eds.)., *Research Technical Communication: A bibliographical sourcebook.* Westport, CT: Greenwood Press, 381–405.

Hager, P. J., and Scheiber, H. J. (1992). *Report writing for management decisions.* New York: Macmillan.

Hayes, L. O. (1991). Beating the paranoia of presentations. *Lodging Hospitality,* October, pp. 62.

Hayes, L. O. (1991). Overcoming your fear of public speaking. *Restaurant Hospitality,* November, pp. 46–47.

Hillman, R, and Jewell, D. L. (1986). *Work for your voice.* Murfreesboro, TN: Copymate.

Holcombe, M. W., and Stein, J. K. (1990). *Presentations for decision makers,* 2nd ed. New York: Van Nostrand Reinhold.

Holtz, H. (1991). *The executive's guide to winning presentations.* New York: John Wiley & Sons.

Holtzman, P. D. (1980). *The psychology of the speaker's audiences.* Glenview, IL: Scott, Foresman.

Kenny, P. (1985). *A handbook of public speaking for scientists and engineers.* Bristol, UK: Institute of Physics Publishing.

Kizer, D. F., Mays, L. K., and Plung, D. L. (1989). *How to effectively deliver or moderate a technical presentation.* Commuguide, No. 3. New York: IEEE Press.

Kloph, D., and Cambra, R. (1979). Apprehension about speaking in the organizational setting. *Psychology Report,* **4,** p. 58.

Knapp, M. L. (1978). *Nonverbal communication in human interaction,* 2nd ed. New York: Holt, Rinehart, and Winston.

Leavitt, H. J., and Mueller, R. A. H. (1951). Some effects of feedback on communication. *Human Relations,* **4,** pp. 401–410.

Leventhall, H., Singer, R., and Jones, S. (1965). Effects of fear and specificity of recommendations upon attitudes and behavior. *Journal of Personal Social Psychology,* **2,** pp. 20–29.

Mair, A. (1985). *How to speak in public.* Edmonton, Alberta: Hurtig Publishers.

Mehrabian, A, and Ferris, S. R. (1967). Inference of attitudes from nonverbal communication in two channels. *Journal of Consultive Psychology,* **31,** pp. 248–252.

Page, W. T. (1985). Helping the nervous presenter: Research and prescriptions. *Journal of Business Communication,* **22**(2), pp. 9–19.

Public speaking for engineers and scientists. (1980). Special Issue. *IEEE Transactions on Professional Communication,* **PC-23**(1).

Reardon, K. K. (1987). *Interpersonal communication: Where minds meet.* Belmont, CA: Wadsworth.

Roloff, M. E. (1981). *Interpersonal communication: The social exchange approach,* Vol. 6, Sage CommText Series. Beverly Hills, CA: Sage.

Scheiber, H. J., and Hager, P. J. Oral communication in business and industry: Results of a survey on technical, scientific, and managerial presentations. *Journal of Technical Writing and Communication,* **24**(2), pp. 161–180.

Solomon, J. (1990). Executives who dread public speaking learn to keep their cool in the spotlight. *The Wall Street Journal,* May 4, B1, B6.

Stettner, M. (1989). How to speak so facts come alive. In D.F. Beer (Ed.), *Writing and speaking in the technology professions,* pp. 225–228. New York: IEEE Press.

Vassallo, W. (1990). *Speaking with confidence: A guide for public speakers.* Crozet, VA: Betterway Publications.

Warlum, M. F. (1989). Improving oral marketing presentations in the technology-based company. In D. F. Beer (Ed.), *Writing and speaking in the technology professions,* pp. 219–222. New York: IEEE Press.

Weiss, H., and McGrath, J. B., Jr. (1963). *Technically speaking: Oral communication for engineers, scientists, and technical personnel.* New York: McGraw-Hill.

White, J. R. (1991). Suggestions on public speaking. *The Appraisal Journal,* January, 71–75.

Part V

Professional Presentation Models

10

Model #1: A Technical Presentation from NCR Corporation

The technical presentation we are exhibiting in this chapter as Model #1 was given to "selected marketing and sales managers" and "VPs of industry marketing" within NCR Corporation's Applied Digital Data Systems (ADDS) Division (now AT&T Global Information Solutions). Entitled, "X-Stations: Problem/Opportunity," the presentation was developed by Carmen T. Reitano and delivered on two different occasions by Robert W. (Bob) Oliver, divisional General Manager, the X-Station Business Unit.

"X-STATIONS: PROBLEM/OPPORTUNITY"—SOME BACKGROUND

The central purpose of the technical presentation, "X-Stations: Problem/Opportunity," according to Bob Oliver, was twofold:

(1) *"To convince* . . . key [marketing and sales] managers that the X-Station product was a viable product and would be a valuable addition to the NCR product line."[1]

(2) *"To convince* the USG [United States Group] resource owners to invest in developing and participating in the rapidly developing X terminal opportunity."[2] [italics added]

---

[1] We want to thank both Bob Oliver, now of AT&T Global Information Solutions, and Bruce Cone, formerly of NCR, for providing us with this presentation script and for permission to use this material (in full) here in Chapter 10. (We should note, too, that this "statement of purpose" was extracted from a letter from Robert Oliver, dated April 15, 1994.) We have chosen to retain the acronym "NCR" throughout this chapter because the presentation was made during the period of NCR's control of the division and because of the references to NCR throughout the script.

[2] Within the NCR Corporation's Applied Digital Data Systems Division, the USG, or United States Group, comprised the domestic sales force of the organization.

Based on the ultimate success of the marketing posture advocated by Bob Oliver throughout the accompanying presentational script, and the industry-based "sense" he has relied upon, the NCR Corporation's Applied Digital Data Systems Division (now ADDS/AT&T) has increased its market share significantly in the X terminal sector of the computer industry.[3]

Located in Heathrow, FL, the ADDS Division of NCR currently manufactures a variety of X terminal systems, including the "X-Stations" product line—that is, the NCR 3533/3534 Family of X-Stations (Release 2.0) and the TN3270/X Local Terminal Emulation. At this juncture in their manufacturing and development cycle, NCR's X-Stations can best be described as

> intelligent, high resolution X Windows display stations that provide easy access to a variety of network computing platforms. The user interface is optimized to provide a new level of ease-of-use while providing universal access to such diverse environments as UNIX, 3270, and DOS/Windows.
>
> . . . The X Window System is built on the client/server model of *distributed processing* [italics added] allowing it to operate over a Local Area Network (LAN). This permits an X-Station to connect into a network of computers[,] from many system vendors, and simultaneously display applications from multiple computers on a single screen.
>
> . . . The X-Stations represent a new, industry-leading level of performance, operational reliability and ease of use.[4]

The TN3270/X Local Terminal Emulation is, simply, "an optional software package for the NCR 3533 and 3534 X-Station product family that allows . . . [a user] to interact with the 3270 environment." The TN3270/X, therefore, does the following:

- It ensures for 3270 communications to IBM or compatible mainframes (when "loaded and executed as a local client" within the NCR X-Station).
- It provides what NCR calls a "migration path" enabling the "move from proprietary systems that access the 3270 environment to Open Systems."[5]

"X-STATIONS: PROBLEM/OPPORTUNITY"—THE CAFTA VARIABLES

As you will shortly discover, the "arguments" that Bob Oliver advances in his presentation, "X-Stations: Problem/Opportunity," are rooted in the following set of key industry-related postulates:

(1) X terminals are the most *cost-effective* mode for delivering X to the desktop environment (based on "life cycle" costs of ownership).

---

[3] For additional details about the X Window System (e.g., applications, costs, installation, support, and maintenance), see the paper entitled "The Cost of X—Color X Desktops," developed by The X Business Group, Inc., Fremont, CA, 1994. This industry-related paper was supplied to us by Bob Oliver in conjunction with a variety of NCR X-Station brochures and related materials.

[4] This descriptive material was extracted from NCR's "Creating Value" brochure series for its 3533/3534 Family of X-Stations, Release 2.0.

[5] For additional information, see NCR's "Creating Value" brochure, entitled NCR X-Station, emphasizing the features and technical specifications of TN3270/X Local Terminal Emulation.

(2) Administration and upgrade costs connected with PCs make them appreciably more costly X desktop devices than the low-price PC ads would lead users to believe.

(3) Due to falling prices, it appears that initial acquisition costs associated with mid-to-high end (color) X terminals are considerably lower than those of workstations and even PCs.

(4) Energy costs vary significantly between X terminals and PCs/workstations.

(5) Hardware maintenance costs for X terminals involve appreciably lower ongoing "costs of ownership" than for workstations—in some cases being half those associated with workstations.

(6) X terminals present a real opportunity for addressing the network administration problems related to LANs in general and hybrid (PC/UNIX) LANs in particular.[6]

The technical presentation that we spotlight in this chapter as Model #1 has been included here for a variety of professional, industry-related reasons. First, the core assumptions out of which this presentation has grown devolve from (a) useful technology-based research and (b) pragmatic, real-world, complementary marketing data. Second, the presentational script forcefully articulates basic computer industry assumptions, marketing strategies, and evolving corporate short- and long-range goals. Third, the presentation contains clear and relevant visual information and statistical data garnered from sources throughout the high-tech world of computer (and electronics) organizations.

Finally, in both our view and that of NCR, the presentation succeeds at convincing audience members of the position advocated by the speaker owing to the following factors:

(1) Carefully etched organizational structure

(2) Vital content (both textual and visual)

(3) Team-oriented ("we") posture adopted throughout and emphasized in the final portion, or close, of the script.

We examine the CAFTA variables associated with this presentation in the next five subsections of this chapter. The complete text of "X-Stations: Problem/Opportunity," along with all "stage directions" and 17 visuals, directly follows our discussion of the presentational script—its organization (rhetorical plan or structure), visuals, and style.

Content

The *content* or subject matter of this marketing-oriented, technical presentation consists broadly, as has been suggested above in our background section, in an examination of the overall viability of X terminal technology—the hardware, related software, product enhancements, and business strategies (in the domains of sales and marketing, specifically). In particular, the presentational content focuses on the X-Station product, NCR's proprietary version of X terminal technology. The presenter addresses the central issues (problems, benefits, and prospects) surrounding the X-Station product as a "valuable addition" to the NCR product line.

---

[6] Additional conclusions and "key findings" concerning X terminals can be found in the report entitled, "The Cost of X–Color X Desktops," The X Business Group, Inc., pp. 3–4.

Audience

NCR's "X-Stations: Problem/Opportunity" was designed for, and delivered to, two similar groups of technically trained marketing and sales professionals on two separate, and equally important, occasions. In addition, several "offshoots" of the "X-Stations" presentation were given before groups of two to three individuals comprising what NCR calls their "account teams."

According to NCR divisional General Manager, Bob Oliver, audience membership on *both* "major" occasions could be characterized as follows:

- All participants were NCR and USG (i.e., NCR's "United States Group") professional-level staff.
- Each group contained about a half dozen individuals: VPs of industry marketing; selected marketing and sales managers; and USG "resource owners."
- All audience members were considered to have had similar industry-related experiences, comparable "high-level" technical (corporate) training, and relevant (technical) undergraduate degrees (e.g., in electrical engineering, computer engineering, or computer science).
- All audience members were "degreed"; some (perhaps as many as half) held MBAs.
- All audience members would have been fully acquainted with the technical terminology and industry-related jargon used consistently throughout the presentation.

Form/Format

NCR's Bob Oliver delivered the "X-Stations" presentation on all occasions—*major* occasions and "offshoots"—within a (small) corporate conference-room setting. All participants were seated (comfortably) around a large conference table. An overhead projector (or *viewgraph,* referred to as the *apparatus* in the "Script Writer's Notes") was used to project on-screen a select set of 17 "visuals" displaying useful data and information tailored to the script and highlighting portions of it.

According to Oliver, a brief question-and-answer (Q & A) session followed delivery of the formal presentation on both major occasions and followed the various "offshoot" presentations (considered as *less* formal "talks") as well.

Time Frame

On each of the major occasions, the "X-Stations" presentation lasted approximately 45 minutes with about 15 minutes of Q & A. The "offshoots" presentations were condensed versions of the more formal presentation on certain occasions; on other occasions, the "offshoots" were slower-paced, more leisurely versions of the two originals. Following the "offshoots," Q & A sessions varied widely but generally lasted between 20 minutes and a half hour.

Aim(s)

Based on documentation we received from NCR granting us permission to use "X-Stations: Problem/Opportunity" and based on the thrust of the script exhibited (in full) below, we can break down the aims—purpose, objectives, stated or implied goals—of this presentation into two general categories, *primary* and *secondary*:

(1) **Primary aims** = *to persuade* . . .

    (a) To communicate in such a way as to convince others—say, members of an audience—to adopt your point of view.

    (b) To move others to some kind of action—if only to adopt your point of view (your position) and thus live or work according to its dictates.

In the case of NCR's "X-Stations" presentation, the primary aim can be identified specifically as follows:

- *To convince* selected marketing and sales managers within NCR that X terminal technology is a viable technology and that the X-Station product "would be a valuable addition to the NCR product line" (i.e., to support a position).
- *To convince* USG "resource owners" to invest in developing and participating in the rapidly developing X terminal opportunity (i.e., to take action).[7]

(2) **Secondary aims** = *to inform, to motivate* . . .

    (a) *To share* data and information—particularly statistical data, marketing strategies, sales trends, divisional goals, and product applications.

    (b) *To arouse interest, to provide with an incentive,* or even *to impel* or *drive forward* toward some kind of action (however limited).

In the case of NCR's "X-Stations" presentation, secondary aims can be identified as follows:

- *To share* data and information with senior marketing and sales staff—for example X terminal shipment data (by supplier), system providers, business objectives, homogeneous/heterogeneous computing networks—so that they might (1) support the position advocated on X terminal technology and (2) "invest" in developing the X-Stations product line.
- *To impel* (*urge, motivate*) senior marketing/sales staff to join the NCR (or USG) X-Stations' "team" organized to beat NCR's competition (and, thus, "to win").

"X-STATIONS: PROBLEM/OPPORTUNITY"—PRESENTATIONAL SCRIPT: ORGANIZATION, VISUALS, AND STYLE

The script used for NCR's "X-Stations" presentation is rich in details, supported with lots of current statistical data and relevant industry-based information, and enhanced by a wide

---

[7] We recently learned that Bob Oliver did, in fact, succeed in convincing members of the NCR marketing and sales community to (a) support X terminal technology as a "viable" technology to invest in and develop and (b) "buy into" his proposal to develop the "X-Station" product and add it to the NCR product line. However, he informed us that while audience members were receptive to his ideas and willing to support his position as a direct result of the presentation, they proceeded to act on the proposal at a much slower rate than he thought they would. Indeed, Oliver's experience seems to jibe with that of James McAlister (1991), who suggests that, in "selling" our ideas, we shouldn't necessarily "expect quick results." In reference to computer and management topics, for example, he notes that ". . . Some ideas take a long time—maybe even years—to take root. Instead of proposing a full-blown policy change, you may do better . . . suggesting a pilot program. Offer a trial period of a few months: A small bite is harder to argue against" (p. 11). See McAlister's brief article, "Ten Tips to Sell Your Ideas," in *Supervisory Management,* December 1991.

range of visuals which underscore major points while graphically revealing strategic directions. All of this material seems particularly valuable in developing the X terminal, or X-Stations, "argument" and in persuading listeners of its cogency. Indeed, this material aims to convince audience members via appeals of two kinds inherent in the presentational script: (1) an appeal based on *ethos*—that is, the development of credibility, character, sense of authority, or "professionalism" and (2) an appeal based on *logos*—the buildup of facts, data, or empirical evidence and the use of rational argument, or logic, to persuade.

While this technical-marketing presentation might be judged, at least in part, as an appeal to listeners' emotions—that is, "If we don't buy into this marketing strategy now and invest in X technology, we'll lose significant market share . . ."), overall the "case" advocated within the presentational script is incrementally built through a marshaling of *evidence.* Logical appeals are consistently offered to members of the audience based on facts, supported by data, and illustrated (in graphs, charts, bulleted lists) by what seem to be *objective trends.*[8]

Organizational Structure

"X-Stations" is organized according to what we would call a modified "3-T" structure.[9] (See Chapter 4 for a broader discussion of this and other organizational types, arrangements, and approaches.) What follows delimits the typical 3-T approach to organizing a presentation:

Introduction or "Opening"

T-1: Tell your audience what you are about to tell them.

Body or "Middle"

T-2: Tell your audience what you said you were going to tell them—that is, deliver the proverbial "goods."

Conclusion or "Close"

T-3: Tell your audience briefly what you just told them.

This approach, primarily *deductive,* is structured to begin with a statement of the central presentational topic, followed by specific facts, data, details, and, finally, an interpretation(s) that supports and develops the central topic statement. The *introduction* of a deductively arranged presentation serves as a contextual framework for the data and information that will follow. In essence, the central topic statement (a) introduces listeners to the subject matter at hand and (b) forecasts the topical focus of the evidence that will be marshaled incrementally throughout to build the speaker's "case."

---

[8] See Table 4.4 in Chapter 4 for a complete list, with descriptions and examples, of "fallacies of misdirection" in arguments.

[9] The "3-T" approach, as we define it here, dates back to the public speaking pronouncements of the ancient Greeks (most notably, those outlined in Aristotle's *Rhetoric*). The approach was adopted and put into widespread use in this century through such practical public speaking manuals as those published (or disseminated) by Dale Carnegie, as early as 1926.

"X-Stations" begins with the following statement (the latter part, in *question* form) which supplies the contextual framework for the presentation:

I want to share . . . some significant insights into competitive activity that we have learned as a by-product of simply managing our business.

I hope all of the information that I am about to present to you will enable you to more effectively answer this question:

Are X terminals a *problem* or obstacle to you in achieving your individual objectives . . . because they are increasingly confusing buyers, delaying decisions, expanding buyers' system options . . .

OR

Are they a major *opportunity* that can provide the leverage needed to exceed your goals?

Next, the presentational script immediately tells audience members exactly what the speaker intends *to do* or *to tell* them, T-1 of the 3-T approach:

In order to empower you to answer this questions, we plan to

- give you a brief retrospective of the industry—a trends view.
- tell you about some of the very strategic decisions, plans, and programs your competitors have made with respect to X terminals.
- show you the results of those actions . . .
- give you a view of the size of the X opportunity as others see it.
- tell you how . . . we can help you exceed your 1992 goals . . . and seed an investment . . . .

In the next main section of the presentational script, the body or middle (T-2), the speaker delivers the "beef"—the data and information supporting each of these announced subtopics—and provides all of the *evidence* necessary to build his "case."

For example, he provides information about "market share" in the X terminal industry (including statistical data on X terminal shipments by supplier), the X "declaration of independence" and X terminal benefits, a discussion of homogeneous versus heterogeneous computing environments, a review of which vendors/suppliers are "doing this [X terminal] business," and so forth. Each subtopic is carefully introduced, supported by data or information, and placed in a cumulative "body" of developing evidence until the speaker determines that the case has been sufficiently, and conclusively, made.

We have referred to the organization of "X-Stations" as a *modified* 3-T approach because the speaker does not actually tell the audience what he just told them in closing. Rather, he simply, but powerfully, sums up his message with the following concluding remarks (functioning, in the overall structure, as T-3):

Ladies and gentlemen, with your help we can all win. We can win by:

- getting incremental X business not built into our 1992 quota plan.
- increasing our X business market share so the world views us as a key player.
- strengthening our overall corporate posture in the competitive marketplace.
- cutting into our competitors' share and slowing down their advance.

In 1993, we'd like to have an approximately equal share with HP, DEC, and IBM. We can't do it alone; we'd sure like to count on you as part of the TEAM.

A rough outline of the organizational structure of the modified 3-T approach as it is used in the "X-Stations" presentation just described might be the following:

T-1   *Opening*
T-2   *Middle*
  • **Topic 1.0**
    —Subtopic 1.1
      Evidence [data/verbal, visual]
      Evidence
    —Subtopic 1.2
      Evidence
      Evidence
  • **Topic 2.0**
    —Subtopic 2.1
      Evidence [data/verbal, visual]
      Evidence
    —Subtopic 2.2
      Evidence
      Evidence
  • **Topic 3.0**
    —Subtopic 3.1
      Evidence [data/verbal, visual]
      Evidence
    —Subtopic 3.2
      Evidence
      Evidence
T-3   *Close*
  • **Final Remarks**
  • **Q & A**

Visuals

The NCR "X-Stations" presentation is supported and enhanced by 17 visuals for use along with what the script labels a "viewgraph," or overhead projector. These visuals posit supporting statistical data and useful marketing/sales and industry-specific information. A set of *script writer's notes* provided throughout the script indicates precisely *where, when,* and sometimes even *how* the presenter should show the visuals and reveal their contents.

Displayed primarily in bar graphs and pie charts, these data reflect trends in X terminal supplier shipments, worldwide X terminal shipments, and U.S. marketing shipments by industry group. The presentation also incorporates bulleted lists, sometimes in combination with (assorted) graphics, identifying such information as system providers, HP's X terminal business objectives for FY 92, X terminal "benefits," and even an X terminal "Declaration of Independence." Other kinds of X terminal information and industry-based data are portrayed in the following graphic formats:

  • Pictorial images as in the presentation "cover" graphic, X Problem . . . Opportunity
  • Screen captures as in the visual "Why X"

- Conceptual "system flow" (and procedural) diagrams as in the two contrasting visuals, "Homogeneous Computing Environment" and "Heterogeneous Computing Environment"
- Textual tables in combination with conceptual diagrams as in the "Industry Segments" visual
- Modified flow charts (with both figures and textual material) as in the visual labeled "Opportunity = 700,000 Seats Per Year" (subtitled "Migration into Commercial Segment Significant").

Script Style

The script style adopted for NCR's "X-Stations" presentation is, appropriately, a mix of the technical, training, and consultative styles. Certainly this mixture of styles seems fitting for the particular combination of data and information—technical, marketing, sales, and mission-oriented—delivered throughout the presentation to an audience made up predominantly of highly experienced, "initiated" technical marketers. It is reminiscent of the technical style that we explore in Chapter 5 in the sense that the script writer

(1) relies on technical terms and phrases, such, as "X terminal topology," "homogeneous computing environment," and "host connect segment";

(2) employs some passive constructions, such as "This was clearly seen and understood as a message that . . ." or "Oral bacteria were evaluated as biological indicators of dental asepsis . . ."

(3) uses nominalized expressions such as "the planning and implementation," "true interoperability," and "mixed computing environment."

However, the style adopted here also reflects the "training-consultative" style we describe in Chapter 5. On the one hand, it is collegial and friendly, rather confident and business-like, while, at times, tending toward the more "formal" end of the stylistic spectrum:

- "*I want to take this opportunity to share some significant insights into competitive activity* that we have learned as a by-product of simply managing our business." [italics added]

On the other hand, the style is quite informal throughout, with lots of personal pronouns (such as, "I," "we," "you," "us") and folksy contractions ("I'm," "we'd," "let's"):

- "Unless I'm mistaken . . . these opportunities "map" your organization!"
- Let's look at the unit growth in some of the industries you and your people sell into."

Two additional features manifested in this presentation's stylistic mix involve the following:

(1) Active verbs and verb phrases ("X terminals *provide* . . ." or ". . . users *choose* X-stations over . . ." or "Four of the players *shared* 14% . . .")

(2) Informal, personal "announcements" and "appeals" that reinforce the folksy, low-key nature of the presentation and function as stylistic "tags" or identifiers:

- "Let us briefly examine . . ."
- ". . . let me point out that . . ."
- "Let me share . . ."
- "Let's look at . . ."
- "I'm going to use this . . . [visual] and the next to talk about . . ."
- "Unless I'm mistaken . . ."

Finally, two stylistic devices employed in NCR's "X-Stations" presentational script seem worthy of special attention. The first, serving as a mode of organizing and "orchestrating" the presentation for the speaker, consists in the use of the stage directions deployed consistently throughout the script. Set in the left-hand margin of each page of the script are the following "markers":

Script Writer's Note

Visual # [1–17] . . .

Presenter Comments

What is particularly noteworthy about these stage directions is that they not only tell the speaker what to *say* or *do,* and *when,* but also sometimes tell him *how to deliver* a message conveyed on a given visual. For example, one Script Writer's Note includes the following instruction:

Script Writer's Note: Presenter assumes a demeanor suggesting a *fait accompli*—i.e., that these are "the facts" as the world sees them. He proceeds to remove the [previous] visual and places Visual #13 on the viewgraph.

Also worthy of special mention, a second stylistic device found in this script involves the speaker's tendency to communicate the following subtext to members of his audience: That they—because they are his listeners, here and now—are, somehow, exceedingly special people, part of an NCR elite "team." The speaker assumes the guise of the *bearer* not only of essential information he is willing *to share* but of important, rarefied "intelligence"—"top secret," *covertly* obtained within the industry—that he is willing to release. The following items seem to illustrate this presentational (stylistic) technique:

- "Let me *share some intelligence with you* . . ."
- "Let me *share a small piece of competitive intelligence* with you."
- "Here is *the situation* . . ."
- "Here's *what HP is telling its people* . . ."
- "Was it good fortune? An accident of Fate? Or the result of *serious, calculating, informed strategic planning?*" [italics added in above examples]

PRESENTATIONAL MODEL #1

In this section we provide the complete presentational script of "X-Stations: Problem/Opportunity," developed, as mentioned earlier, by Carmen Reitano and delivered by NCR divisional GM, Bob Oliver. We have arranged the script model on the pages that follow as closely as possible to the original NCR text. Arranging the presentational script in this manner enables us to showcase its "user-friendly" style, reveal its general fluidity, and illustrate its sequence and structure. The script, as we present it here, therefore includes the following items which serve as stage directions throughout:

(1) Brief notes provided by the script writer regarding presentational content and also delivery pace
(2) Topic(s) to "cover" in response to each visual displayed
(3) The presenter's comments.

"X-Stations: Problem/Opportunity"

Presenter: Bob Oliver
Audience: USG VPs of Industry Marketing
Objective: To convince the USG resource owners to invest in developing and participating in the rapidly developing X terminal opportunity.

[This heading was attached to the NCR script for identification and archival purposes.]

Script Writer's Note: Place the first visual on the viewgraph.

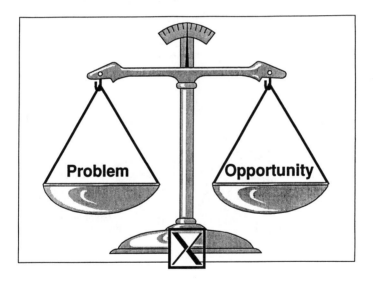

Visual #1: X-Stations: Problem/Opportunity ["Cover" Visual]

Presenter Comments:

Good morning, ladies and gentlemen. I'm Bob Oliver, GM of NCR, Orlando, FL. I want to take this opportunity to share some significant insights into competitive activity that we have learned as a by-product of simply managing our business. I hope all of the information that I am about to present to you will enable you to more effectively answer this question:

Are X terminals a problem or obstacle to you in achieving your individual objectives . . . because they are increasingly confusing buyers, delaying decisions, expanding buyers' systems options . . .

OR

Are they a major opportunity that can provide the leverage needed to exceed your goals?

In order to empower you to answer this question we plan to

- give you a brief retrospective of the industry—a trends view.
- tell you about some of the very strategic decisions, plans, and programs your competitors have made with respect to X terminals.
- show you the results of those actions by your competitors.
- give you a view of the size of the X opportunity as others see it. AND
- tell you how we believe we can help you exceed your 1992 goals . . . and effectively seed an investment that will pay you an above average return over the next five years.

If you agree that these things [items, trends, etc.] are important to all of us, then we ask you for your undivided attention and active participation in this presentation/discussion.

Script Writer's Note: Presenter places the 1989 X Terminal Shipments visual on the view-graph.

X Terminal Shipments
By Supplier

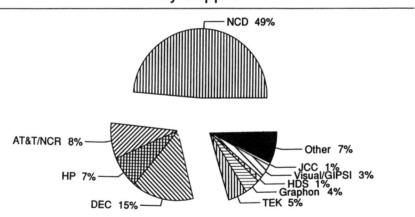

Source: X Business Group **1989 -13,000 Total Units**

Visual #2: 1989 Market Share [Total Units by Supplier]

Presenter Comments:

In 1989, the total market was 13,000 X terminal units. There were 15 or so active players supplying equipment. This chart divides the players into independents and system providers. There were three system providers sharing 30% of the market. There were 12 or so independents sharing 70% of the market. Of these 12, one—NCD—was the dominant player with a 49% share. Four of the players shared 14% with the balance sharing 7%. [When] viewed as Independents VS System Providers, the Independents shared 70% [of the market] and the System Providers shared 30%.

We call this the *dabbling phase*.

Script Writer's Note: Presenter removes Visual #2; Visual #3 is placed on the viewgraph with a cover on top of it so that it is not projecting onto the screen. With the visual in this "BLIND" position he continues.

X Terminal Shipments
By Supplier

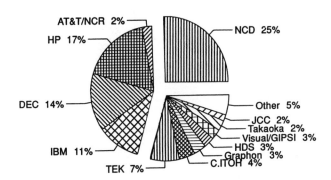

Source: X Business Group   **1991 - 121,733 Total Units**

Visual #3: X Terminal Shipments by Supplier

Presenter Comments:

In 1991, a significant . . . [change occurred] on the part of the system providers. The change moved the system providers from "dabbler" status to serious players and the shift in the balance of power would change X business from a technical curiosity (an interesting technology phase) to a serious alternative processing posture.

Script Writer's Note: Presenter removes the mask/cover and begins to explore the contents of the [pie] chart on Visual #3, X Terminal Shipments by Supplier.

Presenter Comments:

First, let me point out that in just two years the market grew from 13,000 units to 121,733 units. This is approximately 9 times growth.

Second, the total number of X providers grew to about 35. The system providers stayed level at 4.

The independents grew from 6 measurable players to 8 measurable players with the balance sharing just 5%.

The balance of power really shifted because the changes impacted both absolute and relative standings. For example:

NCD—the strongest and most dominant player, and the leading independent—went from 49% market share (with 6,500 units) to 25% market share (with 30,000 units), while still growing slightly in absolute terms. The total market mix shifted so that the system providers now held approximately 45% share, while the independents dropped from 70% to 55%.

Script Writer's Note: Presenter places the following visual on the viewgraph; he continues to hold it by the edge. As he removes the visual, he quickly speaks what follows.

X Terminal Shipments
By System Provider

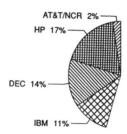

1991 - 121,733 Total Units

Visual #4: X Terminal Shipments by System Providers

Presenter Comments:

   It is interesting to explore what drove this performance. Was it good fortune? An accident of fate? Or the result of serious, calculated, informed strategic planning?

Script Writer's Note: Presenter places Visual #5 on the viewgraph and continues at his usual pace.

System Providers
4–Year Retrospective (1988–1991)

- # DEC

- # HP

- # OKI

- # IBM

- # NCR

Visual #5: System Providers—4-Year Retrospective

Presenter Comments:

   Let me share some intelligence with you:

DEC—In 1988 at DECWORLD in Boston, MA, DEC openly displayed X terminals as the interface of choice to its visiting customer base. This was clearly seen and understood as a message that X was here to stay in the DEC environment. During the year that followed, DEC quickly refined and enhanced its family of X terminals—and the message was X can deliver true interoperability today.

HP—During the last quarter of 1990, HP began planning and implementing their 1991 workstation/X terminal strategy. They developed alternative solutions based on the client–server architecture. They did serious configuration performance testing and were able to demonstrate superior performance at a lower cost per seat when a high performance workstation was used as a host for a number of X terminals. Most of these systems are being sold into [non-technical] departments or are running commercial applications marking a movement away from the technical and scientific market to the commercial and office automation market segment.

[There is a chart of the recommended ratios in your handout package.]

OKI*—OKIDATA spent a year developing a "Leap Frog" strategy for its I 860-based workstation family. It is based on the premise that workstation prices will come down to the point where they will be a viable alternative competing for the desktop in the commercial marketplace. In support of that belief, OKI has identified the ten largest vertical market segments that they believe will support their very aggressive business plan and is funding the porting of specific ISV solutions to their platform.

[* OKI MicroSystems is based in Framingham, MA.]

We predict that your sales force will begin to encounter OKI [sales representatives] in the last half of 1992.

IBM—Like HP, IBM has been quietly penetrating their own customer base using their workstation products as hosts in client/server application environments.

NCR—In this time frame, we [ATT/NCR/ADDS] were basically rudderless! [What with] . . .

- Merger Madness
- MIPS—X86 architecture
- NCR—ADDS

Script Writer's Note: At this point, the audience might feel a bit uncomfortable. With Visual #6 on the viewgraph, the presenter delivers a literal reading of the bulleted items, as follows:

HP's X Terminal Business Objectives FY92

- **Dominate the HP–host connect segment: >75%**

- **Establish presence in SUN–host connect segment: >20%**

- **Launch initiative for other host connect segment**

Distribution Partners have SIGNIFICANT role to play in ALL segments.

NETWORK SYSTEM GROUP
dst10 dec91

 HEWLETT
PACKARD

Visual #6: HP's X Terminal Business Objectives FY92

Presenter Comments:

Let me share a small piece of competitive intelligence with you. This one HP slide says it all. I will read it verbatim and translate for you.

—HP's X Terminal Business Objectives for FY92—

• Dominate the HP-host segment: > 75%

Translation: Penetrate your customer base. This is smart, easy business.

• Establish presence in SUN-host connect segment: > 20%

Translation: Slow down or block the competition from either developing their business in your accounts or creating a new presence in your accounts. SUN's mix of business is now 60% scientific and engineering and 40% in commercial. They have developed the commercial segment from 7% to 40% in just three years.

• Launch initiative for other host connect segment

Translation: Execute a parasitic strategy and become the X terminal front-end to other hosts in the mixed computing environment. Preach interoperability.

• Distribution partners have SIGNIFICANT role to play in all segments

Translation: Don't try to do it all by yourself.

Script Writer's Note: Presenter places Visual #7 on the viewgraph.

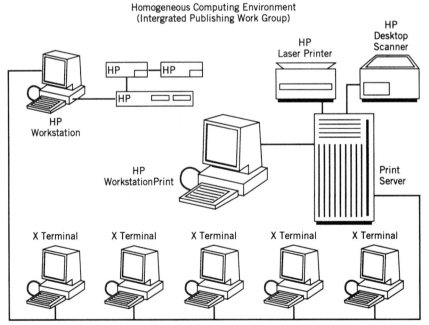

Homogeneous Computing Environment
(Intergrated Publishing Work Group)

Visual #7: Homogeneous Computing Environment

Presenter Comments:

I'm going to use this visual and the next to talk about homogeneous VS heterogeneous computing. I'm going to use these visuals to talk about two very real installations and how they are both appropriate for X terminals. This visual shows the final and winning configuration [adopted] at Sikorsky Helicopter in Connecticut. The application was technical documentation publishing. The original configuration was 256 DEC workstations, organized in 25 clusters of 10 workstations each. In particular, the application was Zyvision's technical publications software.

The high graphical content of the material being published, and the heavy demands for the print function, brought the system to its knees. The winning solution involved upgrading the hosts to more powerful workstations, building clusters of 9 X terminals to each workstation, and beefing up the print function with dedicated print servers. The result was a very high performance system and a much more effective solution. The savings over the originally proposed solution was in excess of $350,000.

Technically, homogeneous computing is simple. Most of the workstations come equipped with the appropriate connectors and all workstations support X. This is where HP and IBM have made significant gains in market share.

Now, with the advent of higher performing 386s and 486s, PCs and X are beginning to look like they could provide an alternative solution in the commercial market segment. [This trend] . . . could signal the entry of companies like Compaq into the fray.

Script Writer's Note: Presenter quietly places Visual #8 on the viewgraph.

Heterogeneous Computing Environment
(Hospital Information Systems Network)

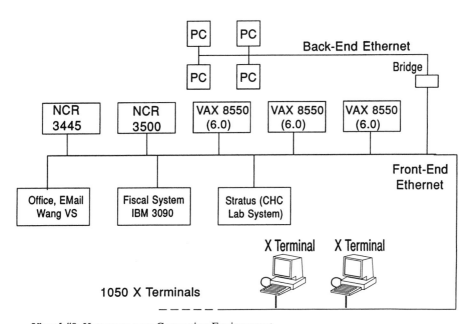

Visual #8: Heterogeneous Computing Environment

Presenter Comments:

Heterogeneous Computing, Disparate Networked Computers, Mixed Brand Networked Computing Environment all mean the same thing. This is the environment where the network is viewed as or becomes the supercomputer. Again, this installation [shown in Visual #8] is real. The facility is the largest health care [operation] . . . in the south. The decision to install X is often described as an "Organizational Decision." This example gives you a clear insight into the process.

Here is the situation: You have a large workforce of mobile, medical professionals. Their work environment can change daily—by work shift, by assignment, by specialty. At any time, [these individuals] . . . might find themselves at any location in this very large medical campus environment in need of data that resides on a large network of mixed computers. In the old environment, they [needed] . . . to know how to access each of the systems or to be conversant in the various technical emulators available to them. This workforce resisted [because] . . . it had no interest in becoming computer literate [to that extent].

The hospital management directed the MIS group to find a more acceptable solution. The solution was X terminals. There are now in excess of 1,000 terminals front-ending the networked computer. The composite value of the front-end computing hardware and software was approximately $350,000.

Additional interesting "notes": The hospital spun off a VAR organization that is currently selling this solution to other hospitals. There is virtually no graphical content in any of the applications running in this environment. The true benefit is one standard interface: true interoperability. There is the suggestion here that a well-oiled sales "machine" could have a parasitic strategy of selling X [-Stations] front-end to competitive networked computer environments. And through this window of opportunity begin to displace some of the installed systems.

Script Writer's Note: Presenter offers the following question preparatory to placing Visual #9 on the viewgraph:

- Simultaneous Applications Through Multiple Windows
- Access to Workgroup Productivity Software–Simplifiers Use

ASCII Terminal

Customer Order

Customer ID: _____

Name: _____

Address: _____

_____

_____

PO# _____

Item#	Qty	Description	$ ea.	Amount
───	──	────────	──	─────
───	──	────────	──	─────
───	──	────────	──	─────
───	──	────────	──	─────
───	──	────────	──	─────
───	──	────────	──	─────
───	──	────────	──	─────
───	──	────────	──	─────

Total: ─────

One application–Sequential

X Terminal

Customer Order

Customer ID: [123456789]

Name: [ ]

Address: [ ]

PO# [ ]

Item	Qty	Description	$ea.	Amount
1.	[ ]	[ ]	[ ]	[ ]
2.	[ ]	[ ]	[ ]	[ ]
3.	[ ]	[ ]	[ ]	[ ]
4.	[ ]	[ ]	[ ]	[ ]
5.	[ ]	[ ]	[ ]	[ ]
6.	[ ]	[ ]	[ ]	[ ]
7.	[ ]	[ ]	[ ]	[ ]

Total: [ ]

(Next)   (Quit)

Email

User: [ ]

Mail Status: [ ]

(Read)   (Quit)

Accounts Receivable

Customer ID: [123456789]

< 45 days $450.62
45-60 days   5032
60-90 days   136
>90 days   1333

Dow Jones Credit Service

Customer ID: [123456789]

Credit ratings: _____

_____

_____

Multiple applications–Simultaneous

Visual #9: Why X?

Presenter Comments:

What is X and why are people buying into it?

Script Writer's Note: Presenter places Visual #9 on viewgraph just as he completes asking the above question.

Presenter Continues:

The immediate benefit to entry level users is simultaneous access to existing applications provided through multiple windows with each window capable of displaying data from different applications running on different computers in the network.

In the hospital example that we just discussed, an operator could be looking at a patient's lab data in one window, the surgical schedule in another window, a review of doctors' notes in a third window, while entering data into yet another, a fourth window. Compare that with a serial hook-up of different data, in different applications, running on different systems in the same networked environment.

Script Writer's Note: Presenter changes to the next Visual, #10, and simply reads the bulleted items.

X Declaration of Independence

X Is:

- Display Independent

- OS Independent

- Host and/or Server Independent

- Network Independent

UNIX Today!/X-Window System Forum

Visual #10: X Declaration of Independence

Presenter Comments:

—The X Declaration of Independence—X is:

- Display independent
- OS independent
- Host and/or server independent
- Network independent

Script Writer's Note: Presenter quickly changes visual, placing Visual #11 on the viewgraph and continues his literal reading of the bullets.

X Terminal Benefits

- **Lower Cost Per Seat VS Traditional Workstations**

- **Lowest Life-Cycle Cost**

- **Can Run Multiple Applications On One Screen**

- **Part of Interoperable Network**

- **Distributed Performance**

- **Greater Security And Control**

- **No System/File Management**

Visual #11: X Terminal Benefits

Presenter Continues:

—X Terminal Benefits—

- Lower cost per seat VS traditional workstations
- Lowest life-cycle cost
- Can run multiple applications on one screen
- Part of interoperable network scheme
- Distributed performance
- Greater security and control
- No system/file management responsibility

Script Writer's Note: Presenter slows down the pace again and quietly announces:

Presenter Comments:

Here is another piece of competitive intelligence.

Script Writer's Note: Presenter places Visual #12 on viewgraph.

WHY USERS CHOOSE X STATIONS OVER OTHER PRODUCTS

Alpha Terminal users

▶ Want a standard GUI

▶ Need faster performance

▶ Low-cost upgrade path

▶ Want simultaneous access to multiple applications

▶ Desire increased functionality

X Station

▶ A low-cost standard GUI

▶ The best X price/performance

▶ No local operating system to maintain

Workstation and PC users

▶ Want centralized system admin.

▶ Low-cost per seat access

▶ Identical workstation "look & feel"

▶ Don't need local storage or processing

▶ No need for 3-D graphics

▶ Faster performance than PCs

NETWORKED SYSTEMS GROUP
RX15 OCT'91

HEWLETT PACKARD

Visual #12: Why Users Choose X-Stations Over Other Products

Presenter Comments:

Here's what HP is telling its people [in reference to]:
"Why users choose X-stations over other products!"

Alpha Terminal Users:

• Want a standard GUI
• Need faster performance
• Would like a low-cost upgrade path
• Want simultaneous access to multiple applications
• Desire increased functionality

Workstation and PC Users:

• Want centralized system administration
• Would like lower cost per seat
• Desire identical workstation look and feel
• Don't need local storage or processing
• Don't need 3-D graphics
• Want faster performance than PCs

X-Stations:

• Provide a low-cost standard GUI that can display text-based applications and graphics
• Ensure the best X price/performance ratio
• Eliminate the need to maintain a local operating system

Script Writer's Note: Presenter assumes a demeanor suggesting a *fait accompli*—i.e., that these are "the facts" as the world sees them. He proceeds to remove the [previous] visual and places Visual #13 on the viewgraph.

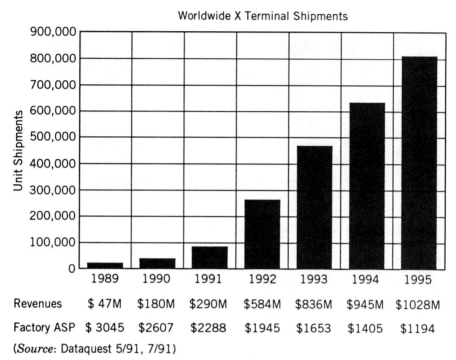

	1989	1990	1991	1992	1993	1994	1995
Revenues	$ 47M	$180M	$290M	$584M	$836M	$945M	$1028M
Factory ASP	$ 3045	$2607	$2288	$1945	$1653	$1405	$1194

(*Source*: Dataquest 5/91, 7/91)

Visual #13: Worldwide X Terminal Shipments

Presenter Comments:

How big is this opportunity now and in the foreseeable future?

	1989	1990	1991	1992	1993	1994	1995
Revenues	47M	180M	290M	584M	836M	945M	1028M
ASP	3045	2607	2288	1945	1653	1405	1194
[Revenues & ASP in U.S. $]							

- During 1992, for example . . .

  The market will just about double revenue from 290M to 584M; and based on Average Sales Price [ASP] projections will increase from 126K units to 300K units.

- During the next four years, from 1992 through 1995 . . .

  The market will again double in revenue size and triple unit shipments to approximately 850,000 X terminals.

Let's briefly examine who is doing this business . . .

Script Writer's Note: The presenter removes Visual #13 and places Visual # 14 on the viewgraph.

Commercial Market U.S. Shipments
By Industry Group

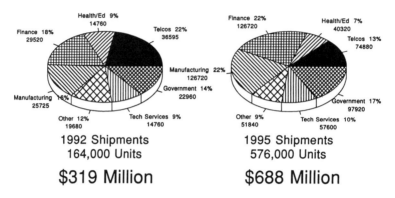

1992 Shipments
164,000 Units

$319 Million

1995 Shipments
576,000 Units

$688 Million

Source: X Business Group

Visual #14: Commercial Market for U.S. Shipments—By Industry Group

Presenter Continues:

Let's look at the unit growth in some of the industries you and your people sell into:

- Manufacturing will grow [roughly] from 25K units to 125K units, five times growth in only four years.
- Finance will enjoy similar growth from 29K units to 126K units.
- Telcos [telecommunications] will double in four years.
- Government will grow three times in four years to 97K units.

Script Writer's Note: Presenter quickly exchanges Visual #14 to Visual #15 and says, simply:

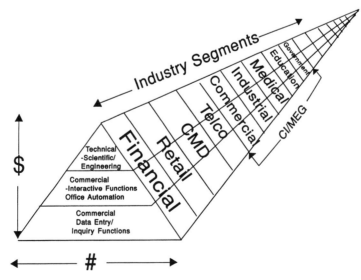

Visual #15: Industry Segments

Presenter Comments:

Unless I'm mistaken, ladies and gentlemen, these opportunities "map" to your organizations!

Script Writer's Note: As soon as he delivers the above sentence, the presenter removes Visual #15 from the viewgraph and replaces it with Visual #16

Opportunity = 700,000 Seats Per Year
Migration Into Commercial Segment Significant

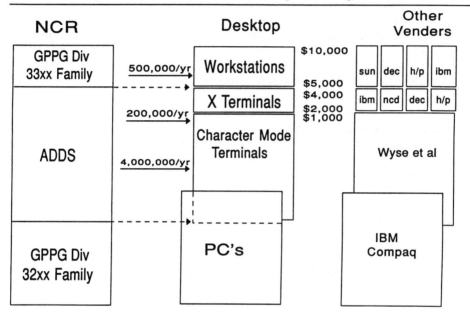

Visual #16: Opportunity = 700,000 Seats per year

Script Writer's Note: Visual #16 is covered with a three-part "mask." The presenter positions the visual on the viewgraph "BLIND," with all sections covered. As he speaks the first sentence below, he uncovers the first section of the visual revealing the "banner":

Opportunity = 700,000 Seats Per Year

Presenter Comments:

Ladies and gentlemen, I said I came here today to present you with an opportunity. I believe that I have identified that opportunity. Now, let me tell you how we can play in this marketplace and WIN!

Script Writer's Note: Next, the presenter uncovers the second section of the visual, revealing the middle and righthand sections, entitled "Desktop" and "Other Vendors."

Presenter Comments:

Here is how the current providers are supplying the various market segments.

Script Writer's Note: The presenter reviews portions of these two sections, reading much of this material verbatim. After having examined this material, he uncovers the lefthand section of the visual, entitled "NCR."

Presenter Comments:

Now let's look at how we are positioned to play in this marketplace.

We believe that ADDS [refer to left side, middle of Visual #16] has the most complete family of terminals of any vendor currently serving the market. We have a full line of ASCI terminals and X terminals.

- NCR's 32XX family can certainly satisfy its customers' needs in the PC arena.
- On the high end, it is our belief that the 32XX family of machines has an above average chance to succeed as hosts for X terminals in the rapidly developing *commercial* market segment.

We believe that if we work together we can help you

- protect your existing base, and
- create new net-add business by . . .
  —executing a parasitic front-end to mixed computer networks strategy;
  —offering better price/performance with our PC/SCO/X terminal alternative configurations; and
  —selling X into competitive environments.

Script Writer's Note: The presenter removes Visual #16, places Visual #17 on the viewgraph, and continues:

1993 Projected
350,000 Units

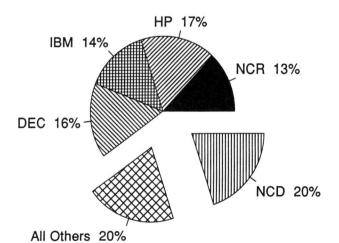

Visual #17: 1993 Projected—350,000 Units

Presenter Comments:

Ladies and gentlemen, with your help we can all win. We can win by

- getting incremental X business not built into our 1992 quota plan.
- increasing our X business market share so the world views us as a key player.
- strengthening our overall corporate posture in the competitive marketplace.
- cutting into our competitors' share and slowing down their advance.

In 1993, we'd like to have an approximately equal share with HP, DEC, and IBM. We can't do it alone; we'd sure like to count on you as part of the TEAM.

SUGGESTED READING

Beer, D. F. (Ed.). (1992). *Writing and speaking in the technology professions: A practical guide.* New York: IEEE Press.

Bender, P.U. (1991). Secrets of power presentations. *Canadian Manager/Manager Canadien,* **16**(3), 16–19, 27–28.

Carnegie, D. (1956). *How to develop self-confidence and influence people by public speaking.* New York: Pocket Books. (See especially Chapters 8, "How to Open a Talk"; 9, "How to Close a Talk"; and 10, "How to Make Your Meaning Clear.")

D'Aprix, R. (1996). *Communicating for change: Connecting the workplace with the marketplace.* San Francisco: Jossey–Bass Publishers.

Dawson, R. (1992). *Secrets of power persuasion: Everything you'll ever need to get anything you'll ever want.* Englewood Cliffs, NJ: Prentice-Hall.

Mambert, W.A. (1985). *Effective presentation,* 2nd ed. New York: John Wiley & Sons.

Martel, M. (1994). *Fire away! Fielding tough questions with finesse.* Burr Ridge, IL: Irwin.

McAlister, J. (1991). Ten tips to sell your ideas. *Supervisory Management,* **36**(12), 11.

Stevenson, J. J., and Stevenson, J. (1988). Writing and presenting a technical paper. *Cost Engineering,* **30**(11), 26–29.

Whalen, J. (1990). Winning presentations: Less talk is more convincing. *Supervisory Management,* **35**(10), 1–2.

11

Model #2: A Scientific Presentation from Pfizer Inc.

The science-based presentational script, Model #2, which we exhibit and examine in this chapter was developed by Dr. John A. Lowe III, a Principal Research Investigator working primarily in the area of medicinal chemistry at the Central Research Division of Pfizer Inc. (Groton, CT).[1] Dr. Lowe's presentation, "Nonpeptide Tachykinin Antagonists: SAR and Receptor Interactions," explores the history of his research team's "discovery of the first nonpeptide substance P receptor antagonist, CP-96,345."

We should point out here that Pfizer Inc. is a worldwide, research-based manufacturer and marketer of health care products and pharmaceuticals, with four basic "business segments": (1) health care, (2) consumer health care, (3) food science, and (4) animal health. The "mission" of the organization, as described in Pfizer's *1993 Annual Report (AR),*

> . . . is to discover and develop innovative, value-added products that improve the quality of life of people around the world and help them enjoy longer, healthier and more productive lives.

With a "product portfolio" considered "to be one of the strongest in . . . [the] industry," Pfizer "spent close to $1 billion on R&D in 1993" and submitted six new health care products to the Food and Drug Administration, including *Enable,* "a very promising new treatment for arthritis" (*AR,* p. 11).

[1] We are extremely grateful to Dr. Lowe for his interest in our project: for sharing this presentational script with us; for providing us with several published (background) articles reporting his research team's discovery of the first nonpeptide substance P antagonist; and for spending a considerable amount of time (with one of us) explaining both the "global" implications of his research work at Pfizer, as well as its particulars (i.e., from the "biological activity" of substance P to the issue of "nomenclature" currency stemming from his discovery). We'd also like to extend our appreciation to Dr. John L. LaMattina, Vice President of U.S. Discovery Operations at Pfizer's Central Research Division, who originally put us in touch with Dr. Lowe.

Dr. John Lowe is, of course, a distinguished Pfizer researcher; he is also a scientist with a genuine interest in the clear and effective *communication* of his ideas, the results of his work. Dr. Lowe is currently a member of an interdisciplinary research team studying the chemistry and molecular structure of Alzheimer's disease with a goal, ultimately, of arresting its development at a "diagnosable" stage; it is within this rich and productive R&D community that his original work on the substance P antagonist emerged.

"NONPEPTIDE TACHYKININ ANTAGONISTS"—SOME BACKGROUND

The various pieces of the "puzzle" surrounding the discovery of the first nonpeptide substance P antagonist—its origin, evolution, and significance—were reported to the scientific community by John Lowe and members of his research team between 1991 and 1993.

These research results appeared in a number of discipline-specific journal articles[2] as well as in two journal articles addressing a more multidisciplinary audience.[3] According to Snider et al. (1991), as reported in their *Science* article, substance P (or SP)

> . . . was the first discovered and is the best characterized member of the family of structurally related *peptides* [italics added] known as tachykinins. . . . These peptides and their receptors are widely distributed in the body and are involved in numerous physiological activities . . . such as smooth muscle contraction . . . and stimulation of salivary secretion. . . . There is . . . evidence supporting a role for SP as a neurotransmitter . . . particularly in the transmission of painful stimuli. . . . Substance P also plays a role in the activation of cells of the immune system. . . . (p. 435)

(*Note:* For nonchemists among our readers, *The American Heritage Dictionary* (3rd edition, 1992), defines *peptides,* symbolized by [PEPT(ONE) + -IDE], as natural or synthetic compounds containing two or more linked amino acids.)

Additionally, a review article was published by Lowe ("Substance P Antagonists," *Drugs of the Future,* **17**(12), 1992, pp. 1115–1121) discussing (a) his team's discovery and initial characterization, (b) its context and development, and (c) related studies on topics

---

[2] The published, discipline-specific literature included the following articles authored by Dr. Lowe and members of his research team at Pfizer Inc. in Groton, CT: J. A. Lowe III et al., "Discovery of CP-96,345 and Its Characterization in Disease Models Involving Substance P," *Regulatory Peptides,* **46**, 1993, pp. 20–23; "Nuclear Variations of Quinuclidine Substance P Antagonists: 2-Diphenylmethyl-1-azabicyclo[3.2.2]nonan-3-amines," *Bioorganic & Medicinal Chemistry Letters,* **3**(5), 1993, pp. 921–924; "The Discovery of (2S,3S)-*cis*-2-(Diphenylmethyl)-*N*-[(2-methoxyphenyl) methyl]-1-azabicyclo[2.2.2]-octan-3-amine as a Novel, Nonpeptide Substance P Antagonist," *Journal of Medical Chemistry,* **35**, 1992, pp. 2591–2600; and "Preparation and Radiolabelling of CP-96,345, the First Non-Peptide Substance P Antagonist," *Bioorganic & Medicinal Chemistry Letters,* **1**(2), 1991, pp. 129–132.

[3] The two articles addressing multidisciplinary audiences within the broader scientific community are as follows: U. Gether et al., "Different Binding Epitopes on the NK1 Receptor for Substance P and a Non-Peptide Antagonist," *Nature,* **362**, 1993, pp. 345–348; and R. M. Snider et al., "A Potent Nonpeptide Antagonist of the Substance P (NK1) Receptor," *Science,* **251**, 1991, pp. 435–437. The latter article served as the initial disclosure for the discovery of the CP-96,345 receptor antagonist.

within the field (e.g., *in vivo* studies involving rat salivation, cat dorsal horn neurons, and guinea pig trachea; initial studies on CP-96,345; and studies of other nonpeptide NK1 receptor antagonists).[4]

In this review article, "Substance P Antagonists," Dr. Lowe provides background material which we felt might prove of some value to *nonscientist* readers of this book. We thought this material would be particularly useful to include for those lay readers who might be interested in additional contextual information and a summary of the broader consequences of Lowe's team's research. Moreover, we thought readers of our book might appreciate the opportunity to look over the collective shoulders of professional scientists— the real-world readers for whom this material was intended—and directly engage information disseminated to the scientific community at large.

We offer here two brief but complete sections taken from Lowe's 1992 review article so that you can (a) explore relevant information, articulated in summary fashion, about the significance of the substance P discovery and (b) examine the language and style of written scientific discourse:

[1] Introduction

Substance P (SP), an undecapeptide neurotransmitter with diverse biological activities in the immune and central nervous systems, has intrigued investigators for many years as a potential target for novel therapeutic agents. Recently, a number of nonpeptide SP antagonists have appeared, offering the possibility to better understand SP pharmacology and evaluate the role SP plays in various disease states. This article will describe both the development of these novel SP antagonists and their impact on our ability to evaluate disease-relevant roles of SP. (p. 1115)

[2] Summary and Conclusions

Early studies with SP and its peptidic antagonists pointed to SP's role in pain, inflammation and asthma. The advent of nonpeptide SP antagonists, and in particular CP-96,345, has allowed confirmation of these earlier findings by establishing the role of the NK1 receptor in these three areas. CP-96,345 has extended these findings by establishing that a key activity of SP *in vivo* is in the control of endothelial permeability, measured as plasma protein extravasation, focussing SP's role on the chronic aspects of pain and inflammation. The structural diversity of the new nonpeptide SP antagonists reported more recently adds a new dimension to this area. Together with CP-96,345, these compounds will hopefully soon lead to clinical testing of the hypothesized role of SP in analgesic and inflammatory diseases. (p. 1120)

---

[4] For an examination of the place of the review article in the literature of science—its rhetorical, narrative, and stylistic dimensions—see Greg Myers, "Stories and Styles in Two Molecular Biology Review Articles," in *Textual Dynamics of the Professions: Historical and Contemporary Studies of Writing in Professional Communities,* Madison, WI: University of Wisconsin Press, 1991, pp. 45–75. In this article, Myers submits that the review article writer "shapes the literature of a field into a story in order to enlist the support of readers to continue that story" (p. 45). While the review article does *not* report original work—what the scientific community calls "first disclosures"—these articles, much like John Lowe's "Substance P Antagonists," contextualize the literature of a given scientific field and, according to Myers, draw readers "into the writer's view of what has happened and, by *ordering* the recent past [italics added], suggest . . . what can be done next" (p. 46).

"NONPEPTIDE TACHYKININ ANTAGONISTS"—THE CAFTA VARIABLES

The science-based oral presentation we provide in this chapter reflects, to a large extent, what might (and did) appear in a standard scientific review article. However, Dr. Lowe has obviously gone beyond the boundaries of that standard (written) form of summarizing and contextualizing research reported within a field. The oral presentational form enabled him to introduce evidence not only of a verbal or symbolic (formula-based, quantitative) nature, but *pictorial* evidence as well—including, for example, highly sophisticated color slides of *in vivo* biological phenomena and three-dimensional models made through computer simulation techniques.

Thus, the oral presentation allowed John Lowe to share information with members of his audience in a richer, verbal–visual context wherein he could more comprehensively

- "describe" his team's discovery
- represent their findings
- persuade audience members of the discovery's significance
- stimulate further experimentation.

That is, in the oral arena, to invoke the formulation of the rhetorician Greg Myers (1991), Dr. Lowe could more fully and dramatically tell his story— "a narrative with actors and events but still without an ending"—and thus "enlist the support" of his listeners "to continue that story" (pp. 45–46).

While the organizational structure of Lowe's oral presentation does not parallel that of a typical journal article reporting the initial disclosure of the results of original research, the script *does* resemble in structure his, or any standard, review article. (We will have more to say about the organization, structure, and style of Dr. Lowe's presentational script later on in this chapter.)

Content

Overall, Dr. Lowe's presentation at the 34th Annual Buffalo Medicinal Chemistry Symposium—"Nonpeptide Tachykinin Antagonists: SAR and Receptor Interactions"—concentrates on the history, or chronology, of the discovery of the first nonpeptide substance P receptor antagonist. The script's initial section clearly delineates the content of the presentation, specifically addressing what information will be delivered. Subsequent sections of the presentation, Dr. Lowe immediately announces, will do the following:

(1) Provide "some background on substance P"

(2) Show why substance P "represents an attractive target for novel therapeutic agents" (i.e., *disease relevance*)

(3) Describe the "discovery of the first nonpeptide substance P receptor antagonist, CP-96,345"

(4) Outline "SAR work in two areas designed to probe the interaction between the receptor and the quinuclidine nucleus"

(5) Depict the molecular biology used "to define the binding site for CP-96,345" and to convey "something about the mechanism of competitive receptor antagonism."

An examination of the presentational content reveals information of a decidedly inter-disciplinary character, encompassing such fields as chemistry, molecular biology, bio-chemistry, medicinal chemistry, pharmacology, genetics, and molecular modeling.

Audience

"Nonpeptide Tachykinin Antagonists" was presented by John Lowe, in different forms and to somewhat different audiences, at various scientific meetings between 1991 and 1993.

Initial disclosure of the discovery of the CP-96,345 receptor antagonist in the journal *Science,* in January 1991, suggested that the compound "may prove to be a powerful tool for investigation of the physiological properties of substance P and [for] exploration of its role in diseases" (p. 435). Results of the discovery based on *in vitro* and *in vivo* studies "demonstrated that CP-96,345 is a potent, competitive, and highly selective antagonist of the SP (NK1) receptor." These results elicited numerous invitations for speaking engage-ments for Dr. Lowe, most notably at the New York Academy of Sciences (November 1991); at congresses in France and Japan; and at symposia in Cambridge, England and Buffalo, New York.

The present form of the talk, the version exhibited here as a presentational model, was given at a *second* symposium in Buffalo—the "34th Annual Buffalo Medicinal Chemistry Symposium"—jointly sponsored by the Department of Medicinal Chemistry at the University of Buffalo (SUNY) and the Western New York Section of the American Chemical Society. Held June 6–9, 1993, the central theme for this symposium was desig-nated "Receptor Structure and Function in Drug Design."

Approximately 500 people registered for the three-day symposium and some 450+ at-tended the Lowe presentation scheduled on day two. Composed principally of professional scientists working in both academic and industry (research-based) environments, Lowe's audience reflected a fairly wide range of backgrounds:

- Some undergraduate science students at SUNY Buffalo
- Chemists and biologists with bachelor's-level training only
- Researchers with PhDs in chemistry or biology
- Scientists and managers at pharmaceutical companies
- Academicians and faculty members representing a variety of disciplines

In planning for, and designing, this presentation, Dr. Lowe had assumed that all attendees would be familiar with BS-level

> . . . chemistry and had some background in biology, including molecular genetics, so that I could explain not only the chemical reactions used to make compounds, but also the biologi-cal results and the molecular genetics experiments and results. [Excerpt from letter dated March 29, 1994]

Comprising a decidedly *multidisciplinary* group, a large number of listeners, Lowe con-jectured, would not have actually read in full the various articles discussing his team's re-search. Some audience members might have "skimmed" one or more of the published ac-counts of his team's discovery; but only those working in a related field would have been "familiar with the fact that Pfizer [researchers] had discovered the SP antagonist."

To be "convincing"—to project a sense of credibility, or *ethos*—before a multidiscipli-nary audience of chemists, biochemists, molecular biologists, and so on, Lowe believed he had to ensure that all of the details of his presentation were correct, no matter how minute and how specialized. He acknowledged the fact that presenting before a multidisciplinary group of specialists representing a number of traditional scientific disciplines was particularly risky and difficult. Lowe recognized that he simply couldn't afford to make an error and thus undermine his own credibility and that of his research team. He didn't want an oral presentation showcasing his team's work to elicit disparaging comments about him (like, "oh . . . well, *he's* only a chemist . . . and couldn't possibly . . .") triggered by what listeners might consider a professional, discipline-specific, limitation(s).

According to Lowe, audience members seemed to be interested in the presentational subject matter; that is, they displayed a level of interest, or "neutrality," that he characterized as typical for this sort of scientific gathering. No one, he acknowledged, seemed to have fallen asleep during his presentation.

Following the presentation, a brief Q & A session elicited essentially favorable responses from audience members. Two listeners, however, who had given presentations earlier, on somewhat related subject matter, were identified as *defensive* or *contentious.* He suggested that a disagreement might have arisen due to territorial or turf-inspired differences in received opinion and vocabulary—the almost inevitable clash between two disciplines when the picture of reality one discipline brings to bear on observed behavior conflicts with that of another.

Apparently, material that Dr. Lowe had discussed involved what he called *counterintuitive* phenomena—in terms of the evolution of ideas—that were described by his research team according to a "new" nomenclature. Lowe and his team had introduced the term *surmountable antagonist* to represent this newly observed phenomena rather than adhere to the more traditional term *competitive inhibitor,* which had been in use within the enzyme field to describe the behavior.

Thus, the source of contention during the Q & A segment was as follows: In the presentation itself, in documenting how substance P binds to its receptor, Dr. Lowe illustrated how molecules that compete and thus seemingly cannot occupy the same space at the same time have, now, been observed to display counterintuitive, or *surmountable,* behavior suggesting that they do, in fact, bind at the same site.

Form/Format

At the 1993 Buffalo Medicinal Chemistry Symposium, the occasion for the delivery of the version of John Lowe's presentation, "Nonpeptide Tachykinin Antagonists," we exhibit here, the form/format consisted of a traditional script-based lecture coupled with some 50 slides to highlight or summarize information and to examine pictorial evidence. (We describe the form and content of the visuals used in this presentation in the next section of this chapter, "Presentational Script: Organization, Visuals, and Style.")

The lecture/presentation was held in a large (~500-seat) auditorium, a lecture hall on the SUNY Buffalo campus. The speaker did not (and generally does not) stand behind a lectern but tended to move around, to wander a bit, in an effort to engage members of the audience more completely. The speaker reported that the use of a clipped on microphone, slide projector, attached computer-based apparatus, along with numerous floor-level wires, combined to restrict, somewhat, his natural tendency to move beyond the confines of the lectern.

Additionally, the speaker reported that he did not read from the text of the script because he had committed the entire presentation to memory. He finds he is able to deliver a presentation, such as this one, in a very natural way, in a relatively leisurely manner—

speaking the material, not reading from a prepared text—incorporating ad-libbed, extemporaneous material at planned intervals along the way.

In addition to the 1993 presentation given at the Buffalo Symposium, other talks—both formal and informal—were made "while the discovery of the role of substance P was evolving." Formats included lecture-style presentations made at international conferences and symposia (in New York, Japan, and Cambridge, England), as well as *posters* (in France). Posters involve informal talks coupled with displays of textual information, data, and chemical schemes arranged on 8″ × 10″ paper and mounted on posterboard panels. These industry-based posters promote one-on-one interchanges with attendees at professional forums, conferences, or trade fairs concerning the context of the subject matter under review.

Time Frame

John Lowe's presentation at the Buffalo Symposium was timed at 50.5 minutes, precisely. The Q & A session that directly followed his program segment lasted about 5 minutes. Lowe had thoroughly rehearsed his presentation, in-house, on several occasions, integrating the visuals with his commentary on them and simulating actual conference conditions. He reported that the final, "dress" rehearsal for the event took 51 minutes, a mere 30 seconds more than it would actually last "on stage" in Buffalo. Obviously, he had prepared thoroughly for this symposium presentation. Indeed, it seems that he routinely prepares well in advance of an oral presentation he is scheduled to make. He seems utterly convinced of the value of rehearsing a presentation—the script along with the visual–"pictorial" material—in depth, many times, prior to an event to ensure for the clarity of his message and maximum precision in its ultimate delivery.

Aim(s)

Based on conversations with Dr. Lowe, as well as on an examination of his published work, we can identify the aims of his "Nonpeptide Tachykinin Antagonists" presentation as follows:

(1) **Primary aim = to** *inform* . . .
   (a) To *educate* members of his audience about all aspects—genesis, evolution, chronology, current status—of the Pfizer team's "discovery of the first nonpeptide substance P receptor antagonist, CP-96,345."
   (b) To *share* summary information, research results (data), chemical codes and "schemes," compound behaviors, molecular phenomena. And, specifically, to describe: the "physiological properties of substance P" (its "SAR and pharmacology"); "SAR work" in areas relative to receptor/quinuclidine nucleus interaction; molecular biology exploring "the binding site for CP-96,345 and . . . the mechanism of competitive receptor antagonism."

(2) **Secondary aims = *to motivate* + *to persuade*** . . .
   (a) To *kindle interest* in the "current state of our understanding" of the substance P (NK1) receptor (see Snider, *Science,* 1991); to stimulate interest in the Pfizer discovery, generally; and to generate further experimental research ("to unravel this [binding site] puzzle" via molecular modeling and computer simulation techniques).

(b) To *convince* a multidisciplinary audience of professional scientists of the legitimacy of a discovery; of the *efficacy* of the behavior(s) observed; and, specifically, of the fact that a new "stage in [our] understanding" of a phenomenon is "forming" and is providing "a more complete picture of *receptor antagonism*."[5] (In a sense, this secondary aim might be construed as a political one. For a brief look at the political context, see the "Audience" subsection, above.)

"NONPEPTIDE TACHYKININ ANTAGONISTS"—PRESENTATIONAL SCRIPT: ORGANIZATION, VISUALS AND STYLE

As you will soon see, the script developed by John Lowe and used to deliver his presentation, "Nonpeptide Tachykinin Antagonists," is detailed, extensive, well organized, deftly summarized, *listener*-centered, and, to a large extent, linguistically informal (*"We've* used . . ."; *"We've* prepared . . ."; or "The results suggest *some very exciting* . . ."; *"This story continues* with . . ."). The visual material is equally comprehensive; in addition, it appears to be precise, relevant, and "readable," whether summarizing textual information (in lists or charts), or displaying symbolic, formulaic, or pictorial "evidence."

Organizational Structure

As far back as, say, the publication in 1830 of John Herschel's influential text, *Preliminary Discourse on Natural Philosophy,* we've been told much about the "context of discovery" (i.e., from observation of "complex phenomena" to the construction of theories) and the "scientific method" (see Losee, 1980, pp. 114–120). Indeed, we have learned how the scientist works—inductively testing hypotheses, representing schema, deducing models, and so forth; but many of us remain unfamiliar with how the scientist communicates the results of research leading to a discovery.

While scientists gather data and information primarily through observation and inductive activity—that is, by way of experimentation—they report results in an essentially deductive fashion in journals that form a kind of public archive of their research. According to Ziman (1976), the "standard means of communicating new scientific discoveries . . . has remained almost unchanged in three centuries" (p. 100).

Within the framework of "a few pages of print," information "summarizing the work of a few weeks or months" is presented (Ziman, p. 100). The "typical" scientific article, such as that published by Lowe et al. in the journal *Regulatory Peptides,* conforms to the following deductive organizational plan:

- **Abstract**
- **List of Key Words** [optional]
- **Introduction**
  Context—with citations to relevant studies.

---

[5] As mentioned above, in the audience subsection, this stage in the evolution of our understanding of receptor antagonism is both counterintuitive and controversial and thus might, according to Dr. Lowe, "take a little while" (perhaps five or more years) to be fully accepted.

- **Body . . . Discussion**

  Original contribution or initial "disclosure," often divided into *Methods* or *Results* sections and subsections—for example, "Pharmacological Characterization."

- **Summary and Conclusions**
- **References**

A typical review article, though, as the "Contents" section of Lowe's (1992) review article demonstrates, does not conform precisely to this organizational plan:

- **Opening (Introduction)**
- **Middle (Body)**
  - —Substance P as a target . . .
  - —Peptidic antagonists
  - —CP-96,345
  - —Discovery and initial characterization
  - —*In vivo* studies
  - —Other nonpeptide antagonists
- **Close (Summary and Conclusions)**
- **References**

(From "Substance P Antagonists," *Drugs of the Future,* **17**(12), 1992, pp. 1115–1121.)

The organizational structure represented by the the review article "Contents" (shown above) closely parallels the essentially deductive arrangement of Lowe's presentational script. With an overall arrangement that recalls the technical presentation we exhibit in Chapter 10, "Nonpeptide Tachykinin Antagonists" is organized just a bit more traditionally, according to a true 3-T plan:

T-1 Opening (Introduction) [Section #1]

". . . *I'll begin with* some background on substance P and show why it represents an attractive target. . . . *Then I'll* describe our discovery . . . and discuss its SAR and pharmacology. *We'll next look at* SAR work in two areas. . . . *And finally, I'll* describe our efforts in molecular biology. . . .

T-2 Middle (Body) [Sections #2–49]

Background on substance P . . . details on "our" discovery . . . discussion of various experiments . . . related studies . . . data on three specific interactions . . . SAR studies, pharmacological studies . . . molecular biology studies . . . and interim summary. . . .

T-3 Close (Summary) [Section #50]

"*So, in summary,* what we've shown is that the SAR for CP-96,345 has led to. . . ."

Within the *body* [T-2] of the presentation, the various pieces of the substance P "puzzle" are defined, discussed, reviewed, described, and revealed—in an effort to tell the complete story behind the Pfizer discovery. The details and examples shared in these sections (#2–49) are woven together, piece by piece, to form a complete narrative quilt representing the history, current status, and evolution of the discovery.

Finally, we'd like to identify two rhetorical features found consistently throughout the body of this script which function to move the narrative forward:

(1) The accrual of what we might call inductive *metonymic* details in every section, on every page—for example, concrete details like "the NK1 receptor," "the G-protein-coupled receptor," "the quinuclidine nucleus," and so forth[6]

(2) The use of transitional phrases, or narrative "links," like the one which begins Section #29: "*This story continues* with the discovery of the piperidine substance P antagonists by Dr. Manoj Desai. . . ."

A rough outline of the organizational structure for the "Nonpeptide Tachykinin Antagonists" script would recall that constructed for NCR's "X-Stations" presentation. It might be arranged as follows (where + simply means "more than," or "in addition to," as in *more than* three details):

Opening [Introduction]—Section #1

["I'd like to begin . . ."] List . . .

- Topic 1
- Topic 2
- Topic 3
- Topic 4

Middle [Story]— Sections #2–49

- Topic 1.0
  —Subtopic 1.1: Experimental Data
  —Subtopic 1.2: Evidence
  —Subtopic 1.3: Details [+]
- Topic 2.0
  —Subtopic 2.1: Experimental Data
  —Subtopic 2.2: Evidence
  —Subtopic 2.3: Details [+]
- Topic 3.0
  —Subtopic 3.1: Experimental Data
  —Subtopic 3.2: Evidence
  —Subtopic 3.3: Details [+]
- Topic 4.0 +

---

[6] For an examination of how *metonymic* details function to create, and move forward, narrative, see David Lodge, "Metaphor and Metonymy in Modern Fiction," *The Critical Quarterly,* Spring, 1975, **17**(1), pp. 75–93. For a broader discussion, see Lodge, *The Modes of Modern Writing: Metaphor, Metonymy, and the Typology of Modern Literature,* Ithaca, NY: Cornell University Press, 1977. See also Roman Jakobson and Morris Halle, *Fundamentals of Language,* The Hague: Mouton, 1959.

Close— Section #50

["So, to summarize . . ."] List . . .

- Topic 1
- Topic 2
- Topic 3
- Topic 4 [future]

Acknowledgments— Section #51

List . . .

- Chemistry [Ack. 1, 2, 3+]
- Pharmacology [1, 2, 3+]
- Molecular Biology [1, 2, 3+]
- Molecular Modeling [1]

Q & A . . .

Visuals

The script of "Nonpeptide Tachykinin Antagonists" is supported and enriched by 51 slides, including an "Acknowledgments" slide, displaying a wide variety of verbal, symbolic, and visual–"pictorial" information. With the exception of 12 color slides, all of the visuals used by Dr. Lowe in delivering his presentation at the Buffalo Symposium were made available to us for use in this chapter. (Copies of these visuals, Slides #1 through #51, have been inserted at intervals within the script, below.)

Slides missing from this version of the presentation, according to Dr. Lowe, involve photos (or pictorial data) that support the efficacy of compounds described or that focus on speculative material shared to stimulate future experimentation. This group of slides, for example, illustrates phenomena, processes, or pictures such as the following:

(1) The biological activity and pharmacology of substance P
(2) *In vivo* biological tissue (e.g., brain slices, parts of a lung, guinea pig bronchial tissue treated with "antagonists")
(3) Computer modeling of compounds using the Nemesis program on a Macintosh IIsi
(4) A computer-simulated three-dimensional model showing the NK1 receptor at the proposed binding site when the CP-96,345 compound *binds* to (or *docks* in) the receptor
(5) Other manipulations involving computer-based molecular modeling techniques.

The slides which have been duplicated for inclusion in the presentational script we exhibit in this chapter serve the following functions:

(1) They illustrate in graphic and formulaic terms the genesis and "evolution" of the Pfizer research team's ideas.
(2) They provide additional background on substance P from an interdisciplinary perspective.

(3) They document aspects of the discovery of the first nonpeptide substance P receptor antagonist, CP-96,345 (e.g., Slide #28, which diagrams the binding of CP-96,345 at the NK1 receptor).

(4) They highlight chemical compounds, schemes, or reactions germane to a discussion of the research (e.g., Slide #9, which presents key elements for NK1 receptor recognition).

(5) They summarize research findings (e.g., Slide #4, which lists tachykinin receptors by receptor (NK1, NK2), ligand (SP, NKA), location (spinal cord, endothelium, neurons, brain), and role (stress, inflammation, asthma, incontinence, pain).

Script Style

The style adopted in "Nonpeptide Tachykinin Antagonists" is consistent with the objective-impersonal scientific style we illustrate in Chapter 5 (Sample 5). As we suggested, this style has traditionally been used within the scientific and engineering communities to report research results and technical information. This objective-impersonal style continues to dominate the scientific literature, appearing consistently in journals, transactions, conference proceedings, abstracts indexes, and databases.

A science-based prose style is characteristically precise, plain, impersonal, cold, routinely coherent, richly detailed, and densely packed; it is, generally, clear to an initiated audience, yet often opaque and impenetrable to the lay reader.[7] Scientific prose contains a mix of stylistic features similar to those we isolated in reviewing the NCR technical script, highlighted as our Model #1. These stylistic features can be summarized in the four categories that follow:

(1) **Passive constructions**—for example, ". . . the binding of CP-96,345 was shown to be enantioselective . . ."; or "In the current state of our understanding it is not yet possible to design . . .").

(2) **Nominalized expressions** (or noun "strings")—for example, "*dose-dependent inhibition* of *mustard oil-induced edema*"; or ". . . *computer-assisted molecular modeling* has not yet produced a *high-affinity, receptor-active nonpeptide ligand*").

(3) **Weak, linking verbs**—for example, "congeners *were prepared* by"; "*are* widely *distributed* in"; or "*has been* the focus of an intense."

(4) **Scientific nomenclature and technical notation** (densely packed, in substantial amounts)—for example, "neurokinin B as NK_1, NK_2, and NK_3, respectively"; or "a potent inhibitor of $[^3H]SP$ binding to bovine caudite membranes."

The prose passages we exhibited earlier in this chapter, which appeared in the journal *Drugs of the Future,* typify this objective-impersonal, or scientific style.

Much as the objective-impersonal style dominates the *written* forms of scientific communication (journal articles, review articles, abstracts), the identifying features of that style tend, naturally, to surface in science-based presentation scripts as well, such as in Lowe's "Nonpeptide Tachykinin Antagonists."

---

[7] For a discussion of the nature of scientific prose and its linguistic character, see Theodore H. Savory, *The Language of Science,* London: Andre Deutsch, 1953, pp. 80–119.

Within an *oral* context—for example, in a script constructed for use at a conference or symposium—still other, different, stylistic features can frequently be identified. These include the following which appear throughout Lowe's script on a regular basis to militate against the standard level of formality characteristic of scientific prose:

- **Informal locutions,** such as . . .
    —*Personal pronouns* ("we begin," "we hoped," "our SAR study")
    —*Contractions* ("we've used CP-96,344," "what we've shown," and, even, "I'll describe," "I'll concentrate on our studies," "I'd like to review," "I'd like to finish")
    —*"Lite" expressions* ("So, in summary," "What Jim finds," "As shown by Mike Snider," "but the next question is whether," "As I showed a moment ago.")
- **Active verbs,** such as . . .
    —"We *decided,*" "the synthesis . . . *relies* on homoquinuclidine," "The synthesis of CP-99,994 *begins* with," "Jim *finds,*" "*causes* release."
- **Names of scientists/researchers** (acknowledged *within* the script's text) in these and other instances . . .
    —"Tom Seeger at Pfizer has carried out autoradiography experiments."
    —"This story continues with the discovery . . . by Dr. Manoj Desai and his co-workers at Pfizer."
    —"Jim Rizzi at Pfizer has constructed this three-dimensional model of the NK1 receptor. . . ."

PRESENTATIONAL MODEL #2

The complete script for Model #2, our science-based presentation—entitled "Nonpeptide Tachykinin Antagonists: SAR and Receptor Interactions"—is exhibited below and appears throughout the remainder of Chapter 11. We have rendered the script faithfully on these pages according to John Lowe's original arrangement of this material. Thus, you have before you a duplicate of the script presented by Dr. Lowe to an audience of participants in the Medicinal Chemistry Symposium held at SUNY Buffalo on June 8, 1993. We have simply incorporated—within the script text—the prepared visuals (labeled Slide #1, #2, etc.) he used to

- support the evolution of his team's research
- examine key aspects of the discovery of "the first nonpeptide substance P antagonist"
- model relevant chemical compounds, "schemes," or phenomena.[8]

---

[8] Of the 51 slides used during Dr. Lowe's original presentation to support and enhance material he discussed, 12 could *not* be reproduced for inclusion in this chapter because of the complex process involved in creating copies of color photos from, in some cases, highly sophisticated computer simulations. These missing slides (numbers 3, 11, 13, 19, 20, 22, 26, 27, 34, 40, 48, and 49) are identified with the letters "*NR*" throughout the script.

Nonpeptide Tachykinin Antagonists: SAR and Receptor Interactions

John A. Lowe III

Central Research, Pfizer Inc.

Groton, CT 06340

A presentation at the 34th Annual Buffalo Medicinal Chemistry Symposium,
SUNY Buffalo, June 6-9, 1993

[*Note:* Dr. Lowe's original script is divided into 51 sections, with corresponding slides labeled 1–51. Ellipsis marks *do not* indicate omitted text; rather, they identify transitional points between textual material and slides, or signal spots where Dr. Lowe provided extemporaneous, ad-libbed material.]

1—I'd like to begin by thanking Dr. McCall and the organizers for the opportunity to present some of our work in the area of substance P receptor antagonists. I'll begin with some background on substance P and show why it represents an attractive target for novel therapeutic

Nonpeptide Tachykinin Antagonists: SAR and Receptor Interactions

- **Substance P - Disease relevance**

- **CP-96,345 - SAR/Pharmacology**
  - *[3.2.2] Analogues*
  - *2-Phenyl Quinuclidines*

- **Molecular Biology and the NK1 Receptor**
  - *Construction of Chimeric Receptors*
  - *Antagonist Binding Site*
  - *"Competitive" Antagonism*

CP-96,345

Slide #1

agents. Then I'll describe our discovery of the first nonpeptide substance P receptor antagonist, CP-96,345, and discuss its SAR and pharmacology. We'll next look at SAR work in two areas designed to probe the interaction between the receptor and the quinuclidine nucleus. And finally, I'll describe our efforts in molecular biology to define the binding site for CP-96,345 and to understand something about the mechanism of competitive receptor antagonism.

2—Substance P [SP] is an undecapeptide discovered in 1931 and sequenced in 1970 and is a member of the tachykinin family of peptides which includes neurokinins A and B. The tachykinins bind to a series of three neurokinin, or NK, receptors, with SP having highest affinity at the NK1 receptor from this family. Thus, it is through the NK1 receptor that SP carries out its biological effects *in vivo*.

Tachykinin Peptide	Receptor
Arg-Pro-Lys-Pro-Gln-Gln-Phe-Phe-Gly-Leu-Met-NH$_2$	**NK$_1$**
Substance P	
His-Lys-Thr-Asp-Ser-Phe-Val-Gly-Leu-Met-NH$_2$	**NK$_2$**
Neurokinin A	
Asp-Met-His-Asp-Phe-Val-Gly-Leu-Met-NH$_2$	**NK$_3$**
Neurokinin B	

Slide #2

3—The NK1 receptor is a member of the G-protein-coupled receptor family, and so SP binding to the receptor causes release of the G protein from the third cytoplasmic loop of the receptor. The G protein then stimulates phospholipase C to hydrolyze its substrate PIP$_2$ to form the two second messenger molecules, IP$_3$ and diacylglycerol. These then set off a cascade of biochemical events within the cell, which in turn lead to the *in vivo* effects observed for SP . . .

{ Slide #3—not reproducible; hereinafter *NR* }

4—And these effects enable SP to play a major role in coordinating the pain and inflammation response, as depicted here. We begin with a wound or other trauma, which is communicated to the CNS via these afferent C-fibers which use SP as one of their primary neurotransmitters. . . . Any mediator which is centrally involved in coordinating pain and inflammation is likely to be implicated in the pathophysiology of numerous diseases, and some of the diseases in which SP is thought to play a role . . .

5—. . . are shown here. And this is what makes SP such an attractive therapeutic target, and a SP receptor antagonist such a worthwhile goal. Early workers in this field sought to discover a SP antagonist by modifying the peptide structure of SP itself, but the resulting peptidic antagonists had insufficient selectivity and oral bioavailability to be clinically useful. Thus we began a program to find a nonpeptide SP antagonist which we hoped would be useful clinically.

6—To that end, we set up a screening protocol, using bovine caudate membranes as a source of NK1 receptors.

We screened a collection of compounds we have in-house for such purposes, measuring their ability to displace tritiated substance P from its receptor. After screening about 800 com-

Tachykinin Receptors

Receptor	Ligand	Location	Role
NK_1	SP	Spinal Cord	Pain Transmission
		Brain-Dopamine Areas	Stress
		Endothelium	Plasma Extravasation
		Neutrophils	Inflammation
		Smooth Muscle	Relaxation
NK_2	NKA	Smooth Muscle – Lung	Asthma
		Smooth Muscle – Bladder	Incontinence
		Neurons	Pain
NK_3	NKB	Brain	?
		Spinal Cord	?

Slide #4

Diseases Involving Substance P

- Arthritis
- Asthma
- Migraine
- Inflammatory Bowel Disease
- Pain

Slide #5

Screening Program for a Nonpeptide SP Receptor Antagonist

- [3H]-SP Binding in Bovine Caudate Membranes

↓

- Identification of a Lead Structure

↓

- Optimization of Potency

⟶ CP-96,345

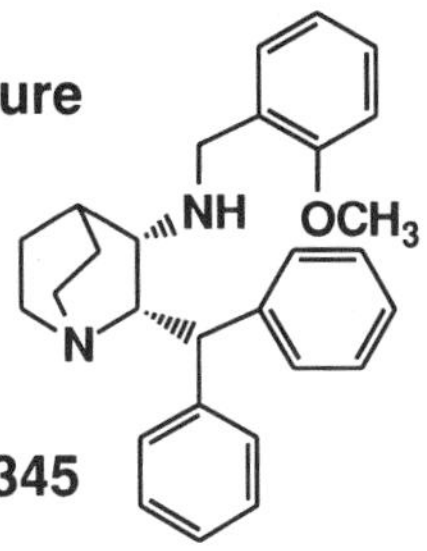

Slide #6

pounds, we identified a lead structure with the desired activity, and my lab began the chemistry effort to improve the potency of the lead compound, which led to the discovery of CP-96,345. I'd now like to review briefly the SAR and pharmacology of CP-96,345 . . .

Synthesis of Quinuclidine SP Antagonists

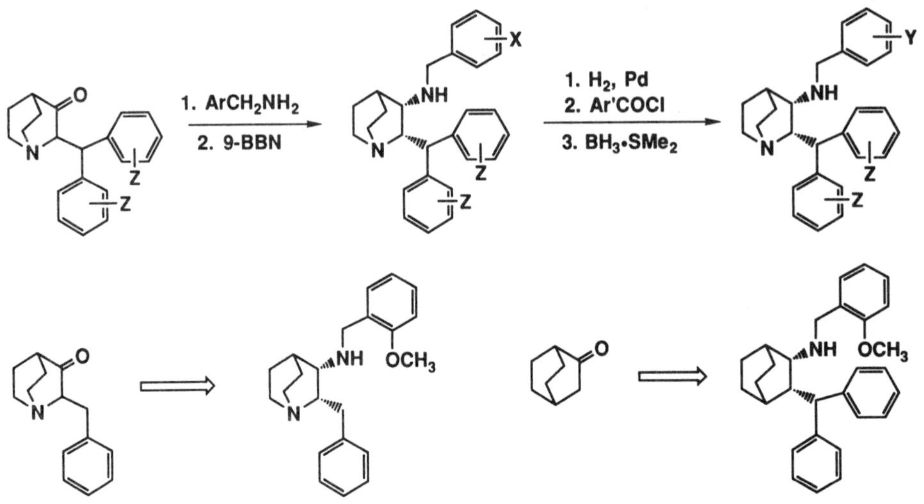

Slide #7

7—The synthetic chemistry used in making the analogs for our SAR program is shown here, starting from the known 2-benzhydryl quinuclidone, via imine formation and 9-BBN reduction, which affords the desired cis stereochemistry. We also found it useful to remove the benzyl group and then acylate the resulting amine followed by reduction to afford another series of benzyl derivatives. Other compounds for the SAR study were prepared as shown here starting from 2-benzyl quinuclidone and bicyclo[2.2.2]octanone.

8—The chemistry used to prepare optically active CP-96,345 is shown here, which relies on this chiral isocyanate reagent, commercially available from Aldrich. One diastereomer crys-

Preparation of CP-96,345

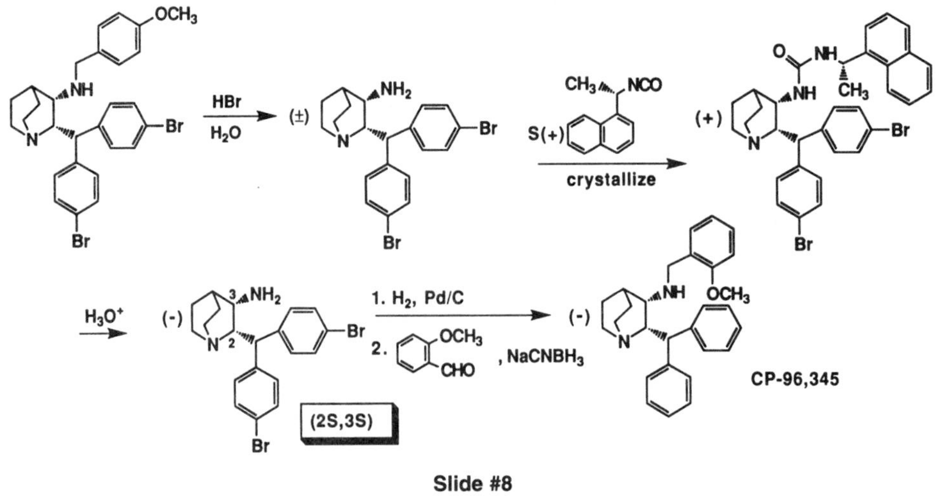

Slide #8

tallized directly from this reaction, and then removal of the chiral auxiliary and preparation of single crystals allowed determination of the absolute configuration by X-ray analysis as $2S,3S$ for the $(-)$ isomer. This intermediate was then converted to CP-96,345, which is thus the $2S,3S$ isomer. The $2R,3R$ enantiomer was prepared starting from the opposite isomer of the chiral isocyanate, and we'll see how this reagent is useful even though it is not a substance P antagonist.

9—Our SAR study identified three key elements in this quinuclidine series which are important for recognition by the NK1/substance P receptor. The first involves the benzylamine side

Key Elements for NK$_1$ Receptor Recognition

OCH_3 IC_{50} = 343 nM

OCH_3 IC_{50} = 20 nM

H IC_{50} = 16 nM
OCH_3 IC_{50} = 2.2 nM
Cl IC_{50} = 33 nM
Et IC_{50} = 17 nM
OEt IC_{50} = 16 nM
$NHCH_3$ IC_{50} = 68 nM

IC_{50} = 487 nM

IC_{50} = >32,000 nM

IC_{50} = 68 nM

2-Methoxybenzylamine Side Chain
①

Benzhydryl Group
②

Bridgehead Nitrogen
③

Slide #9

chain, where substitution plays a large role in determining receptor affinity. As illustrated by the methoxy group, *ortho* substituents provide far better activity than meta or para substituents. In addition, the methoxy group proved superior to other groups in the *ortho* position, even those very similar in terms of size, electron-donating capacity, or hydrogen-bonding ability. So the first SAR point indicates the importance of the 2-methoxy benzylamine side chain for receptor recognition. The second involves the benzhydryl group, where you can see that removal of a phenyl ring results in a considerable loss of receptor affinity, as does substitution on the phenyl rings. This was true for a wide variety of substituents, so the receptor prefers an unsubstituted benzhydryl group. Finally, the importance of the bridgehead nitrogen is demonstrated by the inactivity of the compound lacking it. These three key elements for receptor recognition can be summarized in a three-point binding model . . .

10—. . . shown here. Two of these elements, the ion-pairing interaction with the bridgehead nitrogen and the accessory binding site interaction with the benzhydryl group are common features of antagonist interactions with G-protein-coupled receptors, and have been introduced in the literature before. The third interaction, with the 2-methoxybenzylamine side chain, seems to be unique to the NK1 receptor, and is thus termed the specificity site interaction. I'll describe in a few minutes our SAR studies aimed at elucidating more of the interactions between CP-96,345 and the NK1 receptor, but first I'd like to turn to the biochemical and pharmacological characterization of the compound.

CP-96,345/NK$_1$ Receptor Interactions

Slide #10

11—As shown by Mike Snider, CP-96,345 is a very potent and selective ligand for the NK1 receptor, with little interaction with a wide variety of other receptors. This makes the compound a very valuable tool for studying substance P's effects *in vivo*. The enantioselectivity of receptor binding is shown here, with the *2R,3R* enantiomer, CP-96,344, having some four to five orders of magnitude lower affinity for the receptor than CP-96,345. This makes CP-96,344 a valuable control for studying SP pharmacology as well, because in any *in vivo* test in which we wish to attribute the activity of CP-96,345 to its binding at the NK1 receptor, we should be able to show that the enantiomer is inactive.

{ Slide #11—**NR** }

12—We've used CP-96,345 to characterize the relevance of substance P's *in vivo* activity in three disease areas: pain, inflammation, and asthma. I'll concentrate on our studies in the inflammation area, and then summarize results from the other two.

Disease Models Involving Substance P

- Pain
  - Formalin response
  - Dorsal horn neuron response to noxious stimulation

- Inflammation
  - SP-induced plasma protein extravasation
  - Acetic acid-induced writhing

- Asthma
  - SP-induced plasma protein extravasation
  - Cigarette smoke-induced edema

Slide #12

13—SP can be proposed to play a role in inflammation based on its control of endothelial permeability, as shown on this slide.

{ Slide #13—NR }

Thus SP, released by a proinflammatory stimulus, can increase the permeability of the endothelial lining of blood vessels, allowing neutrophils to pass from the circulation into adjacent tissue, where they migrate to the site of the trauma and initiate the inflammatory response. To establish which receptor mediates this event, we inject Evans blue dye into the circulation, apply SP, and then quantitate the dye that leaks or spreads into peripheral tissue in the presence of CP-96,345.

14—The first model studied involves injection of SP itself into guinea pig dorsal skin, and you can see that the dye leakage is dose-dependently blocked by CP-96,345 with an ED_{50} value of 0.83 mg/kg p.o. At the highest dose tested, CP-96,344 had no effect, demonstrating activity is due to blockade of the NK1 receptor.

CP-96,345 in Neurogenic Inflammation

- ED_{50} = 1-3 mg/kg i.v. for blockade of SP-or antidromic nerve stimulation-induced plasma protein extravasation in the rat

- ED_{50} = 4 mg/kg p.o. for blockade of mustard oil-induced plasma protein extravasation in rat paw

- CP-96,344 has no effect up to 10 mg/kg p.o. in mustard oil-induced extravasation

Lembeck and Nagahisa,
Br. J. Pharmacol., 1992

Slide #14–16

15—In the next experiment, capsaicin, a releaser of endogenous SP, was administered to guinea pigs and dye-spreading measured in the ureter, with CP-96,345 again providing dose-dependent blockade, with an ED_{50} value of 0.83 mg/kg p.o., and CP-96,344 showing no activity.

16—Finally, mustard oil, another releaser of endogenous SP, was applied to the rat paw, producing this control dye-spreading response, which was inhibited by CP-96,345, with an ED_{50} value of 4 mg/kg p.o., and again, CP-96,344 had no effect. These experiments provide definitive evidence for the NK1 receptor as the site which mediates SP control of endothelial permeability. But the next question is whether or not this phenomenon is really relevant to inflammation. To answer that question, Dr. Nagahisa and his colleagues studied a classic model of pain and inflammation used to profile NSAIDs, the acetic acid-inducing writhing model in mice.

17—Here is the control writhing response in mice to an injection of acetic acid, and here is the dose-dependent blockade of that response by CP-96,345, with an ED_{50} value of 10.7 mg/kg p.o. Again, CP-96,344 has no effect at the highest dose tested, indicating activity is due to blockade of the NK1 receptor. Now since SP had never been shown to be involved in this model, Dr. Nagahisa's group carried out one additional experiment, shown by the bar

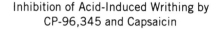

Inhibition of Acid-Induced Writhing by
CP-96,345 and Capsaicin

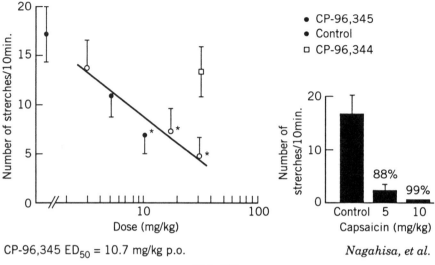

CP-96,345 ED_{50} = 10.7 mg/kg p.o.

Nagahisa, et al.

Slide #17

graph on the right-hand side of the slide, involving animals administered capsaicin, which depleted their afferent C-fibers of sensory neuropeptides including SP. In contrast to the control response, these animals showed little or no writhing response when dosed with 5 or 10 mg/kg of capsaicin, invoking a role for SP in this model. These results strongly imply a role for SP in pain and inflammation based on its control of endothelial permeability and thus its control of neutrophil access to proinflammatory sites. They also indicate a new therapeutic role for SP antagonists in the clinical management of pain and inflammatory disease.

18—The *in vivo* work with CP-96,345 has established the following roles for substance P: SP facilitates nociception, rather than being a primary pain transmitter, and thus plays an indirect

CP-96,345 In Vivo - Summary

- **· SP facilitates nociception**

- **· Controls endothelial permeability -
  Controls neutrophil access to inflammatory site**

- **· Role in:**
    - **· Chronic pain**
    - **· Inflammation**
    - **· Edema component in asthma**

Slide #18

role in pain. Through its control of endothelial permeability, SP plays a role in inflammation and asthma by allowing neutrophils access to a proinflammatory site where they can initiate either inflammation or edema in the case of asthma. The results suggest some very exciting therapeutic potential for SP antagonists, and this potential is now being evaluated by Pfizer, and others, in the clinic.

19—CP-96,345 has also been used to prepare other reagents useful in the study of SP pharmacology. The radiolabeled version shown here was prepared from an intermediate in the resolution chemistry by conversion to the dibromo analog of CP-96,345, then bromine/tritium exchange to prepare doubly labeled CP-96,345 of high specific activity.

{ Slide #19—*NR* }

20—Using this reagent, Tom Seeger at Pfizer has carried out autoradiography experiments. Briefly, Tom incubates a slice from a guinea pig brain with the tritiated compound; then, after a certain time, [he] washed away nonspecifically bound material and exposes the slice to tritium sensitive film. The binding pattern produced is shown here, with areas of high binding, in red, in the caudate nucleus, the area from which we derived our receptor preparation for the original screening protocol, and areas of low binding in blue out here in the cortex. The pattern matches that shown by tritiated SP, indicating both reagents bind to the same site, namely the NK1 receptor. We're using this technique to follow changes in the NK1 receptor during various animal models of CNS disease in order to identify new therapeutic applications for a SP antagonist in the central nervous system.

{ Slide #20—*NR* }

[11-C] CP-96,345 as a PET Reagent

- **Radiochemical Yield = 30-50%**
- **Specific Activity > 1000 Ci/mmole**
- **Biodistribution Studies - % dose/g @30 min**
  - *Lung - 2.06*
  - *Spleen - 0.71*
  - *Hippocampus - 0.042*   **Wieland, et al**

Slide #21

21—In a related study, we've prepared C-11 labeled CP-96,345 in collaboration with a group at the U. of Michigan. They're using the reagent in conjunction with PET technology to study levels of the SP receptor during various animal models of inflammation, again in order to identify new therapeutic applications for a SP antagonist. Finally, we've prepared this photoaffinity labeled version of CP-96,345 to identify amino acid residues at the binding site for CP-96,345 in the NK1 receptor. A group at Boston U. has shown that it specifically labels the NK1 receptor, and is now carrying out proteolytic fragmentation which will lead to sequencing of the radiolabeled fragment. We hope this approach will enable us to locate the binding site for CP-96,345 within the NK1 receptor. I will discuss an alternative approach to this problem, using molecular genetics techniques, in a few minutes, but first I'd like to return to our SAR discussion.

22—As I showed a moment ago [see Slide #10], three interactions were found to be important for recognition of CP-96,345 by the NK1 receptor. This model, however, doesn't tell us anything about interactions between the receptor and the quinuclidine nucleus, and in order to answer this question, . . .

{ Slide #22—**NR** }

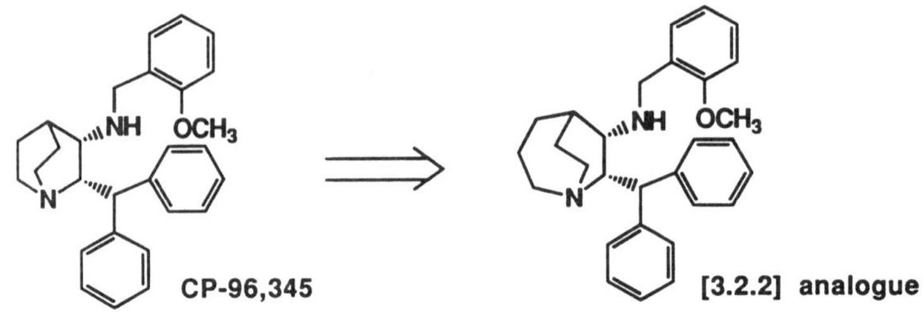

Slide #23

23—. . . we decided to probe this area with an analog of CP-96,345 in which one of the two-carbon bridges of the nucleus has been expanded to a three-carbon bridge. We felt this would only minimally disturb receptor interactions and so provide compounds with similar receptor affinity.

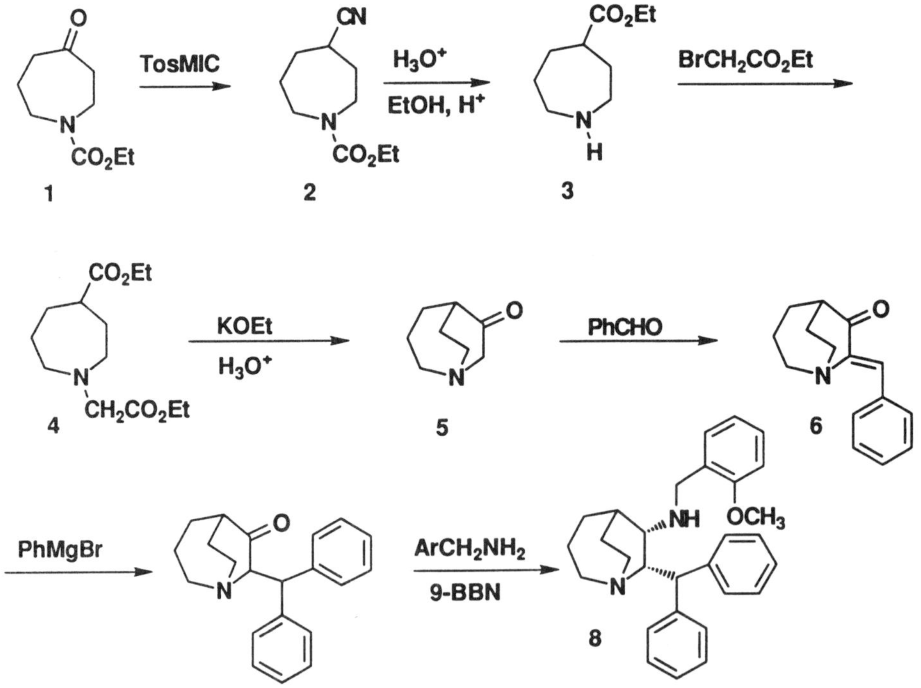

Slide #24

24—The synthesis of the [3.2.2] system relies on homoquinuclidone as an intermediate, which is prepared starting from this homopiperidine ketone using tosylmethylisocyanate as a homologating reagent to afford the corresponding nitrile. After conversion to the ester, the nitrogen is alkylated to afford the requisite diester which is then closed by a Dieckmann condensation. The rest of the synthesis proceeds as in the parent case, with benzylidene formation followed by 1,4-addition of an aryl magnesium halide, and then imine formation followed by 9-BBN reduction. Unlike the parent system, in this case we can get two diastereomers, but we only observe one. NMR and X-ray studies were unsuccessful in assigning the stereochemistry of this product, and we assume that it is as shown since calculations on the [benzhydryl homoquinuclidone] precursor show that the benzhydryl group prefers to lie up against the less sterically demanding two-carbon bridge, which would then place both substituents here in the final product.

CPD	X	Y	IC_{50}, nM*
8a	H	2-OCH$_3$	24
8b	H	2-Cl	43.7
8c	H	2,4-diOCH$_3$	12.7
8d	F	2-OCH$_3$	8.06
CP-96,345			0.27

*IC_{50} value in nM units for displacement of [^{3}H]SP in human IM-9 cells.

Slide #25

25—The SAR for this series of compounds is summarized here, and the direct comparison between the [2.2.2] and [3.2.2] systems shows an eightfold loss in receptor affinity in going to the larger system. The SAR pattern, however, remains the same as in the parent series, with a 2-chloro substituent leading to a significant loss in affinity, a *para* substituent offering no advantage, and fluorine substitution on the benzhydryl group also decreasing affinity just as chlorine did in the parent. So these molecules seem to bind just as the parent system does, yet there is a significant loss of receptor affinity.

26—To understand why, I used the Nemesis program on a Macintosh IIsi to model the [2.2.2] and [3.2.2] compounds. The conformation of CP-96,345 comes from its X-ray coordinates, and the [3.2.2] system represents an energy minimized conformation. As you can see, there is very little difference between these two molecules, and if I didn't label them, you'd have trouble telling which is which.

{ Slide #26—*NR* }

27—Overlapping the two using Nemesis, however, is more revealing and shows that the extra methylene in the [3.2.2] system protrudes into a region of space not occupied by the parent system, indicating the receptor is sensitive to steric bulk in this region.

{ Slide #27—*NR* }

28—Thus we can amend our receptor model to include this steric constraint in binding of the nucleus, and this completes the interactions of CP-96,345 with the receptor. We'll see in a little while how molecular genetics is coming at this problem from the point of view of the receptor, trying to define the residues which make up these contact points with CP-96,345. But first I'd like to finish the SAR story for these nonpeptide substance antagonists.

Binding of CP-96,345 at the NK1 Receptor

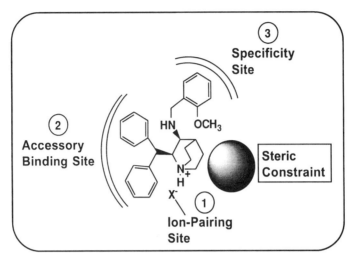

NK1 Receptor

Slide #28

29—This story continues with the discovery of the piperidine substance P antagonists by Dr. Manoj Desai and his co-workers at Pfizer. In fact, CP-99,994 is the most potent nonpeptide substance P receptor antagonist yet described.

Piperidine SP Antagonists

CP-96,345   **CP-99,994**

Slide #29

30—The synthesis of CP-99,994 begins with 4-phenylazetidinone, which is alkylated to afford the *trans*-chloropropyl derivative. When the ring is then cleaved open, this side chain closes on the liberated amine to form the new piperidine, with the substituents in the desired *cis* orientation. The methyl ester is then converted to the requisite benzylamine side chain by, first, protection with Cbz chloride, then conversion to the amide by the Weinreb procedure, followed by Hofmann degradation using lead tetra acetate in *t*-butanol, and finally removal of the resulting *t*-BOC group and then reductive amination using 2-methoxybenzaldehyde. Removal of the Cbz group with ammonium formate then completes the synthesis. The beauty

Synthesis of CP-99,994

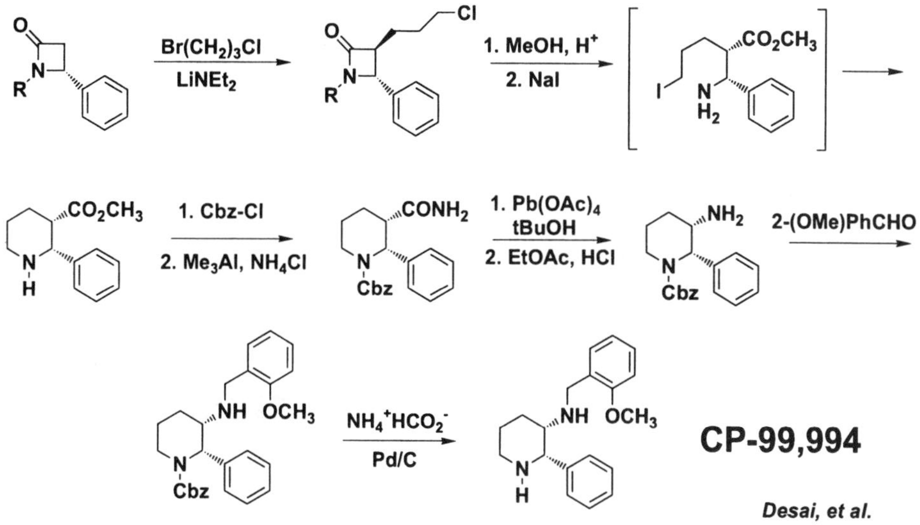

Slide #30

of this approach lies in the availability of 4-phenyl azetidinone in both optically active forms. (One of the elegant features of this approach is the fact that the starting material, 4-phenylazetidinone, is available commercially in both optically active forms.)

31—Thus, each enantiomer can be prepared from the appropriate R or S 4-phenylazetidinone, and, as was found in the parent series, only the 2*S*,3*S* enantiomer is a substance P antagonist.

Enantioselectivity of CP-99,994

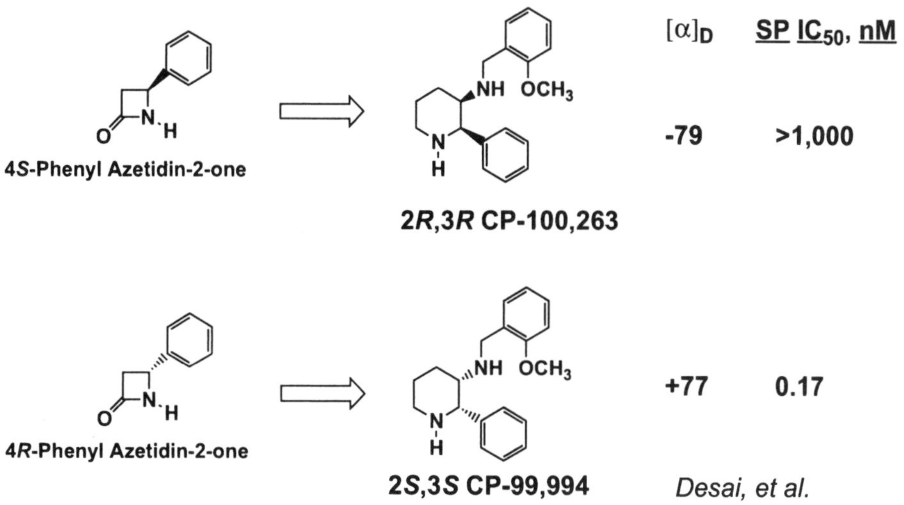

Slide #31, 33

32—SAR slide for CP-99,994

{ Slide #32 *left out* in the final presentation }

33—The biochemical characterization of CP-99,994 shows it to be potent and selective for the NK1 receptor, . . . (in fact, the most potent SP receptor antagonist discovered to date.)

{ Slide #34—*NR* }

34—. . . and to be useful in the characterization of substance P pharmacology. Thus CP-99,994 blocks cell firing of locus coeruleus neurons induced by substance P, it blocks Sar-9, Met-11 dioxide-induced hypermotility activity, and it blocks capsaicin-induced Evans blue dye leakage in guinea pig bronchial tissue, all of which are NK1-mediated effects. Hence this compound is proving to be a very useful tool for characterizing substance P pharmacology *in vitro* and *in vivo*.

A "Hybrid" SP Antagonist

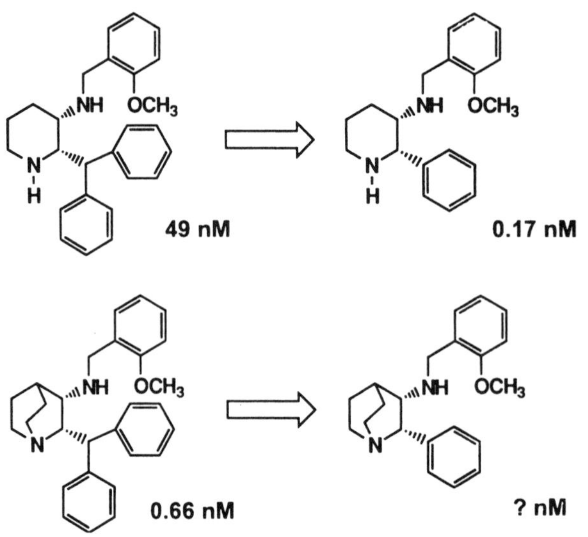

Slide #35

35—Based on the discovery of CP-96,345 and CP-99,994, where a phenyl ring serves as a surrogate for the benzhydryl group, I wondered if the phenyl ring would also be a useful surrogate in the quinuclidine series. To answer this question, I set out to synthesize and evaluate the corresponding 2-phenyl quinuclidine system, which was at that time unknown in the literature.

36—The synthesis we developed was based on a precedented approach in which the quinuclidine is formed by transannular ring closure of an appropriately substituted piperidinyl bromoketone. The requisite precursor was prepared in straightforward fashion, and then brominated and stirred in a two-phase mixture of methylene chloride and aqueous sodium bicarbonate to effect the ring closure. The success of this reaction depends on the presence of the *N*-benzyl group, and, to see why, we need to consider the transition for this reaction, as depicted here. When the piperidine flips into a boat conformation to close the ring,

Synthesis of 2-Phenyl Quinuclidines

Slide #36

the *N*-benzyl group holds the nitrogen lone pair in the axial orientation so that it will attack the bromoketone and close the quinuclidine ring. Once its job is finished, it is easily removed by hydrogenolysis, and the side chain is appended by imine formation followed by borane/methyl sulfide reduction. In this case, 9-BBN is too hindered to reduce the imine, so we take a *cis/trans* mixture and separate them by column chromatography.

37—Resolution is carried out as it was in the parent series, using the commercially available chiral isocyanate reagent. Once again, a single diastereomer crystallizes directly from the reaction mixture, and can be purified to a constant rotation value with a single recrystallization. The chiral auxiliary is then removed, and X-ray analysis of single crystals of the resulting intermediate was used to determine the absolute configuration of the (+) isomer as 2*S*,3*S*. This was then converted to the final target, and the resulting compounds were tested for NK1 receptor affinity.

38—First of all, the direct comparison between CP-96,345 and its 2-phenyl analog shows a 70-fold loss of receptor affinity, indicating phenyl is not a surrogate for benzhydryl in this series. Once again, the *cis* isomer is more potent than the *trans*. Further SAR investigation revealed, however, that substitution of the 2-phenyl group with a 3-chloro substituent enhances receptor affinity, which is different from results in the parent series where this type of substitution was not tolerated. Other substituents provided no increase in receptor affinity, so the 3-chloro group seems to be special in this regard. Once again, a 2-chloro substituent on the benzylamine side chain leads to a loss of receptor affinity, and additional *para* substitution does not increase activity. Finally, most of the biological activity resides in the 2*S*,3*S* enantiomer, as is the case with previous series. When this enantiomer was tested for functional activity in

Resolution of Phenylquinuclidines

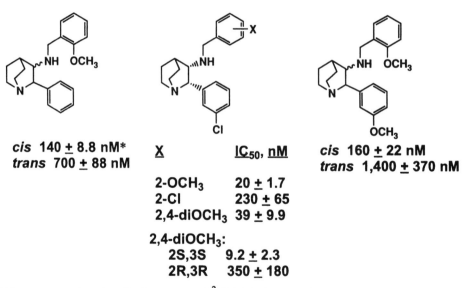

Slide #37

SAR for Phenylquinuclidine SP Antagonists

cis 140 ± 8.8 nM*
trans 700 ± 88 nM

X	IC$_{50}$, nM
2-OCH$_3$	20 ± 1.7
2-Cl	230 ± 65
2,4-diOCH$_3$	39 ± 9.9

2,4-diOCH$_3$:	
2S,3S	9.2 ± 2.3
2R,3R	350 ± 180

cis 160 ± 22 nM
trans 1,400 ± 370 nM

*IC$_{50}$ ± sem values for displacement of [^{3}H]-SP in human IM-9 cells. *Snider, et al.*

Slide #38

the dog isolated carotid artery model, however, it proved to have tissue contractile activity of its own, complicating the determination of a pA2 value and precluding further work in this series. The SAR data indicate, however, some potential for expanded investigation.

39—Our SAR studies can thus be summarized as shown here, with the three key elements for receptor recognition which we determined in studies on the parent series, followed by defin-

SAR of CP-96,345 and Its Analogues

- **Key Elements for NK1 Receptor Recognition**
  - *2-Methoxybenzylamine Side Chain*
  - *Benzhydryl Group*
  - *Bridgehead Nitrogen*

- **Steric Constraint in Binding the [3.2.2] Nucleus**

- **Flexibility at the C-2 Position in the Phenylquinuclidines**

Slide #39

ition of a steric constraint in interactions between the receptor and the quinuclidine nucleus, and finally the new SAR findings at the 2-position in a series of 2-phenyl quinuclidines. This rounds out the SAR picture for the quinuclidine substance P antagonists.

40—Now I'd like to turn to the final section of the talk and discuss how molecular genetics is beginning to reveal aspects of the interactions of CP-96,345 with the NK1 receptor. The opportunity to unlock the details of these interactions has been made possible by recent work in which the genes for all three neurokinin receptors were cloned, sequenced, and expressed, and are thus available for further manipulation by molecular genetics techniques.

{ Slide #40—*NR* }

This slide shows the proposed topology for the NK receptors, featuring the seven *trans*-membrane helical motif for receptors in the G-protein-coupled receptor family, and indicates by the lettered circles those residues which are conserved among all three NK receptors. It is thus understandable that SP binds to all three of these receptors. But, as we've seen, CP-96,345 binds only to the NK1 receptor, and thus some nonconserved residues, indicated by the red circles, must be responsible for recognizing CP-96,345. There are far too many nonconserved residues to identify which ones bind CP-96,345 by changing each of them one at a time, so we adopted a different strategy: to narrow down the region involved in CP-96,345 binding by the construction of chimeric receptors.

41—These chimeras can be constructed beginning with the wild-type NK1 and NK3 receptor genes. The genes are cleaved at a common endonuclease restriction site, and these restriction sites can be engineered in by PCR technology [which] is necessary; the fragments are then recombined, one from each of the corresponding parent receptor genes, to afford a chimeric receptor gene, which is expressed. And we can then identify the region of the NK1 receptor to which CP-96,345 binds by seeing where incorporation of the NK3 receptor sequence interferes with its binding.

42—The results from the first studies, carried out by Ulrik Gether and Thue Schwartz at the U. of Copenhagen, are shown here. The chimeric receptors are shown in the top panel, and the binding numbers for substance P and eledoisin indicate that the chimeric receptors all fold normally into the membrane. In addition, all these receptors show a normal PI response when stimulated with substance P, indicating they are fully functional receptors and that any loss of affinity for CP-96,345 is not due to improper folding or function. The results with CP-96,345 show that incorporation of TM7 from the NK3 receptor has little effect on its affinity, whereas with incorporation of TM6 and TM7 along with the intervening sequence, a significant loss

Construction of Chimeric NK Receptors

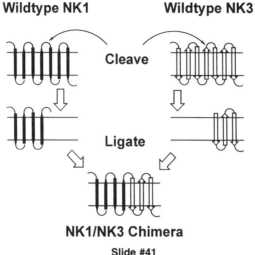

Wildtype NK1   Wildtype NK3

Cleave

Ligate

NK1/NK3 Chimera

Slide #41

of affinity for CP-96,345 occurs. Incorporating the portion of the NK3 receptor including TM5 to the carboxy terminus abolishes affinity for CP-96,345, demonstrating that the binding site is in this region of the receptor. A second important point from this study is that the binding of substance P is not affected by these changes, indicating that its binding site is in the N-terminal domain of the receptor. Other studies support this result, showing that the peptide agonist and nonpeptide antagonist bind to different sites within the receptor, even though their interaction is fully competitive. We'll return to this point later, . . . since it is a very important one if we are to understand how antagonists function at G-protein-coupled receptors, but first . . .

[Additional extempore, explanatory material was introduced here suggesting how "receptors" work in a manner "at odds" with findings described in previously published research.]

Binding to Chimeric NK Receptors

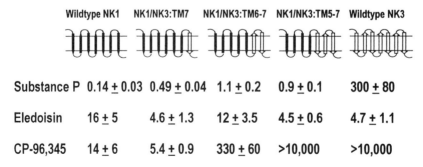

	Wildtype NK1	NK1/NK3:TM7	NK1/NK3:TM6-7	NK1/NK3:TM5-7	Wildtype NK3
Substance P	0.14 ± 0.03	0.49 ± 0.04	1.1 ± 0.2	0.9 ± 0.1	300 ± 80
Eledoisin	16 ± 5	4.6 ± 1.3	12 ± 3.5	4.5 ± 0.6	4.7 ± 1.1
CP-96,345	14 ± 6	5.4 ± 0.9	330 ± 60	$>10,000$	$>10,000$

Displacement of 125I-BH-SP in nM units

Slide #42

43—We next wanted to define more precisely the location of the CP-96,345 binding site and thus made smaller substitutions from the NK3 receptor into the NK1 receptor. Again, all these chimeras were properly folded and fully functional receptors. We began by incorporating a small segment from the extracellular loop just above TM domain 5 from the NK3 receptor into the NK1 receptor, and, as you can see, affinity for CP-96,345 is abolished. The corresponding segment on the next extracellular loop above TM domain 6 facing this first one also has a profound effect on affinity for CP-96,345, and thus the binding site resides in this small domain just above TM domains 5 and 6. To further demonstrate this, this small region, just above TM domains 5 and 6, was transferred from the NK1 receptor into the NK3 receptor, affording a chimera with good affinity for CP-96,345.

NK1 Binding Site for CP-96,345

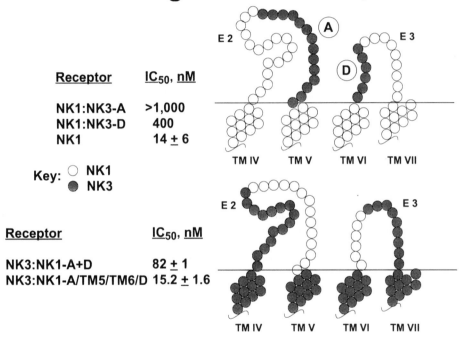

Receptor	IC$_{50}$, nM
NK1:NK3-A	>1,000
NK1:NK3-D	400
NK1	14 $\pm$ 6

Key: ○ NK1
      ● NK3

Receptor	IC$_{50}$, nM
NK3:NK1-A+D	82 $\pm$ 1
NK3:NK1-A/TM5/TM6/D	15.2 $\pm$ 1.6

Finally, when the intervening sequence of TM helices 5 and 6 is included, fully wild-type affinity for CP-96,345 is restored to a previously unresponsive receptor. We believe this is the first time this experiment has been successfully carried out (. . . the binding site for a nonpeptide antagonist has been transferred from the wild-type receptor to a previously nonresponsive receptor . . .), and it provides convincing evidence for the location of the CP-96,345 binding site within the NK1 receptor.

44—Experiments to determine the actual residues which contact CP-96,345 within this binding site are currently ongoing, and results of two of these studies are shown here. The group under Dr. Fong at Merck has demonstrated the involvement of His-197 in recognizing CP-96,345, since its mutation to an alanine residue leads to a significant loss of affinity for CP-96,345. Studies by Bruce Sachais in Jim Krause's lab at Washington U. in St. Louis have demonstrated the importance of Ile-290, which shows a significant loss of affinity for CP-96,345 when it is mutated to serine. These two residues seem to lie just outside the actual binding site, so they may not be in direct contact with CP-96,345. Rather, they seem to

NK₁ Residues Involved in CP-96,345 Binding

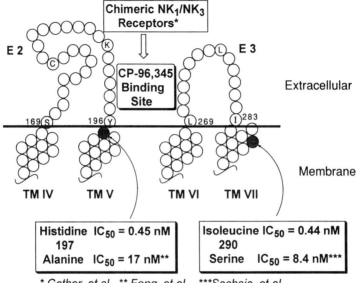

Slide #44

be involved in folding the binding site into the proper conformation during its recognition of CP-96,345. Studies to define the actual residues in contact with CP-96,345 are in progress.

45—We next wondered whether this finding could be generalized to all the NK receptors, and the opportunity to study this was afforded when Sanofi Research announced the discovery of the first nonpeptide NK2 antagonist, SR 48,968. As you can see, this compound is quite selective, in addition to being a very potent NK2 antagonist.

Potent, Selective Tachykinin Antagonists

	NK1	NK2
CP-96,345	8.1	> 10,000
SR-48,968	> 10,000	0.7

Slide #45

46—Chimeric receptors were now constructed between the NK1 and NK2 receptors, and, once again, binding studies with peptide agonist ligands demonstrated they were properly folded and fully functional receptors. As before, incorporation of TM domain 7 from the NK2 receptor has little effect on the binding of CP-96,345, but it already has incorporated affinity

Binding Site for Tachykinin Antagonists

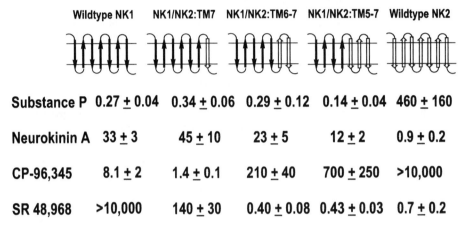

	Wildtype NK1	NK1/NK2:TM7	NK1/NK2:TM6-7	NK1/NK2:TM5-7	Wildtype NK2
Substance P	0.27 ± 0.04	0.34 ± 0.06	0.29 ± 0.12	0.14 ± 0.04	460 ± 160
Neurokinin A	33 ± 3	45 ± 10	23 ± 5	12 ± 2	0.9 ± 0.2
CP-96,345	8.1 ± 2	1.4 ± 0.1	210 ± 40	700 ± 250	>10,000
SR 48,968	>10,000	140 ± 30	0.40 ± 0.08	0.43 ± 0.03	0.7 ± 0.2

Displacement of 125I-BH-SP or 125I-BH-NKA (for wildtype NK2) in nM units

Gether and Schwartz

Slide #46

for SR 48,968. Inclusion of the section from TM domain 6 to the carboxy terminus now significantly decreases the affinity of CP-96,345 and restores fully wild-type affinity for SR 48,968 to a previously unresponsive receptor. Inclusion of the section from TM domain 5 to the carboxy terminus furthers this trend, and these results demonstrate that the binding site for nonpeptide antagonists is at the carboxy terminus of both the NK1 and NK2 receptors.

Summary of Molecular Biology Results

- **SP and NKA interact with the N-terminal portions of their respective receptors**

- **CP-96,345 binds to epitopes near the top of TM5 and TM6 and adjoining loops E2 and E3 of the NK1 receptor**

- **SR-48,968 binds to a similar region of the NK2 receptor**

- **Peptide agonists and nonpeptide antagonists interact in a competitive manner with different portions of the NK receptors**

Slide #47

47—So to summarize the results of our molecular biology studies, we've shown that, while peptide agonists bind at the amino terminus of their respective NK receptors, the nonpeptide antagonists bind near the carboxy-terminal end. We've further defined the binding site for CP-96,345 to a small region in the extracellular loops just above TM domains 5 and 6 of the NK1 receptor and are currently trying to pinpoint the residues which actually make contact with the antagonist. Finally, let me discuss this point that, although their binding interactions are fully competitive, peptide agonists and nonpeptide antagonists do not bind to the same receptor sites. Competitive binding is usually pictured as occurring by displacement of one ligand by another at the same site, which is clearly not possible here.

48—Molecular modeling may provide a clue to unravel this puzzle. Jim Rizzi at Pfizer has constructed this three-dimensional model of the NK1 receptor, with the proposed binding site for CP-96,345 indicated here. (. . . and when he docks CP-96,345 into its binding site . . .)

{ Slide #48—NR }

[Additional extempore material was interpolated here speculating about how "computer simulation" of the "docking process" might "stimulate further experiments."]

49—What Jim finds is that there is a conformational change in this extracellular loop region when it binds CP-96,345, which is transmitted to the N-terminal extracellular by means of this disulfide bond. This disulfide is an obligatory structural feature of the receptor, and binding and signal transduction do not occur without it. This extracellular loop makes up a significant part of the binding site for substance P, and so what seems to happen here is that binding of one ligand induces a conformational change in the binding site for the other ligand preventing its binding.

{ Slide #49—NR }

Thus, the peptide and nonpeptide ligands are competitive, even though they occupy different sites, because they alter the conformation of the entire binding region of the receptor. We hope this insight will lead to greater understanding of the mechanism by which nonpeptide antagonists block the function of G-protein-coupled receptors, and enable us to design antagonists at new G-protein-coupled receptors in the future.

Summary

- **CP-96,345 SAR → 3-Point Binding Model**

- **Nuclear Modifications:**
    - *[3.2.2] Analogues*
    - *2-Phenyl Quinuclidines*

- **Binding Site for CP-96,345 in NK1 Receptor**

- **Mechanism of Competitive Receptor Antagonism**

Slide #50

50—So, in summary, what we've shown is that the SAR for CP-96,345 has led to a three-point binding model which has been further refined with SAR around the quinuclidine nucleus.

Molecular biology studies have enabled us to define the location of the binding site for CP-96,345 at the NK1 receptor, and these studies are providing the first indications of a possible mechanism describing how nonpeptide antagonists block the function of G-protein-couple receptors. We hope the insight from these studies will be useful in the future in the design of antagonists at new G-protein-coupled receptors.

Acknowledgements

- *Chemistry*
  Sue Drozda and Frank Ewing
  Manoj Desai, Sheri Lefkowitz, Peter Thadeio
- *Pharmacology*
  Mike Snider and Kelly Longo
  Atsushi Nagahisa and Megumi Nakagaki
- *Molecular Biology*
  Ulrik Gether and Thue Schwartz
  Bruce Sachais and Jim Krause
- *Molecular Modeling*
  Jim Rizzi

Slide #51

51—I'd like to close by thanking the people who carried out the work I described today. Sue Drozda and Frank Ewing carried out the quinuclidine chemistry, and Manoj Desai, Sheri Lefkowitz, and Pete Thadeio carried out the piperidine chemistry.

The *in vitro* biochemistry was carried out by Mike Snider and Kelly Longo, and the *in vivo* pharmacology by Atsushi Nagahisa and Megumi Nakagaki.

The molecular biology studies were carried out in collaboration with Ulrik Gether and Thue Schwartz at the U. of Copenhagen and with Bruce Sachais and Jim Krause at Washington U. in St. Louis.

Finally, Jim Rizzi carried out the molecular modeling studies. I'd like to thank these people for their hard work and you for your kind attention.

SUGGESTED READING

Anholt, R. H. (1994). *Dazzle 'em with style: The art of oral scientific presentation.* New York: W. H. Freeman.

Bazerman, C. (1988). *Shaping written knowledge: The genre and activity of the experimental article in science.* Madison, WI: University of Wisconsin Press.

Booth, V. (1993). *Communicating in science: Writing a scientific paper and speaking at scientific meetings,* 2nd Ed. Cambridge: Cambridge University Press.

Cook, E. B. (1968). Oral presentation of a scientific paper. In F. P. Woodford (Ed.), *Scientific writing for graduate students: A manual on the teaching of scientific writing,* pp. 150–166. New York: The Rockefeller University Press.

Day, R. A. (1994). *How to write & publish a scientific paper,* 4th ed. Phoenix, AZ: Oryx Press.

Garvey, W. D. (1979). *Communication: The essence of science.* Oxford: Pergamon Press.

Fleck, L. (1979). *Genesis and development of a scientific fact* (T. J. Trenn, R. K. Merton, and F. Bradley, Eds. and Trans.). Chicago: University of Chicago Press.

Foster, J. (1963). *Science writer's guide.* New York: Columbia University Press. (See especially Chapter 1, "Principles and Practices," pp. 1–35.)

Harre, R. (1965). *An introduction to the logic of the sciences.* London: Macmillan. (See especially Chapter 4, "Scientific Explanation," pp. 82–110.)

Holcombe, M. W., and Stein, J. K. (1986). How to deliver dynamic presentations—Use visuals for impact. *Business Marketing,* June, 162–165.

Kapp, R. O. (1960). *The presentation of technical information.* New York: Macmillan.

Kenny, P. (1992). *A handbook of public speaking for scientists and engineers.* Bristol, UK: Institute of Physics (IOP) Publishing.

Losee, J. (1980). *A historical introduction to the philosophy of science,* 2nd ed. Oxford: Oxford University Press.

Montgomery, S. L. (1996). *The scientific voice.* New York: Guilford Publications.

Nies, J. I., and Tas, R. F. (1991). How to add visual impact to your presentations. *The Cornell H.R.A. Quarterly,* May, 46–51.

Savory, T. H. (1953). *The language of science: Its growth, character and usage.* London: Andre Deutsch.

Toulmin, S. (1974). Postscript: The structure of scientific theories. In F. Suppe (Ed.), *The structure of scientifc theories,* pp. 600–614. Urbana, IL: University of Illinois Press.

van Fraassen, C. B. (1980). *The scientific image.* Oxford: Oxford University Press. (See especially Chapters 5, "The Pragmatics of Explanation," pp. 97–157; and 7, "Gentle Polemics," pp. 204–215.)

Ziman, J. (1976). *The force of knowledge: The scientific dimension of society.* Cambridge: Cambridge University Press. (See especially Chapter 5, "Scientific Communication," pp. 90–119.)

12

Model #3: A Management-Based Presentation from Grumman Technical Services

The third and final model script we want to present in this section involves a managerial presentation entitled "Journey to Excellence" designed and delivered by J. L. "Skip" Olson, a Vice President of Grumman Technical Services (A Division of Grumman Corporation) operating in Titusville, Florida at the Kennedy Space Center (KSC). We should point out here that a number of technical writers/editors and engineering support staff aided in the development of both the script and visuals connected with this project—a formal presentation focusing on Grumman's commitment to quality (and quality-oriented processes) at KSC.[1]

"JOURNEY TO EXCELLENCE"—SOME BACKGROUND

For the most part, this organization's "journey to excellence" presentation takes listeners through what Grumman Technical Services (GTS) calls their "companywide effort to facilitate total quality."[2] This corporate effort, known as *Grumman Quality,* or *Process GQ,*

---

[1] We'd like to publicly acknowledge the complete cooperation of this group of technical writers/editors and engineering support staff during our research process and the writing of our book. We are particularly indebted to Skip Olson, Program Vice President, Shuttle Processing Contract; Ray McCormick, Deputy Director, Integrated Ground Operations (Engineering Support); and Deirdre A. Sheetz, Supervisor of Operations and Maintenance Documentation.

[2] Much of the background material presented here on GTS quality (and excellence) programs was compiled via on-site visits to the Grumman facility at KSC during the spring of 1992. Additional details about these programs are explored in a variety of useful pamphlets and brochures provided to us by Skip Olson and members of the Grumman staff. We found the following two documents especially useful for understanding the quality "agenda" at Grumman: (1) *Grumman Quality* (Grumman Corp., n.d.), a pamphlet detailing the quality process from 1983 through 1991, the year GTS won the George M. Low Trophy, NASA's Quality and Excellence Award (an award signifying the "Best of the Best" in the aerospace industry, sponsored by the National Aeronautics and Space Administration); and (2) *1991 Highlights: George M. Low Trophy—NASA's Quality and Excellence Award* (1992).

has identified the following six goals that are maintained on a consistent basis:

(1) Emphasize the customer.

(2) Stimulate leadership among our people.

(3) Make total quality a *way of life* where we do right things right the first time every time.

(4) Streamline decision-making and operating processes.

(5) Enhance communications within our company and with our customers and suppliers.

(6) Reinforce the idea that each of our employees has a stake in our company's success.

In addition, in their ongoing quest to achieve total quality, GTS management highlights nine "elements" of Process GQ which, they contend, help focus all Grumman activities toward the preceding six goals:

(1) Leadership

(2) Training

(3) Work process management

(4) Customer involvement

(5) Supplier involvement

(6) Communication

(7) Policy deployment

(8) Employee reward and recognition

(9) Awards

"JOURNEY TO EXCELLENCE"—THE CAFTA VARIABLES

The goal-setting and maintenance activities, the isolation of key strategic and logistical "elements," and the integration of continuous quality processes—all carefully adopted and rigorously supported by management and staff—have become the basis for Vision '95 which delimits Grumman's long-term goal: "to be recognized as one of the best areospace, transportation, information, and electronics systems and services companies in the world."

We consider the management-based script included here as Model #3 particularly important because it fully, and successfully, articulates a major corporation's (Grumman's) long-term goal. In doing so, in laying out and examining that goal, Skip Olson's presentation

- delineates the major components of Grumman Quality (or Process GQ)
- describes Grumman's most significant quality improvement initiatives
- reviews the history of the quality "movement" at Grumman from, roughly, 1983 to 1991.

In precise, concrete, and dynamic language—and graphically, as well, with the deployment of equally clear and relevant visuals—this VP shares both Grumman's "tradition for quality" and their "journey to excellence." In a single, highly coherent management presentation, that's quite a triumph, indeed.

A discussion of the CAFTA variables we want to isolate and briefly examine for this management-oriented presentation appears in the next five subsections of this chapter. The entire presentational script for "Journey to Excellence," along with visuals (i.e., slides) used, directly follows our rhetorical "plan," or outline, of the presentation.

Content

The *content* or subject matter of this formal, managerial presentation is, as we've noted in some detail in the background material on "Journey to Excellence," Grumman Quality (or Process GQ). The presentation focuses on all aspects of the quality "movement" and commitment to quality at Grumman: the tradition of quality; quality programs and initiatives; relevant goals, elements, and strategies; the award process and winning the George M. Low Trophy (for 1991), NASA's Quality and Excellence Award; and creating an environment for "continuous improvement" through process assessment, documentation, and constructive feedback.

Audience

Grumman's "Journey to Excellence" was presented on a number of occasions (more than 10), during (approximately) an 18-month period, to professional groups within a variety of industry-based, academic, and professional (quality-related) conference settings. Many of the forums addressed were supported, sponsored, or endorsed by NASA and NASA contractors, the Johnson Space Center *Quarterly Quality Review,* the Total Quality Management (TQM) Seminar for Aerospace and Defense, and the American Society for Quality Control (ASQC).

According to Grumman, audience membership of the various groups addressed by Skip Olson included the following: CEOs, presidents, and VPs from a wide range of industries and the military; senior-level executives; upper- and mid-level management; quality professionals; NASA contractor professionals (e.g., engineers, managers, and quality-related personnel); and academics specializing in some facet of "quality" as a discipline.

The various conference audiences ranged from a minimum of approximately 30 upper- and mid-level managers and quality professionals attending a Johnson Space Center forum to a maximum of 200 at Skip Olson's presentation within the context of a special interest session on "TQM issues" at a NASA/Contractor event. Other conference presentations made by Olson involved, for example:

- 90 middle managers and quality personnel at the Electric Power Resource Institute (sponsored by the electric power industry);
- 100 senior executives, upper- and mid-level managers, and quality personnel from the defense and aerospace industry, as well as "high-tech" representatives at all levels from the military, attending a TQM Seminar for Aerospace and Defense; and
- 150 middle managers and "top-level" executives (with some international representation) from TQM departments out of "a wide spectrum of industries" attending the annual meeting of the ASQC.

Additionally, and of considerable importance to the present discussion, audience members for this series of quality-related presentations—delivered on a variety of occasions (described above)—might best be characterized as

- *aware of,* or *familiar with,* either quality-based issues or the professional field of TQM; or
- *receptive* to the principles and practices of the quality movement (i.e., somewhat "initiated," if not wholly "converted").

Moreover, as a group they were considered to be

- eager, like-minded professionals interested in, or knowledgeable about, quality-based issues and TQM; and
- college-educated (in engineering, technical, or business areas), with advanced degrees (MBAs, PhDs) or significant amounts of technical training or relevant professional development activity.

As we have insisted throughout this book, when presenters can accurately forecast the composition of their intended audience(s) during planning and development stages of any project, the resultant presentation is much more likely to succeed. Precise knowledge and information about the makeup of the groups who would attend these industrial, government, and academic forums resulted, we were told, in the (increasing) effectiveness of each presentation and in the ultimate satisfaction—for both Skip Olson and GTS—that a job had been particularly well done.

Form/Format

On the more than 10 occasions that Skip Olson delivered "Journey to Excellence" for GTS, the primary form (or format) of the event consisted of an individual, lecture-style ("frontal") presentation. Delivered within the context of industry-related, governmental, or academic/professional "conference" settings, the presentations were generally held in large-scale auditorium (or "ballroom-type") venues, seating 100+ to 200+ attendees. Two smaller-scale events, with audiences of approximately 30 attendees (one, at the Johnson Space Center, Houston, TX; a second, at the Manned Space Flight Center in Huntsville, AL), were held in training-type "classroom" settings typical of those found in hotels and on university campuses on the professional conference circuit.

Time Frame

Two slightly different versions of the "Journey to Excellence" presentation were developed. While both contained virtually the same content, one (somewhat longer) lasted approximately 25–35 minutes; a second, the "short version," was clocked at 20–22 minutes. (The version of the script we include in this chapter is the foundation for the longer presentation.)

We should point out that *both* versions of the delivered script were enhanced, quite effectively, by a substantial number of explanatory visuals (a total of some 35 slides), presenting such material as the following: a "mission statement"; a "team motto"; a wheel depicting the spectrum of employee-generated communication lines; photos of GTS program-related events and staff; and relevant data (in graphs and charts), "bulleted" information highlights, and process diagrams.

Aims(s)

From our conversations with Skip Olson and those Grumman staff involved with the "Journey to Excellence" project, we believe that the *aims,* and overall purpose, of these presentations can be summed up as follows:

(1) ***To inform***—to share data and information (i.e., statistics, strategies, goals, processes, systems) about the tradition for (total) quality at Grumman and its full integration into the work environment at the Kennedy Space Center—that is, to share with a variety of presentational audiences the results and ongoing nature of Grumman's Process GQ.

(2) ***To teach/train***—to organize, structure, and define the various components of Grumman Quality, Process GQ, and Vision '95—Grumman's "total quality initiatives"—so that audience members themselves might, at some future point, be able to adopt these same (or similar) components (goals, "elements," processes) and incorporate them as "initiatives" within their own organizations for the common good (and not, simply, for a "run" at winning NASA's Quality and Excellence Award, the George M. Low Trophy).

(3) ***To motivate***—to kindle interest, and, to a certain extent, *entertain.* While much can, indeed, be shared and taught within a compact 30-minute presentation, because of the high degree of *ethos,* or credibility, a speaker at the VP level possesses relative to a subject like quality, much of what he or she has to say will necessarily prove motivational as well. That is, conference attendees (managers, senior managers, VPs, and CEOs) are as likely to be

- *motivated,* and even "entertained," by quality-oriented ideas, and
- *aroused* about values, goals, initiatives, processes, and ultimate benefits that might accrue to their own organizations . . .

as they are likely to be affected by the "rapid-fire" abilities of even a skilled "trainer-teacher" sharing important, high-level organizational data and information.

"JOURNEY TO EXCELLENCE"—PRESENTATIONAL SCRIPT: ORGANIZATION, VISUALS, AND STYLE

The script for Grumman's "Journey to Excellence" is detailed, complete, and rich in content and ideas. As we note in Chapter 5, in reference to another management-oriented presentational script, this one clearly transmits authority. Although it appears friendly, eager, and even a bit low-key and casual—and it truly is all of these—the script is fundamentally business-like; it evokes that sense of professionalism we described earlier in this book as a combination of industriousness, involvement, commitment, skill, and the sincere concern for an enterprise of mutual interest and benefit.

Organizational Structure

"Journey to Excellence" is organized according to a deductive scheme at the "macro" (or overall) level with brief introductory remarks serving as a contextual framework for delivering the data and information (that comprise "the journey") to follow. The presentational script immediately launches into a *statement of purpose:*

We are encouraged by NASA to speak to others about Grumman's total commitment to quality and the road to receiving the George M. Low Trophy.

Forecasting the topical focus ("Grumman's *total commitment to quality*") and chronological order ("the *road to*" attaining NASA's Quality and Excellence Award) of the script to follow, the introductory remarks even contain a (seemingly) lighthearted but incisive and illustrative story about the nature of the phrase "total commitment"—a concept to be explored and examined throughout.

A rough outline of the organizational structure (topical) and logic/order (chronological, linear) of "Journey to Excellence" might look like the following (where + simply means "more than," or "in addition to," as in *more than* three details, examples, or slides are employed in relation to a given topic):

T-1   *Story . . .   *[story]**

T-2   *Body*

- **Topic 1 . . .**
  [narrative]
  [detail 1.1, detail 1.2 . . .]
  [examples+]
  [slides+]
- **Topic 2 . . .**
  [narrative]
  [detail 2.1, detail 2.2 . . .]
  [examples+]
  [slides+]
- **Topic 3 . . . +**
  [narrative]
  [detail 3.1, detail 3.2 . . .]
  [examples+]
  [slides+]

T-3   *Close . . .*
- **"Wrap Up"**
- **Q & A**

Note: An optional "story" resides about midway through the original presentational script narrative; that story is identified above as ***[story]*** and is included in the script version presented here.

Visuals

An extensive network of *visuals* complements the data and information delineated, via vivid (verbal) details and examples, in the central *story* of "Journey to Excellence." Numerous slides sprinkled throughout the presentation add depth and breadth to the chronological narrative of "the journey" to quality and excellence.

These visuals highlight, and also forecast, succeeding sections of the narrative. They depict key points in "the journey" graphically (see the George M. Low Criteria slide below) and, also, verbally (see the "Journey to Excellence" slide, a brief bulleted list forecasting the whole story to be explored in the presentation). An assortment of photos shows the Grumman people "behind the scenes," who daily take part in "the journey." Still other slides contain a wide spectrum of supporting details—data and information—in a variety of visual formats:

- Bulleted lists identifying quality processes, the "Team Charter" concept, and available NASA recognition awards
- Conceptual diagrams and flow charts clarifying and concretizing the "Process Management" system, the "Process Improvement" cycle, and the notion of "Team Excellence" at KSC
- Line charts depicting the "Steering Team" concept and circular charts indicating spheres of employee-generated communication
- A time line highlighting "Quality History" at Grumman
- Line graphs, bar charts, and multiple-bar graphs exhibiting relevant data and trends, such as the dramatic increase in the number of "approved" employee suggestions since 1990.

Script Style

The script style for "Journey to Excellence" seems to jibe well with, and effectively reinforce, its presentational content. That is, it is high-quality, fluent, fluid, business-like prose, appropriate to a professional discussion about an organization's history of, and commitment to, quality. The script style is unadorned, relatively plain, and spare (in the sense of lean and trim), conveying (overall) an aura of personal and professional integrity, honesty, openness, and pared-down simplicity.

Moreover, because the language chosen for this script so carefully reflects, even elevates, its content, the style used seems to work well in inviting potential listeners to (a) participate fully and equally in the discussion and (b) accept the message, or "news," conveyed on its own terms.

All of the stylistic options chosen, all of the stylistic "markers" we identify below, seem to promote and transmit the strong sense of authority and credibility conveyed in this presentation:

- *Forceful, straightforward syntax of the written script* (followed in the *oral* version)—exhibited in sentences such as "The NASA Excellence process was vital to us—not just to winning an award, but as a gauge to measure our progress."
- *Sentence structure and word order*—many short to medium-length, strategically placed, fast-paced, noun-phrase/verb-phrase, simple and compound sentences, such as these:
  —"We engineer and install special instrumentation for flow and launch operations." OR
  —"We developed complete diagnostic capabilities for quickly identifying problems and returning the hardware to operating status."
- *Active verb forms and action verbs*—for example, "shows," "proves," "engineer and install," "serve," "examine," "meet," "monitor," and "automated."

- *Brevity and clarity of definitions articulated*—such as "Impact time is the percent of required support time we miss because of hardware or operational problems."

- *Concrete words and technical terms used throughout the script*—for example, "teamwork," "management team," "post-launch," "post-test analysis," "calibration support," "tape certification."

- *Planned informality of the prose*—for example, the use of expressions, phrases, or short sentences such as "Well, now . . ."; "Don't fret . . ."; "My personal favorite . . ."; "Man, the chicken was ready!" or "Quite a platform for TQM—eh!"

- *Regular use of personal pronouns and contractions*—such as "we," "our," "I'd," "I'm," "I'll," or "isn't."

- *Delivery of important information in parallel lists*—such as the following, for example, structured to share pieces of the quality "puzzle": "This is a valuable way for us to work with our Lockheed teammates to integrate efforts, define shared processes, identify and track key measures, and move forward in a *consistent* way toward total quality."

- *Easy-to-spot and clear identification of new topics* introduced throughout the presentation—with transitional words and phrases such as these: ". . . Grumman's first attempts at TQM . . ."; "First . . ." "Second . . ." Third . . ."; "Our mission statement spells out what we do best . . ."; "In addition to routine maintenance . . ."; "A key element in assuring TQM success is improving communication."; "Another key element . . ."; "The next key element of GQ I'd like to talk about . . ."; My final comment is . . ."; "Let me close by saying . . . ."

All these stylistic features, taken together, coupled with the understated *power* of the speaker and the *clarity* of his ideas—and tempered with a sense of genuine concern, openness, friendliness, even avuncularity—constitute the hallmarks of what we call the "consultative" presentational style (a style solidly within the middle range of the list of stylistic options we present in Chapter 5).

One final comment about this script: While "Journey to Excellence" was crafted with care, precision, and attention to detail, as well as with much concern for linguistic fluency in an oral context, we should point out that some room had been left for improvised, off-the-cuff remarks, "ad-libs," and spontaneous additions or deletions (depending on the time frame allocated to a particular presentation and specific audience needs determined prior to a conference "event").

PRESENTATIONAL MODEL #3

What follows in this section is the complete presentational script of "Journey to Excellence," developed by GTS staff and Grumman Program VP for Shuttle Processing, J. L. "Skip" Olson. As we have noted earlier in this chapter, Skip Olson delivered this presentation on a number of occasions before a variety of professional audiences.

"Journey to Excellence"

We are encouraged by NASA to speak to others about Grumman's total commitment to quality and the road that led to receiving the George M. Low Trophy. To begin, I'd like to share a little story about a country pig and a chicken.

Grumman Technical Services

Journey to Excellence

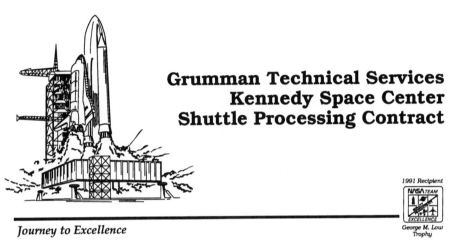

**Grumman Technical Services
Kennedy Space Center
Shuttle Processing Contract**

1991 Recipient

NASA TEAM

EXCELLENCE

*George M. Low
Trophy*

Journey to Excellence

Slide #1

Well, it seems the two of them were walking along one day when the pig realized that he hadn't had breakfast. Just as he mentioned that to the chicken, the chicken noticed a restaurant across the street. As they were walking across the street, they saw a sign on the restaurant window that said, "Special: Ham and Eggs—99 cents."

Man, the chicken was ready! She practically flew up them steps. The pig, on the other hand, paused. The chicken shouted back, "Come on pig, I'm hungry." The pig replied, "Ham and eggs for you chicken is a *contribution,* for me it's a *total commitment.*" [italics added]

. . . *pause* . . . Don't fret, it took me two days to get it.

Well now, Grumman's first attempts at TQM over four years ago were sort of like the chicken's, a contribution. But we quickly learned that to make it work, we had to make a total commitment. It didn't happen all at once and not without a lot of effort first from management, then from our employees. Fortunately, we got a lot of outside help along the way from involvement in various award programs.

The NASA Excellence process was vital to us—not just [for] winning an award, but as a gauge to measure our progress. What better way to know how you are doing than to be evaluated by your customer!

We had the opportunity to learn from the experiences of other NASA contractor finalists and recipients on their quality programs.

The additional insight provided by Florida Power & Light [FP&L], a Deming Award winner, convinced us TQM really does work. A tour of their facility allowed us to incorporate several of their lessons learned that really helped smooth some of the bumps in our journey.

Today I hope to give you some ideas to take back to smooth your own journey to excellence.

George M. Low Criteria

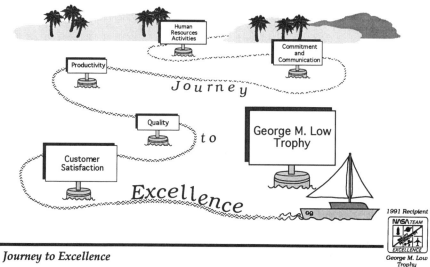

Journey to Excellence

1991 Recipient

George M. Low
Trophy

Slide #2

Grumman Technical Services

Journey to Excellence

- **Grumman's Commitment to Quality**
- **Grumman's Quality Process at KSC**
- **Results**
- **Lessons Learned**

1991 Recipient

George M. Low
Trophy

Journey to Excellence

Slide #3

I'll do this by sharing with you: Grumman's commitment to quality; how the quality process works for Grumman at the Kennedy Space Center; the results we achieved; and what we've learned from our efforts.

We are very proud of the fact that Grumman was recently named recipient of NASA's highest award for contractors and subcontractors, the George M. Low Trophy. We participated in the award process for the past three years, attaining finalist status each year. Being named recipient of this award is important to us for many reasons.

Grumman Technical Services

1991 Recipient

George M. Low
Trophy

Journey to Excellence

Slide #4

First, our people deserve to be recognized as the best of the best. They consistently perform at a superior level in an environment where excellence is mandatory. Isn't that the American way and what the quality movement is all about?

Second, this is the first time a subcontractor is a recipient. It shows that subcontractors are important to the success of the space program. We encourage other subcontractors to participate in what we consider an important process.

Third, it proves that focusing on total quality processes to achieve customer satisfaction works. Furthermore, that it applies to service organizations as well as manufacturing organizations.

So you'll understand the culture at the *rocket ranch,* I'll describe the origins of our contract and the work we do. In the early '80s, NASA combined multiple contracts at KSC into several large contracts. Among those was the Shuttle Processing Contract, the SPC. Lockheed Space Operations Corporation [LSOC] formed a team to pursue a contract. We, along with Thiokol [MTI] and Pan Am World Services (now Johnson Controls), joined Lockheed on the winning team. Although we are a subcontractor, Lockheed has always recognized us as an equal teammate and they continue to treat us that way.

Origins of SPC

- **Consolidation of Multiple Contracts**
- **Teamed with LSOC, MTI, Pan Am**
- **Partners with NASA**

1991 Recipient
NASA TEAM
EXCELLENCE
George M. Low Trophy

Journey to Excellence

Slide #5

Likewise, we function as a team with NASA. At KSC, we accomplish what we do because of the attitude that everyone works for the same team and safely launching the Space Shuttle is our goal. To quote one of our NASA teammates, "Our guys work so well together that the only way to tell who works for who is the name on the bottom of their badges."

Unquestionably, this has been the best year for SPC. In the past 12 months, SPC launched eight shuttles, landed three at KSC, integrated into the fleet and launched the newest shuttle, Endeavor, and brought on-line a third Orbiter Processing Facility. Records for processing time continue to be broken each "flow" while, at the same time, our safety record continues to improve. For these and many other reasons, we're proud to be part of the SPC team.

Our mission statement spells out what we do best: We provide safe, reliable, and on-schedule operations & maintenance support for launch processing, instrumentation systems, and calibration support for shuttle processing. For the past eight years we have been committed to continuous improvement. Unquestionably, we achieved our success through communication and teamwork with our customers.

In everyday terms, we do a host of functions for the SPC team. Our work force of about 700 people operate, monitor, and maintain over 400 computer subsystems in what is called the Launch Processing System. In addition to orbiter processing, this system processes shuttle payloads and reaction control systems and monitors KSC facilities and the Shuttle Avionics Integration Lab at Johnson Space Center. I'm very proud of our team for accomplishing a flawless record for supporting all shuttle tests and launches since 1983.

In addition to routine maintenance, our technicians and field engineers respond when Launch Processing System hardware requires unscheduled maintenance. We developed complete diagnostic capabilities for quickly identifying problems and returning the hardware to operating status. [And there are] lots of opportunities . . . [with]

Mission Statement

- Provide safe, reliable, and on-schedule support for Launch Processing System O&M and Instrumentation & Calibration assigned to the Shuttle Processing Contract.

- Secure this commitment by integrating continuous improvement methods.

- Maintain open lines of communication with our customers and suppliers to meet common goals and objectives toward an effective shuttle program.

1991 Recipient

Journey to Excellence

George M. Low
Trophy

Slide #6

1991 Recipient

Journey to Excellence

George M. Low
Trophy

Slide #7

1991 Recipient

George M. Low
Trophy

Journey to Excellence

Slide #8

- 400 subsystems,
- '70s vintage equipment, [and]
- parts obsolescence.

We do in-place calibration on more than 15,000 critical ground support components, special spacecraft tools, precision measuring equipment, and facility support systems.

We engineer and install special instrumentation for flow and launch operations. We also operate and maintain the Permanent Measurements System. This system monitors and records critical ground measurements used in a variety of tasks such as Solid Rocket Booster stacking, main engine over pressures, and vehicle lift-off loads.

Likewise, we have lots of opportunity here. For example, when cracks are discovered in the crawler way tunnels or hypergolic leaks that need to be isolated.

And, we provide post-launch and post-test wave analysis data for Lockheed, NASA, and many other contractors. Over 1,300 data plots are used to evaluate facility performance and structural integrity of mobile launch platforms, rotating service structures, and, most recently, the orbiters themselves through a new modal analysis system that we operate and maintain.

Other support responsibilities include logistics engineering, supply support, safety, security, test engineering, intermediate level maintenance [ILMF], and tape certification [tape cert] and storage. We have made significant productivity improvements in each of these areas. For example:

> *Tape Cert*—[We] . . . provided new equipment and better procedures and are processing about the same number of tapes with 10 . . . [fewer] people.

Grumman Technical Services

Journey to Excellence

1991 Recipient

George M. Low
Trophy

Slide #9

Grumman Technical Services

Journey to Excellence

1991 Recipient

George M. Low
Trophy

Slide #10

ILMF—[We] . . . automated the production control process using bar coding and are providing better tracking with three or fewer people.

Our TQM initiative, which began in 1988, is known as Grumman Quality or simply GQ. Our GQ plan, called Vision '95, is actively used throughout the Grumman Corporation. Vision '95 contains the nine elements you see listed here. The plan describes specific actions for each element. The Corporate Quality Council evaluates each division twice a year on their progress in achieving specific goals of this plan.

Grumman Technical Services

Grumman Total Quality Process

- **Leadership**
- **Training**
- **Work Process Management**
- **Customer Involvement**
- **Supplier Involvement**
- **Communication**
- **Policy Deployment**
- **Employee Reward and Recognition**
- **External Awards**

1991 Recipient

George M. Low Trophy

Journey to Excellence

Slide #11

GQ requires a team approach to our work and empowering employees to make decisions about their work processes. All our teams are united under one motto that describes the KSC attitude: "Here's how we can, not why we can't."

But GQ is much more than a motto. GQ is totally integrated into our work processes and, as our NASA Validation Team told us, "It's become the way we do business." Our GQ effort is built on the principle that every employee and every team contributes to continuous improvement. We established a multi-level team structure that defines a role for everyone: senior management, middle management, and every work team.

My staff and I make up the Steering Team responsible for creating the right environment for total involvement. We meet for an hour and a half each week for short, productive sessions. In the meetings, we define plans, allocate resources, monitor key indicators, and charter teams when improvement opportunities are identified. We review improvement plans for teams and help them when needed. Most importantly, we recognize team efforts and show our appreciation with awards, certificates, and a sincere thank you after their presentations.

Grumman Technical Services

Kennedy Space Center
Space Shuttle Team Motto

"Here's how we can,
not why we can't."

Journey to Excellence

Slide #12

Grumman Technical Services

Steering Team

Natural
Management
Team

Natural
Management
Team

Natural
Management
Team

Natural Work
Teams

Natural Work
Teams

Natural Work
Teams

Journey to Excellence

Slide #13

Communication

Management/
Employee
Dialogue

Goals and
Objectives

Morning
Meetings/
Telecons

Team
Building

Hot Line/
Open Door
Policy

Employees

Suggestion
Program

Annual
Employee
Opinion
Survey

Job
Shadowing

Newsletter

Weekly Staff
Meetings

Skip Level
Meetings

Journey to Excellence

1991 Recipient

EXCELLENCE

George M. Low
Trophy

Slide #14

A key element in assuring TQM success is improving communication. We found that management needed to establish better paths to promote open, two-way communication. By listening to the employees, we became instantly aware of what we needed to do to improve. This chart shows the various paths established to promote open communication and the change of emphasis from telling to listening.

Another key element assuring TQM success is our commitment to training. We developed an effective in-house, quality training capability to augment our existing technical and management training. Between 1988 and 1991, training hours per employee doubled as our quality process advanced. After a thorough review of all training programs at KSC, NASA decided to use our training for their teams.

In regard to customer involvement, our Steering Team is also a link to our Lockheed customer and the SPC continuous improvement process [CIP] which began in 1991.

I serve on the Lockheed Natural Management Team for our Support Operations directorate. This is a valuable way for us to work with our Lockheed teammates to integrate efforts, define shared processes, identify and track key measures, and move forward in a *consistent way* toward total quality.

Similarly, we interface with NASA's TQM Process. We serve on the KSC TQM Integrated Working Group and the TQM Coordinators' Council. We are also working with our NASA partner to integrate TQM efforts and work-shared processes.

For example, 18 months ago we formed a joint Grumman/NASA Quality Action Team to examine processes in Tape Certification. The team focused on issues relating to tape procurement, storage space, and their latest project—data integrity.

Commitment to Training

Employee Training

- Quality Process
- Employee Development
- Techniques for Improvement
- Group Process
- Manager Development
- Job Skills

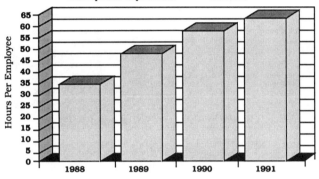

1991 Recipient

Journey to Excellence

George M. Low
Trophy

Slide #15

Team Excellence at KSC

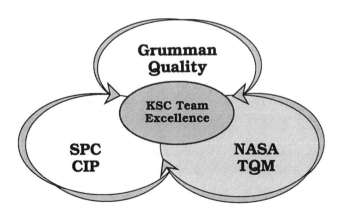

1991 Recipient

Journey to Excellence

George M. Low
Trophy

Slide #16

Continuous Improvement Through Total Involvement

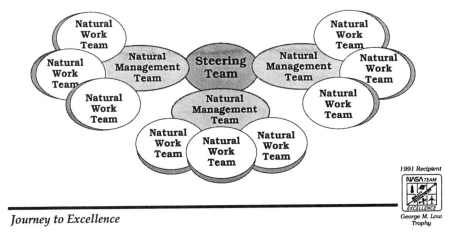

Journey to Excellence

1991 Recipient

George M. Low
Trophy

Slide #17

Even though our approach to TQM didn't require the much-talked-about culture change, it isn't a miracle cure that happened overnight either. Rather, it's been an ongoing evolution that began with our contract award in 1983. At that time, we inherited a team of super people who knew their job[s], shared a common goal—of launching shuttles, had pride in their work, wanted to do it better, and loved working as a team with their customer—NASA. Quite a platform for TQM—eh! We built on that over the years by adding other techniques of Total Quality [as follows]. [In . . .]

'83— Instituted Quality Circles. Quality circles worked well through 1988, especially when management actively participated.

'84—NASA/Contractor Quality Conferences. From the beginning, our top management committed to supporting NASA's focus on quality by attending these conferences. Out of this came, in 1985, the NASA Excellence Award Process (later renamed after George M. Low). However, even though we couldn't apply for the Award until 1988 ([as a] subcontractor), we remained committed and involved!

'85—Q/PI Seminar and Teams. NASA and contractor teams began attending two-day sessions to learn group dynamics and work Q/PI projects. Today, we are still sending work teams.

[We]. . . really got going in '88 with 2 processes: [the] *GQ process* **and** *NASA Excellence Award* **[NEA]** *process.* We introduced the Grumman quality process and, for the first time, we were eligible for the NASA Excellence Award.

'89—MBNQA and NASA Excellence Finalist. As part of a company wide requirement, we used the Malcolm Baldrige National Quality Award [MBNQA] criteria to assess our quality program. We continued the NEA process and were chosen as a finalist.

Quality History

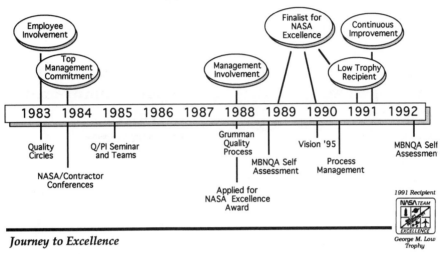

Journey to Excellence

1991 Recipient
George M. Low
Trophy

Slide #18

'90—Vision '95. Grumman Corporation implemented a long-range plan for our quality processes. After going off and working [out] some of our weaknesses . . . for the second consecutive year, we were a finalist for NEA.

'91—Low Trophy. Our quality program evolved to where we are today: Work Process Management and Continuous Process Improvement. We feel this directly led to our receiving the George M. Low Trophy, NASA's Quality and Excellence Award.

But [that's] not the end: '92—MBNQA. This year, we performed a second Malcolm Baldrige Award assessment of our quality program and are currently developing improvement plans to correct our weaknesses.

optional story [. . . to follow]

What is process management? This chart was put together for the *old timers* at KSC who contend that TQM "ain't nothin' different than what we been doin' all along!" Fact is, we've found the approach of focusing on long term Process Management is quite a bit different than problem or people management. True, we had gotten very good at reacting to crises, but our methods hardly ever kept problems from reoccurring.

[For example—Buffer Tiger Team Story]

We think process management is really just a systematic way to apply common sense. It involved a change in our approach as we evolved from quick response problem resolution by a limited number of people to a new environment where teams identify, measure, and improve processes without a lot of help from management. Now we use everyone's efforts and ideas

Process Management:
A Systematic Way to Apply Common Sense

Tiger Teams		**Natural Work Teams**
Investigations		**Ongoing Improvement**
Fire Fighting	Process Management →	**Prevention**
Guesswork		**Measurement**
Hindsight		**Foresight**

1991 Recipient

George M. Low Trophy

Journey to Excellence

Slide #19

for continuous improvement and are learning to anticipate and correct problems *before* they occur.

For us, process management has become a cycle for continuous improvement. In the cycle, teams monitor their processes, use measurements to define improvement opportunities, charter improvement teams to analyze the process, and develop and execute improvement plans.

Using this approach, we no longer depend solely on management skills or gut feelings to identify problem areas. The teams monitor their processes by charting key indicators. They use measurements to define and identify specific areas of improvement. Fortunately, not all our processes needed repair and we learned you should not rush out to try and fix them. Rather, they should be monitored to ensure they stay within control limits.

Here's another example of something we didn't start with, but quickly discovered that we should be doing—chartering teams. When through key indicators we find a broken process, our natural management team forms an improvement team. Seven to ten people are selected for this team based on their knowledge of the process.

But instead of just throwing them at it, the team is given a specific *charter* that defines the process, problems associated with the process, team members, and what measures and support are important to improvement. The charter also provides guidelines for the length of time we anticipate the team needs. The benefit of using charters is that they help teams reduce their problem-solving time by avoiding confusion during team start up.

The team is assigned a *process owner* who helps gather information, review possible solutions, and provide other help. The *facilitator* guides the team through problem-solving techniques.

Grumman Technical Services

Process Improvement Cycle

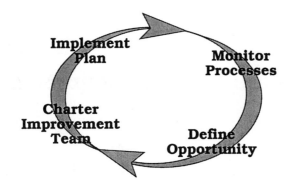

Implement
Plan

Monitor
Processes

Charter
Improvement
Team

Define
Opportunity

Journey to Excellence

1991 Recipient
NASA TEAM
EXCELLENCE
George M. Low
Trophy

Slide #20

Grumman Technical Services

Team Charter

- **Process Opportunity**
- **Team Members**
- **Measurements and Supporting Data**
- **Process Owner and Facilitator**
- **Timelines, Expected Milestones**
- **Special Resources**

Journey to Excellence

1991 Recipient
NASA TEAM
EXCELLENCE
George M. Low
Trophy

Slide #21

Now I'd like to talk about another key element of GQ, recognition. We believe it is absolutely essential to show timely appreciation for our employees' achievements. Therefore, continuous improvement has also been applied to our awards program. Not only are we personally handing out more awards, but our awards board and morale committee are continuously coming up with better ways to recognize employees. And I can attest to what many surveys reveal: The good old-fashioned pat on the back, especially in front of one's peers or family, goes just as far [as]—or even further than—money.

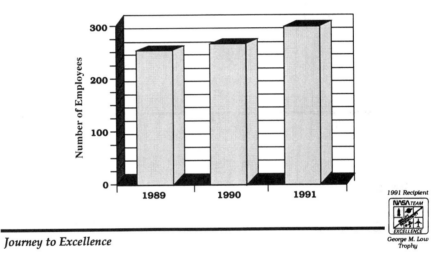

Slide #22

As I mentioned, we continually strive to find new ways to show appreciation. A lot of thought and effort has gone into coming up with more timely, meaningful, and personalized awards.

For example, before we present gift certificates, we find out what . . . award recipient[s] would like—a meal at their favorite restaurant or perhaps a gift from a particular department store.

As you can see, we present the usual variety of awards but have added some which are unique: Quiet Excellence for the person who always does super but goes unnoticed; and Customer Satisfaction for anyone receiving . . . [oral] or written appreciation from their customer.

My personal favorite, perhaps, is our Colleague Recognition Award Program. This program openly encourages all employees to nominate their co-workers or even their bosses. You'd be surprised at how many actually do!

And, if that isn't enough—and it never can be—our employees are also recognized through us by the NASA and SPC awards program. These awards are both prestigious as well as exciting. The two most coveted are the Silver Snoopy, which is presented in the work place by an astronaut, and the Manned Flight Awareness Award, NASA's highest honor. This award is

Grumman Technical Services

Employee Recognition

 Grumman Awards

- **Employee of the Month/Year**
- **Supervisor of the Month/Year**
- **Manager Recognition**
- **Manager of the Year**
- **Quiet Excellence**
- **Individual Performance**

- **Group Performance**
- **Customer Satisfaction**
- **Colleague Recognition**
- **Perfect Attendance**
- **GQ Suggestion**

Journey to Excellence

Slide #23

Grumman Technical Services

Employee Recognition

 NASA and SPC Awards

- **Silver Snoopy**
- **Manned Flight Awareness**
- **Employee of the Month**
- **Supervisor of the Month**
- **SPC Team Award**
- **SPC Suggestions**
- **NASA Team Award**

Journey to Excellence

Slide #24

a week-long affair that includes a trip to Houston for a special tour of the Johnson Space Center, a dinner and reception with astronauts, and, back at KSC, a first-class seat at the VIP launch site to view a launch.

The next key element of GQ I'd like to talk about is Employee Involvement. With the natural teamwork environment that exists at KSC, the only problem associated with getting people involved was "Too many, all at once!" Following our initial TQ Awareness Training, we really

Grumman Technical Services

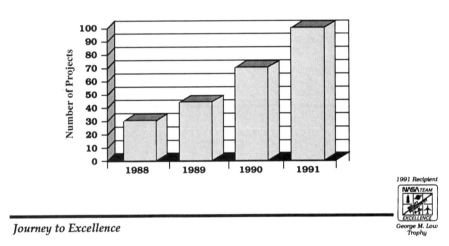

Employee Involvement is Gaining Steady Momentum

Journey to Excellence

1991 Recipient
NASA TEAM
EXCELLENCE
George M. Low
Trophy

Slide #25

had to scramble to handle all of the volunteers who wanted to be on teams. But we got it all worked out and during our last evaluation, the validation team said it was obvious that not only is everyone *aware of our process* but most are *actively involved* in it! As you can see, the number of projects completed has more than tripled in 3 years.

Another form of employee involvement has been the Suggestion System; but guess what? . . . we found it wasn't working so well. So, a corporate Quality Action Team streamlined the process in 1990 and you can see the results. We adopted the philosophy of encouraging all ideas for improvement with the motto that "No idea is too simple it if makes us more efficient."

By empowering our supervisors to approve suggestions (if they would implement), we improved turnaround time from nearly 9 months to fewer than 20 days. Our goal is 5 days. Many process improvements resulted from the added flow of these suggestions. We are now able to implement suggestions and reward suggesters rapidly, providing a catalyst for additional suggestions. Incidentally, we also went from giving monetary awards to $50 gift certificates.

Now let's talk results from our quality program and its focus on processes. As you can imagine, the *paper* process at KSC is tremendous. In fact, it has often been said that one way to

Employee Suggestions

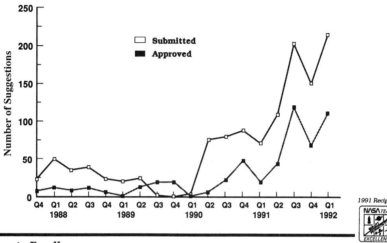

Journey to Excellence

1991 Recipient
George M. Low
Trophy

Slide #26

know when it's time to launch is when the paperwork outweighs the payload. One of our improvement teams examined the process of distributing our work documents, called Standard Practice Instructions, or SPIs. The team discovered that we could consolidate volumes in many work areas. With a surprisingly simple solution (and most are), the team reduced the number and cost of maintaining SPIs by more than 60%.

Here's one that no doubt you all can identify with, the priority material request process. Priority 02 procures materials needed within 2 hours. Priority 05 procures materials within 6 hours, and nonpriority items are procured within 72 hours. The team discovered that the priority request system wasn't working. Orders were backlogged because requesters were circumventing the lead time for normal delivery of both priority and nonpriority materials by attaching a priority 02 to all orders. This resulted in long lead times for all material deliveries. The team developed solutions that allow priorities to be used effectively and appropriately. The *amount of priority requests decreased* significantly (85%) while the *number of priority materials delivered "on time" increased* to over 90%.

Yet another team does depot-level maintenance on computers and peripheral equipment by processing approximately 6,000 Line Replaceable Units per year. By tracking key indicators, talking with their internal customers, and using written feedback cards on repair quality, this team reduced defects in repaired LRUs from an average of 3% per month to an average of 1% per month.

In the Instrumentation area, one of our teams is responsible for installing strain gages in the Mobile Launch Platform holddown posts which support the Solid Rocket Boosters and the Orbiter. While this chart doesn't go back that far, on Columbia's first launch in 1980, 100% of these gages failed in the launch blast and had to be replaced. The team began

Reduced SPI Volumes

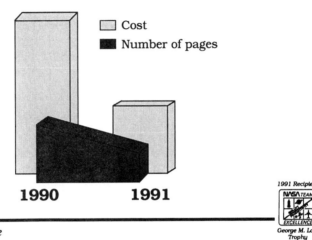

Journey to Excellence

Slide #27

Priority Material Improvements

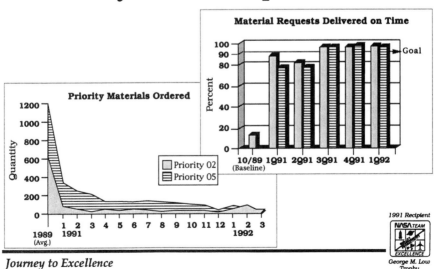

Journey to Excellence

Slide #28

Defects in Repaired LRUs

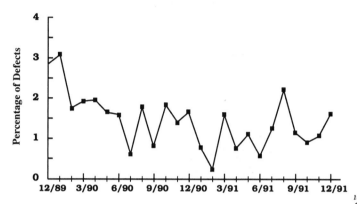

1991 Recipient

George M. Low Trophy

Slide #29

Hold Down Post Strain Gage Failures

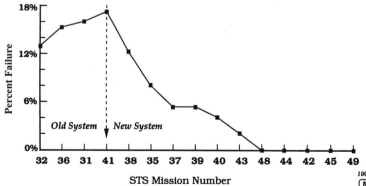

1991 Recipient

George M. Low Trophy

Slide #30

a series of unrelenting improvements in the gage installation process. Over time, they achieved a zero failure rate in what has to be the most severe environment I can think of.

To celebrate our technicians' completion of the refurbishment of all 28 holddown posts, we had a BBQ with the rest of the pig. Both our Lockheed and NASA counterparts were on hand to show their pride and appreciation for what turns out to be a major schedule and cost improvement in vehicle processing.

The most important measure of our success in operating and maintaining the Launch Processing System is impact time. *Impact time* [italics added] is the percent of required support time we miss because of hardware or operational problems. I'm sure you can relate this to your office or personal computer, when it goes down at that critical time when you need it most.

Grumman Technical Services

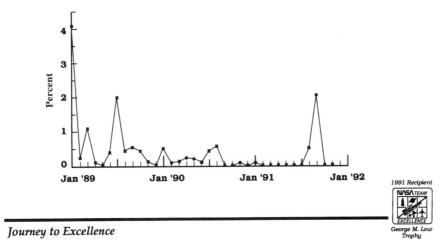

Launch Processing System
Customer Impact Time

Journey to Excellence

1991 Recipient
George M. Low Trophy

Slide #31

At KSC when the system responsible for monitoring the heartbeat of an orbiter goes down, that orbiter doesn't get powered up. We quickly learned that is not the way to satisfy our customers. To avoid this, we closely follow preventative maintenance schedules and procedures, develop redundant capabilities, and plan for every contingency that could be envisioned. We measure our performance carefully. When there is a change we analyze it, understand it, and improve the process as necessary. This was the case in September of 1991 when we installed newly designed memory boards without sufficient lab testing.

Through process improvements and efficiencies gained by implementing our TQM process, we not only managed an average of 9% below budget, but we have achieved cost savings of over 17 million dollars over the past 4 years. At the same time, we have absorbed a significant number of new tasks without increasing staff. . . . Our real measure of productivity.

Award fee evaluations are the ultimate measure of customer satisfaction in our business. Since our performance is reflected in the SPC team's ratings, I am very proud of our accomplish-

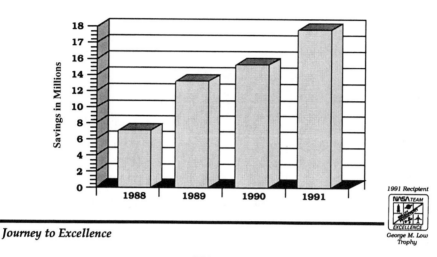

Cost Savings
(Cumulative)

Journey to Excellence

1991 Recipient
George M. Low Trophy

Slide #32

ments. Shown here are the semiannual ratings for the last several years. What the chart doesn't show is . . .

How We Got There, Through

- Reduced cost

- Reduced incidents and accidents

- Greater emphasis on teamwork

I demonstrated but a few examples of how our total quality process is working and how we achieved superior performance. I would like to share many others with you, but time is limited. Allow me to wrap up with a few lessons learned.

First, make sure you have a well-defined plan with clear goals. You and your people need to understand why you are doing TQM and what you expect from the effort. In all honesty, we jumped into it for all the right reasons. But not having a clear plan when we started caused us some grief.

Second, define responsibilities for everyone on your team. TQM takes a *total* team effort and *everyone* needs to know what . . . [he or she is] expected to do. Like the pig in the opening story, everyone has to make a total commitment. Keep it simple and keep everyone informed. Encourage management to listen to their employees. Establish various paths of communication to stimulate employee feedback.

Third, define your processes fully along with their measures. This is necessay to establish priorities for continuous improvement and customer satisfaction.

Customer Satisfaction

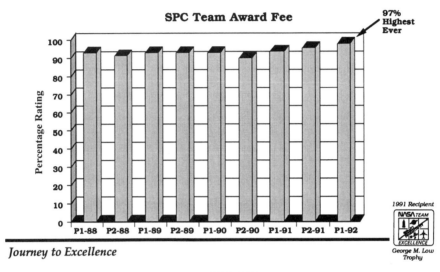

SPC Team Award Fee

97% Highest Ever

Journey to Excellence

1991 Recipient
George M. Low Trophy

Slide #33

Grumman Technical Services

Lessons Learned

- **Have overall multistep plan with clear goals**
- **Define team responsibilities**
- **Define and measure processes**
- **Be responsive to your customers' evolving TQM initiatives**
- **Be patient and persistent**
- **Use the criteria and feedback from an award process**

1991 Recipient
George M. Low Trophy

Journey to Excellence

Slide #34

Fourth, be aware that your customers and suppliers are probably trying to spread their TQM wings. Collaborate and learn with them. You'll both be richer for the effort.

Fifth, be persistent. Patience is tough at times, but keep pressing—good things will happen. As FP&L taught us, TQM is a long-term process—not a program.

My *final* comment is a suggestion to use the criteria and feedback from an external source, such as the NASA Excellence Award or the Malcolm Baldrige Award. The criteria of either is an excellent road map to success in TQM. The ASQC [American Society for Quality Control] and NASA Excellence Award Team provided us the direction we needed for significant process improvement. If there's any magic to this, it's the power of listening and responding to your customer.

We've been successful in our journey toward excellence. However, we know there is no finish line. Although we are excluded from applying for the Low Trophy for the next three years,

 Grumman Technical Services

1991 Recipient

George M. Low
Trophy

Journey to Excellence

Slide #35

we do not intend to sit back on our laurels and just relax. We are using the Malcolm Baldrige Award criteria in hopes that it will help us become even better.

We are working hard to achieve the goals of our Vision '95 plan that includes improving total cycle time for each of our critical processes by 25% every two years and eliminating defects in all our operations.

Likewise, other Grumman Divisions are also achieving success in their TQM efforts. The Long Life Vehicle Division that builds postal delivery trucks recently received a Quality Supplier of the Year Award from the Postal System and our Aircraft Systems Division [in] Stuart, Florida was awarded Boeing's Suncontractor Quality Award each year for the past seven years.

Let me close by saying thank you for listening to our *journey*. I sincerely hope that I've provided you some light to help guide your way to excellence.

SUGGESTED READING

Alessandra, T., and Hunsaker, P. (1993). *Communicating at work: Improve your speaking, listening, presentation, and correspondence skills to get more done and to get what you want at work.* New York: Fireside/Simon & Schuster. (See especially Chapter 14, "Presentation Power," pp. 169–186.)

Bartolome, F. (1989). Nobody trusts the boss completely—Now what? In Harvard Business Review Book Series (Eds.), *The articulate executive: Orchestrating effective communication,* pp. 3–16. Boston: Harvard Business School Publishing Group.

Beckhard, R., and Harris, R. T. (1987). *Organizational transitions: Managing complex change,* 2nd ed. Reading, MA: Addison-Wesley (OD Series).

Caporali, R. (1992). TQM is well worth the effort. *Key Speeches,* **5**(5), 4–8.

Deming, W. E. (1986). *Out of the crisis.* Cambridge, MA: MIT Center for Advanced Engineering Study.

Fairhurst, G. T., and Sarr, R. A. (1996). *The art of framing: Managing the language of leadership.* San Francisco: Jossey–Bass Publishers.

Larson, C. E., and LaFasto, F. M. J. (1989) *Teamwork: What must go right / What can go wrong.* Newbury Park, CA: Sage Publications.

Mattimore, B. W. (1994). *99% inspiration: Tips, tales & techniques for liberating your business creativity.* New York: AMACOM/American Management Association. (See especially Chapter 25, "Word Picturing and Associations: How to Be a More Creative Business Presenter, Speaker, and Writer," pp. 130–133.)

Nanus, B. (1992). *Visionary leadership: Creating a compelling sense of direction for your organization.* San Francisco: Jossey–Bass.

Spitzer, D. R. (1995). *SuperMotivation: A blueprint for energizing your organization from top to bottom.* AMACOM/American Management Association. (See especially Chapter 8, "Supermotivating Communication," pp. 113–131.)

PART VI

Presenting in International Environments

13

Internationally Speaking . . .

Nancy C. Corbin[1]

AT&T encountered many challenges in developing and maintaining its SKYNET®
International Service to Moscow. We discovered that while the technical issues were easy to
identify and build a plan to address, the human communication challenges were not. . . .
—*D. L. Flaherty Kizer*

As I have tried to identify key points that I believe will ensure your success in addressing
international audiences, I have fondly recalled the particular experience that drives each
point. This chapter is sprinkled with real-life experiences I have had with audiences in
Canada, England, Russia, the Baltics, and Mexico. I have also summoned up the expertise
of several of my professional colleagues who, like myself, have presented to and taught
foreign audiences.

Working with an international audience will undoubtedly be an experience you will
never forget. It will be a growth experience, perhaps even a turning point in your career. I
am hopeful—and, at the same time, a bit anxious—that your experiences with international audiences be both pleasant and profitable.

---

[1] I have had a great deal of pleasure preparing this "guest" chapter for you and would like to dedicate it to the
board members of the Professional Communication Society of IEEE.

INTRODUCTION

So you've been asked to make a technical (scientific, or management-based) presentation to an international audience. Your first thought will probably be to get out all of those speech books you have been saving in your bookcase for just such as occasion. Your frustration will start to mount as you frantically search through the Table of Contents and Indexes for the word *international* and will probably climax when you discover that few textbooks address this subject at all. The one thing that you must not do is opt to use your normal presentation techniques because you can find so little information on the subject. That would be a disaster. Rather, you must build on those techniques you have learned in the past for planning, preparing, and presenting "top notch" technical presentations.

If you have not had the experience of addressing an international audience, the idea is not all that remote. Such an opportunity is likely to be in your not-too-distant future. The historical changes in Russia, in Eastern Europe, and in many other nations, as well as the North American Free Trade Agreement, have opened up a large, untapped market for European and Latin American business. The shift of many commodities from the United States to Japan and other countries has paved the way for more and more business people to find themselves entrenched in foreign lands, foreign languages, and foreign cultures. In order to solve complex business issues, we must quickly bridge the communication gaps that separate new players in the international marketplace. Global competition, changing values, informed shoppers, complex lifestyles, and new technologies make it necessary for us all to consider the international marketplace.

There is no better time to study up on preparing for these audiences than now.

PLAN, PREPARE, PRACTICE, AND PRESENT—THE FOUR Ps

When addressing an international audience, you will follow many of the same guidelines that you have learned for addressing your native audience. As with your native audience, much of the success of your presentation depends on proper planning and proper preparation. Unlike presentations prepared for your native audience, there will be obstacles in communicating with your foreign host(s) and language barriers to overcome. You will want to plan early to overcome these obstacles, thus ensuring for the success of your presentation. Developing a solid presentation is actually a four-step process: plan, prepare, practice, and present. As shown in Figure 13.1, each of these steps builds on the previous step; in actuality, each step lays the foundation for the next step. And, the degree to which the elements contained in the previous step are addressed will directly affect the success of the next step. The following sections will define these four steps in enough depth to ensure that if you follow these steps, your international presentation will not only be successful but will be a pleasant experience as well.

Step 1: Plan

Identify Your Audience. Audience analysis is the first step in planning your international presentation. When planning your presentation for an international audience, your first goal is to identify everything you possibly can about that audience. This is not easy

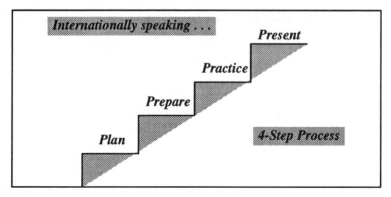

FIGURE 13.1. *A four-step process for developing international presentations.*

and, in fact, may almost seem like a futile effort. According to Michael Goodman (1993), the needs of the customer take precedence over any other factor. Audience analysis is a fundamental step toward following Goodman's communication model to determine the customer's knowledge, ability, and needs.[2]

Thus, you must determine what are the primary interests of your intended audience, what is their language, and whether you will address this audience through a translator. Of equal importance, you will need to know the amount of time allotted for your presentation. And, as with any presentation, you must determine what audio or visual equipment will be at your disposal, what is the projected size of your audience, and what is the size of the room in which you will be making your presentation.

You should be able to obtain all of this information from your foreign host. However, you must not get discouraged if responses to your questions are slow in coming. Remember, the more you can determine about the demographics of your audience, and the more you know about the equipment that will be at your disposal, the more successful your presentation will be. Of course, this is much easier said than done. Whether or not these questions are answered adequately, there *are* measures that you must take to ensure the success of your presentation.

Develop Your Timeline.   Another important part of the planning process is to develop a timeline for your presentation (Figure 13.2). Once your host has identified for you how much time has been allocated in the program for your presentation, you must plan how to use that time most productively. When developing this part of your plan, you must allow time for translation. Your host should tell you whether your translation will be serial or parallel. In all likelihood, you will be working with *serial translation.* This means that your message will be heard twice: first in your language and then in the native language of your audience. Serial translation has a seesaw effect, but I prefer this method over *parallel* or *simultaneous translation* for two interrelated reasons: (1) It involves the translation of discrete, more easily digested units of language, and (2) it is generally clearer and, overall, less distracting to listeners.

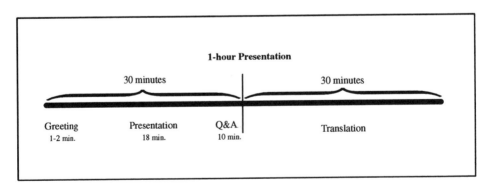

FIGURE 13.2. *International presentation timeline.*

[2] For a complete discussion of Goodman's communication model, see M. B. Goodman, "Implications of a Market Economy for Technical Communications in Russia," *IPCC '93 Conference Proceedings,* Philadelphia, PA, 1993, pp. 145–151. This paper was presented on a panel entitled "The New Face of Technical Communication: People, Processes, Products."

If serial translation is the case, you must divide your time by at least 50 percent or perhaps even a little more. Remember, English translated into another language generally requires many more words to express the same thought. If, for example, you are allotted one hour for your presentation, you have about 30 minutes of actual speaking time as I've shown in Figure 13.2.

When planning your presentation timeline, you'll want to allocate some portion of this 30 minutes to address questions from your audience—perhaps 5 to 10 minutes at the conclusion of your presentation. Keep in mind that all questions and answers will pass through two languages as well. Consequently, 10 minutes will not allow for many questions and answers. In reality, an hour on an international program translates into only about 20 minutes for delivering your technical message.

Don't forget to save 1 or 2 minutes of your time for a warm and friendly greeting for your audience. You will want to thank them for the opportunity to speak to them. Do not steal time from your greeting. It's a critical warm-up period for both you and your audience.

Identify Key Topics. Presenters speaking to an international audience often fall into the same trap as presenters speaking to their own native audiences. We simply try to tell our audiences too much or all that we know on a given subject. By developing your timeline, you immediately see that you must identify two or three main points that you want to share with your audience. Select three key points or work in groups of three points. An audience's retention of data delivered in *triads* is far greater than information delivered in any other numerical combination.

Begin by listing every point that you want to make:

- Point 1
- Point 2
- Point 3
- Point 4
- Point 5
- Point 6

Your list will decrease as you begin to combine your thoughts, eliminate ideas, and organize your material. These key points will be the ones you stress when you

- Tell your audience what you are going to tell them,
- Tell them, and
- Tell them what you told them.

Of course, you'll want to flavor your presentation with some words or phrases in the language of the audience to whom you will be speaking (e.g., in French, words like *ordinateur* [computer] or phrases like *énergie hydraulique* [hydroelectric power]). These key words or phrases might then become major points that you will reinforce with presentation media.

Develop a Proper Greeting. Be prepared to open your presentation with friendly body language and a warm, sincere greeting from your country. Forego any jokes as "ice breakers." Humor simply does not cross international boundaries very well. The only person laughing may be you. On the other hand, you might share some special moment or incident that you have encountered since arriving in your audience's country.

Ron Blicq (1993), author, senior consultant, and owner of RGI International in Winnipeg, Canada suggests that your audience will particularly appreciate any attempt you make to speak to them in their language. Based on his teaching experiences with Russian and German audiences, Blicq admits that while this is not an easy task, it is thoroughly worthwhile attempting. You will need to learn a little about the host country's language and, sometimes, its alphabet—just enough so you can pronounce words correctly. Blicq suggests that you be coached by someone who knows the language so that you will speak your opening words with the correct pacing and inflections.[3]

You might plan to begin your presentation to a foreign audience by asking a few questions—questions that directly relate to your subject matter and that require a response from your audience either orally or by gesture(s). This opening strategy will not only help to set the stage for your presentation technically, but will also help to ensure that you are successfully communicating with your audience. You may "level the playing field," so to speak, by asking a few questions and/or making a few statements that ensure that you and your audience are "in sync" technically.

The time spent delivering your greeting will also allow you to get in sync or in rhythm with your translator and your audience. Speaking through a translator is definitely going to be a unique experience.

Step 2: Prepare

Write Out Your Entire Presentational Script. Once you have identified your key topics, write out your entire presentational script. I have never insisted that speakers write out their presentations when addressing native audiences for fear they would resort to memorizing their presentation, or, worse yet, reading their presentation. However, my experiences with foreign audiences have shown me how important this step is. International presenters cannot afford to ad lib their technical messages—at least not in the beginning.

---

[3] For additional linguistic "hints" on working with international audiences, see Ron Blicq's paper entitled "Strategies for Preparing and Teaching a Course on Technical and Business Communication to a Foreign-Born Audience," *IPCC '93 Conference Proceedings,* Philadelphia, PA, 1993, pp. 156–161. Blicq's paper was also presented as part of the forum entitled "The New Face of Technical Communication: People, Processes, Products."

Instead, they need to know exactly what they plan to say and then test their data to ensure the integrity of their technical message. The importance of this step cannot be overemphasized.

Keep sentence structure simple. When you address your audience, you'll want to speak in simple sentences as well. A sprinkling of compound sentences is certainly okay. But, complex and compound–complex sentences, as well as sentence fragments, should be avoided—again to protect the technical integrity of your message.

Cleanse Your Presentation. After developing the best possible draft of your presentational script, you will want to have it reviewed by someone totally familiar with the language of your intended audience. This individual can help you "cleanse" your presentation of all idioms, acronyms, slang, and jargon that will not handily go through translation. Humor, especially jokes, is yet another type of information that generally does not cross international or cultural boundaries. Linguists that can ensure the translatability of your presentation are available through your local colleges and universities. In order to ensure the clarity of your technical message, you should plan to spend some time with such an individual. It is imperative that you do everything possible to ensure that your technical message does not get lost in translation.

Develop Supporting Visual Aids. After you have developed your oral presentational script, you are ready to develop your supporting visual aids. Plan to use two sets of visual aids—one in English and one in the language of your intended audience as shown in the samples that follow. Depending upon the complexity of your data, you may combine both languages onto one set of visuals as shown in the sample below. The translator who verified the integrity of your presentation can also translate your visual aids. If you do not translate all of your visual aids, you will, at the very minimum, want to flavor your title page with the language and culture of your foreign audience.[4]

[4] I review the importance of visual aids in "breaking through the sound barrier" created by different languages in my paper "Visualization Breaks the Sound Barrier," *IPCC '88 Conference Proceedings,* Seattle, WA, 1988, pp. 211–215.

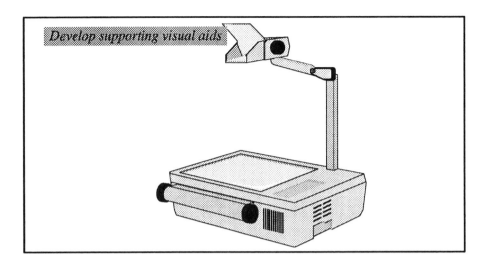

Sample – Bilingual Visual Aid

Cautions

ご注意

o **Do Not Store under High-Humidity Conditions**

○湿気の多い所はさけて保管してください。

o **Store on the Level Surface**

○水平面上に保管してください。

Sample – Bilingual Visual Aid

Sample – Bilingual Visual Aid

***Show Them What You Want Them to Hear!*[5]** The importance of good visual aids that project your technical message cannot be overemphasized. Remember, audiences retain very little of what they hear. But, to *show* an audience "what you want them to hear" practically doubles the understandability and future retrievability of the information you present.

Reaching any audience is difficult. Reaching an international audience is a real challenge. You can take no shortcuts. You must prepare your message not only in words, but in pictures as well. Inflation has not yet decreased the value of a picture; a good picture is still worth a thousand words. However, the picture is not good and shouldn't be used if it takes a thousand words to explain it.

Because of time limitations imposed on a presenter when addressing an international audience, good visual aids allow the presenter to provide more material than would otherwise be possible. Keep your visuals simple. Keep your type size large enough to be read from the back of a very large room. Follow the same rules you would follow in preparing for your native audience. A wide range of visuals is, of course, available to select from. Listed below are just a few choices you have for preparing visuals for an international audience with a brief explanation of how each can best be used. You should refer to earlier chapters in this book for other suggestions on the effective use of visuals and for presentation techniques.

Photographs. Photographs project reality and leave nothing to the imagination. Photographs involve the most cost-effective method for developing visual aids. All you need is a relatively good camera and a roll of film and you are in business. A photographer can give you some tips on capturing your technical message on film.

Cutaway Art. Cutaway art allows the presenter to isolate an area of an object from its host. Cutaways are extremely useful when describing any type of equipment, terminals, or even large computer systems.

Graphs. Graphs are best used for projecting trends. Because an audience retains so little of the information they hear—especially numeric information—speakers find it helpful to package their numeric information in graphs. Graphs depict trends. Generally, the trend is the important information that the speaker wishes the audience to understand and retain. Keep graphs simple and limit line graphs to no more than three lines. Color enhances the effectiveness of graphically depicted data. There are, of course, a wide variety of graph types to choose from. Study the small assortment below for the graph type that best projects the kind of data or information you need to share. Your imagination is the only limitation in developing meaningful graphic data.

---

[5] I review the use and importance of visual aids in developing presentations for foreign audiences more extensively in my paper "Show Them What You Want Them to Hear," *IPCC '91 Conference Proceedings,* Orlando, FL, 1991, pp. 413–419.

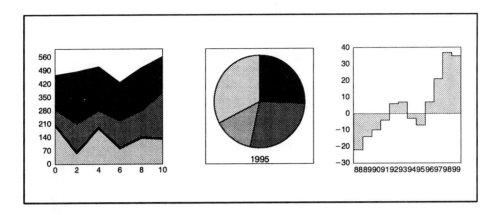

Pictograms. Pictograms enliven horizontal or vertical bar charts by replacing the straightforward bars with symbols that provide a more graphic representation of the data. Using this technique can save valuable translation time. Pictograms work best with single bar charts. Clustered and stacked bars are too complex to be displayed as a pictogram.[6]

Flow Charts. Flow charts establish direction for an audience and are probably the best visual for depicting processes. As you are well aware, we place a tremendous amount of emphasis these days on processes. Having a clear-cut process in the workplace seems to be the secret to business success—especially a process that allows you to take measurements along the way. You will probably find yourself using a number of flow charts for delivering technical information not only to international audiences, but to all audiences. As more and more business moves internationally, flow charts will become a preferred delivery tool for the international presenter. Be careful when "flowing" information not to let your chart become too busy and confusing. Use more than one visual if necessary; keep your boxes and all information contained in the boxes legible for your audience.

Remember, your ability to *flow* information is only limited by the reach of your imagination. Perhaps you will be speaking about a continuous process flow such as we find in management. You may want to use a flow chart, such as the one that follows, to make your point that there is no beginning or end to improving such a process.

---

[6] Other helpful techniques for developing graphics can be found in Willian Saunders' book, *Business Presentations with Freelance Graphics for DOS,* New York: Lotus Books/Brady Publishing, 1991.

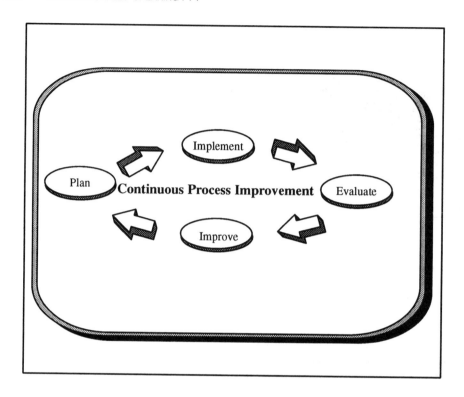

A graphics designer can help you turn your technical message into clear, concise pictures that will reach any audience. Remember: Use plenty of visual material. You can cut down on the amount of time necessary for translation by including as much of your technical message as possible in visual form. Make up for the time you lose to translation by using effective visuals. Ensure, however, that the technical message you wish to project is absolutely clear on your visuals.

Arrange in Advance for Visual Equipment. Notify your host well in advance about the type of audio or visual equipment you will require for your presentation. However, don't be surprised if such equipment isn't available. Much of the visual projection equipment that you take for granted is but another newfangled technological achievement that many abroad have only heard or read about. Be sure you know what options are available to you. But, be prepared for anything.

Remember to tell your host that you will need two overhead projectors if you elect to translate one set of your view foils (or transparencies) into the language of your audience. Also, you will want to ask for help in placing your view foils on the projector. Trying to deliver your presentation while working with two sets of foils can be cumbersome, distracting, and confusing. If you choose to use 35-mm slides, you may want to consider taking along your own projector. The quality of slide projection equipment in many foreign countries is somewhat inferior. Keep in mind that you will require an electrical converter in most parts of Europe and Asia if you plan to use your own equipment.

Step 3: Practice

Nothing will substitute for practice! No matter how well you plan, no matter how well you prepare, only practice will position you to deliver a winning presentation. In his book entitled *10 Seeds of Greatness,* the well-known Dennis Waitley claims that we spend more time on our life's hobbies than we do on our chosen profession. Making winning presentations is essential to our career development and growth. Therefore, we must follow planning and preparing stages with practice. When practicing a presentation for an international audience, ensure that your pauses for translation follow complete thoughts that your translator can easily understand and relate to the audience. Have someone, perhaps a coworker, critique your presentation for tone, inflection, pronunciation, enunciation, continuity in your technical message, and time. Identify what body language feels most comfortable for delivering your message and seems most relevant to the words as you intend to speak them.

Meet with Your Translator. Regardless of how well you have planned your presentation and how well you have prepared your visual aids, the acid test of an international presentation is whether it successfully communicates via translation.

In addition to alerting your host of your visual equipment requirements, be sure to make arrangements to meet with the individual who will be translating for you prior to your presentation. This practice step is absolutely essential for maintaining the integrity of your presentation. Ensuring that an audience understands our spoken message is far more difficult than ensuring that they understand our written message. The spoken word allows no opportunity to back up or reread. Your translator is going to serve as your voice in reaching your foreign audience. You must be certain that this individual totally understands your visual materials and your script. Therefore, you will want to meet and review your entire presentation with your translator. Well-planned visual aids will assist your translator in reaching your audience.

Plan to spend some time explaining to your translator the science or technology about which you will be speaking. Discuss any words or phrases that are truly foreign—words that the translator may not be at all familiar with. Discuss the speed at which you should speak. Let the translator become familiar with your voice, your delivery, and your accent. Even though the translator may be fluent in your native tongue, he or she may find your particular accent a bit challenging. Alert the translator to any questions that you may pose to the audience. The translator can help to elicit a response.

Also, to ensure that none of your body language will create unexpected cultural problems, you should alert the translator to any particular body movements or gestures that you plan to use and their symbolism. Review your intended pauses with the translator to ensure that you are covering your materials in complete translatable segments. You don't want to say too little or too much that the translator feels burdened in trying to convey your message in intelligible and complete thoughts. Plan your movements so as not to turn your back on your translator or not to position yourself so your translator cannot see your face. Discuss any bold or unusual movements with your translator so that he or she can be prepared to accommodate such movements.

Preview the Facility. In addition to meeting with your translator before your presentation, you will want to preview the facility in which you are to present so that you can check out the equipment and the space that you will be using. This procedure will also eliminate any unwelcome surprises at the podium.

In checking the equipment, ensure that extra projection bulbs are available. Test your visuals to ensure that they are visible from every section of the room. Check to see that there is no unwanted natural lighting, such as uncovered windows, that will detract from the projection power of your visuals. Opt for a pin-on microphone if one is available to ensure that your voice remains audible as you move between the podium and the screen.

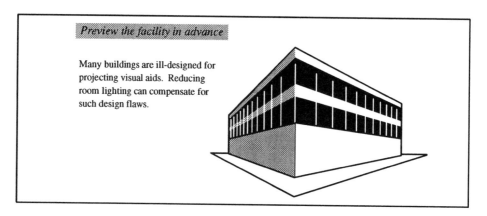

Preview the facility in advance

Many buildings are ill-designed for projecting visual aids. Reducing room lighting can compensate for such design flaws.

Step 4: Present

Delivering Your Presentation. Now that you have planned your presentation thoroughly and you have meticulously prepared all of your presentation materials, the actual presentation should be a cinch. I wish I could tell you that, but, in all fairness to you, such a statement would certainly be misleading. No presentation is ever a cinch. You have, however, taken all of the necessary steps to position your presentation for success. With your well-thought-out presentation in hand and your carefully prepared visual materials, you will certainly step to the podium far more confidently than the speaker who has not taken such pains to prepare.

One of the first things you will probably recognize is a much more somber audience than you are accustomed to. Don't mistake their somberness for lack of interest. Although some foreign audiences may seem silent and unresponsive, this does not mean that they are uninterested in what you have to say. In fact, these audiences generally see you as an expert in any technical area they want to know more about. Don't be surprised if you are bombarded with questions (both during and after your presentation) that are totally unrelated to your area of expertise. Keep in mind that many foreign audiences are new to the global marketplace and are hungry for all types of information. On the other hand, do not take a lack of questions to mean an uninterested or unappreciative audience. Foreign audiences are generally less likely to address questions to a speaker than are American audiences. These audiences do, however, appreciate the opportunity to talk with a speaker after the program is over. When you complete your presentation, extend an invitation to your audience to spend some time with them following the program if this fits within your (and their) schedule.

You will very likely find yourself anchored to the lectern as you deliver your presentation. In fact, your presentation will resemble that of a dramatic script once you have divided each complete thought with a pause. First you will speak; then you will pause while your translator speaks. Your opening greeting will help you develop the rhythm you need to work effectively with your translator. As you make your presentation, be sure to mark the spots where you intend to pause. Placing your finger on the spot where you just left off will keep you from losing your place when you start to speak again and will ensure that you are ready to speak once again the instant your translator is finished speaking. You will probably find yourself engrossed in what your translator is saying along with trying to "read" your audience's reactions to your materials. Be careful not to interrupt your translator before he or she is finished speaking. Use the time your translator is speaking to review your next thought. Thus, you can deliver your material without the appearance of reading your presentation. You will look like an "old pro" in front of your foreign audience. Don't be surprised if you find this seesawing back and forth with your translator a bit awkward at first. It's only natural that you will.

While presenting, speak in clearly constructed simple sentences avoiding more complex sentence structures as well as sentence fragments. Take special care to pronounce and enunciate your words properly. Avoid contractions. Many languages do not use contractions at all or have a limited number of contractions. Likewise, avoid idioms. Machines do not run. People run. Machines *operate*. The ordinary, everyday language that we are accustomed to using can distort your entire technical message and leave your audience completely baffled. Translators are handicapped by dialects and different pronunciations for, and enunciations of, the same word. Although your audience may not understand a word you are saying, your inflection is still important. Your inflection, like your body language, flavors your presentation.

Don't feel uncomfortable asking your translator whether you are making your point clearly or whether the audience understands. In fact, you can address such questions directly to your audience. It is perfectly acceptable to ask questions such as: "Am I making this clear?" or "Do you understand the point I am trying to make?" Offering to be available after the presentation for additional discussion is generally appreciated by any audience.

Because a higher level of concentration is required when working with a translator, you will want some assistance with placing your view foils on the projector. Agree beforehand as to how you will indicate when you want your next view foil. This will eliminate any awkwardness and save you a few of your too-few minutes for delivering the presentation.

Don't be surprised if your audience showers you with trinkets or books in appreciation for sharing your knowledge with them. International audiences are generally very appreciative and are not generally reluctant to show their appreciation.

Monitoring Your Body Language. Body language is key to any presentation. However, you may feel a bit strange using body language in front of an audience that does not understand a thing you are saying. Remember, too, that your translator will translate your technical message but will probably forego your body language in the process. So, should you use body language when addressing an international audience? I strongly recommend that you use your normal body language—that is, the body language that feels natural and comfortable in front of your own native audience. Body language is a universal language. Many of our body gestures cross international boundaries. Body language is the one language that is rarely misleading. A smile is a smile in any language. All of our feelings and emotions can be easily interpreted by our foreign audiences. It is not difficult for our audience to translate our excitement, our concern, or our disgust regardless of the language they speak.

Even though your body language will not be seen when your message is translated into the language of the audience, your audience will relate to your body language as they listen to your message in their language. Don't be discouraged, though, when your translator uses little or none of your body language. Body language is much like verbal language. Once spoken, it is also impossible to retract. Consequently, your body language will carry your message even if your translator does not mimic it. Arm yourself with enthusiasm and sincere, heartfelt body language. Equipping yourself with this "universal" language will surely aid you in delivering a winning presentation.

Responding to Questions from the Audience. If you have planned properly, you have allocated some time at the end of your presentation for questions from the audience. When a foreign audience asks questions, you will probably hear a much longer question from the audience member than the one the translator gives you in English. Unless the question is straightforward, describe your interpretation of the question and ask (through the translator) if you have understood the question correctly. This procedure, Blicq (1993) suggests, can prevent you from unknowingly providing an answer that does not properly respond to the question.

Don't go over your allocated time. Professional speakers keep to the schedule! Do make yourself available to answer other questions after the session is over. By doing so, you will reach those members of the audience who are uncomfortable with addressing questions for all to hear but would really appreciate some private time with you.

Managing Handouts. Audiences are always pleased when the presenter makes handouts available. You will need to start early in preparing your handouts because these, too, should be translated into the language of your intended audience. A good "sanity check" would be to have a second translator translate the handouts back into your language to ensure that the integrity of your data and information was not undermined during the initial translation.

Being Flexible. The key to a successful international presentation is to stay calm and be flexible. Have a contingency plan ready before you arrive. The situations you encounter may be grossly different from those you had envisioned or anticipated. You may face a different audience, be presented with strange, awkward, or nonexistent platform equipment (or equipment that arrives late), or discover that the length of your presentation timeframe is now scheduled to be longer or shorter than you have planned for. The key, according to Blicq (1993), is to be flexible, to be ready to quickly adjust to change, and yet to keep your audience unaware that you have had to make last-minute changes (often, right in front of them).[7]

SUGGESTED READING

Brislin, R., and Yoshida, T. (1994). *Intercultural communication training: An introduction,* Vol. 2, W. B. Gudykunst and S. Ting-Toomey (Series Eds.), series entitled *Communicating Effectively in Multicultural Contexts.* Thousand Oaks, CA: Sage Publications.

Corbin, N. C. (1988). Visualization breaks the sound barrier. *IPCC 1988 Conference Proceedings,* pp. 211–215. Seattle, WA.

---

[7] In this paper (pp. 156–161), Blicq underscores the importance of "being quick on your feet" when working with international audiences (see footnote 3, above, for complete source citation).

Gray, J. G., Jr. (1993). *The winning image: Present yourself with confidence and style for career success,* 2nd ed. (with intercultural focus). New York: AMACOM/American Management Association.

Hasling, J. (1988). *The message, the speaker, the audience,* 4th ed. New York: McGraw-Hill.

Hoft, N. L. (1995). *International technical commuication: How to export information about high technology.* New York: John Wiley & Sons.

Kizer, D. F. (1989). *How to effectively deliver or moderate a technical presentation* (Commuguide, Number 3). Piscataway, NJ: Institute of Electrical and Electronics Engineers (IEEE/Professional Commuication Society).

Leeds, D. (1991) *PowerSpeak.* Englewood Cliffs, NJ: Prentice-Hall.

Walters, L. (1993). *Secrets of successful speakers: How you can motivate, captivate & persuade.* New York: McGraw-Hill.

Wiseman, R. L., and Shuter, R. (Eds.). (1984). *Communicating in multicultural organizations* International and Intercultural Annual, Vol. XVIII. Thousand Oaks, CA: Sage Publications.

Postscript

Now that you've wended your way through all of the substantive material this book has to offer, we believe you'll agree that you are holding in your hands a useful "prospectus" for designing and delivering successful presentations whatever environment you currently work in—whether technical, scientific, or management—and no matter what professional presentation-related contingency you might be confronted with, domestic or international.

We've examined a wide range of information and strategies key to designing and delivering your next technical, science-based, or managerial presentation. We hope that, having digested all of this material we've assembled for you, we've given you the confidence to restructure and reframe complex data, information, and issues into valuable presentational content.

We hope, too, that we've given you the confidence to deliver that content in a wide variety of professional situations and environments—within your own organization ("in-house") and beyond it—to your peers, staff, customers, or "trainees"; to senior management and executive-level decision makers; to groups of fellow scientists, corporate researchers, government policy analysts, or academic specialists; and, finally, to those individuals within your audience(s) who are just now being initiated into an esoteric new field, skill, activity, or technology you understand.

We've provided you with much material to review, digest, internalize, and, then, put into practice—as early as tomorrow:

- Preparation methods and planning stages
- Presentational language, styles, and scripts
- Full-blown, real-world model presentations
- Research strategies for developing your presentation
- Approaches to organizing and refining your subject matter or presentational content
- Knowledge about crafting dynamic visuals, and, as Edward Tufte has put it, envisioning information

- Techniques for integrating visuals (from slides to computer displays) into your presentation
- Pragmatic and logistical advice for presentational occasions (from note cards to script writer's notes, from stage presence and body movement to seating arrangement and use of a microphone).

We've even guided you toward building obligatory "bridges" for communicating before international audiences—across what media expert Marshall McLuhan called the "global village." What else? What next? Well, we think that's, appropriately enough, up to you. Go ahead, design and deliver your next professional presentation. We know you'll be successful no matter how complex your subject matter, no matter what audience(s) you plan to address, no matter what environment—technical, scientific, or managerial, at home or abroad.

We believe we've provided you with a detailed, practical, and richly illustrated guide for both designing and delivering real-world, work-world, speeches and presentations. We'd like to think you've read this fund of material with interest and patience and care.

Now, simply, go out and regularly reap rewards . . . on all sorts of occasions . . . those signally special as well as those daily and routine.

Appendix A

TABLE A.1. Number of Respondents by Participating Organization

Organization	Number of Respondents
Harris Corporation (two government sectors)	30
Storage Tek Printer Operations	24
NASA/KSC	12
Level Five Research	9
Computer Science Raytheon (CSR)	9
Metretek, Inc.	7
McDonnell Douglas Space Systems (MDSS/KSC	5
Grumman/KSC—Space Systems Division	2
Sandia National Labs	1
Bell Atlantic	1
NCNB (National Bank)	1
Caterpiller, Inc.	1
3M Corp.	1
BDM Corp.	1
Reynolds Metals Co.	1
Boeing Defense & Space Group— Helicopter Division	1
Total	106

TABLE A.2. Survey Respondents by Job Title or Profession

Job Title or Profession	Number of Respondents
Vice Presidents	3
Corporate Training Directors	1
Senior Managers	7
Managers (including Engineering)	30
Senior or Lead Engineers	18
Project Leaders	3
Engineers (Staff, Aerospace, Design, Computer, Electrical, Mechanical, Software)	25
Computer Scientists	2
Physicists	2
Senior Systems Programmers/Analysts	2
Designer/Analysts	1
Training Specialists	1
Planners (Engineering)	3
Lab Staff	1
Engineering Tech Support Staff (Quality Assurance, Engineering Support, Advisory Engineering, Logistics)	7
Total	106

TABLE A.3. Survey Respondents by Academic and Professional Degrees[a]

Degree	Number of Respondents
PhD	3
DPA	1
MBA/MPA	14
MS/MA	31
MSEE/MSME	
BS/BA/BBA	45
BSE/BSEE	
BSME	
AS (Associate)	2
No degree	10
Total	106

[a] Only respondents' highest degree is reported here; however, survey respondents reported all degrees held.

TABLE A.4. Survey Respondents' Years of Professional Experience

Professional Experience	Number of Respondents
Under 1 year	1
1–5 years	16
6–10 years	21
11–15 years	23
16–25 years	30
Over 26 years	15
Total	106

TABLE A.5. Survey Respondents by Sex

Sex	Number of Respondents	Percent
Males	91	85.8
Females	15	14.2
Total	106	

Appendix B

Rating Guide for Team Presentations

The Team

_____ Poised
_____ Sincere
_____ Concerned with message
_____ Eager (apt) to convince audience
_____ Reflect positive self- (team) image

The Message

_____ Introduced well
_____ Concluded well (concise recommendations made)
_____ Balanced presentation, with clear sections (or subdivisions)
_____ Audience led from point to point
_____ Subject matter tailored to audience (e.g., VPs, managers, researchers)
_____ Position clear and significant
_____ Use of clear language (unambiguous, concrete)
_____ Use of careful, forceful language

The Transmission

_____ Voices (of team members)—clear, varied, conversational, loud enough for facilities
_____ Faces (team members)—alert, attentive, expressive
_____ Gestures (team members)—nondistracting, reinforce meaning, reinforce positive attitude(s)
_____ Pace (team members)—controlled delivery speed (e.g., not rushed)

The Audience (Your Listeners)

_____ Audience (prior) knowledge taken into account
_____ Audience attitude(s) taken into account
_____ Audience interest aroused, needs satisfied
_____ Full audience addressed (all questions answered with care)
_____ Audience members clearly acknowledged (even complimented)

FIGURE B.1 *Rating guide for team presentations.*

Checklist for Presentation Visuals

When visual aids are clear and easy to understand, they aid communication by focusing the audience's attention on your message and clarifying your major points. Poor visual aids obstruct the message by confusing your listeners, forcing them to decipher the visual rather than absorbing the message, and eventually causing loss of interest. Through careful planning and audience analysis, you can make sure you are using visual *aids* rather than visual *deterrents*.

In preparing visuals for your presentation, have you

☐ Targeted the visuals for the topic to be covered, the audience that will hear the presentation, and the physical surroundings?

Don't try to "force fit" a presentation around available visuals. Create or modify existing visuals to enhance a specific presentation.

☐ Determined that each visual is essential to the point you are trying to make?

Visuals can highlight or clarify key concepts. Avoid the temptation to use too many visuals; sometimes verbal explanation is sufficient.

☐ Made sure that each visual presents only one major idea or concept?

A viewer can absorb only a limited amount of information in the brief time the image is shown. A visual that requires longer than a one or two minute showing may be too complicated. For complex information, consider using overlays or splitting the material into two visuals. Eliminate extraneous information. Use color, typeface, or contrast to emphasize key points.

☐ Used only key words or phrases rather than complete sentences?

Listeners are irritated when presenters read full sentences aloud, and with good reason. We speak at about 150 words per minute; the audience can read the message three times faster.

☐ Considered the production time? Cost?

Include rehearsal time with the final product and the actual equipment to be used.

☐ Projected a professional image?

Be consistent with type size, style, and placement. For readability, use a sans serif typeface (such as Helvetica or Univers). Use a "caps and lowercase" format. In a team presentation, all presenters' visuals should appear to be part of the same "family." Have visuals prepared professionally if possible.

☐ Organized and analyzed the visuals in terms of their collective effect on the audience?

FIGURE B.2. *Evaluation form for presentation visuals.* Source: The Technical Presentation *(a workbook, by N. Burleigh and A. McMakin, Pacific Northwest Laboratory, Richland, Washington (Courtesy of Batelle), 1992.*

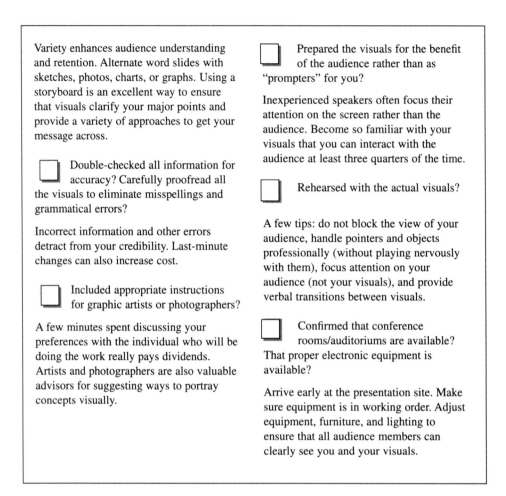

Variety enhances audience understanding and retention. Alternate word slides with sketches, photos, charts, or graphs. Using a storyboard is an excellent way to ensure that visuals clarify your major points and provide a variety of approaches to get your message across.

☐ Double-checked all information for accuracy? Carefully proofread all the visuals to eliminate misspellings and grammatical errors?

Incorrect information and other errors detract from your credibility. Last-minute changes can also increase cost.

☐ Included appropriate instructions for graphic artists or photographers?

A few minutes spent discussing your preferences with the individual who will be doing the work really pays dividends. Artists and photographers are also valuable advisors for suggesting ways to portray concepts visually.

☐ Prepared the visuals for the benefit of the audience rather than as "prompters" for you?

Inexperienced speakers often focus their attention on the screen rather than the audience. Become so familiar with your visuals that you can interact with the audience at least three quarters of the time.

☐ Rehearsed with the actual visuals?

A few tips: do not block the view of your audience, handle pointers and objects professionally (without playing nervously with them), focus attention on your audience (not your visuals), and provide verbal transitions between visuals.

☐ Confirmed that conference rooms/auditoriums are available? That proper electronic equipment is available?

Arrive early at the presentation site. Make sure equipment is in working order. Adjust equipment, furniture, and lighting to ensure that all audience members can clearly see you and your visuals.

Figure B.2. (Continued).

Index